LIBERAL PARTY GENERAL
ELECTION MANIFESTOS 1900–1997

LIBERAL PARTY GENERAL ELECTION MANIFESTOS 1900–1997

Edited by Iain Dale

With an introduction by
Duncan Brack

Routledge
Taylor & Francis Group

LONDON AND NEW YORK

First published 2000 by Routledge
and Politico's Publishing
2 Park Square, Milton Park, Abingdon, Oxfordshire OX14 4RN

Simultaneously published in the USA and Canada
by Routledge
711 Third Avenue, New York, NY 10017

First issued in paperback 2014

Routledge is an imprint of the Taylor and Francis Group, an informa business

© 2000 Selection and editorial work Iain Dale
© 2000 Introduction Duncan Brack

Typeset in Times by RefineCatch Limited, Bungay, Suffolk

British Library Cataloguing in Publication Data
A catalogue record for this book is available from the British Library

Library of Congress Cataloging in Publication Data
British political party manifestos, 1900–1997 / edited by Iain Dale.
p. cm.
Contents: v. 1. Conservative Party general election manifestos /
with an introduction by Alistair B. Cooke – v. 2. Labour Party
general election manifestos / with an introduction by Dennis
Kavanagh – v. 3. Liberal Party general election manifestos / with an
introduction by Duncan Brack.
1. Political parties – Great Britain – Platforms – History – 20th
century. 2. Great Britain – Politics and government – 20th century.
I. Dale, Iain.
JN1121.B78 2000
324.241'009'04 – dc21   99–25226
CIP

ISBN 13: 978-1-138-87407-7 (pbk)
ISBN 13: 978-0-415-20591-7 (hbk)

CONTENTS

CONTENTS

EDITOR'S PREFACE

In compiling and co-publishing this series of twentieth century General Election manifestos I am conscious that I owe a great debt to F. W. S. Craig, the doyen of political reference book compilers. Before his untimely death in 1989 Fred Craig had published three separate collections of manifestos, the latest containing all manifestos published between 1959 and 1987. As we enter the new millenium it seems appropriate to continue Craig's work by publishing a three-volume series containing all the General Election Manifestos of the three main political parties published during the twentieth century.

It should be noted that the publication of an official party manifesto is a relatively new invention. At the beginning of the century the Party's manifesto normally consisted of a statement of policy issued by the Leader of the Party in his election address to his own constituents. Nowadays it is not quite so simple. Manifestos go through umpteen drafts and are carefully worded to appeal to the maximum number of electors. The pictures selected often tell the voter more than the words.

The manifestos in this collection are reproduced verbatim in their original style. There are naturally changes to the textual layout, particularly for latter day manifestos where the use of pictures is more commonplace.

I would like to thank the Liberal Democrats for their co-operation in this project and all those Liberal supporters who have been involved in drafting their manifestos down the years. This book is for them.

Iain Dale
Politico's Publishing
London, 1999

INTRODUCTION

Duncan Brack[1]

Of the three main British political parties, the Liberal Party has experienced the most dramatic swings in fortune over the last hundred years. The nineteenth century was in many ways a Liberal century, with the Victorian Liberal values of economy, self-help, free trade and religious and political toleration accepted as the governing orthodoxy, particularly after the extension of the franchise to the middle classes in 1832. The Liberal Party itself, founded in 1859, governed for twenty-two of the following thirty-six years, until Gladstonian Liberalism finally reached its limits and the party went down to crushing defeat in 1895. In the succeeding ten decades, the party swung from landslide victory and reforming government to dissension and disintegration, virtually to disappearance and then to successive revivals, each one ultimately frustrated but leaving a stronger foundation for the next to build on. But even when denied the chance of power, Liberals often acted, albeit involuntarily, as a source of ideas for other parties to implement.

This volume charts the progress of the party and its ideas through the medium of the twenty-six Liberal election manifestos of the century, from 1900 to 1997. Two 'health warnings' are necessary. First, manifestos in their modem form are a relatively recent invention; those produced in the 1990s, for all parties, were far more detailed (and far more professionally presented) than earlier versions. In particular, before 1931, with a few exceptions, the Liberal 'manifesto' was a statement of policy issued by the leader of the party in his own election address. Being briefer than modern election addresses, far shorter than modern manifestos, and frequently concentrating on criticism of opponents, these statements are not particularly helpful in identifying Liberal proposals and themes – particularly unfortunate, given that this period covered not just the only Liberal governments of the century, but also the Liberal platform of 1929, an important milestone in the development and acceptance of Keynesian economics.

Second, even when manifestos have been drawn up and presented more systematically, their impact should not be exaggerated – an easy mistake to make in a book dedicated solely to their content. For almost half of the post-1945 period, what the Liberal Party claimed in its election manifestos was of almost no relevance whatsoever to British politics. And even when it did start to matter, it should be remembered that only a very small proportion of the electorate ever read the manifesto. It forms only one part of the kaleidoscope of impressions that forms the party's overall *image.*

What follows is a brief guide to Liberal fortunes since 1900, placing the Party's manifestos in context. For the more modern period, some description of the manifesto-making process is included. The section ends with an analysis of the role of the manifesto – and of 'policy' – in the Liberal Party and the Liberal Democrats.

Liberals in government: 1900–18

After predictable defeat in the 'khaki election' of 1900, where Liberal fortunes barely improved from the disaster of 1895, the party staged a spectacular recovery, pulling off the greatest electoral landslide of the century in 1906.[2] The Liberal leader Campbell-Bannerman's election address, however, provided no hint of what was to come – arguably the most brilliant reforming administrations of the century, demonstrating that Liberalism had adjusted successfully to the new demands of the industrial age. His address stuck to excoriating the Unionists; its major positive point was a defence of free trade (a cornerstone of Liberal policy for the preceding sixty years), and an assault on protectionism, or 'tariff reform', the issue that had split the Unionist government and forced Balfour's resignation in December 1905. The address referred back to the 'public declaration' Campbell-Bannerman had made shortly after assuming office, but in fact this speech at the Albert Hall on 21 December was hardly more informative. As with Tony Blair ninety years later, the Liberal leader was determined to avoid the internal conflicts and hostages to fortune that could result from the publication of a detailed policy programme – harking back in this case to the troubled reception of the Liberals' Newcastle Programme of 1891. The *Times* thought Campbell-Bannerman's address a 'very remarkable document', declaring that all of it, 'except an introductory sentence or two at the beginning and some twenty lines at the end, is devoted to a diffuse and inaccurate review of the acts of the late Government'.[3] Nevertheless, it worked. Liberal candidates in the country largely followed Campbell-Bannerman's lead, concentrating on tariff reform and free trade; their main secondary issues all related to actions of the previous government which Liberals condemned: licensing, education, Ireland, 'Chinese slavery'.[4] Dislike of the outgoing government, coupled with the Gladstone–MacDonald pact with the newly created Labour Party, swept the Liberals into power.

For the first two years the new government stuck to the reversal of Unionist legislation and traditional Liberal enthusiasms such as reform of the licensing laws, but most of their legislative efforts were blocked by the House of Lords. Change came only with the pressure of by-election defeats and Asquith's elevation to the premiership following the death of Campbell-Bannerman, in turn opening the Exchequer to Lloyd George. The Liberal government radicalised in office, as Liberal governments, unlike Labour ones, have tended to do. The Cabinet increasingly adopted 'New Liberal' policies of social, fiscal and economic reform, laying the foundations of the welfare state Attlee was to build on after 1945. The introduction of old age pensions, health and unemployment insurance, labour exchanges, school meals, and progressive taxation, all paid tribute to the government's willingness to intervene in the operation of the market, promote state welfare provision, and secure a modest redistribution of income and wealth (all in sharp contrast to Gladstonian Liberal principles of self-help). Constitutional reform came too: fanatical Tory opposition pushed Asquith into limiting the powers of the Lords, and the pivotal role of the Irish Nationalists once the 1910 elections had removed the Liberal majority led to the Irish Home Rule Bill, a measure which arguably would have prevented decades of bloodshed had war not intervened to halt its progress.

The two elections of 1910 were triggered by the Lords' rejection of the Finance Bill,[5] an event that had not occurred for more than 250 years. Goaded by Lloyd George's inflammatory speeches, the Lords voted the Bill down on 30 November 1909; Asquith, describing this as a 'breach of the constitution and a usurpation of the rights of the Commons', dissolved Parliament. Unsurprisingly, his election address focused almost entirely on this issue, together with the standard references to free trade. He stressed the need to limit the Lords' veto, a pledge he had made at his Albert Hall speech on 10 December in terms which implied that he had obtained a promise from the King to create, if necessary, enough new peers to remove the Unionists' inbuilt majority in the upper house. In fact, the King had refused to accede to this proposal until after a second election, which rather blunted the subsequent Liberal campaign in the country.

Back in government after the January 1910 election, the Liberals tabled the Parliament Bill, which limited the Lords' veto to two sessions, and removed it altogether for money bills. The Lords amended the bill out of recognition in November and Asquith once again dissolved Parliament, having this time acquired a firm pledge from the new King, George V, to create new peers if required. The electoral outcome was virtually the same, the Parliament Bill was reintroduced, and, once the Unionist leaders were informed of the King's position, enough of their peers abstained to allow it to become law in August 1911. In the end the Lords' strategy during 1909–11 proved a massive blunder: their opposition helped the government through one of its more difficult periods, when increased taxation was beginning to bite but before many of the resulting social benefits had been fully realised, and in the end largely destroyed their own power – an eventuality of which the Liberal leadership had been hopeful from the beginning.

The four years following the 1910 elections placed Asquith's government under increasing strain, with ministers under pressure over Irish Home Rule, women's suffrage and labour unrest. Nevertheless, the Liberals, together with their Labour partners in the 'progressive alliance',[6] looked well placed to win the election due in 1915. The Great War changed everything. Possibly Liberalism as a philosophy was simply incapable of coping with the strains of fighting a modern war; in any case, the governmental crisis of December 1916, when Asquith was overthrown by a new coalition under Lloyd George, dealt the party a fatal blow. By his refusal to serve in the new government, Asquith created a serious split in the Liberal ranks, but not one that was easily definable ideologically. Lloyd George, not Asquith, was the natural leader of the radicals, but the main bulk of his support came from Conservatives and right-wing Liberals. Thus many party members became progressively more and more alienated. Many drifted into retirement; many more moved towards Labour. Party organisation in the country deteriorated during the war; to an extent, a problem which afflicted all parties, but the Liberals had no firm leadership to pull it back into line.

Three-party politics: 1918–31

The Liberals entered the December 1918 election campaign split into two camps, though fighting on barely indistinguishable programmes (see Lloyd George's and Asquith's election addresses). The result was a right-wing landslide; probably only the

3

'coupon' negotiated between Lloyd George and the Conservatives for coalition candidates saved the Liberals from crashing into complete ruin. As it was, Labour emerged as the opposition, with twice the votes and seats of the Asquithian Liberals, largely because they fought more constituencies. Both Liberal and Labour candidates in 1918 commented on the numbers of ex-Liberal constituency activists running Labour campaigns. The steady departure of Liberal activists – generally radicals and pacifists – to the Labour Party had become a flood, and subsequent Liberal revivals could never be made to survive at the grassroots.

The succeeding six years saw both Conservative and Labour parties effectively conspire to eliminate the Liberal Party as a serious contender for power. This was clearly in both their interests: Labour because they could hope to benefit from the transfer of allegiance of radical Liberal voters and activists, the Conservatives because Labour was likely to be an easier opponent to beat in an election.[7] Both were also probably motivated by a dislike of Lloyd George, a man who, as Baldwin explained, had a 'morally disintegrating effect' on all who dealt with him.[8] Thus Coalition Liberal ministers had their schemes opposed by their ostensible Conservative supporters in Parliament and were one by one forced to retire; in 1922 Lloyd George himself was overthrown. The election which followed capitalised on Lloyd George's confusion and removed many of his supporters; the Asquithian Liberals, although recovered in numbers, still trailed behind Labour. Asquith's election address, which for the first time included a 'Programme of the Liberal Party', was not particularly inspiring, sticking to policies such as free trade, land value taxation and reform of the licensing laws which were by now seeming distinctly dated.

The two elections of 1923 and 1924 were the final acts in the Liberals' destruction. Baldwin's calling of an election on the issue of tariff reform in 1923, superficially an odd decision, in practice managed both to reunite the Conservative Party and to permanently isolate Lloyd George from it (a renewed coalition being still a possibility). At the same time it forced the Liberal Party, improved in seats but still unable to escape from third-party status, to choose between Conservatives and Labour. Ramsay MacDonald was then presented with the chance he had been hoping for: the first Labour Government, strong enough to govern by itself but not so strong as to be able to implement dangerously radical measures. The Liberals were perpetually placed in the position of either voting with the government, and appearing as a mere appendage to Labour, or voting against it, probably on an issue which most Liberals supported anyway, and facing an election which they could ill afford to fight. In practice they split, repeatedly and disastrously. The outcome of the 1924 election was a catastrophe, with the Liberals collapsing from 158 seats to forty-two, with half Labour's share of the vote. The Liberals were now permanently trapped as a third party within a two-party system; they were never to recover.

Probably the only beneficial outcome of the 1924 election was to remove Asquith from the Commons; along with almost all the Liberal leadership, he lost his seat in the debacle. The 1923 election, with Baldwin's threat to free trade, had reunited the two Liberal factions, and in December 1924 Lloyd George was elected as chairman of the parliamentary party (Asquith remained leader, but moved to the Lords). After two years of bitter infighting, and in failing health, Asquith resigned the leadership in October 1926. There was no credible alternative to Lloyd George, much as the Asquithians hated him; and, as Masterman admitted, 'I've fought him as hard as anyone, but I have to confess, when Lloyd George came back to the party, ideas came back to the party'.[9] He used his political funds (derived from the sale of honours) to finance major policy studies, beginning with *The Land and the Nation* and *Towns and the Land* (both 1925) as the basis for his new land campaign. The Liberal Industrial Inquiry (1926–28) involved many of the liveliest Liberal minds, including J. M. Keynes, Ramsay Muir, Walter Layton and F. D. Simon, and was published as *Britain's Industrial Future* (1928) – the famous 'Yellow Book'.

These studies' ideas for government planning, cooperation between capital and labour and a reflationary financial and fiscal policy were developed into a election programme set out in the 1929 pamphlet, *We Can Conquer Unemployment*, referred to in Lloyd George's own election address. According to the historian Robert Skidelsky, it was the most intellectually distinguished manifesto ever put before British voters.[10] The Liberal campaign had some impact: in the 1929 general election the party's vote rose from the 2.9 million of 1924 to 5.3 million. But the Liberals were now too firmly established in third place: the first-past-the-post system delivered the first indication of what it would do to a vote spread too evenly across the country, and the number of Liberals MPs rose from forty only to fifty-nine.

The impact of the second Labour government (1929–31) on the Liberals was very much the same as in 1924: they split repeatedly in the division lobbies, suffered defections to both Conservative and Labour parties, and saw their grassroots organisation disintegrate. In June 1931, a breakaway group of 'Liberal Nationals' resigned the whip to oppose the government more consistently. After the financial crisis of August 1931, the party initially welcomed the formation of the National Government, and four Liberals joined MacDonald's cabinet. But they were unable to prevent the holding of the general election the Conservatives (the bulk of MacDonald's support) so strongly wanted. The November 1931 election saw Conservative numbers rise by over 200, while Labour suffered the worst defeat in its history. The Liberals fought in no less than three groups: the official party, now led by Samuel and still part of the Government, fell to thirty-three (they fought only 112 seats); Simon's Liberal Nationals, generally unopposed by Conservatives, won thirty-five; and Lloyd George's family group of independent Liberals, firmly opposed to the Government, won four. The manifestos reprinted here are Simon's election address (which attacked both Labour and his former party and announced his conversion to protectionism), and the first recognisably party manifesto, from Samuel's official Liberals – though it had little to contribute other than a high-minded appeal to sacrifice, a return to the natural Liberal refuge of free trade (though import restriction was contemplated as an emergency measure), and a call, the first of many, for electoral reform.

Nadir: 1931–55

For the following twenty years the Liberal Party became steadily more and more irrelevant. Only two Liberal ministers were reappointed to the Cabinet after the 1931 election, alongside two Liberal Nationals. The National Government's decision to introduce protectionism forced Samuel's Liberals first out of government, in September 1932, and then into formal opposition, in November 1933. Although this may have helped improve the party's distinctiveness, it did nothing to revive its collapsing organisation. The Liberals lost seats at every one of the next four elections, ending with a mere six in 1951 (only 109 seats were fought), the result of 2.5% of the vote. Samuel lost his seat in 1935; his successor, Sinclair, lost his in 1945.

Free trade, still the central plank of the 1935, 1945 and 1950 manifestos, seemed the echo of a bygone age, particularly since after 1933 the economy recovered relatively strongly despite protection. Yet the party could not abandon it, since it was virtually the only issue it could call its own,[11] and was vital to internal cohesion. In the absence of Lloyd George, the Liberal leaders were too financially orthodox to develop his proto-Keynesian programme further. Indeed, they returned almost to a Gladstonian degree of fiscal rectitude, arguing for lower taxes and more thrift, particularly in the 1950s. This in turn helped to push the left of the party out towards Labour.[12] Only the 1945 manifesto bucked the trend, with a more collectivist and radical approach, in keeping with the general tenor of post-war reconstruction. Although in that election the Liberals were able to field Sir William Beveridge as a candidate, his famous report, *Social Insurance and Allied Services*, was not seen as a Liberal cause; it was the product of the coalition government and was supported by all three parties. Furthermore, Labour was clearly more likely to implement it, not least because the Liberals, fighting less than half the seats, could not possibly form a government whatever the outcome.

The party lacked any coherent image: it was split ideologically between those in favour of greater state intervention and those opposed to it. Neither Sinclair, who devoted most of his time to his ministerial post in the wartime coalition, nor his successor, Clement Davies, were able to give a clear lead, and as a consequence Liberals tended to describe themselves in terms of the other two parties, as a moderating influence on the extremes of socialism and Conservatism (the 1951 manifesto referred to the need to 'strengthen the liberal forces in both parties'). This was not an electorally appealing position, particularly since the defections of Liberal activists to both the other parties since the 1920s appeared to have made each of them more liberal in any case. Commentators suggested that the party could usefully transform itself into a civil liberties pressure group.

Clement Davies did at least manage to keep the party alive during its darkest days. A major reorganisational effort led to 475 candidates in the 1950 election, but the outcome was a mere 0.1% increase in the vote, and a net loss of three seats. Demoralised and exhausted, the party sunk even further in 1951. Perhaps the greatest service Clement Davies performed for it was to refuse the offer of coalition, and a Cabinet post as Minister of Education, made by Churchill (still sympathetic to his erstwhile colleagues) after the narrow Tory victory of 1951. The Liberals thus avoided likely absorption into the Conservative Party, and the 1955 election at least saw no further decline.

The party was very lucky to survive the 1950s at all. Only one of its six MPs in 1951 had won a three-cornered contest and four would probably have lost if opposed by Conservatives. Paradoxically, Liberal weakness was a help; for most of this period Conservative Central Office thought the party too ineffective to be worth trying to absorb. Maintained by a relatively recent tradition of parliamentary strength, and a few pockets of support, geographically and socially isolated from mainstream Britain, the Liberal leadership never really adjusted to minority status. In retrospect their pretensions – such as the anticipation of 80–100 gains in 1945 – look ridiculous. But they kept the party alive.

Revival: 1955–81

The disaster of 1950 did at least trigger more fundamental reforms in party organisation. In the face of their inability to win parliamentary contests, activists began to concentrate on local elections, and from 1953 the party's long decline in council representation was halted and then reversed. By-elections became of much greater importance to a party suffering from a serious lack of publicity, and a by-election team was in operation by the mid 1950s. From late 1954, Liberal by-election performance did indeed pick up, culminating in the first gain for a generation, at Torrington in 1958, followed by the stunning victory at Orpington in 1962. Such resources as there were began to be targeted more effectively. Above all, the party gained a new leader, when Clement Davies was persuaded to retire in 1956. Jo Grimond was charismatic, idealistic and imaginative, an inspiring speaker and a good communicator, especially for young voters. He was able to capitalise on the electorate's growing disenchantment with the other two parties, particularly after the Suez adventure of 1956 made it clear that the Conservatives were *not* Liberals in disguise. Furthermore, he was interested in ideas, and in his books and pamphlets he gave political Liberalism a new direction and purpose; almost half of the 1959 manifesto was his personal statement, an innovation at the time. He made the Liberals a respectable party to join once more, and attracted experts who contributed to a real renaissance in party thinking.

The outcome can be seen in the three election manifestos of 1959, 1964 and 1966, all distinctly more radical and coherent than their predecessors. The 1964 and 1966 manifestos in particular built on the work of a new Research Department, headed by Harry Cowie, and its series of policy committees, run with money from the Rowntree Trust, made available as the Liberal revival gathered pace. This was a change from earlier practice, which was for the parliamentary party to play the main role in drafting.[13] Although some of the key Liberal ideas of the period – such as opposition to Britain's independent nuclear deterrent – emanated from the leadership, they were all debated by Liberal assemblies, particularly in 1963, when virtually the entire platform for the following year's election was debated and endorsed.[14]

In fact, Grimond himself was little involved in drawing up the manifestos. He preferred the broad sweep, presenting the party in general terms as the 'radical, non-Socialist alternative,[15] and left the details to others, mainly Mark Bonham Carter and Arthur Holt (chairs of the party's research committee) and Frank Byers (chair of the general election committee). He was also nervous of creating too many hostages to fortune.[16] But the manifestos brimmed over with new ideas and new developments of old themes: entry into Europe (one of the key issues for the many new recruits to Liberalism, and a natural development of the enduring Liberal belief in internationalism), industrial co-ownership and profit-sharing, home rule for Scotland and Wales and regional government in England. Particularly after Orpington, political journalists enthusiastically reported Liberal policy initiatives, contrasting them with the stale approaches of Tories and Labour. On the eve of the 1964 election, even the *Times* stated that the Liberals had the best policy programme of the three.

The internal left–right debates seemed to be settled, as Grimond and Suez brought a new generation of radicals into the party, and the 'economic liberals' departed. The central theme of Grimond's leadership was realignment of the left, the uniting of Britain's progressive forces around the nucleus provided by the Liberal Party, basing politics on ideas rather than class interests. The approach seemed appropriate for a period of rapid social change and class dealignment, but it was premature: the split in the Labour Party which Grimond foresaw was not to occur for another twenty-five years. Although his leadership saw a substantial Liberal revival, with the party's vote roughly doubling between 1955–59, and doubling again between 1959–64, the end result was a disappointment. Spurred by the growing Liberal threat, the new Labour leader Harold Wilson adopted his own modernisation programme and proved just as effective as Grimond in putting it over in the media. The narrow Labour victory in 1964 held it together, and the 1966 election, when the Liberals gained three seats but lost votes, dashed Grimond's hopes for good. He resigned the leadership in 1967.

His successor, Jeremy Thorpe, was an accomplished organiser, fund-raiser and speaker, but displayed little interest in party policy. The 1970 Liberal manifesto had very little to add to the Grimond legacy, and was generally ignored by the media; the party failed to capitalise on the widespread radical disillusionment with the failures of the Wilson government that spawned a host of single-issue pressure groups. New thinking *was* going on, but in contrast to the Grimond era it was concentrated at the grassroots. An abortive revolt against Thorpe's leadership in May 1968 led to the establishment of the Liberal Commission, charged with translating the party's principles into a coherent programme. Its report, *Liberals Look Ahead*, produced for the 1969 Assembly, revealed some innovative thinking, including proposals on environmental policy, then just emerging as a serious issue – though most of them were not reflected in the manifesto.

New ideas stemmed particularly from the Young Liberals and the new breed of community politicians. Unlike many of the recruits of the early 1960s revival, they did not leave when political circumstances shifted for the worse, towards the end of the decade. They endured the disappointment of 1970, when the party lost half its seats, and stayed on to form the backbone of the next revival. Many of them organised as a separate entity within the party, standing candidates for key posts, organising seminars and publishing their own journals. Throughout the early 1970s the Young Liberals constituted the largest single voting block in the assembly, numbering on average one in four delegates.[17] In 1972 a radical was elected as Party President, defeating the leadership's candidate.

In the wake of the 1970 defeat, the party formally adopted the community politics approach. 'Our role as political activists', resolved the Assembly, 'is to help and organise people in communities to take and use power; to use our political skills to redress grievances; and to represent people at all levels of the political structure'. The widening commitment to local campaigning spurred the beginnings of revival. Local election gains started in 1971, and rapidly accelerated; Liberal councillors reappeared in areas where they had been absent for decades. From October 1972 to November 1973 the Liberals won no less than five parliamentary by-elections. Some of these were fought on community politics-style campaigns, but not all: the party also benefited from the rapid slide into unpopularity of Heath's crisis-and U-turn-ridden government, and Thorpe's performances in the media compared well with Wilson's. Liberal hopes were therefore riding high when Heath abruptly called a general election in February 1974.

The 1974 manifestos were notable largely because for the first time in a generation their content mattered to the outside world, as neither of the other two parties seemed likely to be able to win a majority. The February document was prepared by the party's

Research Department, based on the paper *Forward with the Liberals*, written by Lord Banks and adopted by the 1973 Assembly. It built on earlier Grimond-era themes such as decentralisation (reinforced by the party's community politics credentials) and industrial partnership, and added a permanent prices and incomes policy (not a particularly Liberal approach, but seen as essential to deal with the inflation crisis), and a comprehensive overhaul of welfare policy, including the right to a minimum income. The October version was written by the party's former Research Director Tony Richards (then secretary to the parliamentary party) after consultation with various key committees (the chairs of some of whom complained that there was too little time to consult with colleagues) and spokesmen. It was a shorter summary of the Liberal approach, and Thorpe recommended at its launch that it should be read together with the more detailed February manifesto – though many activists complained that they would rather have a longer document, a sign of the growing importance of the manifesto in campaigns[18] and within the party.

The results of both elections were an even bigger disappointment than 1964 and 1966. Despite winning six million votes, only fourteen Liberal MPs were returned in February, and thirteen in October. The failure to win a substantially greater number of seats ensured that the parliamentary party remained to the right of the activists, though not so much that it was willing to accept Heath's offer of a coalition. Labour returned to power and was able to win a small majority in October 1974, ending once again Liberal hopes of participation in government. The party's performance in by-elections and local elections declined, and, as more and more details of the Scott affair leaked out, Thorpe took the decision to resign the leadership in May 1976. After a leadership election in which all party members were able to vote – the first of its kind in British politics – David Steel took over in July.

As a leader, Steel shared many characteristics with Thorpe. He was an able communicator to the outside world, but was less effective in internal party management, generating activists' respect but not much affection, in contrast to Grimond. He was not particularly interested in the details of policy, concentrating instead on broad strategy, where his main aim was to show that Liberals could exercise power by working with politicians of other parties (the EEC referendum of June 1975 being an important example of this approach) – which he saw in any case as a logical outcome of the party's objective of electoral reform. In March 1977, accordingly, he took the party into the Lib-Lab Pact with the Callaghan Government, now in a minority in the Commons following byelection losses. The outcome, however, was disappointing; policy achievements were limited and the government's unpopularity rubbed off on the Liberals. The pact was terminated in August 1978, the party having started in March to prepare for the election that finally came, in the aftermath of the winter of discontent, in May 1979.

Once again the leader played relatively little part in the preparation of the manifesto,[19] which was put together by the party's Research Department, overseen by the Standing (later Policy) Committee; a subgroup chaired by William Wallace did the work, and the drafting (including Steel's introduction) was carried out by Wallace and the Research Director Peter Knowlson. After the political instability of the previous five years, the manifesto stressed constitutional reform, presenting it as the essential prerequisite for the industrial and economic reform that the electorate clearly wanted. The statutory incomes policy still featured, though it caused some controversy within the party, and a new area of policy distinctiveness opened up, with a major section on environmental protection. In the wake of the Lib-Lab Pact, the manifesto was reported more systematically in the press; the *Economist* complimented the party on having once again produced strikingly the best party manifesto.[20] But it was not the programme the country wanted, as Britain swung decisively away from run-away inflation, industrial strife and national bankruptcy. After a difficult campaign, the party could thank its community politics base, and skilful leadership by Steel, for 14 per cent of the vote and a loss of only three seats – a set-back, but not a collapse.

Alliance: 1981–88

Although the 1970s did not see the major policy innovations of the Grimond era, they were nevertheless a period of steady policy development. Even while the Liberal Party was building its image as a moderate centrist force, controlling the extremes in the other two parties, at the same time it was becoming increasingly radical and distinctive in its policy platform, adding a detailed programme of constitutional reform and grow-ing environmentalism to continued internationalism as areas where it was more differ-ent from Labour and the Conservatives than they were from each other. This was largely a grassroots, rather than a leadership-driven development; it carried on after the 1979 election, with a series of papers for debate at assemblies, systematically developing a policy platform starting from the party's basic philosophy. All this was overtaken, however, as the political scene underwent the dramatic upheaval of the foundation of the Social Democratic Party in March 1981, and the formation of the Alliance between the SDP and the Liberals six months later.

The two manifestos of 1983 and 1987 were joint policy statements agreed between the SDP and the Liberal Party (though the procedure differed radically in each election). As such, they were the outcome of a series of negotiations between the leaderships and policy committees on both sides, and therefore reflected not just the policy positions of the two parties, but their relative skills in the internal bargaining process. The parties themselves developed policy in different ways. Liberal policy derived largely from ini-tiatives from the grassroots and the Standing Committee (which reflected and responded primarily to the party in the country), with key decisions taken by the assembly, while the SDP was far more leadership-dominated, with most policy initia-tives stemming from the MP-dominated Policy Committee.[21] Despite this difference, and despite the generally more radical tone of Liberal policy, there were relatively few major policy disputes. Joint meetings of policy panels were able to hammer out com-mon programmes without too much difficulty, and a number of joint commissions, for example on unemployment and constitutional reform, operated harmoniously. In Jan-uary 1983, as SDP policy slowly developed, a Joint Policy Resolution Group, headed by John Horam for the SDP, and Richard Wainwright for the Liberals, was established to reconcile points of disagreement.

The 1983 manifesto was deliberately put together in a hurry. Preparations for the election had begun in late 1982, but the two leaders, Jenkins and Steel, postponed any decision over a joint manifesto until April 1983, when it became increasingly clear that an election was likely to be called. The joint coordinating committee of the parties agreed with Jenkins' proposal, supported by Steel, that the document had to be pro-duced urgently and by one person – Christopher Smallwood, the SDP's policy coordinator. The draft was considered on the same day (4 May 1983) by separate Liberal and SDP policy groups, by the joint committee, by a small group (mostly MPs) from both sides, and finally by the two chief whips, Alan Beith and John Roper. The two leaders met the next day to resolve the remaining problems (demands by the Liberals for stronger sections on the environment, agriculture and minority rights). This procedure diverged sharply from that which the Liberal Standing Committee believed it had agreed, which was for Smallwood to produce an outline only, which would then be expanded by Alan Watson, a Liberal candidate. The two leaders' desire to avoid protracted discussions and negotiations between committees caused considerable resentment amongst Liberals, who complained at the lack of consultation, and the tone of the final document, which they saw as too SDP-dominated.[22] It appeared – not for the last time – as though Steel had sided with the SDP against his own grassroots.[23]

Apart from the process by which it was put together, however, the manifesto (subtitled, as the Liberals had not been able to do for decades, 'Programme for Government') caused relatively little dissension within the Alliance. It was clearly less radical than a Liberal-only version would have been, harking back to the consensus days of Butskellism – the *Financial Times* commented that to read it was to 'suffer something very like nostalgia'[24] – but it retained a clear commitment to comprehensive constitutional reform, and to sweeping overhaul of the welfare state. The broad themes were clearly centrist, stressing the need to avoid extremism and confrontation politics and to promote 'partnership' and national unity. This was the platform which Liberals had tried to put forward for most of the post-war period, on which the SDP was founded and to which the electorate had seemed to respond so positively in the preceding two years. But it still suffered from the long-running Liberal problem that it defined the party not as what it was but as what it was not – not the right-wing Conservatives, and not the left-wing socialists. Given also that the Falklands War had helped generate a considerable spirit of national unity, the Alliance platform managed to look both dated and indistinct – as John Cartwright put it, the voters 'don't know what tune we're whistling'.[25] Together with the disorganisation of the campaign, where the two parties worked in parallel but not together, and the normal effects of the first-past-the-post system, it helped ensure that the Alliance remained in third position – winning the largest third-party share of the vote since 1923, only two points behind Labour, but with only twenty-three MPs.

The period from 1983 to 1987 was one of growing cooperation at the grassroots of the Alliance and growing tension at its centre. In most areas, campaigners found they could work together effectively and without serious dispute; several seats opted for the practice of joint selection of parliamentary candidates. Yet the new SDP leader David Owen was determined not to let the two parties drift together. Originally viewed as the most left-wing of the SDP's founding Gang of Four, he rapidly accommodated himself to Thatcherism, and indeed came increasingly to believe that strong leadership was what the Alliance needed – whereas for Steel and most Liberals, Thatcherite Conservatism was the opposite of everything they stood for. Owen had few firm policy principles, using policy positions – including his much-trumpeted but largely meaningless 'social market economy'[26] – purely as weapons with which to hammer the opposition, whether that happened to be Labour, the Liberals or the Jenkinsites within his own party. Thus he took the SDP further to the right on issues such as the application of markets to public services.[27] He opposed joint policy-making with the Liberals until it became clear that it was the only way to resolve the problems over defence policy. When joint discussions could not be avoided – for instance, over the 1987 manifesto – he attempted to dominate the process, presenting wording previously agreed with Steel, on a take-it-or-leave-it basis to the joint policy committees.[28]

Although it was the best known of the divisions within the Alliance, the split over defence in fact existed primarily within the Liberal Party; the SDP were largely united behind the hawkish Owen. But Steel had already been defeated twice by Liberal assemblies (in 1981 and 1984) over the siting of US cruise missiles in Britain. With the British Polaris nuclear submarines scheduled for replacement in the near future, it was clear that the Alliance had to reach an agreed position for the 1987 election. A joint policy commission was established in 1984 and reported in 1986. A casual comment from Steel led to an inaccurate press report stating that the Liberal position (no replacement for Polaris) had won out in the final draft. Owen reacted furiously and the draft was amended slightly; the final version said merely that no immediate decision needed to be taken over replacement, a position which may well have been acceptable without the rows which had preceded it. But the leaders felt it necessary to find some additional way to demonstrate harmony. For Owen, this meant working Alliance policy back to the SDP's position (for the UK to remain a nuclear weapons state); for Steel it meant reaching an agreed Alliance position, the precise details of which were unimportant. They hit on the possibility of creating a joint Anglo-French deterrent, and visited France to discuss it. The French government was too polite to turn them down flat, but the Liberal Assembly had no such compunction. The combination of an unconvincing proposal and deep unhappiness at the way Owen appeared to be bouncing Steel into decisions led to a narrow defeat for the leadership on the issue of European nuclear cooperation, though the joint commission's report itself was endorsed.[29] In fact, after an intensive round of consultation within the Liberal Party – and against a background of a steady slide in the opinion polls in late 1986, as the Alliance was portrayed in the media as deeply divided – the 1987 manifesto did in the end contain a commitment to maintaining Britain's nuclear deterrent, though it did not specify through what system.

The tragedy of this episode is that it need never have happened. Owen became more and more incapable of negotiating rationally, as he became convinced that the Liberals were conspiring against him with his opponents in the SDP, an eventuality which his own behaviour made more likely. Steel paid too much attention to creating agreed Alliance positions, and too little to shoring up his own standing within the Liberal Party. The genuine policy disagreements between the two parties were very limited in number, but the Alliance had no way of resolving them except through weeks of time-consuming and demoralising negotiations and high-profile dissension at conferences.

The 1987 manifesto was the outcome of an eighteen-month exercise, of which the first twelve months was spent preparing a detailed joint policy document, *The Time Has Come*, launched in January 1987. The two policy committees set up a team of fourteen people to draft the manifesto, but this was soon delegated to Alan Beith. *Britain United: The Time Has Come* reflected the compromises of its predecessor, and, indeed, of the 1983 version. In policy terms it was not at all radical, except over constitutional reform; as a document negotiated between two teams it hardly could have been.[30] The press thought so too: 'as a rallying cry', the *Independent* concluded, 'moderate dirigisme is not frightfully inspiring'.[31] Coupled with the shambles of the election campaign, trying to implement a non-existent joint strategy with media operations that didn't coordinate, it is perhaps surprising (or it shows that not too much stress should be placed on manifestos as determinants of election outcomes) that the Alliance managed to retain twenty-three per cent of the vote and twenty-two seats.

For most Alliance activists, it had become clear that the existence of two parties, initially seen as an appealing novelty, was now a handicap, and merger campaigns took off strongly in both parties. The process finished both leaders. Owen's final miscalculation was to assume that he could use the internal SDP referendum on opening negotiations to drive out his opponents within the party; when he lost the vote, by a margin of almost three to two, he resigned and was replaced by Robert Maclennan. Steel's undoing was his habitual disregard for policy detail, leading to the disastrous farce of the 'dead parrot' draft of the founding policy statement of the merged party, a document which he should have known would have been unacceptable to the Liberals, and indeed to many Social Democrats.[32] Although the document was scrapped and a new one prepared, Steel's position was fatally undermined, and he could not have hoped (and in any case may not have wanted) to become the leader of the new party launched in March 1988.

1988–97: Liberal Democrats

The short history of the merged party, the Liberal Democrats, has been almost as dramatic as that of the Liberal Party of the previous eighty years. Born out of the failures of the Alliance and the bitterness of the merger, it had an unhappy beginning, being beaten into fourth place by the Greens in the 1989 European elections, and falling in opinion polls to within the statistical margin of zero. Yet just fifteen months later it won the first of a string of by-elections, some gained by spectacular majorities. From 1991–97, the party overtook the Conservatives in local government, fought two highly professional general election campaigns, won a higher number of MPs than at any time since 1929, and entered, through a joint cabinet committee with Blair's New Labour government, at least into the fringes of government.

In most matters, the Liberal Democrats can be seen as a modernised Liberal Party, with a policy platform built around Liberalism.[33] The legacy of the SDP lay primarily in organisation, with the policy-making process in particular borrowing from the SDP model. The key element is the Federal Policy Committee, whose composition carefully balances the different elements within the party: activists, councillors, MPs and the 'state' parties in Scotland and Wales; but the conference is sovereign, and on a number of occasions has not hesitated to vote down Policy Committee proposals of which it disapproved. In comparison to the pre-merger SDP, power has shifted from the leader and the Policy Committee to the conference; in comparison to the Liberal Party, power has shifted from both the conference and the leader (with his formal veto) to the Policy Committee. Yet although the potential for conflict between the various elements clearly exists, as with the party's predecessors it has only rarely emerged. This has been reinforced by the absence of policy-oriented factions within the party; although there has been disagreement on particular policy details, there has also been wide consensus on the overall direction, and no coherent and consistent critique of the policy programme. The policy-making structure itself, which incorporates most potential critics through the structure of policy working groups established by the Federal Policy Committee, has helped to maintain this state of affairs.

The other key element in policy-making is the leader. Unlike Steel and Thorpe, but in common with Grimond, Paddy Ashdown displayed a consistent interest in ideas. In the early years of the Liberal Democrats, he had a crucial role to play in drawing together a coherent policy programme out of the wreckage of the Alliance. His views largely helped to determine the direction and main themes of the party in the run-up to and during the 1992 election. Although this led to a few clashes with the Policy Committee and the conference (who both tended to be less market-oriented in economic and social policy), he was able to stamp his ideas firmly on the party largely because of the respect and admiration he enjoyed amongst members – 'ordinary party members will take things from him for which they would have lynched David Owen,' commented the *Economist* in 1991[34] – and also because of his position as chair of the Policy Committee, and that body's key role in determining policy. He became somewhat less engaged during the 1992–97 Parliament, as the main policy issues seemed to be settled, and he pursued his project of establishing links with the Labour Party.

The procedure by which the election manifestos were put together was a painstaking one. In mid-1990, the Policy Committee appointed Richard Holme as the manifesto coordinator, and he presented an outline structure of the document for approval soon afterwards. Most of the initial drafting was carried out by the Policy Director, Duncan Brack, drawing on the large pool of proposals contained in the party's various policy papers, which were prepared by working groups appointed by the Policy Committee and then debated by conference. Holme would amend the drafts, which would then be submitted to Paddy Ashdown for his comments; the leader was fully involved in the process from the beginning.

The first stage was the drafting of a 'pre-manifesto' paper, *Shaping Tomorrow, Starting Today*, which was discussed and amended by the Policy Committee and debated at the spring conference in March 1991. The paper met with general approval, and its basic structure was repeated in the manifesto, modified by various points made during the debate on the earlier paper. This process was an important one. After the Alliance years, party activists had had enough of being caught out by policy bombshells emanating from the leadership, and Ashdown and Holme were determined to ensure that the party understood and accepted the broad thrust of the manifesto well before it was finalised.

Drafting of the manifesto proper started in spring 1991, and the different chapters were submitted to parliamentary spokesmen for their comments and then debated at the Policy Committee. The rewritten and tidied-up version could have been ready – just – for an election in summer 1991, but the Conservatives' decision to soldier on into 1992 removed the pressure, and enabled the autumn 1991 conference to debate important papers on economic, environmental and European policy. Drafting was returned to in late 1991, and the final draft was discussed by the Parliamentary Party, and then approved by the Policy Committee, on the evening of the day after the 1992 Budget (11 March), which by then was fairly obviously going to be the signal for the election campaign. The final artwork was delivered to the printer late the next day, and the document was launched five days later, ahead of both the other parties'.

Although the procedure was a long drawn-out one, there were no real clashes on any major policy issue throughout it, although both MPs and Policy Committee (which included several candidates) displayed an increasing nervousness about some of the more radical proposals as the campaign approached. The manifesto was accompanied by a 'costings programme' (an innovation introduced in 1987 and copied by Labour in 1992) showing the party's proposed variation from forward government spending plans and the implications for taxation and borrowing. Far more care was lavished on its design and presentation than in earlier years (Holme and Brack worked together with a design company from the beginning) – a development common to the other parties, and a sign of the growing professionalisation of politics. Welsh and Scottish versions were produced by the state parties' policy committees, in coordination with the Federal version. The procedure was much the same in 1997, with William Wallace being appointed to coordinate the process, Neil Stockley (Policy Director) doing much of the drafting, and the 'pre-manifesto' paper, *The Liberal Democrat Guarantee*, being debated at the autumn 1995 conference.[35]

Both manifestos' content was much more coherent, and radical, than their Alliance predecessors. Once again, constitutional reform, environmentalism and internationalism (in the context of the renewed debate over Europe) featured as strong and distinctive sections, but on both occasions they were joined by a new theme, the need to invest in public services (particularly in education) and the necessity of raising taxes to pay for it (the famous penny on income tax for education). Initially viewed by commentators in 1992 as a risky move, the campaign proved it to be a popular selling point, and the message was given a much higher profile in 1997, and hammered home repeatedly in a highly focused campaign. Both manifestos were also far better received by the media than their Alliance predecessors. 'The Liberal Democrat essay far out-distances its competitors with a fizz of ideas and an absence of fudge,' stated the *Guardian* in 1992.[36] 'Across a spectrum of issues,' commented the *Independent*, 'the Liberal Democrats are more in sympathy with the spirit of the times than either of the two big parties.'[37] In 1997 the *Independent* called the party's manifesto the most challenging of the three, saying that politics without the Liberal Democrats would be 'intolerable'. Peter Riddell in the *Times* enjoyed its 'refreshing candour' and admired Ashdown's willingness to leap where Tony Blair feared to tread.[38] To what extent this boldness in policy will survive the party's engagement with the Labour Party – and possible coalitions at least in Scotland and Wales, if not at Westminster – remains to be seen.

Manifestos in Liberal politics

What use is a manifesto? Most obviously, it represents a party's promise to the electorate, the proposals it intends to implement when it achieves power. It is also a statement of the themes on which the party leadership thinks the election should be fought. But the vast majority of the electorate never read one, and most probably do not even pay much attention to the newspapers' summaries of them. The manifesto forms, at best, only one part of the kaleidoscope of impressions that together create the overall image of the party – alongside the party's record in central and local government, the qualities and behaviour of its spokesmen and representatives at national and local levels (most importantly its leader), and the way in which it is portrayed in the media.

Manifestos are also of some interest to the party's opponents – most obviously as a source of policy positions on which the party can be attacked, but also as an initial negotiating platform, should the party end up in a position of influence after the election. From 1974 onwards, Liberal manifestos was subject to systematic analysis by the other two parties for precisely this reason, and of course the party itself conducted a similar analysis of Conservative and Labour positions, comparing the different manifestos with each other.[39]

For the Liberal Democrats and its predecessors, however, the manifesto has also had an important third role: as a tool of communication *within* the party. For much of the present century, Liberals have lacked a firm base of class or interest around which to unite. They have had to rely on a shared ideological heritage – the expression of their political philosophy – to hold the party together, and election manifestos have been the most important expression of this *credo*. In turn this has resulted in a party which in general has been more interested than its main opponents in ideas.

Even when not in power, the Liberal Party and the Liberal Democrats have possessed a continuing record of influencing general political debate in Britain. 'Possibly the Liberal Party cannot serve the state in any better way,' said Keynes in 1926, 'than by supplying Conservative Governments with Cabinets, and Labour Governments with ideas.'[40] Seventy years later, the Conservatives no longer succeed in attracting Liberal Democrat defectors (rather, the reverse), but Labour has consistently borrowed the party's ideas, and under Tony Blair, has even implemented some of them, in the constitutional reform arena. Much to Liberal Democrat irritation, many political commentators have written as through this is the party's only *raison d'être*. 'To deserve to be taken seriously, Liberal Democrats must put forward radical ideas,' stated the *Financial Times* in 1994. '. . . . that above all is their role'.[41] It is a long tradition: even when out of power after the First World War, they still managed to provide the country with the political genius of Lloyd George, the economic radicalism of Keynes, and the administrative imagination of Beveridge.

The election manifesto, and, more broadly, the whole process of making party policy, has been an important part of this function. The development and debate of a relatively detailed policy programme has played a noticeably more important role within the Liberal Democrats and its predecessor parties than it has in the Labour or Conservative Parties. Policy development was an important factor in three out of the four post-war Liberal revivals: Grimond's ideas brought the party back into real politics in the 1960s, the successes of community politics underpinned the revival of the 1970s, and the resolution of policy differences inherited from the Alliance was crucial in cementing the merger, and resolving the conflicts, between Liberals and Social Democrats in the 1990s. Only the achievements of the Alliance in the 1980s were not based on any new policy thinking.

Policy has been important to the Liberal Democrats and their predecessors because the party has been largely composed of people for whom policy debate matters. Partly this is because since the 1920s the Liberal Party, SDP and Liberal Democrats have been third parties: they did not, and could not realistically expect to, form the government of the country. The party could not promote its message, or boost the morale of its own supporters, in terms of its government record; it had to rely instead on developing, refining and publicising its policies. And the pursuit of power and personal ambition, or the management of government, could not be motivations for Liberals in the same way as they could be for Conservative and Labour politicians. Policy development and debate offered an alternative driving force. This is, of course, a self-reinforcing process: since policy is important to the party, the organisation is structured so that policy debate is encouraged. And because policy is seen to be important, policy intellectuals are more likely to be attracted to the Liberals than to either of the other two parties, both as members and voters.

This process has been strongly reinforced by party members' social and educational backgrounds. The impetus for the social reformism of the New Liberals of the turn of the century came from the professional middle classes: journalists, writers and lecturers, lawyers and doctors with a social conscience. The Liberal Summer Schools and Lloyd George's 'coloured books' showed the intellectual strength of the Liberal Party of the 1920s despite its electoral decline. The first post-war revival under Grimond once again attracted the same elements into the Liberal Party. And in the 1980s, the membership of the new Social Democratic Party, as Hugh Stephenson argued, 'appear . . . . to be the professional middle classes jumping at the chance to have their interests represented and protected in the political system by a party they have themselves created, thus ending their effective exclusion from existing party politics.'[42] The SDP proved a magnet for policy intellectuals – most likely to be alienated by the instinctual and dogmatic Thatcherite approach to politics – who created a structure of rigorous, technocratic and detailed policy-making which was largely inherited by the Liberal Democrats.

For much of the post-war period the Liberal Party was little more than a party of policy enthusiasts pure and simple, kept alive only by its long parliamentary tradition coupled to a few local pockets of support. But since the 1960s it has enjoyed increasing success in local government and now possesses a highly effective campaigning ability that has delivered electoral success in an increasing regional concentration of support. In effect the Liberal Democrats now displays a mixture of cultures, of policy puritanism plus campaigning ruthlessness: people for whom elections are to be won to put policies into practice, together with people for whom policies exist to help win elections. The policies each group desires to develop are different, and are developed and promoted in different forums. Tensions between the two have occasionally surfaced, and seem likely to do so with ever-increasing frequency as the Liberal Democrats become electorally more successful. The two cultures can coexist, however, because the Liberal Democrats do not exercise power at national level, and have done so widely at local level only recently. The constraints that accompany the realities of power have therefore not yet infected the policy process to any great extent. When and if they do, one can expect much greater tension, and associated clashes, within the party structure.

But equally it is this mixture of cultures that gives the Liberal Democrats their real political strength. Policy-making without campaigning would result in a party that really was nothing more than a source of ideas for others. Campaigning without policy development would be mere local populism. If the party can succeed in integrating these different abilities, realising their strengths while avoiding their weaknesses, then the policy inheritance of Liberalism may yet come into its own.

Notes

1 The author would like to express thanks and appreciation to William Wallace and Harry Cowie, who were interviewed in connection with this Introduction; and also to Neil Stockley, whose analysis of Liberal manifestos 1945–79 (*Journal of Liberal Democrat History*, 1999) proved very helpful.

2 Several other elections saw a greater swing in terms of votes, but none matched 1906 in terms

of seats changing hands: the Liberals achieved a net gain of 216 and Labour of 28; the Conservatives lost 245, falling to a historic low of 157.

3 Quoted in Peter Rowland, *The Last Liberal Governments: The Promised Land, 1905–10* (1968), p. 23.

4 The introduction of Chinese labourers, poorly paid and badly treated, to the Rand. The Unionists complained that the Liberals had exaggerated the horror stories: 'for one seat lost by tariff reform', said Joseph Chamberlain on 18 January 1906, 'ten have been lost by libels and baseless stories about Chinese labour' – quoted in Rowland, *The Last Liberal Governments*, p. 24.

5 Lloyd George's 'People's Budget' of 1909, containing increases in income tax and excise duties, new taxes on cars, petrol and land, and a new supertax for those with incomes above £5,000 – all designed to raise revenue for higher social and defence spending.

6 Throughout this period, Labour never appeared likely to survive on its own. In 1913, exploratory talks were held on closer cooperation; possibly only the outbreak of war prevented a merger of at least the trade union 'Lib-Lab' section of the Labour Party with the Liberals.

7 They were right. In the period 1859–1918, when Liberals fought Conservatives, the latter were in power (alone or as the largest party) for only 27 out of 59 years (46 per cent); from 1918–99, when Labour was the Tories' main opponent, the Conservatives retained power for 56 out of 78 years (72 per cent).

8 Quoted in Martin Pugh, *The Making of Modern British Politics 1867–1939* (second edition, 1993), p. 222.

9 Lucy Masterman, *C. F. G. Masterman* (1939), p. 346.

10 Robert Skidelsky, *Politicians and the Slump* (1967), pp. 51–56.

11 In 1942, according to Mass Observation, it was the only Liberal policy electors recognised.

12 For instance, Lloyd George's daughter Megan, a Liberal MP from 1929–51, who defected in April 1955, and subsequently became a Labour MP from 1957–66.

13 By 1955, this was causing some dissastisfaction amongst party activists; Party Council adopted a motion calling upon the Executive to 'formulate proposals for new arrangements more in keeping with democratic principles', though the Executive managed to avoid doing this until after the election – Jorgen Scott Rasmussen, *The Liberal Party: a study of retrenchment and revival* (1965), pp. 144–45.

14 Harry Cowie, 'The Liberal Party in the General Election of 1964', in Rasmussen, *The Liberal Party*, p. 284.

15 1964 manifesto (*Think for Yourself – Vote Liberal*), first sentence.

16 Even then, Conservative Central Office was in the habit of 'costing' opponents' manifestos, and publishing wildly inaccurate estimates of their impact on public expenditure and taxation. Grimond initially opposed publishing the policy committees' papers at all, but was eventually persuaded by Mark Bonham Carter (personal communication, Harry Cowie).

17 Ruth Fox, 'Young Liberal influence and its effects', Liberal Democrat History Group Newsletter 14, March 1997, p. 17.

18 Spokesmen for the other two parties noted that sections were omitted and implied that the policies did not exist – David Butler and Dennis Kavanagh, *The British General Election of October 1974* (1975), p. 69.

19 The party leader had a formal veto over the inclusion of any item in the manifesto, a power which excited opposition from the radicals, who made sporadic attempts to remove it from the party's constitution. But its importance should not be exaggerated; at least until the 1980s, the party and the leader were never so far apart that there were any major internal policy disagreements.

20 See David Butler and Dennis Kavanagh, *The British General Election of 1979* (1980), p. 159.

21 As David Steel commented in 1982, 'The Liberal Party is not an authoritarian party and the SDP perhaps is'. The SDP leadership was determined to avoid the kind of takeover by small bands of extremists to which they believed the Labour Party had been subject; the objects of area parties (groups of constituencies, in theory large enough to avoid domination by a small clique) for example, included only the promotion, and not the discussion, of policy.

22 See David Butler and Dennis Kavanagh, *The British General Election of 1983* (1984), p. 79.

23 This triggered, after the election, another attempt to remove the leader's veto on the manifesto contents (see above, n19); once again, it failed.

24 Quoted in Ian Bradley, *The Strange Rebirth of Liberal Britain* (1985), pp. 173–74.

25 Quoted in Ivor Crewe and Anthony King, *SDP: The birth, life and death of the Social Democratic Party* (1995), p. 214.

26 For a full analysis, see Duncan Brack, *The Myth of the Social Market: A Critique of Owenite Economics* (1989).

27 The SDP supported an internal market within the NHS before the Conservatives.

28 On one occasion, the Liberals requested a ten-minute adjournment to discuss the new wording with which they had been confronted. Owen refused, threatening to terminate the meeting, whereupon the redoubtable Lady Seear stated that she proposed to make an eleven-minute intervention. Owen gave in (William Wallace, personal communication). It was domineering tactics like this that helped undermine Owen's position inside his own party.

29 The result was widely presented, at the time and subsequently, as a unilateralist vote against any UK nuclear weapons. This is wrong. For a full account see Michael Meadowcroft, 'Eastbourne revisited', *Radical Quarterly* 5 (Autumn 1987).

30 'Negotiated manifestos are not a good idea ... they tend towards the lowest common denominator rather than the highest common factor. . . . Whereas I am proud of my part in the 1992 and 1997 Liberal Democrat manifestos, I cannot say the same of the last Alliance platform. It was bland and uninspiring.' Richard Holme, 'Alliance days', *Journal of Liberal Democrat History* 18 (Spring 1998), p. 12.

31 Quoted in Crewe and King, *SDP*, p. 374.

32 The document's title was *Voices and Choices for All*. It gained its much better-known name when Des Wilson, the chair of the group appointed by the Liberal and SDP Policy Committees to draw up its replacement, declared that it was 'as dead as John Cleese's parrot' (a reference to an old Monty Python sketch in which John Cleese played a pet shop customer sold a dead parrot).

33 The policy and policy-making of the Liberal Democrats is more fully explored in Duncan Brack, 'Liberal Democrat policy', in Don MacIver (ed.), *The Liberal Democrats* (1996).

34 'Paddy's people', *Economist* 14 September 1991.

35 The main differences in policy terms between 1992 and 1997 were that education was given a higher profile, and constitutional reform a rather lower one, in 1997; and the taxation and expenditure policies were more cautious in 1997. For a good comparison, and an explanation of the 1997 process, see Alex Wilcock, 'The Manifesto – how it happened', *Liberator* 245 (July 1997).

36 Leader, *Guardian* 19 March 1992.

37 Leader ('The case for the Lib Dems'), *Independent*, 8 April 1992.

38 David Butler and Dennis Kavanagh, *The British General Election of 1997* (1984), p. 178.

39 Even in 1979, the Liberals were viewed as potential partners by the Conservatives should they fail to gain a majority (William Wallace remembers a conversation with Chris Patten (then in the Conservative Research Department) about it. In 1992, the author helped conduct a comparative analysis of the three manifestos. In both elections, it was not clear until the last few days of the campaign, if then, what the outcome would be.

40 'Liberalism and Labour', reprinted in J. M. Keynes, *Essays in Persuasion*, (1931), p. 343.

41 Leader, *Financial Times* ('The role of a third party') 21 September 1994.

42 Hugh Stephenson, *Claret and Chips: The Rise of the SDP* (1983), p. 173.

THE LIBERAL PARTY GENERAL ELECTION MANIFESTO 1900

Manifesto of the National Liberal Federation

Date of Election	September 28–October 4
Party Leader	Sir Henry Campbell-Bannerman
Candidates	406
MPs	184
Votes	1,568,141
% of vote	44.6%

Yielding to pressure from the less scrupulous of his colleagues and supporters, Lord Salisbury has recommended the Queen to dissolve Parliament as and from today. When Lord Beaconsfield was blamed for not taking a General Election in 1878 on the conclusion of the Berlin Conference, he declared that:

'A Minister with a large majority in the House of Commons has no business to dissolve merely with the object of gaining an advantage at the polls due to transitory circumstances. It is said I have lost a golden opportunity. I am not so sure of it. The English people do not like breaches of Constitutional practice.'

It would seem that Her Majesty's present advisers are less scrupulous than Lord Beaconsfield, and a 'Khaki' Election in the month of October is accordingly ordered.

The Nation will not soon forget the dark days of less than a year ago following the miscalculation of a Government that had risked a war without first counting the cost. The manner of conducting the negotiations had, at least, not made for a peaceful solution. For years this Government, without remonstrance, had allowed the Transvaal to arm itself to the teeth, and yet continued to underestimate its military strength. Disasters in the field fell like thunderclaps upon our country and overwhelmed it with shame, apprehension, and distress. Out of this state of humiliation it has been lifted, not by the statesmanship and administration of the Government, but by the genius of Lord Roberts and the bravery and endurance of officers and men; while the whole people, without distinction of Party, calmly, patiently, stubbornly facing their adversity, have cheerfully yielded up those they love best to hardship and to death in the service and for the honour of a common country.

And now this Government are scheming that in the achievements of a great General and a brave army their own negligence, miscalculation, and manifold misdoing shall be forgiven and forgotten. They are seeking to prostitute the sacrifices of a whole people to the interest of one political Party. By a Dissolution on a stale Register and a point-blank refusal of such special legislation as would put the new Register in force – sharp practice unprecedented since the great Reform Bill – they deliberately disfranchise half a million of electors, and their appeal to the nation for a verdict of acquittal and confidence is so far a delusion and a sham. Liberals, whatever their differences of opinion, must unite in indignant protest against such an obvious and discreditable electioneering trick, and call upon their fellow-citizens not to be blinded to the vast and varied interests at stake by the dust of a false and partial issue. Not Lord Roberts and his soldiers, but Lord Salisbury and his colleagues ask for the Nation's confidence, and that in all departments, for the next six years.

What have they done to deserve it? Have they other credentials than the mismanagement of negotiations and of war?

Abroad, where it was prophesied for them by one of themselves that the advent of this Heaven-sent Government would shed an unwonted feeling of calm and security over Europe, their career has been marked by a continuous series of wars and rumours of war. In theories and complications with which they have been called upon to deal, they have shown neither clear purpose nor resourceful diplomacy, nor any true sense of the greatness and dignity of the country whose destinies and traditions had been committed to their keeping. In the Near East, thanks to the feebleness and ineffectiveness with which the voice of this country was heard in the Councils of Europe, we have seen the Armenian Christians slaughtered and unavenged, Greece humiliated, the Sultan triumphant, and Crete only delivered from his sway by a happy accident, of which admirals were able to take advantage where Statesmen had failed. In India the wanton breach of the country's pledged word and the abandonment of the wise policy of their predecessors kindled the whole frontier into a flame. In Siam, Tunis, and Madagascar British interests were gratuitously sacrificed by a series of what were called 'graceful concessions'.

Finally, in the Far East the Government subjected the country to a succession of humiliation. They entered into a futile and unnecessary contest with Russia, on which they were at every point worsted. They neglected golden opportunities which might have been seized with effect, and finally were forced to console themselves and the country with Wei-hai-Wei, the possession of which has imposed an additional burden on our already over-taxed military resources, and is a source of naval weakness rather than strength. And in this, as in all other matters, the Government so unskilfully represented the interests and presented the case of this country, that the nations of Europe now stand towards us in an attitude of hostility and suspicion.

At home, the lavish and grandiloquent promises with which the confidence of the country was wooed have issued in a singularly bare and exiguous performance. The great social programme has evaporated into air. The scheme for Old Age Pensions, which was so simple that anyone could understand it,' and which 'any Liberal Unionist agent' was prepared to explain, has disappeared in a vanishing vista of Committees of Inquiry. The great question of Temperance Reform, which bulked so largely in election addresses, has also been shelved. In the early days of the Government it was pushed aside, the profits of the Brewers being preferred to the prayers of the Bishops, and of late, when revived by the highly significant Report of his own licensing Commission, it was dismissed by the Prime Minister with cheap jibes about 'free indulgence.' The scheme of Employers' liability which was to compensate 'every man for every accident,' 'as a matter of right and certainty, without the risk of litigation,' has resulted in a scheme which, though revolutionary in its character, is arbitrary and partial in its incidence, and has proved the most litigious Act of modern times.

22

There is one section of their policy to which the Government have devoted themselves with zeal and persistence – that of administering doles from the public exchequer to the classes on whose support they rely. That policy appears to have been pursued with all the more gratification because it involved the emphasis and extension of the principle of Sectarianism in Education, and preserved the so-called 'Voluntary' Schools from that public control which should always follow the grant of public money. In doles of this sort to Agricultural Landowners, to Clerical Tithepayers and to Denominational Schools, the whole of the magnificent revenue derived from Sir William Harcourt's great financial reforms has been uselessly and mischievously dribbled away; during years of peace and increasing income there has been no substantial remission of taxation; while, to complete the picture of the Government's financial recklessness, the Sinking Fund, the reserve of the country against the time of war, was wantonly raided, in the teeth of his own financial principles, by the Chancellor of the Exchequer.

Is it likely that the nation will forget this record of the Government's unskilful handling of its interests abroad, and the vicious principles of its legislation at home? Shall we not all unite in condemnation of a Ministry which, for the five years of its existence, has kept the Empire in a ferment, has squandered its resources, and in legislation and administration has shown neither the will nor the power to pursue or to initiate a policy of progress and reform?

The military conquest of the Orange Free State and the Transvaal is said to be over, and those territories have been formally annexed to the dominions of the British Crown. But to annex a territory is one thing, to settle it is another. There remains before this country a task of delicacy and difficulty which throw mere operations of war into the shade. It is a task which calls for tenacious purpose, discriminating judgement, broad and liberal sympathies. It consists in the reconciliation of a humbled but brave people to the conditions of a new flag, and in the reconstruction of free institutions within the bounds of an Empire for men who before owed no direct allegiance save to themselves. Is such a task to be left to a Party with Tory ideals and Tory traditions, and a Government with the personnel and the record of the present administration? Is it reasonable to expect that those who so little understood the task before them at the beginning of the war, will be able to cope with the far heavier and more complicated problems presented by its sequel? These are the questions connected with South Africa which the electorate of these islands have now the opportunity and the responsibility of determining.

There are, moreover, far-reaching questions affecting the relations between the Colonies and the Mother Country to which new attention has been directed by the attitude and action of the Colonies in this war. These are questions which ought not to be left for solution to the Tory Party, whose record in these matters in times past has never been happy, and has sometimes been disastrous.

But we do not forget that questions of Foreign Policy and the Government of our Empire across the seas are by no means the only matters for Liberals to ponder. Nor does our duty end with opposition to the class legislation which this Government has forced upon us. It is sometimes said by cynics that the work of the Liberal Party is done, but he who thinks this must be blind indeed to the grim and menacing group of subjects which has been called 'the Condition of the People Question.' So long as the Housing Problems both of the Town and of the Rural Districts remain unsolved; so long as our Land Laws are unreformed; so long as the evils of intemperance continue unchecked; so long as complete Religious Equality is denied; so long as the doors of Parliament are open only to the wealthy; so long as some men have many votes while many have none; so long as the Peers may arbitrarily overrule the Commons – so long must there remain work which the Liberal Party alone can do.

To secure that the government of the Empire shall be conducted upon liberal principles, to maintain a firm but non-provocative policy abroad, to forward social progress at home, and to provide strong business-like administration in all the great Departments of the State, is as much the duty of Liberals today as it ever was, and it is to strenuous endeavour to secure that liberals shall have the power to perform these duties that we call upon our Federated Associations to devote themselves. Every seat won from the Tories is a gain to the cause of the people.

LIBERAL PARTY GENERAL ELECTION MANIFESTO 1906

Sir Henry Campbell-Bannerman's election address

Date of Election	January 12–February 7
Party Leader	Henry Campbell-Bannerman
Candidates	539
MPs	400
Votes	2,757,883
% of vote	49.0%

The dissolution of Parliament imposes upon you the duty of returning a representative to the new House of Commons, and I respectfully place my services at your disposal. I do so with confidence, bearing in mind the eight successive Parliaments through which our relations have been unbroken, and having a vivid sense of the kind indulgence which during that long time you have uniformly extended to me.

I make this appeal, however, not merely as your Member in past Parliaments, but as the head of the Administration recently appointed by His Majesty the King; and I am confident that in undertaking those duties I had your approval.

After ten years of Unionist rule, the country has now an opportunity of saying whether it desires a further period of government at the same hands, or whether the Administration which has been called on to fill the gap created by Mr Balfour's unexpected resignation shall be confirmed in office.

In coming to a decision, the electors will, I imagine, be largely guided by the consideration, in the first place, of the record of the late Government; and, secondly, of the policy which the leaders of the Unionist party are now submitting to them for their judgement.

With respect to their record, it will hardly be disputed that they had advantages such as few Governments in recent times have enjoyed. For ten years they have been supported by an immense majority in the House of Commons; and throughout this period the House of Lords, by its docility, has done its part to facilitate their task. But, as if these advantages were not enough, they have further, by an unprecedented use of restrictive powers, curtailed the freedom of discussion in the House of Commons, and impaired its authority, reducing the Legislature, so far as was in their power, to a machine for registering the decrees of the Executive.

Of the opportunities so secured we have to ask ourselves what use have they made? What have they accomplished for the benefit of the country and the Empire? What claim can they establish on the strength of their performances to the confidence of the electors which they are about to solicit?

The period over which we are looking back presents itself to me, I confess, as a well-nigh unbroken expanse of mismanagement; of legislation conducted for the benefit of privileged classes and powerful interests; of wars and adventures abroad hastily embarked upon and recklessly pursued. The legacy which they have bequeathed to their successors – and I say it in no partisan spirit, but under a full sense of responsibility – is in the main a legacy of embarrassment, an accumulation of public mischief and confusion absolutely appalling in its extent and its ramifications.

The last general election was fought on the single issue of the situation created by the war in South Africa. The Government of the day asked for, and obtained, a mandate for concluding the war, and for settling our newly acquired territories. So far as that settlement has proceeded, I ask you whether it has been conducted in such a manner as to justify the confidence then reposed in them. It seems enough to remind you that the late Prime Minister now declares to us that, as the result of a policy which involved such sacrifices on the part of the people of this country, South Africa has been reduced to a condition in which loss of prosperity, nay, even ruin, can only be avoided by the use of servile labour imported in unlimited quantities from China.

Ten years ago, the incoming Conservative Government found the national finances in good order. The public debt was being steadily reduced, the burden of taxation was moderate. The coffers of the Exchequer were made to overflow year after year, by the operation of the Estate Duty Act, which had been carried in the teeth of their violent opposition. What do we find today? Expenditure and indebtedness have been piled up, the income-tax stands at a shilling, war taxes are continued in peace time, the national credit is impaired, and a heavy depreciation has taken place in securities of every description. You have only to look around to see the result. Industry is burdened, enterprise is restricted, workmen are thrown out of employment, and the poorer classes are straitened still further in their circumstances. Again, I ask whether by their conduct of affairs in this province of administration alone they do not stand condemned as unfit to administer the business of a great commercial State. I confess I am astonished when I find the very men who have so conducted their stewardship appealing for a new lease of power, in order that they may assume a still closer control of our industries, and exercise a free hand on the imposition of yet further taxes.

One word more on this question of expenditure. If the amount of money expended be a criterion of effective administration, then the defences of the country and the Empire should be secure indeed; but let me remind you that our predecessors when they left office, after four years spent in a series of costly and confused experiments upon the Army and the Volunteers, were still engaged in groping after the true principles of Army reform, still speculating and debating as to the objects for which an Army was required at all. These proceedings have had a demoralising and disheartening effect upon our Regular and Volunteer forces, and the country has just cause for indignation at the levity with which they have been carried out.

If we look back on the field of domestic legislation, the retrospect is no less gloomy. Whether we have regard to their treatment of the supreme national interest of education, or to the licensing question, or to the rating system, we find them approaching and dealing with these matters animated more by a desire to propitiate their powerful friends in the country than to settle problems of national consequence with due regard to the needs, the sentiments, and the convictions of all concerned. Of their failure to deal in a serious spirit with the social questions of which so much was heard at the general election of 1895, I say nothing. The constructive social programme served its purpose at the polls; little has been heard of its promises during the ten years that have supervened; and to-day its promoters seem to have forgotten that such a promise ever existed.

So much for the record, the authors of which appear before you to-day burning with indignation at the iniquities of a Government that has been in office for just a month, and evidently very well satisfied with their own handiwork. Assuredly the terms on which they propose that you should recall them to power betray neither signs of repentance nor promise of amendment. The policy which they offer for your accept-ance appears to me indeed to embody the most mischievous characteristics of their past. The thing which they describe as Fiscal Reform, what is it, after all, but another and a larger item in that series of reforms in which the Unionist party have proved themselves adepts – reforms introduced for the benefit of minorities, classes, interests? This policy – and I shall take the liberty of describing it as Protection – which they will consummate if you allow them, I hold to be fraught with incalculable mischief to the nation and the Empire, and I will endeavour briefly to state the grounds of my conviction.

We are Free-traders because we believe that under Free Trade our people and our industries stand to derive greater benefit than under any other system known to man-kind up to the present time; and in this belief we are confirmed by the teachings of our own experience – the safest guide that I know of for a nation to follow. Similarly our fathers abandoned Protection because they found it to be a bad system under which to live and labour. But we are told that conditions have changed since then, and that, inasmuch as certain great industrial States are thriving or expanding under Protection, we should hasten to resume our cast-off garments, with such alterations in their style as modern Tariff fashions may dictate.

I cannot follow the argument. Nothing in the experience afforded by these countries leads me to suppose that the factors in the case have altered, or that what was pro-foundly injurious half a century ago has become vital to our prosperity to-day. Noth-ing in their experience leads me to suppose that by limiting our imports we shall increase our exports, that by raising prices, no matter by what kind of tariff expedients, we shall assist in equalising the conditions of international competition, or in enlarging the area of employment. Still less am I persuaded by the experience of those countries that the taxation of food conduces to the welfare of the people. Heartily as I should welcome the adhesion of other States to Free Trade, I am not prepared to sacrifice conditions which I believe to be indispensable to our social welfare, and our industrial greatness and expansion, because individual industries, here and there, are hampered and obstructed by foreign tariffs.

I hold that Protection is not only bad economy, but that it is an agency at once immoral and oppressive, based as it is, and must be, on the exploitation of the com-munity in the interests of favoured trades and financial groups. I hold it to be a cor-rupting system, because honesty and purity of administration must be driven to the wall, if once the principle of taxes for revenue be departed from in favour of the other principle, which I conceive to be of the essence of Protection – that, namely, of taxes for private beneficiaries. I hold that a method, which, even if it be not deliberately contrived to secure the public endowment of such beneficiaries, including trusts and monopolies, must inevitably operate in that direction, is a most grave menace to freedom and progress, and an outrage on the democratic principle. Last, but not least, in order of importance, I hold that any attempt to rivet together the component parts of the Empire with bonds so forged, or to involve it with us in a Fiscal war against the world, is not, and cannot come to, good. An empire 'united' on a basis of food taxes would be an empire with a disruptive force at its centre, and that is a prospect with the realisation of which, both in the interests of the Colonies and the mother-country, I can have nothing to do.

Let me only add, in case I am told that it is unfair to identify the late Prime Minister, chief of the party of Tariff reform, with the extreme proposals of his leading colleague, that I understand Mr Balfour to be agreed in principle with Mr Chamberlain, and also that the Unionist party is committed to the programme of tariffs and preferences put forward by Mr Chamberlain. This being so, I conceive that the minor Fiscal Policy indicated by Mr Balfour occupies, in the estimation at any rate of the majority of our opponents, little more than a nominal place in the contest in which we shall shortly be engaged. It is the larger policy, therefore, with which we are confronted, and which we are called upon to fight. Our concern in any case is with the results that must flow from the adoption of either of those policies, and not with the question of whether Mr Balfour conceives himself to be a Free-trader, or a Protectionist, or both, or neither.

I am well aware that our opponents claim to be in a position to establish some kind of indeterminate fiscal limbo, in which the advantages of Free Trade and Protection are to be combined with the disadvantages of neither – a Fiscal paradise, perhaps I ought to call it, where tariffs will bless consumer and producer in equal measure, where the workman will find employment by the exclusion of foreign commodities, and the taxpayer will be relieved by the golden stream of tribute with which the foreigner will still – I know not how – continue to provide him. These fairy stories will be dismissed by serious men, and so, I hope, will be the illusory assurances that the protection imposed will be of such a moderate description that nobody will be any the worse for it. The man who sets a stone rolling down a steep place may intend that it shall fall slowly, and stop before it reaches the foot of the slope, but the stone follows its own course. In the same Way, the forces that will determine the course and momentum of the tariff movement, once it is started on its way, are beyond the control of the Tariff propagandists; and we shall do well to remember that every country which started on the Protectionist path set out in a gradual and tentative way, and with the declared intention of executing a strictly moderate tariff policy.

Neither in their past record, nor in their present policy, is there anything to entitle the late Government to a vote of confidence from the country.

One word in conclusion. Our own policy is well known to you, and I need not here repeat the terms of the public declaration which it fell to me to make shortly after assuming office. Should we be confirmed in office it will be our duty, whilst holding fast to the time-honoured principles of Liberalism – the principles of peace, economy, self-government, and civil and religious liberty – and whilst resisting with all our strength the attack upon Free Trade, to repair, so far as lies in our power, the mischief wrought in recent years, and, by a course of strenuous legislation and administration, to secure those social and economic reforms which have been too long delayed.

As to the spirit in which foreign affairs will be conducted, it is satisfactory to be able to say that, by renouncing those undesirable characteristics which we formerly detected in their foreign policy, the Unionist party have made it possible for us to pursue a substantial continuity of policy without departing from the friendly and unprovocative methods which, under Liberal Governments in the past, have determined the relations of Great Britain with her neighbours.

LIBERAL PARTY GENERAL ELECTION MANIFESTO JANUARY 1910

Mr Herbert Asquith's election address

Date of Election	January 14–February 9
Party Leader	Herbert Asquith
Candidates	516
MPs	275
Votes	2,880,581
% of vote	43.2%

I ask you for a renewal of the confidence with which on six previous occasions you have honoured me. Never during the long connection between us, as constituency and member, have issues so grave been submitted to you for your decision.

Four years ago the country gave an emphatic verdict in favour of the maintenance of Free Trade. Since then we have passed through times both of enlarging and of slackening industry, and our fiscal system has stood the test of both. During the last 12 months a further strain has been cast upon it. A large addition had to be found to the provision for National Defence –an addition due to the paramount necessity of keeping our Navy equal to all the demands that may be made upon it, and superior to all the dangers to which, from any quarter, our Empire may be exposed. At the same time, the grant of old age pensions, and the prospect of further and fuller developments of a policy of social reform, involved the State in liabilities, actual and contingent, which could only be satisfied by a substantial increase of taxation. The Budget of 1909 sought to meet both these classes of requirement, within the limits of Free Trade finance, by an equitable distribution of the burdens among the different classes and interests in the community. It apportioned the new taxes between luxuries, superfluities, and monopolies, leaving the necessaries of life untouched. The Budget was freely and exhaustively discussed in the House of Commons, and in the end it received the approval of an overwhelming majority of the representatives of the people.

The supporters of what is called Tariff Reform saw in the passing of such a Budget into law the 'death warrant' of their schemes. They accordingly mustered and set in motion the formidable interests and influences which they can command, either as followers or as allies; with the result that the House of Lords, in defiance of the counsels of the wisest and coolest heads in the Tory party, rejected the whole provision which the Commons had made for the finance of the year.

This is a proceeding without precedent in our history, a wanton breach of the settled practice of the Constitution, and an assumption on the part of the non-representative House of a power to control taxation, which has been repudiated in the past by Tory as emphatically as by Liberal statesmen.

In a sentence, the House of Lords has violated the Constitution in order to save from a mortal blow the cause of Tariff Reform.

If you care either for Free Trade, which has made our country prosperous, or for Popular Government, which has made it free, now is the time to assert your devotion; for in this contest the fortunes of both are at stake.

There is before you a larger issue still. The claim of the House of Lords to control finance is novel, and a mere usurpation. But the experience of the Parliament which has today been dissolved shows that the possession of an unlimited veto by a partisan Second Chamber is an insuperable obstacle to democratic legislation. The will of the people, however clearly and emphatically expressed, is always liable to be rendered inoperative. Given a Tory majority in the House of Commons, the House of Lords interposes no check upon legislative innovations of the most violent and unexpected kind, as we saw in the case of the Education Act of 1902 and the Licensing Act of 1904. On the other hand, a Liberal majority in the House of Commons, as has been demonstrated during the last four years, is, under existing conditions, impotent to place on the Statute-book the very measures which it was sent to Westminster to carry in to law.

It is absurd to speak of this system as though it secured to us any of the advantages of a Second Chamber, in the sense in which that term is understood and practically interpreted in every other democratic country.

The limitation of the veto is the first and most urgent step to be taken; for it is the condition precedent to the attainment of the great legislative reforms which our party has at heart, and which I laid before my fellow Liberals in a recent speech at the Albert Hall.

I appeal to you, in this momentous crisis, with confidence, for the support which during twenty-four years you have never withdrawn from me.

LIBERAL PARTY GENERAL ELECTION MANIFESTO DECEMBER 1910

Mr Herbert Asquith's election address

Date of Election	December 2–December 19
Party Leader	Herbert Asquith
Candidates	467
MPs	272
Votes	2,295,888
% of vote	43.9%

I ask you to renew the unbroken relationship between us, as Constituency and Member, which has now entered upon its twenty-fifth year.

During the whole of this long connection there has been complete confidence both on the one side and the other, and neither you nor I have ever wavered in our allegiance to the great ideals and purposes of which the Liberal Party is the champion and trustee.

I am, therefore, not under the necessity, which would be binding on a new-comer, of making to you any general profession of political faith. As lately as January in the present year, I expounded to you in detail, and you approved by a decisive majority at the poll, the present aims of liberal policy.

The appeal which is now being made to you and to the country at large may almost be said to be narrowed to a single issue. But upon its determination, in one sense or the other, hangs the whole future of Democratic Government.

Are the people, through their freely chosen representatives, to have control, not only over finance and administrative Policy, but over the making of their laws? Or are we to continue the one-sided system under which a Tory majority, however small in size and casual in creation, has a free run of the Statute Book, while from Liberal legislation, however clear may be the message of the polls, the forms of the Constitution persistently withhold a fair and even chance?

You will not, I am sure, be misled in the judgement you are called upon to pronounce by the belated and delusive composition which the House of Lords is, at the last moment, being advised to offer to its critics. The schemes which are now being put forward, in the hope of disguising the real issue, would result, if they were carried into law, in the creation of a Second Chamber predominantly Conservative in character, practically inoperative while there is a Tory majority in the House of Commons, completely independent of the prerogatives of the Crown, and capable of interposing an even more formidable veto than the present House of Lords upon the prompt and effective translation into law of the declared will of the nation.

I ask you to repeat, with still greater emphasis, the approval which only eleven months ago you gave to the proposals of His Majesty's Government.

LIBERAL PARTY GENERAL ELECTION MANIFESTO 1918

Mr Herbert Asquith's election address

Date of Election	Saturday 14 December
Party Leader	Herbert Asquith
Candidates	253 (plus 158 Coalition Liberal Candidates)
MPs	28 (plus 133 Coalition Liberal MPs)
Votes	1,298,808 (plus 1,455,640 Coalition Liberal votes)
% of vote	12.1% (plus 13.5% Coalition votes)

It was in the summer of 1886 that I was first elected member for East Fife. Our boundaries have now been enlarged, and I appeal to the new constituency to grant me a renewal of the confidence which I have enjoyed for an unbroken term of more than thirty-two years. The Parliament which has just been dissolved has been one of the most remarkable in our history. It carried through a series of great political and social changes, and in its later years had sanctioned and sustained to the end with patriotic unity our national part in the Great War. During most of those stirring events it was my privilege to be First Minister of the Crown. It was while I held that office that our Empire entered the war; that our vast voluntary armies, largely through the genius and energy of Lord Kitchener, were raised and organised; that Italy became associated with us as an Ally; that the Military Service Act was passed into law; that the enemy's cruisers and merchant ships were driven from the seas and his ports blocked; and that by rigorous taxation, as well as the use of our unrivalled credit, we were enabled not only to bear our own burden, but substantially to lighten that of our fellow combatants. Throughout the war, whether in or out of office, I have supported every measure for its efficient and successful prosecution. Hostilities have now been brought to a glorious end, and it is impossible to overstate the decisive importance of the part played in the struggle by our own Navy, our Army, our Air Force, and our Mercantile Marine. We can also look forward with confidence to the complete attainment of the common purpose which I set forth on behalf of the Allies at the beginning of the war, and to the bringing into being of a League of Nations, which will, we hope, secure the peace of the world and the reign of international justice and humanity.

With peace we must set our own house in order. We must be on our guard to make secure what has already been won. There must be no tampering with the essentials of Free Trade. Self-government for Ireland must be promptly translated from what it is already – a statutory right – into a working reality. Temporary restraints necessary in war upon personal liberty and the free expression of opinion must be removed without delay. The ties which unite us to our fellow-subjects in the great Dominions have been strengthened by our comradeship in the efforts and sacrifices of the war. Peace will bring with it a call and a stimulus to the inter-Imperial development of our common resources in men and material, and to the more frequent and intimate interchange of counsel, without any impairment of complete local autonomy. To India we owe an early redemption of the pledges which with the assent of all parties, have been given by the Imperial Government.

In the field of creative reform at home, social and industrial – our first duty is owed to those who have won us the victory and to the dependants of the fallen. In the priorities of reconstruction they have the first claim, and every facility should be given them not only for reinstatement, and for protection against want and unemployment, but for such training and equipment as will open out for them fresh avenues and new careers. The war has cleared away a mass of obstructive prejudices and conventions, and with peace will come a realisable prospect of a new and better ordered society. Some of the earliest and most practical steps to be taken in regard to land, housing, health, temperance, the future conditions of industry, were recently indicated by me at Manchester. I summed up their general purpose in the following words: –

'In every chapter of reconstruction I should be prepared to adopt for myself, and to recommend to my friends, as an appropriate watchword the formula of a national minimum. In concrete terms, I understand that to mean that we ought not to be content until every British citizen – man, woman, and child – has in possession or within reach a standard of existence – physical, intellectual, moral, social – which makes life worth living, and not only does not block, but opens the road to its best and highest possibilities.'

But I am not bound (as none of us should be) to any cut-and-dried programme. I will give wholehearted support, reserving in regard to particular measures complete freedom of judgement and action to any policy from any quarter, Liberal, Unionist, or Labour, which proceeds on these lines, and is animated by this spirit. The best security for the successful prosecution of such a policy is that, in accordance with our traditions, it should be subject to full scrutiny in the free atmosphere of a representative House of Commons. For that purpose it is essential that every elector should claim and should exercise unfettered liberty of choice.

LIBERAL PARTY GENERAL ELECTION MANIFESTO 1922

Manifesto to the Nation

Date of Election	Wednesday 15 November
Party Leader	Herbert Asquith
Candidates	328 (plus 162 National Liberals)
MPs	54 (plus 62 National Liberals)
Votes	2,516,287 (plus 1,673,240 National Liberal votes)
% of vote	17.5% (plus 11.6%)

The Conservatives and Mr Lloyd George

The complete collapse of the Coalition Government at length gives the Electors an opportunity of pronouncing their verdict upon its performances, and of deciding where to put their trust in the future. For four years the alliance between Mr Lloyd George and the Conservative Party has dominated the affairs of the nation. This combination has now broken up in general confusion and discredit, leaving behind it an unexampled record of extravagance and failure. It must be remembered that both wings of the Coalition are responsible for its misdeeds, and neither can escape its share of public condemnation.

The circumstances of the Coupon Election were so abnormal that it was easy to be misled by the specious appeal then put forward jointly by Mr Lloyd George and Mr Bonar Law. But the events which have since happened constitute a complete justification of the warning which Liberal leaders then gave that the continuance of Coalition meant the abandonment of principle and the substitution of autocratic for Parliamentary Government.

It is now universally agreed that what the last House of Commons and the country needed was an opposition strong enough in numbers not only to express, but to make effective its criticisms both of expenditure and of policy.

Failures of the old government

Mr Lloyd George and his colleagues have spent as they pleased; their Peace Treaties are impossible of fulfilment; they have shown themselves equally incapable of securing good understandings abroad and of pursuing consistent policy at home. No confidence could be placed in their declarations whether in the industrial or the international sphere.

The nation demands a complete change – conviction instead of compromise, economy instead of extravagance and waste.

The Liberal Party: the only economists

Now that economy – the supreme need of the nation – has become a popular watch-word, its value is everywhere proclaimed. But the Electors will not be satisfied with the belated and coerced repentance of those who have been responsible for wasteful expenditure in the past.

The one Party in the State which has consistently fought waste, challenged estimates, moved reductions and stood for economy is the Independent Liberal Party.

It did so when economy was unpopular, and when the leaders of the late Coalition denied and ridiculed the possibility of retrenchment. The country will judge those who formed and supported the Coalition, not by what they now say, but by what they, when in power, then did.

The Liberal Party and Ireland

The Liberal Party rejoices that there is now general assent to the Irish settlement on the lines of Dominion Home Rule, but it must not be forgotten that for a year the Coalition was engaged in a futile attempt to reduce Ireland to submission by the exercise of undisciplined force. It was the Independent Liberals both in and out of Parliament who aroused the conscience of the country to the criminal folly of such methods, and consistently pressed the policy of conciliation which was too tardily adopted.

When the late Government led the country into disastrous and costly adventures in Russia and Mesopotamia it was again Independent Liberalism which denounced the recklessness of these enterprises.

Free Trade

By the terms of the compact which brought it into being the Coalition was bound to make a breach in our Free Trade system. At every stage in the series of irritating and ill-conceived measures which have hampered our industrial recovery during the last four years, it has been Independent Liberalism that has fought the battle against Protection and Government interference. What is needed in the new Parliament is the full and effective expression of the Liberal spirit.

Liberalism is not Socialism. Liberalism repudiates the doctrine of warfare against private enterprise.

Programme of the Liberal Party

It stands for:

1 Peace and disarmament made secure through the League of Nations.
2 The prompt revision and settlement of Reparations and Inter-Allied Debts.
3 Drastic Economy in public expenditure and the abandonment of the policy of military adventures abroad.
4 Fulfilment by the community of its responsibility for securing the workers against the hardships of unemployment, co-operation between Capital and labour, and honest and fair treatment of organised labour as the only basis of industrial peace.

5 Unqualified Free Trade with the immediate repeal of the Safeguarding of Industries Act and similar protective measures.
6 The defence of such essential social services as Education, Housing, and Public Health.
7 Political and legal equality for women and men.
8 A comprehensive reform of the existing Land System, including the Taxation and Rating of Land Values.
9 The democratic reform of our Licensing System.
10 Re-adjustment of our electoral system by the introduction of Proportional Representation.

Liberals stand for the nation

It would be easy to follow the example of others and attempt to purchase electoral support by displaying a long series of glittering promises. But the country has too much reason to know the difference between promise and performance, and the simple truth is that great and necessary schemes of social reform, involving large outlay of public money, cannot be realised unless and until real Peace has been established by a foreign policy based upon and conceived in the spirit of the League of Nations and National Finance is placed upon sure foundations by a course of rigorous economy. By these means, and by these means alone, can prosperity be promoted, employment assured, and taxes lightened.

The essence of the Liberal spirit is that it sets the well-being of the community as a whole above the interests of any particular section or class. It is this spirit which distinguishes Liberalism from any other political party which is now appealing for electoral support. The moment has come to restore Liberalism to its rightful place in the councils of the Nation.

LIBERAL PARTY GENERAL ELECTION MANIFESTO 1923

A call to the nation

Date of Election	Thursday 6 December
Party Leader	Herbert Asquith
Candidates	453
MPs	159
Votes	4,311,147
% of vote	29.6%

The Government, elected twelve months ago on a programme of five years of tranquillity, has suddenly decided to plunge the country into the turmoil of a General Election, on the allegation – unproved and unproveable – that Tariffs are a cure for unemployment. The Prime Minister has deliberately chosen the earliest possible date for the Polls in order to avoid informing the House of Commons, and through the House of Commons the country, as to the reasons and the scope of his proposals. Tory Ministers profess that they are driven to this precipitate action by a sudden inspiration concerning unemployment, and hope to stampede the country by reviving the musty war-cry that Tariff Reform means work for all.

Failure of the Conservative Government

There is one explanation and one only, for the course which the Government have pursued. It is that in a single year their conduct of foreign policy in great matters essential to our livelihood has signally and disastrously failed. By their own declarations, repeatedly made, the first condition of our recovery is the restoration, not merely of the home market, but of world trade. By their own declarations in Despatches, addressed to our Allies, the growing collapse produced by French policy in Germany, and the reaction of that policy upon trade and credit, throughout Europe, are the main cause of the distress in which our trade is plunged. For at least a century past, no greater economic, political or moral question has confronted Europe than the French and Belgian occupation of the heart of German industry in the Ruhr. In no great European question, for at least a century past, has it ever been doubtful where Britain stood. Yet for a whole year neither our Allies, nor Neutral Powers, nor our late enemies, have known whether in this crucial issue Britain had a voice or mind or conscience of her own.

In January the Government refused to associate the country with the occupation of the Ruhr; but for months they half condoned it and waited on results. Only when its failure was becoming manifest did they declare their view, held apparently since January, that the invasion was a breach of the Treaty of Versailles. In December of last year the American Secretary of State, Mr Hughes, offered American co-operation in an impartial investigation of Germany's capacity to make reparation for damage done in the war. The British Government took no steps for nine whole months to urge acceptance of this offer upon our Allies. In June Germany put forward proposals, largely on Lord Curzon's prompting, for meeting the Allies' demands. The British Government declared, quite properly, that these proposals called for reply. Five months have passed, and no reply has ever been made. British policy was one of the chief rallying powers in Europe after the Napoleonic wars. For the past year its blindness, indecision and impotence have been such that it has ceased to exercise any guiding influence upon European affairs.

In Eastern policy the tale has been the same. It was not enough that we should abandon all for which we fought against Turkey in the war. By the shameless Treaty of Lausanne we have also surrendered all the securities for British commerce in Turkey which we enjoyed before the war. By the policy which we have followed British trade in Turkey is practically at an end. Our weakness has been noted elsewhere, and a similar fate now threatens our hold of valuable markets in the Far East.

By moral indecision, by divided counsels, and by diplomatic incompetence, the Government have failed in Europe and Asia alike, to make one single effective effort to assert our rights, to restore our trade, or to bring back peace and order to a distracted world.

Every serious observer of contemporary affairs knows that Liberal criticism of this policy during the Parliament now dissolved was abundantly justified. Our warnings were left unheeded, and the inaction of the Government has been a potent contributory cause of unemployment at home.

Liberal foreign policy

Liberal policy stands for the prompt settlement of Reparations, with due consideration for the position of inter-allied debts, and for an earnest endeavour to co-operate with the great American Commonwealth in bringing peace to the world. Liberals hold that the economic restoration of Europe is the necessary condition of the revival of our industries and the establishment of peace. They would welcome the reopening of full relations with Russia.

The whole force of the Liberal Party will be thrown into the support of the League of Nations. Our foreign policy should aim at making full use of the League, and enlarging its scope and power, until all nations are included within it, and at substituting international co-operation for the perpetuation of national enmities and the piling up of the means of destruction.

Protection no cure for unemployment

But the return to normal economic conditions must take time, and in the interval unemployed men and women cannot be left to await better times with no prospect but unemployment benefit and Poor Law relief. The schemes of the Government are totally inadequate.

Trade restrictions cannot cure unemployment. Post-war conditions do not justify such restrictions; they merely render it more disastrous. High prices and scarcity can only lower the standard of living, reduce the purchasing power of the country, and thereby curtail production. An examination of the figures shows that the suggested tariff cannot possibly assist those trades in which unemployment is most rife. The last thing which taxation on imports can achieve is to provide more work for those engaged in manufacture for export.

Mr Baldwin asks for a blank cheque, and if he is wrong the country must take the risk. He offers no evidence. He formulates no scheme. In the face of declarations made last year by prominent Tariff Reformers like Mr Bonar Law and Mr Austen Chamberlain, that after-war conditions make proposals for Tariff Reform inopportune and injurious, he asks for power to tax an undefined number of commodities, without any disclosure of the scale or range of the duties, or the industries to be disturbed.

Liberal policy on unemployment

The Liberal Party is equally convinced that the remedies recommended for unemployment by the Labour Party – Socialism and the Capital Levy – would prove disastrous. What is needed is not the destruction of enterprise but its encouragement; not the frightening away of Capital but its fruitful use.

The Liberal Party is not content with criticising the proposals of others. The country has made enormous sacrifices to restore the national credit. A bold and courageous use should be made of that credit on enterprises that would permanently improve and develop the home country and the Empire; such as internal transport by road and water, afforestation, the supply of cheap power secured by the co-ordinated use of our resources of coal and water, reclamation and drainage of land, the development of Imperial resources especially in our Crown Colonies, railway building in the Dominions and India, the facilitation of overseas settlement under the British flag, cheapening the means of transport in order to develop inter-imperial trade, and a freer use of the provisions of the Trade Facilities Act.

Insurance, security, partnership

The Liberal Party proposes thoroughly to remodel the Insurance Acts with a view to providing benefits sufficient to allow a reasonable subsistence to a man and his family without aid from Poor Law Relief. The Poor Law Authorities should not have to bear a burden which ought to be regarded, not as a local, but as a national charge.

The Liberal Party will take all possible steps to promote the co-operation of employers and employed. The worker should be secured a proper status and a fair share in the produce of the industry in which he is engaged. Liberal industrial policy is based upon the principles of partnership between Labour and Capital, security of livelihood for the worker, and public advantage before private profit.

Equal rights for men and women

Women electors should be among the first to recognise and resist the Protectionist attack on the standard of life of the poorest homes in the country. Of all sections of

41

the community they are in the closest and most intimate contact with prices, and no one will suffer more from Tariffs than the Chancellor of the Exchequer of the home. Liberals aim at securing political, legal, and economic equality between men and women. Mothers and Fathers should have equal rights and responsibilities in the guardianship of their children.

Pensions

The thrift disqualification attached to Old Age Pensions should be immediately removed. Liberal policy concentrates upon lifting from the homes of the poor those burdens and anxieties of the old, the sick, and the widow with young children, which the community has the power and duty to relieve.

The farmer and the farmworker

The needs of British Agriculture require special consideration. Import duties on what the farmer buys can only further injure his position. British Agriculture requires a free hand, stability of prices, greater capital resources, security of tenure, adequate means for preventing the exaction of unfair and uneconomic rents, and improved transport. Credit facilities for the farmer, and co-operative marketing on a large scale with Government assistance, which has so successfully helped American agriculture over a great crisis, can also be applied in our own country. Opportunity should be given for the cultivator to become the owner of his own land on reasonable terms by a system of land purchase. A free man on his own land, whether as farmer or smallholder, has always proved the most successful and energetic of producers. Small holdings and allotments should be developed and encouraged.

The agricultural Labourer is engaged in a skilled industry of cardinal importance to the nation, and ought to be adequately remunerated. The State must recognise that the conditions of his work make it vital to secure that his standard of life should be raised, his housing vastly improved, and the amenities of rural life enlarged. Every opportunity should be given to him and his children to improve their position on the land which he has cultivated for so long.

Social reform

Unemployment is also caused by over-taxation and wasteful administration. There is urgent need and abundant scope for retrenchment in the expenditure of the taxpayer's money in some departments of public service. The Liberal Party draws a sharp distinction between the use of the National revenue for purposes which add to the wealth and comfort of the people as a whole and the waste of public money in directions which are unproductive or destructive. Liberals will be no parties to the starvation of, or to false economies in, Education. They believe that no better investment of National Wealth can anywhere be found than in developing the faculties and intelligence of the youth of the country.

For the same reason, Liberal Policy centres upon the promotion of all those things which build up the home – housing, temperance, child-welfare and other social services.

Housing

The rapid and adequate provision of Housing Accommodation is an urgent public duty. It should be treated, not as a local, but as a national problem; and until the present shortage has been overtaken, there should be no decontrol of rents.

Temperance

The excessive consumption of alcoholic drink is one of the main causes of unemployment, disease, and poverty; and the right of the citizens of a locality to decide for themselves the drink facilities in their own area should no longer be withheld.

Land and rating reform

Reforms in local government and rating are long overdue. For some years the Poor Law system has been ripe for legislative revision. The overlapping of Insurance, Old Age Pensions, and Poor Law Relief requires immediate action. The present rating system discourages improvement and penalises those who create industries or provide houses; it must be so altered that as great a part of the burden of rates as is practicable is transferred to those who benefit most by the efforts of the community, namely, the owners of the site value.

The dweller in the town, like the dweller on the land, should be entitled, if he so demands and his terms are fair, to become the owner of his factory, shop or home. Lease-hold enfranchisement has long been an object of Liberal policy. It is time that it became the law of the land.

Mr Baldwin's sudden plunge has thrown his own supporters into confusion and has firmly united the Liberal Forces. The country has now the opportunity of overthrowing a Government whose record is one of unrelieved futility, and of calling for an alternative administration, which will pursue Peace and Reconciliation abroad, Social and Industrial improvement at home, and which is definitely committed to the defence of Free Trade as the best basis upon which to rebuild the life of the Nation.

LIBERAL PARTY GENERAL ELECTION MANIFESTO 1924

The Liberal Manifesto

Date of Election	Wednesday 29 October
Party Leader	Herbert Asquith
Candidates	340
MPs	40
Votes	2,298,747
% of vote	17.6%

The country has been plunged into a General Election for the third time in two years. This election has been forced on us by the Labour Prime Minister and his Government for two reasons.

First, they were not prepared to face an impartial enquiry into the circumstances which led to the withdrawal of a prosecution against a Communist writer for inciting to mutiny in the Navy and Army. Next, they wished to evade Parliamentary discussion of a reckless proposal to guarantee, at the risk of the British taxpayer, a loan to the Communist Government of Russia.

Liberalism in the last Parliament

The Liberal Party in Parliament, whilst they have rejected crude schemes of 'Nationalisation' promoted by the Labour Party, have assisted the Government in every move made by it towards sound social reform, and they regret that the efforts of the Ministry in that direction have been so halting, ineffective and unimaginative.

They have pressed the Government week by week to fulfil its pledges to provide work for the unemployed by schemes of National Development, in order that we might be adequately equipped to meet the competition of our trade rivals. They have urged that the credit of the nation should be used in permanently improving and developing the Home Country and the Empire, such as Power Supply, Afforestation, Reclamation and Drainage of Land, Overseas Settlement under the British flag and development of the Empire's resources. The Government has taken no definite or effective action in these matters.

They have pressed the Government repeatedly to fulfil their election promises to the Ex-Service men, the War fighters in the Civil Service, the ex-ranker Officers and others; again without result.

The Liberal Party are in full sympathy with all efforts for mutual disarmament and for the promotion of international peace. But they have been unable to prevent the

Government increasing Military Estimates by twelve millions over the expenditure of last year, or starting a naval race in the building of new cruisers.

The Russian blunder

The Liberal Party is in favour of re-establishing economic and commercial relations with the Russian people. But at a time when every nerve should be strained to re-establish British credit and equip British industry for the recovery of foreign trade, the Labour Ministry has undertaken to recommend Parliament to ratify a Treaty which contemplates that the British taxpayer should guarantee a loan to a Government whose principles deny the obligations which civilised nations regard as binding between borrower and lender, This was done shortly after the Prime Minister had declared in the House of Commons that only credulous people would believe that he would countenance such a procedure.

The Government and unemployment

In 'Labour's Appeal to the Nation', the manifesto on which the Labour Party fought the last Election, the confident assertion was made that the Labour Party alone had a positive remedy for unemployment. The country has waited in vain for this remedy to be produced, let alone applied. Unemployment is more serious now than when the Government came into power. At that time the number of unemployed persons was 1,153,600. The most recent Return, that of September 29th this year, shows that the number of unemployed has swollen to 1,198,800, and it is still increasing. The Government's policy on this vital question has been one of drift and indecision. Nothing new and effective has been done, and their profuse electoral promises remain to this day unredeemed.

Housing

It has long been obvious that the solution of the Housing Problem depends mainly on a sufficiency of skilled building labour being made available. Mr Wheatley's Housing Act professed to deal, specifically with this part of the problem. But no effective measures have been taken to train young apprentices, or otherwise to increase the number of building craftsmen. Instead of its being possible to say that under the Wheatley Act progress in house building has been made, the fact is that fewer houses are now being begun than when the Government came into office. The Liberal policy on housing is to insist that the reserve of unemployed labour should be utilised to build houses for the people.

The land problem

Liberalism, in pursuance of its historic role of giving equal opportunities to all classes, and of creating the fundamental conditions of economic and political freedom, has a special responsibility for promoting and carrying through great policies of land reform.

Land and agriculture

The long-standing neglect of agriculture in Great Britain must be redressed. Real improvement cannot be achieved either by fantastic schemes for setting officials to control all imported and home-grown food, or by impracticable and mischievous measures for taxing imported food. It can be achieved only by securing to land workers the fruits of their energy and enterprise through a complete alteration in the system of land tenure. That system must be modified in accordance with modern necessities. The Liberal land policy contemplates a land tenure which would combine the advantages of ownership and of tenancy without the disadvantages of either. On the basis of this reform can be built a coherent scheme of agricultural credit with the assistance of the State, of businesslike marketing of produce, of co-ordinating transport services, of draining and reclaiming land for productive uses.

The Liberal policy is to liberate farmers from the restrictions of an out-of-date land system; to liberate agricultural labourers from poverty and lack of opportunity; and to make the best use of all the land of the country in the interest of the whole community.

Towns and the land

A large section of our town dwellers have neither room to live nor room to work, nor room to play. Many of the evils of town life are the result of allowing private owners of land to hold up growing towns by withholding land from use, and selling it yard by yard at exorbitant prices. The Liberal land policy for the towns is to enable towns to assert their rights, to undo the results of past neglect, and to create the conditions necessary for the health of town workers and the efficiency of industry. Land Values, created by the activity and expenditure of the community, must be made to contribute to the expenses of maintaining the conveniences, utilities, and amenities of the town. The degradation and disgrace of our slums must be wiped out, and facilities for all classes of the population to get access to the fresh air and open spaces provided. The leasehold system, which allows landowners to take for themselves the fruits of traders' enterprise, must be reformed. Occupiers of dwelling houses held on lease must be given the right to purchase their freehold at a price which will not confiscate the investment made in building or buying their homes. Occupiers of shops and business premises on short leases must be enabled to obtain from a Land Court compulsory orders for the renewal of their leases on fair terms. In order to control effectively their future development, towns must be given power to acquire at fair prices all land likely to be required in the future for housing, open spaces, and other purposes connected with the health and welfare of their population. The radical cure of slums by building new Industrial Towns, planned from the beginning for healthy living, comfort, amenity and efficient industry, must be taken in hand, and there as elsewhere all increments in value created by the community secured by it.

Coal and power

The hindrances to national prosperity imposed by our present system of land tenure particularly obstruct the development of the great industry of coal mining. Largely owing to the land system our coal resources are wastefully used and wrongly applied. Nothing is more urgent in the national interest than to bring permanent peace to our coal fields, and so to use our coal as to make it a far greater source of wealth and power.

The coal problem is intimately linked up with the power problem, since power is coming more and more to mean electrical power, in generating and distributing which we are falling far behind our leading competitors. The Liberal policy is to make coal what it ought to be and is in many other countries – a great national asset – by empowering the State to acquire all mineral rights, and to provide State assistance and direction in the building of super-power stations. By a levy on the purchase price at which mining royalties are taken over by the State, funds will be provided for rebuilding and bettering the mining villages, many of which are a disgrace to the country and a standing menace to the peace and efficiency of the industry.

Education

The Liberal Party has worked out a ten years' programme of educational advance. If it comes into power it will wipe out the arrears of educational reform which have accumulated in unprogressive areas; it will get rid of the worst buildings, and will reduce the size of the classes in Elementary Schools. It will effect much-needed reform in Rural Education and improve the qualification of teachers. With special concern for young workers in and out of work, and for more Secondary Schools, it will press for large additional provision for pupils over 14 years of age with maintenance allowance in suitable cases. It will extend provision for University Education, and, as regards Technical, Evening and Adult Education, it will seek to collaborate with employers and employed in making a determined effort to increase the efficiency of all schools which prepare the youth of the nation for their vocation in life and fit them for their responsibilities as future citizens. It recognises that the fulfilment of these aims demands such conditions of service and such payment of teachers as shall secure a constant and increasing supply of properly qualified men and women, and believes that satisfactory conditions as regards remuneration can best be secured by national agreement.

Free Trade

The Liberal Party holds unshakeably by its policy of Free Trade. The country gave its verdict a year ago on the policy of Protection, and it may safely be trusted in the present election to give an equally decisive verdict on the Labour Party's policy of Controls and Shackles.

Industrial peace

The alarming increase in recent years of industrial disputes, unless arrested, will inevitably destroy our supremacy in the markets of the world.

The Liberal remedy is the co-operation of all engaged in industry – investor, manager, workman – and the fair distribution of its profits amongst all engaged in it. It is by co-operation and goodwill, and not by Socialism, that prosperity can be restored to

British Trade and better wages and security of employment obtained for British Workmen.

Social insurance

A further extension and a complete co-ordination of the Insurance Acts, which were initiated by the Liberal Party before the War, is now a matter of urgent national necessity. The Liberal policy is that the various schemes of social and economic insurance which are now in operation should be so amended and consolidated as to make certain that the benefits provided shall afford a man and his family a reasonable subsistence, without the necessity for applying for relief from the Poor Law. Old Age Pensions must be freed from the disqualifications attaching to thrift. Pensions for widows and allowances for orphans during their school life must be provided. Breadwinners breaking down in health before the age of 70 must be assured of support outside the Poor Law. All this must be carried out by a comprehensive policy of contributory insurance, maintaining self-respect and giving to all citizens security against destitution.

Temperance

One of the gravest social problems of the day is that of the excessive consumption of alcoholic liquor. It ought to be dealt with, in the light of experiments made at home and abroad, on bold and democratic lines. Here, too, the record of the Government is utterly disappointing. Its attitude to temperance legislation is illustrated by the rejection through Labour votes of the temperance proposals put forward by Welsh Liberal members. This shows how little faith can be placed in the professions which the Labour Party made while in Opposition, but are either unable or unwilling to fulfil when in power.

Electoral reform

The existing machinery for expressing in Parliament the will of the people is delusive and misleading. It is apt to give a decisive majority in Parliament to a pronounced minority of votes in the country. In the last three elections it worked out unequally and unfairly. It is imperative that effective steps should be taken to secure a real correspondence between Parliamentary representation and electoral strength.

Sane progress

In placing Labour in power, Liberalism followed constitutional usage. In voting against the Government, Liberalism has consulted the deepest interests of the country's security, credit, and good government. The people have now a choice to make between three parties. They have an opportunity of putting in power a Liberal Government which will pursue the path of Peace, Social Reform and National Development, avoiding, on the one hand, unthinking resistance to progress, and, on the other hand, unbalanced experiments and impracticable schemes which will destroy the whole social and economic system upon which the prosperity of this country has been built.

LIBERAL PARTY GENERAL ELECTION MANIFESTO 1929

Mr Lloyd George's election address

Date of Election	Thursday 30 May
Party Leader	David Lloyd George
Candidates	513
MPs	59
Votes	5,308,510
% of vote	23.4%

Failure of the Government

The General Election now in progress will have an important and in some respects a decisive influence on the well-being of this great country. The by-elections of the last two years have made it abundantly clear that the nation has lost confidence in the present Government. Its complete failure to grapple with the serious emergency in our trade and the consequent abnormal unemployment has created a general sense of disappointment in all classes of the community. Even Conservatives do not conceal their disillusionment with the Government they succeeded in placing in power five years ago. Whatever the result of this election may be, it is clear that the supporters of the Government will be in an emphatic minority in the next Parliament.

Revival of Liberalism

The issue, therefore, for the electors is whether they will entrust the destinies of the country to the Liberal Party, which can show a long record of great and enduring service to the nation, and which can command to-day amongst its leaders a number of able and experienced men, who in some of the highest offices of the State served their country well, or to the Socialist Party, which, apart altogether from being inexperienced, is committed to proposals which would be disastrous to the trade, commerce, and industry of the land. Reports come in from every part of this island which indicate a sensational revival of the trust in Liberalism and a general desire to see the affairs of the nation once more placed in the hands of a Liberal Administration.

 For the twelfth time I solicit the suffrage of my fellow-electors of Caernarvon Boroughs. Having represented them in the House of Commons continuously since 1890, I need enter upon no elaborate explanation of my political opinions. On all such matters as the urgent importance of restoring agriculture to its proper position in the economy of the nation, the vital need for ampler facilities for education, the temperance question, housing, and the complex problem of giving security, leasehold enfranchisement, opportunities, and independence to the poorer and less fortunate sections of the community, the importance of Empire development, and certainly not least the fair treatment for all questions specially affecting Wales, her language, and her people, my views are well known to you. In this election I only want to stress what seems to me to be major issues which call for urgent treatment.

Peace

The greatest world issue before the country to-day is peace. Everybody wants peace and talks peace, but the acid test of whether covenants, treaties, and pacts of peace mean anything, and whether the Government mean them to mean anything, is disarmament. If the Government has confidence in the League of Nations, in the Kellogg Pact, in the Washington Treaties they will cut their vast and swollen armaments to the police level. If they continue to spend money on armaments and organise conscript nations in arms, it is because they really trust not in peaceful methods, but in war. We are spending £112,000,000 a year on armaments and little more than £100,000 a year on the League of Nations.

My first object, if elected to the new Parliament, will be to urge that immediate steps be taken to give a practical response to the offer, made by President Hoover in his inaugural address, to co-operate with other nations to bring about that large and simultaneous reduction of armaments which is the only sure protection against war, and the only sure foundation for peace. A conference of nations to discuss measures that will lead to drastic reduction in these increasing armaments should be immediately summoned.

Unemployment

The central domestic issue which confronts us is unemployment. There can be no national health, no widespread prosperity, there can be no national happiness and contentment so long as more than a million of our fellow-countrymen are unable to find work and earn wages by their work. The nation ought, and will rally to whatever party can give grounds for believing that it can get rid of this running sore from the body-politic.

The Liberal Party has not simply made election promises. As a result of the only thorough and consistent study which has been given to our national problems during the last few years by some of the ablest economic experts, aided by experienced business men, it has produced a sound, safe, practical programme for every elector to judge for him or her self.

Last February the Prime Minister stated in the House of Commons that 'in the view of the Government the object which we desire can best be attained by perseverance in our policy', by perseverance, that is to say, in a policy which has resulted in unemployment being substantially the same as it was when they came into office in 1924. The Labour Party policy was recently announced by Mr Ramsay MacDonald at the Albert Hall. If they are returned to power they will appoint another committee.

A practical policy

The Liberal policy is a practical policy. In the first place it seeks to restore the prosperity of our industries by breaking down the barriers to international trade, by promoting harmonious relations between employer and employed, by encouraging in every way greater efficiency in industry, and by restoring the Trades Facilities Act, which gave the support of the national credit to industrial enterprise of a substantial and valuable kind and which could not be initiated or carried out without special assistance. Before that Act was abandoned by the present Government, enterprises of the aggregate value of £74,000,000 were put through at an infinitesimal cost to the Treasury.

In the second place, it pledges itself to find immediate employment for those now out of work on works of national utility and development, many of these works, like electricity, telephones, housing, roads, and railways, being long overdue. It is surely better, instead of wasting our substance by spending £70,000,000 a year on 'doles' for which there is no return, to lay out this enormous expenditure in providing work on plans which will leave the nation richer and more efficient for its tasks. The details of these plans are set forth in the liberal pamphlet 'We Can Conquer Unemployment', and need not be repeated here.

Free Trade

I shall continue my life-long opposition to the policy of raising prices at home and impeding foreign trade by Protection. Freer trade for all nations is the only road to national, Imperial, and international prosperity.

The Liberal watchwords

The Liberal programme deals with the immediate and ultimate needs of the nation. Its watchwords are:

- the restoration of prosperity to our industries;
- the conquest of unemployment;
- the cutting down of unproductive expenditure;
- temperance reform;
- the completion of proper housing for the people;
- slum clearance;
- revitalisation of agriculture;
- the emancipation of the leaseholder from harsh and unjust conditions that confiscate his capital and toil;
- a great expansion of education;
- vigorous national development of the resources of the country;
- Imperial unity;
- the devolution of purely national questions within the nation to the nationalities concerned;
- freer trade;

- international peace by the substitution of arbitration for force, and an all-round reduction of armaments.

It is on this programme that I confidently seek re-election.

LIBERAL PARTY GENERAL ELECTION MANIFESTO 1931

Liberal address to the Nation

Date of Election	Tuesday 27 October
Party Leader	Sir Herbert Samuel
Candidates	112
MPs	33
Votes	1,403,102
% of vote	6.5%

The country is faced by an economic crisis of great gravity. Not only has Britain been driven off the Gold Standard, but almost every other nation is reeling under the strain of an unparalleled depression.

Nothing save the highest statesmanship can steer the world back to normal conditions and prevent disasters of the greatest magnitude.

The Liberal Party held that the Government and Parliament should devote themselves to the vast and urgent tasks that faced them, without a General Election at this time. But the Prime Minister has decided to appeal to the country for a mandate to carry through whatever measures may be found to be needed to deal with the emergency, and the electorate is now called upon to give its judgement.

In these circumstances, the Liberal Ministers have felt it their duty to co-operate with the Prime Minister in maintaining a strong and stable Government composed of men of all parties.

Situation still critical

The situation to-day is not less critical than it was when the National Government was formed. Despite the fact that the Budget has been balanced, the nation has gone off the Gold Standard, and the effects of this on national and international credit, and on the cost of our food and raw materials, have yet to be fully felt.

The vital need of to-day is to avoid any inflation of the pound, which would mean a rapid fall in the purchasing power of money, the loss of savings, large and small, and a general lowering of the standard of life of the whole community.

Common action by the countries of the world is urgently required to stabilise currency, to deal with international debts and reparations, and to make a powerful effort to secure a lowering of the tariff barriers to trade which are without doubt one of the principal causes of the universal depression and unprecedented unemployment.

At home it is imperative both to keep the Budget balanced and to secure a favourable balance of trade, by whatever methods, whether related to currency, to the expansion of exports or the restriction of imports, which might be found to be necessary and effective for that purpose. At the same time, energetic action should be taken to promote industrial and agricultural development, with a view to increasing the production of foodstuffs at home and the export of manufactured goods abroad.

The Liberal Party goes to the polls as the vigorous advocate of those Liberal aims and ideals which have rendered the highest service to the country and to the Empire. We are strongly of opinion that no issues of controversy between the parties supporting the Government should have been introduced at this election.

Having regard, however, to pronouncements that have been made, we feel bound to declare our view that whatever emergency measures might be found to be necessary to deal with the immediate situation, freedom of trade is the only permanent basis for our economic prosperity and for the welfare of the Empire and of the world. Protection has not saved those countries which have adopted it from more acute unemployment than ourselves.

Taxation on the staple foods of the people has always been opposed by the Liberal Party and would lay fresh burdens on those least able to bear them.

The abandonment by Great Britain of her free trade policy would aggravate the divisions between nations and would check the growing realisation throughout the world of the disasters towards which they have been leading mankind.

The nation's sacrifices

It is profoundly to be regretted that the financial difficulties of this time have put a check upon measures of social reform and of national development, and have demanded severe sacrifices from the whole nation.

Liberalism, which for generations has played a leading part in the effort to raise the standards of life of the people, and which still stands as the principal bulwark between the country and a disastrous conflict between classes, deeply deplores these events.

But it sees in the maintenance of sound finance, which is the condition of the restoration of industry and commerce, the indispensable steps to the lessening of unemployment and to the resumption of social progress.

Despite the professions in the recent declaration of the Labour Party that it would wish to balance the Budget and to prevent inflation, the programme of expenditure to which that party has now committed itself must defeat both those aims and lead to financial disaster.

The conditions of the present Election are one more proof of the imperative need of a reform in the electoral system if the real wishes of the voters are to be truly expressed at the polls.

An independent party

To safeguard international peace, to maintain and increase the strength of the League of Nations, and to promote the success of the forthcoming Disarmament Conference are among the prime purposes to which the nations should address themselves. The development of responsible government in India through the Round Table Conference is also of the highest importance.

It is as an independent party, standing with undiminished conviction for those causes of individual and national liberty and social progress with which liberalism has always been identified, forming a barrier against both reaction on the one hand and rash and injurious changes on the other, but co-operating now with the Prime Minister in dealing with the crisis which is upon us, that the Liberal Party appeals to the nation.

It asks that the electorate shall use its power to ensure that liberal ideas shall have a powerful expression and an effective influence both in the Government and in the coming Parliament.

LIBERAL PARTY GENERAL ELECTION MANIFESTO 1935

Date of Election	Thursday 14 November
Party Leader	Sir Herbert Samuel
Candidates	161
MPs	20
Votes	1,422,116
% of vote	6.4%

A General Election is being held at a moment of acute international crisis. After long delay the Government have lately been taking definite action at Geneva. All parties support the action. An election is therefore unnecessary.

Upon the success or failure of the League of Nations in its effort to penalise aggression must depend our own future policy, in foreign affairs and as to armaments. If the League succeeds we shall take one course; if it fails, another. The issue is now in the balance. Until we know we cannot judge. This is precisely the moment when the nation ought not to be asked to give a mandate on these matters for the next five years.

National defence

Our aim is to maintain the peace of the world and preserve our own security. Armaments, on however vast a scale, will not bring security or stop war. The national defences must be kept efficient and large enough for the needs of the times, but a colossal, panic expenditure upon arms is not the road to peace. It is the duty of the House of Commons to examine, upon their merits and with the utmost care, all demands for increased expenditure, especially upon armaments, and to insist upon the strictest control of their manufacture and sale, and the elimination of the motive of private profit. It is the duty of the voters to elect a House of Commons that will do this. Through strengthening the League of Nations, and through international disarmament, and there alone, the true path to security lies.

First steps to restored prosperity

Liberals are convinced that a change in the policy adopted in this country during the last four years is essential if the poverty and distress so widely prevailing are to be ended, and if the peril of war which overhangs the world is to be removed. The continued un-employment of 2,000,000; the unrelieved misery –of the depressed areas; the low wages of the miners, of the farm workers, and of many others; the immensely reduced figures of our export trade compared with a few years ago; the plight of our shipping industry – all point to a wrong policy. And the unrest in the world is due chiefly to the hard struggle of some of the great Powers to keep their peoples in proper comfort. All this comes from the disastrous reduction in the volume of world trade. And that is due to the restrictions imposed by Governments. The present Government in Great Britain has been among the most active in increasing these restrictions. While rendering lip-service to greater freedom of trade, and entering into some agreements with other countries for trifling reductions here and there, its actions on the whole have immensely increased the obstacles which hamper world commerce. The Ottawa Agreements – now repudiated by the Canadian people – were among the most disastrous. It is urgently necessary that there should be a change, if our unemployed workers are to be brought back into employment, and if the sources of world unrest, threatening war, are to be removed. To rid commerce of the hindrances that come from tariffs, quotas, subsidies, and unstable currencies is the first step to a restored prosperity and a more tranquil world. The Liberal Party alone has continuously urged the vital importance of this issue. It alone can be trusted to press it forward to a solution.

Liberals stand for a vigorous sustained policy of national development. They have long advocated the employment of idle capital and idle labour upon a great number of enterprises, which are urgently needed – for the housing of the people, the expansion of industry and agriculture, and the better equipment of our country. The present Government has stubbornly rejected that policy.

Revise the Means Test

The Liberal Party condemns the Means Test regulations. It considers that to treat the 'household' as a unit is wrong. The Government has dissolved Parliament without issuing the revised regulations promised eight months ago, and so has refused to submit them to the judgement of the electorate. It ought not to be given a free hand to settle this matter as it chooses in the next Parliament.

Industry and the worker

The Liberal Party has laid before the country a wide and detailed programme, dealing with the organisation of industry and the status of the worker; with the ownership and use of land, the securing for the public benefit of the land values created by the public, the development of agriculture, the reforms that are essential in the coal industry; with the raising of the school age and a great expansion in our educational system; with the inclusion of other classes in National Insurance; with housing, temperance, the extension of leisure, and greater facilities for its use.

Liberty and democracy

The Liberal Party stands, as ever, for personal and political liberty. It has fought against the many encroachments upon freedom which have been made in recent years. It opposed the withdrawal from Parliament of proper control over unemployment assistance, and will not cease to resist the constant attempts to transfer powers from representative bodies to irresponsible boards. It will always strenuously defend democratic institutions against the attacks of Fascists or Communists or others in other parties who set small store by liberty. In order to raise the authority of the House of Commons it would reform our defective and unjust electoral system, and through proportional representation, enable the true desires of the people to be expressed in Parliament.

It would give the same rights to women as to men throughout the political and social system.

Liberals do not recognise the present Administration as a 'National Government'. A truly National Government is one that is supported by all parties and approved by the nation in general. No party supports the present Government except the Conservative. In the by-elections only one elector in three votes for it. Liberals see in the sudden dissolution of Parliament at this moment as an attempt to use the international situation as a means of securing another lease of power for the Conservative Party.

We appeal to the nation to ensure in the next House of Commons an effective representation of Liberal opinion. We think it of vital importance that the existing Conservative Government, for such in effect it is, should not be left in a position of uncontrolled authority. And it is no less essential in the national interest that, when it leaves office, the only alternative should not be a Socialist Party pledged to a reckless scheme of wholesale nationalisation. We present to the electors the Liberal policy here outlined, and we claim for it the active support of all who endorse its general aims and approve its specific proposals.

20 POINT MANIFESTO OF THE LIBERAL PARTY

General Election, 1945

THE Liberal Party, having for five years formed part of the All-Party Government, which has victoriously guided Britain through the dangers of the European war, now appeals with confidence to the new electorate.

The Liberal Party has no responsibility for forcing an early election and, realising that the existing register is imperfect and will disfranchise many thousands of voters, was prepared to continue the Coalition until a new register was ready in October, and had expressed willingness to discuss its continuation until the end of the Japanese war.

Nevertheless, now that the decision has been taken, we welcome the opportunity of submitting our programme to the Nation.

1
FROM VICTORY TO PEACE

Victory in Europe has been won, but the war against Japan calls for unremitting effort. The Liberal Party has pledged itself to support all measures needed to strengthen the arms and shorten the task of our valiant fighting men in the Far East.

The sacrifice and steadfastness of the people of these Islands, the British Commonwealth and Empire—standing alone for a whole year against the insolent might of Germany and her Allies—have saved the world. But victory must be a beginning, not an end—the beginning of a system by which war must be made impossible and through which differences between nations must be settled by just and peaceful means.

We must strive to preserve the common purpose of the United Nations, who have humbled Germany. In particular, the close comradeship in war between Britain, Russia and America must be preserved, fostered and developed in peace. The new World Organisation coming to birth at San Francisco must be supported and strengthened. Nations, like private citizens, must come to acknowledge the rule of law and of impartial arbitration in their dealings with each other. The tasks of peace, like those of war, are too vast for any one nation to accomplish alone. Much patience and self-control will be called for in harmonising various national interests, but the war has taught with tragic clearness that no people can survive in selfish isolation.

The nations determined to preserve peace must have sufficient forces, especially in the air, to crush ruthlessly and immediately any attempt by an aggressive nation to go to war. We ourselves in this country and the Empire must have adequate strength, provided so long as necessary by a system of universal service and with the most modern equipment, to contribute according to our responsibilities as a World Power.

2
THE BRITISH COMMONWEALTH

In pursuing this policy we can look with confidence for the sympathy and support of the great self-governing Dominions. The war has brought them together with us in closer consultation and combined action than ever before. The Liberal principle which inspired the creation of the Commonwealth—that of free and independent nations working together in a common loyalty for a common way of life—must be fostered as an element of stability in the world and a practical example of the way in which liberty can be combined with national freedom.

The Colonies have proved an invaluable source of strength to us in war. It will be our duty, as well as our advantage, to help their development in peace. Basing our rule on the principle of trusteeship, we must consider first the interest of their peoples and encourage economic development and political self-government in association with the Commonwealth.

It will be the object of the Liberal Party to break the deadlock in India, and to bring about a reconciliation between the various elements among Indians themselves may frame a democratic Constitution for complete self-government for India.

3
SERVICE MEN AND WOMEN

Victory in total war has been achieved by the common service of all, by soldiers, sailors and airmen, and also by those working in the fields, factories, ships, mines and offices, and by the steadfastness of the women in the home. Nevertheless, our first thought at this time must be for those who have been fighting in the Services—cut off for many years at a time from their families, many of them fighting in distant theatres. They have carried the heaviest burden of all. The Liberal Party recognises its duty to safeguard the interests of the Servicemen, their wives and families, and especially those of men who are still fighting against Japan. Our influence has been used and will continue to be used to ensure for them the fairest possible conditions of release and rehabilitation; of training for civil life, of gratuities and pensions and of prospects of employment and housing. We are determined to see that no time is lost in providing homes for men returning from the wars. This is a debt the nation owes to its warriors and it must be paid in full.

4
SOCIAL SECURITY

The Liberal Party is fighting independently of all other parties for a radical programme of practical reform.

Though there are brains and hands and resources enough in the world, properly used, to give healthy self-respecting lives to all, mankind is a prey to Fear—fear of poverty and want through unemployment, sickness, accident and old age. With the Beveridge schemes for Social Security and Full Employment, the Liberal Party leads a frontal attack on this Fear.

Freedom from Want can be achieved by Social Security—a defence against unmerited misfortune from sickness, accident or unemployment and from loss of earning power through old age. Social Security is the economics of the good neighbour, and extends and improves the original measures of health and unemployment insurance passed by a Liberal Government.

5
FULL EMPLOYMENT

Full Employment can be maintained in a Free Society. Where there is work to do and men to do it, unemployment is an intolerable waste of wealth, and it imperils healthy family life—basis of the

LIBERAL PARTY GENERAL ELECTION MANIFESTO 1945

Date of Election	Thursday 5 July
Party Leader	Sir Archibald Sinclair
Candidates	306
MPs	12
Votes	2,248,226
% of vote	9.0%

20 Point Manifesto of the Liberal Party

The Liberal Party, having for five years formed part of the All-Party Government, which has victoriously guided Britain through the dangers of the European war, now appeals with confidence to the new electorate.

The Liberal Party has no responsibility for forcing an early election and, realising that the existing register is imperfect and will disfranchise many thousands of voters, was prepared to continue the Coalition until a new register was ready in October, and had expressed willingness to discuss its continuation until the end of the Japanese war.

Nevertheless, now that the decision has been taken, we welcome the opportunity of submitting our programme to the Nation.

From victory to peace

Victory in Europe has been won, but the war against Japan calls for unremitting effort. The Liberal Party has pledged itself to support all measures needed to strengthen the arms and shorten the task of our valiant fighting men in the Far East.

The sacrifice and steadfastness of the people of these Islands, the British Commonwealth and Empire – standing alone for a whole year against the insolent might of Germany and her Allies – have saved the world. But victory must be a beginning, not an end – the beginning of a system by which war must be made impossible and through which differences between nations must be settled by just and peaceful means.

We must strive to preserve the common purpose of the United Nations, who have humbled Germany. In particular, the close comradeship in war between Britain, Russia and America must be preserved, fostered and developed in peace. The new World Organisation coming to birth at San Francisco must be supported and strengthened. Nations, like private citizens, must come to acknowledge the rule of law and of impartial arbitration in their dealings with each other. The tasks of peace, like those of war, are too vast for any one nation to accomplish alone. Much patience and self-control will be called for in harmonising various national interests, but the war has taught with tragic clearness that no people can survive in selfish isolation.

The nations determined to preserve peace must have sufficient forces, especially in the air, to crush ruthlessly and immediately any attempt by an aggressive nation to go to war. We ourselves in this country and the Empire must have adequate strength, provided so long as necessary by a system of universal service and with the most modern equipment, to contribute according to our responsibilities as a World Power.

The British Commonwealth

In pursuing this policy we can look with confidence for the sympathy and support of the great self-governing Dominions. The war has brought them together with us in closer consultation and combined action than ever before. The Liberal principle which inspired the creation of the Commonwealth – that of free and independent nations working together in a common loyalty for a common way of life – must be fostered as an element of stability in the world and a practical example of the way in which security can be combined with national freedom.

The Colonies have proved an invaluable source of strength to us in war. It will be our duty, as well as our advantage, to help their development in peace. Basing our rule on the principle of trusteeship, we must consider first the interest of their peoples and encourage economic development and political self-government in association with the Commonwealth.

It will be the object of the Liberal Party to break the deadlock in India, and to bring about a reconciliation between the various elements so that Indians themselves may frame a democratic Constitution for complete self-government for India.

Servicemen and women

Victory in total war has been achieved by the common sacrifice of all, by soldiers, sailors and airmen, and also by those working in the fields, factories, ships, mines and offices, and by the steadfastness of the women in the home. Nevertheless, our first thought at this time must be for those who have been fighting in the Services – cut off for many years at a time from their families, many of them fighting in distant theatres. They have carried the heaviest burden of all. The Liberal Party recognises its duty to safeguard the interests of the Servicemen, their wives and families, and especially those of men who are still fighting against Japan. Our influence has been used and will continue to be used to ensure for them the fairest possible conditions of release and rehabilitation; of training for civil life, of gratuities and pensions and of prospects of employment and housing. We are determined to see that no time is lost in providing homes for men returning from the wars. This is a debt the nation owes to its warriors and it must be paid in full.

Social security

The Liberal Party is fighting independently of all other parties for a radical programme of practical reform.

Though there are brains and hands and resources enough in the world, properly used, to give healthy self-respecting lives to all, mankind is a prey to Fear – fear of poverty and want through unemployment, sickness, accident and old age. With the Beveridge schemes for Social Security and Full Employment, the Liberal Party leads a frontal attack on this Fear.

Freedom from Want can be achieved by Social Security – a defence against unmerited misfortune from sickness, accident or unemployment and from loss of earning power through old age. Social Security is the economics of the good neighbour, and extends and improves the original measures of health and unemployment insurance passed by a Liberal Government.

Full employment

Full Employment can be maintained in a Free Society. Where there is work to do and men to do it, unemployment is an intolerable waste of wealth, and it imperils healthy family life – basis of the nation's greatness. Our national resources, labour, power and skill of brains, are our most precious national assets, and Government and private initiative alike must ensure that none of them stands needlessly idle.

Housing

There is a house famine in the land, Liberals will not be satisfied until there is a separate dwelling for each family at a reasonable rent. This can be achieved only by a completely new approach, applying to housing the same drive as was used to produce aircraft and munitions of war. The responsibility should be placed on a Minister of Housing and no vested interests can be allowed to stand in the way. Local authorities must be enabled to borrow at a low rate of interest, and in no part of the country be allowed to ignore their obligations. Other agencies who are ready and able to provide houses should be encouraged.

We must control the costs of building materials so as to keep down the prices and rents of the houses we build.

In the countryside the problem is no less urgent than in the towns. Farm workers and fishermen must also share in the benefits of good houses equipped with water, power and sanitation. The next Parliament must drive forward the new housing programme by every available means.

The land

Great Britain is a small country with a vast population. It is therefore essential that the best use should be made of its land.

The full development of our national resources; the protection from disfigurement of the countryside; the balanced location of industry, and a successful housing policy all depend upon comprehensive measures of Town and Country planning.

Development rights outside built-up areas should immediately be acquired for the public and there should be a periodic levy on all increases in site values. Every increase in values due to community action should be secured for the community.

The fullest use must be made of agricultural land for food production. The State should, subject to the owner's right of appeal to an impartial tribunal, have the right to take over all land which is badly managed or badly farmed, and any other land which in the interests of good cultivation and of the population on the land should be in its control.

Farming and fishing

The Liberal Party means to maintain a prosperous and efficient agriculture. The threat of famine in Europe, and our own reduced capacity to pay for imports, mean that more food must be produced at home than before the war. To do this, farmers must have the assurance of stable prices, and the advantage of bulk purchase, and cheap transport. Capital must be available on easy terms for drainage, improvements and modern equipment, and science and research must be freely at the disposal of the farming community.

Farmers should be free to cultivate their land according to their own judgement and at their own risk, subject only to the maintenance of reasonable standards of farming and meeting the food requirements of the nation.

A prosperous free agriculture demands also the location of light industries in country districts, providing alternative employment and bringing greater purchasing power to the rural population. The distribution of industry is of the first importance to the health, happiness and well-being of our people.

Those who have fought for the country must have an opportunity to live on the land and cultivate it. Land Settlement must therefore be encouraged.

The Ministry of Food must remain to ensure the fair distribution of available supplies to consumers, and to offer long-term contracts assuring farmers of fair prices and guaranteed markets over a period of years.

The wages and housing of farm workers must be comparable with those of skilled workers in other industries.

The need for maximum production of food calls for a flourishing fishing industry. Government assistance will be needed in replacing boats and gear and in providing adequate curing and refrigeration facilities at ports so that fish so badly needed on our tables shall not be thrown back into the sea.

Health

People cannot be happy unless they are healthy. The Liberal aim is a social policy which will help to conquer disease by prevention as well as cure, through good housing, improved nutrition, the lifting of strains and worries caused by fear of unemployment, and through intensified medical research. The Liberal Party's detailed proposals for improved health services would leave patients free to choose their doctor, for the general practitioner is an invaluable asset in our social life.

Education

Liberals supported the recent Education Act, and will do all they can to bring it quickly into operation. Our place in the world will depend on the character of our people and on minds trained to understand and operate the complex technical achievements of the modern world. We cannot afford to neglect talent which lies unused because of the poverty of parents. The quality of our teachers must be maintained, but their numbers must be increased so that the school-leaving age can be raised and the size of classes reduced. Day nurseries should be increased and the nursery school system greatly expanded. Playing-fields and opportunities for organised games should be normally provided in all schools.

Industry

British Industry will face new and complex problems after the war. If we are to succeed we must sell the goods which the world wants at the price which the world will pay. We can do this only by achieving justice for the three partners in industry – the Manager, the Worker and the Investor.

Of first importance are the status and remuneration of the worker. He has for too long been regarded as a 'hand'. He must become a partner and acquire economic citizenship, through Works Councils set up by law, and through Joint Industrial Councils in every Trade Board Industry. Profit-sharing should be encouraged, and information on the conduct and finance of business should be readily available to assure workers that wages fixed and profit-sharing schemes in operation are fair and just.

Liberals believe that the controversy for and against nationalisation is out of date. They approach industrial problems without economic prejudice, and since they represent no vested interest of employers or employed, they alone can plan in the interests of the whole community. They believe in private enterprise and the value of individual effort, experiment, and willingness to take risks. Hence their support of the small trader and their desire to diffuse ownership as widely as possible. Hence also their opposition to cartels and price-fixing rings which, often abusing the name of private enterprise, create conditions of monopoly and hold the community to ransom.

But where public ownership is more economic, Liberals will demand it without hesitation. Where there is no further expansion or useful competition in an industry or where an industry or group of industries has become a private monopoly, Liberals say it should be come a public utility. Liberals believe in the need for both private enterprise and large-scale organisation under government control, and their tests for deciding which form is necessary are the service of the public, the efficiency of production and the well-being of those concerned in the industry in question.

Transport and power

Railways, with the large part of road transport controlled by them, are clearly in effect a monopoly, and should be treated as a Public Utility on a national plan. Electric power should also be reorganised as a public utility.

British Civil Aviation must be rapidly expanded both to make consultation and intercourse between all parts of the Commonwealth and Empire swift and easy, and to serve the common interest of mankind.

Coal

Coal is our principal mineral wealth, and most of our industry is based on its use. This fact, and the variety and immense potential value of by-products from coal, demand in the interests of the national economy that the Coal Industry shall not be treated merely as a private profit-making concern. It must be regarded not as one industry among many, but as the key to the health of our basic industries and our export trade. Compared with other countries, the British coal-mining industry is inefficient and is losing ground. Since it is apparent that the necessary increase of efficiency cannot be brought about with the present organisation, the industry should be a public service, in which the miners can feel that they are working for the benefit of the whole community. But the terms on which the coal-mining industry is made into a public-service must be such as to ensure three things:

(a) Decentralisation of operation and freedom to experiment in different coal undertakings.
(b) That the industry pays its way without subsidies from the general tax-payer.
(c) That coal is not made too dear either to industrial or to domestic consumers.

Freedom of trade

Freedom and expansion of trade are the necessary basis of world prosperity. We can secure the imports needed to maintain our standard of life only by selling our exports in the markets of the world. We should therefore press on vigorously with the conclusion of agreements with America and other countries for the progressive elimination of tariffs, quotas, exchange restrictions and other barriers to trade, on the lines of Article VII of the Mutual Aid Agreement between Britain and the United States, which implements the Atlantic Charter.

The traditional policy of the Conservative Party to build up a system of economic isolationism within the Empire is inconsistent with world co-operation, and with our obligations under Article VII of the Lease-Lend Agreement. This policy would not commend itself to the great Dominions; it would be inadequate to maintain the volume of trade needed by Britain, and it would provoke dangerous economic strife.

Taxation

Under the impact of war, ordinary methods of control over expenditure have necessarily been relaxed. The time has now come for a strict supervision of national expenditure in order to eliminate waste and to secure a progressive reduction in the burden of taxation, both direct and indirect. In particular, it will be our aim to remove taxes on the prime necessities of life.

The system of taxation must be designed to encourage the re-equipment and modernisation of British industry.

Controls

This war has forced us all to accept many controls which cannot be suddenly relaxed without incurring the dangers of soaring prices and inflation. While Liberals realise this, they are determined that no control shall remain longer than is absolutely necessary for the welfare of the country and the full employment of its people.

The work and position of women

The family is the basis of our national life. Liberals were the first to demand family allowances and are determined to secure adequate provision for motherhood and child welfare. They are also determined that the benefits of modern scientific and mechanical development shall be used to eliminate needless drudgery in the home.

In public life, the Liberal Party demands for women equality of opportunity and status; it stands for equal pay for equal work, and for equal opportunity of entry into the public services.

Scotland and Wales

The Liberal Party recognises the desire of the people of Scotland and Wales to assume greater responsibility in the management of their domestic affairs, and has long been in favour of suitable measures of Devolution.

The drift of population from those countries to congested cities in England is unhealthy and should be reversed, by measures for a more balanced distribution of industry throughout these islands and by the full development of the agricultural, fishing, industrial and power resources of Scotland and Wales.

A better Parliament

Our present system of voting produces Parliaments which are not representative of the people's will. A party with a minority of votes can secure a majority in the House of Commons. Liberals hold that Members of Parliament should be chosen in such a way as to represent fairly the number of votes cast. They would therefore reform the voting system so as to give electors the opportunity of expressing an additional choice or choices, as well as a first choice, when there are more than two candidates for a seat.

In addition, Liberals consider that it is in the interests of democracy that the scales of the electoral system should not be weighed in favour of wealthy candidates, and that Members of Parliament should be chosen for their opinions and qualities, not for their interests. Accordingly, the Liberal Party favours placing the essential costs of elections on the State, subject to suitable safeguards against frivolous candidatures.

The liberty of the subject

It is always the task of Liberals to exercise that eternal vigilance which is the price of freedom. Before the war our Members of Parliament challenged every encroachment upon the liberty of the subject. When we joined the Coalition in 1940, Sir Archibald Sinclair obtained a promise from the Prime Minister that it was the Government's intention to preserve in all essentials a free Parliament and a free Press, and that the Emergency Powers (such as preventive arrest under Regulation 18b and the power to suppress newspapers) would disappear with the passing of the emergency.

In the next Parliament, whether in or out of office, we shall continue to do our utmost to safeguard and enlarge civil liberties. Power must exist in any modern State. But it need not be arbitrary power. In this country the citizen has two essential safeguards against in justice and oppression, namely: democratic control, through

Parliament and elected local authorities, over all those in official positions, and the right to appeal to the ordinary Courts of Law whenever a Minister or an official exceeds his authority. Both these safeguards we shall strenuously maintain.

To sum up

The Liberal Party submits to the nation the vision of a healthier society in which our people may live full, happy and useful lives and bring up their families in decent homes with out fear of war or of unemployment. At the same time its programme is also a call to hard, strenuous work on the part of all, Government and citizens alike. But the war has shown Britain capable of the task. It has revealed a mighty nation, renewed in its youth, with vast stores of energy and enterprise. It has the skill, the confidence and the determination; what is now needed is a Government wise enough and courageous enough to set the pace of advance.

NO EASY WAY

Britain's problems and the Liberal answers

LIBERAL PARTY MANIFESTO

LIBERAL PARTY GENERAL ELECTION MANIFESTO 1950

No easy way: Britain's problems and the Liberal answers

'I wilt find a way or make one . . .'
Hannibal on crossing the Alps

Date of Election	Thursday 23 February
Party Leader	Clement Davies
Candidates	475
MPs	9
Votes	2,621,548
% of vote	9.1%

The Liberal Party offers the electorate the opportunity of returning a Liberal Government to office. We believe that our Party is more likely to unite the nation than either the Conservatives or the Socialists – locked as they are in what is really a class struggle.

Britain has been brought close to bankruptcy by the effects of two wars, continued world disunity, and aid to friends abroad. The generous help we have received from our Commonwealth partners and the United States has helped us immeasurably, but will not long continue. We can only effect our recovery through our own efforts.

The cause of crisis

Crisis after crisis comes upon us, because we are living beyond our means. The Liberal Party believes passionately in full employment in a free society, and in maintaining the social services. But unless we practise thrift and get full production, lower rations and mass unemployment are inescapable when American aid ends.

A government governs best by example and not by exhortation; Liberals in office not only would demand thrift but would practise it.

Taxation, direct and indirect, takes eight shillings in every pound; more taxation would only reduce incentives and yield less revenue. Taxation at its present level prevents an increase in production by penalising effort, and prevents saving without which we cannot maintain, let alone expand, industrial equipment. We can make enormous savings in government expenditure, but we cannot be dishonest enough to pretend that the whole saving would be passed on at once to the tax-payer. We must budget for an excess of revenue over expenditure, until supply in every direction meets demand. Any

71

immediate tax relief must be directly designed to increase effort. Only when greater production has been reflected in greater exports, can we sensibly relieve the general tax-payer.

Government economies

We demand that the Government should cut its own spending drastically. It should contract or merge many departments of State, reducing staffs wherever possible. The Ministries concerned are Supply, National Insurance, Civil Aviation, Food, Agriculture and Fisheries, and, so far as their Housing functions are concerned, Health, Works, and Town and Country Planning. Under full employment work should easily be found for the Civil Servants thus affected.

We must cut Food Subsidies, now helping many who are not in need of them. But we would help those suffering by the reduction of subsidies – mainly pensioners and large families – by increasing social security benefits. At present nearly £500 million a year is taken in taxation to be returned in subsidies, which is unnecessary and administratively extravagant. Even with increases in pensions and allowances, hundreds of millions of pounds would be saved by progressively cutting subsidies.

We want to take the Government out of business which can be more efficiently and economically operated by private traders. All international marketing agencies, such as the Liverpool Cotton Exchange, should be restored to private enterprise and bulk purchase reduced – though existing bulk purchase contracts would be respected.

Controls

Every control not imposed by the need for fair shares or scarcity must go; every relaxation of control saves costs in Government and business. Similarly, we would abandon any form of limitation of entry into any kind of trade production.

Incentives for production

Liberal Government would set itself to reconcile the interests of workers and employers, whether in state or private trading. Since the Whitley Committee was set up during the first world war, Liberals have striven for joint consultation at all levels of production. Joint consultation is, to a great extent, disregarded in privately-owned companies and its operations hampered in state industries. Remote control imposed by managements and trade union headquarters is largely responsible.

Outside the Socialist Party there is growing belief in the merits of co-ownership and profit-sharing in industry, but there has been no tendency to establish such schemes universally. The Liberal Party is prepared to introduce co-partnership and profit-sharing into major units of industry.

The industrial worker should receive a share of increased profits as a matter of right and not as an act of grace by his employers, and, wherever practicable, be increasingly associated with the business of management.

One immediate concession a Liberal Government would make to benefit production would be to remove profits tax on undistributed profits used to replace capital equipment.

Nationalisation and monopolies

Nationalisation for the sake of nationalisation is nonsense. The Liberal attitude is clear. Monopoly where it is not inevitable is objectionable and should be broken up. If it cannot be broken up it should, if possible, be controlled in the public interest without a change of ownership; only when neither the restoration of competition nor control is possible should nationalisation be considered.

In any case, we are persuaded that there should be no consideration of any further nationalisation of industry for a period of five years, until the results of nationalisation to date have been digested.

In particular we opposed the Act for the nationalisation of the iron and steel industries. This we would repeal. A Liberal Government would free road transport. We would examine the workings of every state industry with the object of decentralising control, creating competition inside the industry wherever possible, and making each industry responsible to Parliament.

We recognise that the breaking of monopoly powers is one of the key problems of our time and we would have a permanent 'watch dog' commission of enquiry into monopoly and restrictive practices.

In the interests of the consumer's purse and the independent trader's livelihood, Liberals would allow no minimum price-fixing unless permitted by the Board of Trade, and we would reform those sections of the patent law which prevent useful ideas benefiting the public.

With the ending of monopolies and cartels, inefficient producers and traders would no longer be protected. Inefficiency is a luxury we can no longer afford. We would enact freedom of entry into trade, freedom from unnecessary controls and form-filling, and freedom, for the worker, from direction of labour.

International trading

The whole strength of this country, which sustained the part Britain played in two world wars and built up the standard of life we have to-day, was due to our free trade and willingness to buy and sell in any part of the world. The protectionist policy of the Conservative and Socialist Parties has handicapped the development of our international trading ever since a Liberal Government was last in office.

Now, barriers grow higher and two-nation agreements, quotas and tariffs, currency restrictions and foreign travel regulations take the place of friendly dealings on a free world market. Obviously we cannot trade freely to-day with the iron curtain countries; obviously the rest of the world must become a free trading area as its only hope for prosperity. If British statesmen say these things and mean them, the prospect will soon improve.

Liberals recognise that protection of industry is a naked confession that we cannot meet in our own markets the competition which we must meet abroad or starve. We would reduce tariffs by stages, until all are abolished.

No industry is harder hit by protection and its higher costs than shipping, which has never received protection. Shipping must flourish or our Merchant Marine will again decline and our invisible exports decrease.

Our defence

We oppose peacetime conscription because it creates inefficiency and denies regular servicemen the pay and conditions to which they are entitled and would receive if we relied on volunteers. Conscription has weakened our economy and impaired family life, and though we spend four times the pre-war amount on the Army, we have far fewer troops ready to fight. We must give the voluntary principle a chance, just as the Americans have done with success. It may be that by abandoning conscription we would make no immediate economies – for Liberals would do nothing to impair the equipment and efficiency of the armed forces – but many men would be released for production.

At the same time, we must make conditions of service in the Territorial forces as attractive as possible to increase recruitment. We must also try to cut down some of our overseas garrison commitments by arrangement with our partners in the Commonwealth.

The nation's food and land

The land is our greatest factory and the healthiest. Those who live by it must have assured markets and guaranteed prices, with notice to be given of any downward trend. We can and must produce a far greater volume of the things for which our soil and climate are best fitted – especially livestock, dairy produce, fruit and vegetables.

A Liberal Government would set up a Land Bank to provide cheap capital and credit for agricultural and horticultural development. It would import the maximum of animal and poultry feeding stuff; it would reduce distribution costs with the encouragement of regional marketing and co-operative machine-buying, storage, grass-drying and local water schemes and reclamation of marginal land. Rural life can be made more stable by the siting of light industries in country towns, and more attractive by an intensive drive for the basic amenities of modern living – piped water, electricity and bus services.

We have many haphazard systems of water supply with local water authorities separately constituted in an uneconomic makeshift way, which is especially detrimental to the countryside. A Liberal Government would make a national geographical and geological survey as a preliminary to creating a national water system.

Housing

The main plan is, first to get people decent living conditions and then to give them the chance to become owner-occupiers, even in Council houses and flats. One Minister must be responsible for the housing drive, to co-ordinate the housing functions at present undertaken by four different Departments – Health, Works, Supply, and Town and Country Planning.

The efficiency of the building industry is 30 per cent below pre-war, while costs have risen steadily. While subsidies are paid for council building they must be made available to private building.

Immediate reforms are necessary in the Rent Restriction and Town and Country Planning Acts to ensure that penalties are not imposed on improvements to property and that the good landlord is not forced to let his property deteriorate through receiving sub-economic rents.

Leaseholders in house and shop properties must be enabled to buy their freeholds at a fair price, and an increasing proportion of the burden of local rates be transferred from building to site values.

Our policy for women

The part played by women in the councils of the Liberal Party is shown by our unanimous adoption of a programme for women drawn up by women Liberals. We are pledged to the principle of equal pay for equal work, a principle a Liberal government would introduce into the Civil Service. We would remove all restrictions on equal opportunity for training and entering all types of employment.

Liberals oppose the bringing into industry of married women with young children, but would not discourage schemes of industrial outwork, to help the family budget by work done at home. The main professional emphasis would be on the pay and conditions of women teachers and members of the nursing service. More opportunity for promotion could be given in both professions, and, in hospitals, more could be done for patients and nurses alike by increased recruitment of foreign domestic labour.

Representative government

The only tried system of completely fair representation according to the voting strength of Parties is through Proportional Representation by the single transferable vote. The present system is not even faintly equitable. That P.R. leads to stability is proved by Sweden and Switzerland, among others.

We are anxious to reform the composition of the House of Lords, so as to eliminate heredity as a qualification for membership, which should be available to men and women of distinction.

We wish to restore the authority of Parliament and the status of its individual Members by reversing the trend towards supreme Executive power. A Liberal administration would give more time in debate and more independence of action to the private Member seeking to bring in non-Party legislation.

A Liberal Government would give the Scottish and Welsh people the right to manage their own affairs by setting up a Scottish and a Welsh Parliament to deal with matters of particular concern to Scotland and Wales respectively, while matters concerning the whole Kingdom would be decided in Westminster.

Security of the individual

Social security can only be established when its benefits can be related to the cost of living. Considering our limited resources, Britain has gone a long way towards this goal, and we are confident a Liberal Government could improve the benefits of social security. But the only definite pledges we can make – and these are considerable – are to extend the family allowance to the first child, to make a concerted effort to improve living conditions for the elderly and to improve the administration of the National Health Service.

Much can be done, through the encouragement of voluntary mutual aid, to improve social welfare and the better use of leisure time. Old Age pensioners who wish to go on working are performing a great public service, and a Liberal Government would revoke the Means Test on the working pensioner. We would also assess war pensions on the merits of the individual case, not on the basis of service rank.

Liberty of the individual

The nation is pledged to the United Nations Declaration of Human Rights and a Liberal Government would make its domestic and colonial administration conform to it. All Ministerial Orders would be made liable to challenge in the Courts and subject to amendment; no one would be tried except in a proper Court of Law; the powers of Government inspectors to enter private premises would be drastically reduced. (At present 17 Government Departments have such powers of inspection.) All unemployed persons would be allowed the right of appeal to the National Insurance Commissioner.

In the Trade Union movement a new Charter is needed, not only to reform the machinery of control, but also to safeguard the rights of the individual Trade Unionist. We would set up a Royal Commission to investigate all questions affecting the movement. But pending a searching examination by a Royal Commission and reflecting on its report, we are already satisfied that contracting-in should be substituted for contracting-out of the political levy.

Education

It is a further restriction on personal liberty that an age limit of 16 should be imposed on children, below which age they may not take the General Certificate of Education.

The Liberal aim is equality of opportunity, which cannot be realised until the size of primary school classes is much reduced. We are as much concerned about the welfare and pay of teachers as we are about the training of their pupils; theirs is an urgent priority case.

We would not raise the school-leaving age to 16 until accommodation and teachers could be found. We would avoid standardisation of teaching, establish separate schools for different branches of education.

The Commonwealth and Empire

The Liberal Party created a Commonwealth out of the Empire, and the Commonwealth and Empire have become the greatest voluntary force for peace in the world. We want to strengthen the ties between ourselves and the Dominions, with increasingly close consultation on investment policy, migration and defence. Liberals warmly supported the granting of independence to India, Pakistan and Ceylon, and look forward to welcoming new Dominions.

Self-government must only be granted to Colonies when in the interests of the majority of the people concerned. Once self-defence and the essential freedoms of all races and groups can be assured, indirect rule, however benevolent, will no longer be necessary. Even then, colonial economic independence is unlikely. More than ever

Britain must establish herself in Colonial eyes as the trustee of a family business to which they will soon be admitted into equal partnership.

World affairs

Our first need is peace. If that fails the Welfare State and all the other domestic issues of this Election will be in vain. The Liberal Party therefore pledges itself to work, in and out of Parliament, to speed the process of creating an international order under the rule of law. U.N.O. must be kept in being. It is carrying out useful international work in spite of difficulties. We must hold on to the Security Council at all costs, for it offers the only machinery through which the development of the hydrogen bomb and other horrors of science can be brought under control.

The other half of the problem is strengthening the organisation of the free world, whose chief components are the United States, the British Commonwealth and Western Europe. Britain is in the unique position of being closely linked with all three and we should develop our association with all of them.

There need be no choice for Britain between Europe and the Commonwealth. Any suggestion of incompatibility between our loyalties was repudiated by the Commonwealth Conference at Colombo and by M. Spaak speaking on behalf of the Council of Europe. Europe does not want partnership with a Britain which has weakened the links with its own family-nations.

Our party will press for quicker action in developing the Council of Europe. We must push on this year to make European currencies convertible with one another and remove restrictions of trade among ourselves. The democratic countries have a joint responsibility to preserve democracy in Western Europe; the fundamental rights of free elections and the right to form an opposition, freedom of speech and freedom from arbitrary arrest should be guaranteed and made enforceable by a European Court.

Liberals believe that Western Germany should soon be invited into the Council of Europe. This would be the most promising way to persuade Germans, many of whom are drifting dangerously again, that their only hope is in association with the liberal world. Let it be understood that Liberals do not conceive of Western Union as an exclusive Anti-Communist Alliance; until we can trade freely with Communist countries, we must strengthen the interests of democracy throughout the non-Soviet world, wiping out the economic misery on which Communism thrives.

LIBERAL MANIFESTO

THE NATION'S TASK

2d.

LIBERAL PARTY GENERAL ELECTION MANIFESTO 1951

The nation's task

Date of Election	Thursday 25 October
Party Leader	Clement Davies
Candidates	109
MPs	6
Votes	730,556
% of vote	2.5%

Great Britain is facing a new crisis – one of the biggest in her history. The people have not yet grasped how vast are the problems we have to solve very soon indeed.

There is still no sure peace between nations. Hanging over the whole world is the fear that some governments are planning aggression. There is still war in Korea, and the dispute in Persia is an immediate danger. We have begun a gigantic programme of rearmament, which will affect the living standards of all of us. At the same time, the Dollar Gap has again opened and that, together with shortage of all foreign currencies, brings the ugly threat that we may not be able to buy the raw materials we must have to keep up the employment of our people. On top of all this is the fact which comes home to every housewife every day: the cost of living keeps going up.

One thing is certain, no matter what the result of the Election. The country will need not only courage but unity. The nation cannot afford another parliament based on open class division, bitter party strife, and the remorseless friction of two great party machines.

A party for all the people

Why is it of vital concern that there should be a strong Liberal Party in the next House of Commons?

First – the Liberal Party has something to say on its own account. It is the only party free of any class or sectional interests. Its influence is far and away greater than its numbers would suggest.

Second – the existence of a strong, independent Liberal Party would strengthen the liberal forces in both parties. Neither of these parties is genuinely united. Both have powerful extremist wings which could do serious damage to the nation's welfare. In the everyday business of Parliament, the Liberals would support the more reasonable elements in both the Labour and Conservative parties. They would act as a brake on class bitterness and create a safeguard against the deadening power of the great political machines. It is their peculiar role to do this in modern society because they are radical without being socialist. For that reason they provide the rallying-point for the saner elements in both modern Conservatism and modern Socialism.

The existence of a Liberal Party, as recent experience has shown, constantly reminds the individual MP that the crack of the party whip is by no means the be-all and end-all of a live democracy.

That is why Liberals are convinced that there should be, and must be, more Liberal Members in the House of Commons. In a supreme effort to bring that increase about, Liberals will contest selected seats in all areas of the country, and concentrate all their resources in those constituencies. By so doing, Liberals offer to the nation an opportunity of sending to Parliament first-class men and women who have a great contribution to make to the solution of our problems; men and women who will fight without fear for the policies they think best for the nation, whether they are popular policies or not.

Liberals, with more Members in the House, can compel Parliament to face the problems squarely and can make sure that the measures taken for their solution are based on common sense and social justice.

World peace through law

We stand firmly, as we have always stood, behind Collective Security and the United Nations Organisation. We believe in the absolute necessity of maintaining the rule of law, and protecting British interests when necessary within the framework of international law.

Because there are other nations who do not accept that rule of law, peace cannot be taken for granted. For this reason, we support with all our hearts the measures which are being taken to build up collective security among the free nations, so that there shall be adequate strength to stop any possible aggressors and oblige them to settle their disputes by peaceful means. We fully support the rearmament programme, but we emphasise once again that it is a mistake to measure the success of rearmament by the amount of money we spend on it. The true test is the number of fully equipped Army, Air and Naval units that are ready for action. More Liberals in Parliament means more Members pledged to demand efficiency and value for money in all our military spending.

A strong Commonwealth

One of the greatest forces for peace is the British Commonwealth. The Liberal Party, which created the Commonwealth, will throw every ounce of its weight behind every effort to improve Commonwealth relations and build up a system of genuine co-operation. Liberals are proud of the Commonwealth. They wholly condemn the colour bar which exists in parts of it.

New design for Europe

The Liberals alone recognise the fact that the world is witnessing the end of the era of national self-sufficiency. Nothing that we can do on our own can completely solve our difficulties. We must act and think on an international plane. In this sphere, the Liberal Party can justly claim to have been the pioneer. It is the only truly international party of the three.

The Council of Europe is a Liberal conception. It is the realisation of a dream of European Liberals for two centuries. We are living in a world in which a great new design for human government is taking form. Our intimate family relationship with the British Commonwealth, our partnership with the United States – a partnership on which all the hopes of world peace depend – and such fresh groupings as the North Atlantic Organisation and the Pacific Pact, are not rival conceptions to one another. They are all part of the shape of things to come. To avoid international anarchy and chaos, everything depends on the willingness to agree to some organ of government larger than the State.

The Liberal Party will campaign continuously for the breaking down of international barriers. Only by working with like-minded peoples shall we secure the greatest prize of all – the peace and growing prosperity of all mankind.

More production – lower prices

At home, after tremendous efforts to recover from the war, we are still faced with appalling difficulties. We used to be the workshop of the world. That position is now seriously challenged. Although we have full employment at the moment – a policy which Liberals largely designed and fully support – the standard of living of our people cannot be maintained unless a very great effort is made and new policies adopted.

For wages to go up is, in the long run, a good thing. For prices to go up is a bad thing. We can keep wages up and bring prices down in only one way – by making more and better things with the same amount of labour, and selling at no more than a fair profit. To achieve this, it is essential that producers should have up-to-date plant – and enough of it – and that manufacturers, farmers, housebuilders – in fact, everyone who makes necessary goods – shall be able to do so in the ways that are most efficient. Only thus can we hope to compete in foreign markets and increase our exports.

Liberals in Parliament, if there are enough of them, can ensure that legislation and administrative action help the producers of goods instead of hampering them. The Trade Unions, too, have a very big part to play, but they must be ready to accept and promote new and better methods in industry. To refuse new methods, with the idea of preventing unemployment, is the surest way to cause unemployment. The American worker lives much better than the British worker, not because he works longer or harder, but because he often has better machinery and better tools, his work is better organised and the industry operates under far less restrictions.

Increased efficiency and production must also be obtained by bonus systems and profit-sharing schemes on top of the standard Trade Union wages. This will encourage the worker to do his best, and will lower the cost of production.

Set industry free

Heavy taxes which prevent business from having enough capital to scrap old plant and put in new must be avoided in the interests of efficiency.

In many industries profits are higher than they need be or should be, because groups of producers combine to limit competition. Parliament must strike at Monopolies, price rings, and other hindrances to trade; in fact, at everything that hits the consumer by forcing up prices.

What we need is a great national drive to bring down the cost of living. It can be done, but it means the fullest co-operation of Government, Parliament, Capital, Management, Labour, to see to it that there is more production per man, greater freedom to produce, greater freedom to sell, greater freedom to buy.

No easy promises

Many promises will be made in this Election. We refuse to join in a dishonest competition to make the nation's tasks look easier than they are. It would be easy to hold out false hopes of lower taxes immediately or that all the houses that are needed could be built in a short time.

Taxation can only be reduced substantially when by hard work and increased efficiency we have raised the national income, so that a lower rate of tax will bring a higher revenue. We shall take care, as Liberals have always done, that the burdens do not fall too heavily on those who are least able to bear them. And at the present time, Liberals will specially champion the interests of pensioners and all with small fixed incomes – just because they are the people most in need.

Widespread misery and suffering is caused by the shortage of Houses. But more houses depend on materials being available, and these can only be obtained as part of the general production drive. We shall continue to advocate our policy of reducing building costs without lowering standards.

The Social Services must be safeguarded. Food subsidies must remain until the increased productivity campaign has brought down the cost of living.

Extravagance and Waste have constantly occurred in public administration. We demand the setting up of a House of Commons Committee on National Expenditure, to prevent the waste of taxpayers' money before the event, instead of leaving the Comptroller and Auditor to discover it two years later.

The difficulties which face us in the field of international trade and in home industries, and the great danger of a world food shortage, emphasise the vital part which British Agriculture has to play if we are to survive. In these unsettled conditions, the system of guaranteed prices and assured markets is essential. Liberals advocate the complete reorganisation of the marketing system of the country so as to eliminate waste and inefficiency and enable producers to get fair prices while ensuring reasonable prices and standards of quality to the consumer.

Scotland and Wales

We repeat our pledge to Scotland and Wales that we will work in every possible way to win for them their own Parliaments. Self-government for Scotland and Wales is necessary to save their vital concerns from neglect, and it is no less necessary to ease the burden on the Parliament at Westminster. It is a step forward in freedom which will not weaken but will strengthen the unity of the Kingdom.

The nation's task

The way out of our difficulties will not be found by relying on governments. Every one of us has a responsibility which we must accept. The British are an adventurous people. They work best when they have the greatest freedom. The duty of governments is not to restrict enterprise but to create conditions in which enterprise can flourish in the interests of the whole nation.

We believe that a Parliament in which these views are not forcefully expressed will serve the nation badly. Only Liberals will resolutely champion this policy as a whole and on every occasion.

We live in difficult times, and no honest man can pretend that there is an easy way ahead. But we know that Britain will rouse herself to accept the challenge of these days. The next few years will be critical for our country. We cannot fail to win through if we meet them with the courage and the initiative that are fostered by a Liberal attitude to life.

GENERAL ELECTION
MAY, 1955

CRISIS

UNRESOLVED

•

THE MANIFESTO OF
THE LIBERAL PARTY

PRICE 2d.

LIBERAL PARTY GENERAL ELECTION MANIFESTO 1955

Crisis unresolved

Date of Election	Thursday 26 May
Party Leader	Clement Davies
Candidates	110
MPs	6
Votes	722,405
% of vote	2.7%

Just under four years ago the Liberal Manifesto opened with the statement that this country was 'facing a new crisis and one of the biggest in our history'.

It would be ungenerous not to admit that since the last General Election we have gone some way to arrest the decay which set in with the second post-war Labour Government; the crisis was confronted but has not been resolved. There are still great problems fraught with danger which cause much concern.

There are some who are so encouraged by the better face of our affairs as to think that halcyon days have come; there are some who feel that it does not greatly matter which Party steers because the winds have abated and the sea is calm; there are some who believe that we have now reached such stability and such assurance of continued prosperity that socialism and other forms of extremism can be counted out; there are some who can persuade themselves against all the evidence that the Conservative and Socialist Parties are liberalised. These ideas are delusions. The Liberal Party stands as a security against the fate that would befall a people whose future depended upon the outcome of a struggle between two class parties seeking power to be used in the service of their own particular clients. The independent mind, the small man and the consumer are neglected by both the great Parties.

War, devastating and possibly final, is a continuing threat. The fear of war enforces the use on a colossal scale of manpower and materials on purposes of defence. The prosperity of Britain hangs in the balance. Continued inflation endangers all the social progress of the last ten years, checks further progress and may defeat our hopes of making full employment in a free society our normal economic condition. To face and overcome external and internal dangers Liberal policies remain essential, and Liberal Members of Parliament alone can effectively advocate them.

Foreign affairs

There is fortunately broad agreement in this country both about the aims of British Foreign Policy and the means by which they are to be realised. The search for a foreign policy which shall be different from that of the Government of the day for the mere sake of opposition is futile and unpatriotic. Liberals have supported European Unity, close association with the Commonwealth and the United States, and the integration of Germany into Western Europe and all measures of defence essential to protect liberty. But we consider that greater effort should be made to bring home to other peoples the sincere devotion of the Western Powers to the cause of peace. Liberals have been constant in their support of the United Nations, but think that it is the duty of Her Majesty's Government to put forward positive proposals for the reform of the Charter designed in particular to restrict the occasions when Five Power unanimity is required, and specially to provide that all Sovereign States shall have a right to membership conditional upon their accepting the terms of the Charter.

The London and Paris agreements are a means and not an end. We needed strength for negotiation with Russia and we must now negotiate for the establishment of European peace and the re-unification of Germany. Liberals will work towards complete disarmament in all weapons, in all countries, under a system of international control which shall permanently ensure the free world and our children against aggression and the infinite horrors of warfare. Liberals maintain that peace in the Far East cannot be achieved until the Chinese People's Republic is a member of U.N.O. They deplore the ungenerous attacks made upon the United States, which imperil that understanding and co-operation between our two countries on which freedom has twice depended and still depends. At the same time they regret present ambiguities in American policy regarding Formosa, and will support all efforts made to remove a danger of conflict in Far Eastern countries.

The Liberal Party has been and will continue to be critical of the timidity and hesitation which both Labour and Conservative Governments have shown about associating this country intimately with the movement to secure some measure of European unification. It advocated wholehearted support for the European Defence Community and for the Coal and Steel Community and it rejects the insincere plea that our Commonwealth responsibilities are any bar to that closer association with Western Europe which is so highly desirable in the interests of both France and Germany and the settlement of their agelong quarrel. The concessions reluctantly made by our Government last autumn to secure the defence of Europe might well have sufficed to save the European Defence Community had they been made earlier. Liberals will continue to goad the Government when they feel that it is reluctant to play its proper role in the evolution of organs such as the Council of Europe and the Coal and Steel Community. A sincere attempt must be made to establish an arms pool. We must not be content to accept the Western European Union as concerned exclusively with problems of defence. We must have positive and constructive policies for economic and social progress in Europe. In particular, it is our duty and in the interests of this country to encourage by every means the establishment of a great free trade area in Europe.

Colonial development

There is general agreement, it may be hoped, on the necessity of training the inhabitants of all dependent territories to govern themselves. Liberals recognise that the conditions vary from colony to colony and that there is no master plan which can be uniformly applied; there must be flexibility. The noble experiment of establishing the principle of real partnership between races in the colonies is imperilled because the indigenous population has lost confidence in the objective. In order to restore this confidence there should be no departure from the principle that development must contribute directly and primarily to the prosperity of, and to higher standards of life for, the resident local multi-racial population. However slow the rate of development, Liberals must set their faces like flint against all forms of racial discrimination in British territories. Particular attention is drawn to the Liberal Party's suggestion for the institution of a Consultative Colonial Assembly, meeting periodically, at which representative delegates from colonial territories can confer upon developments within their territories, freely express their views thereon and work out practical means for the fulfilment of their aspirations.

The economic problem at home

We repeat what was said at the beginning: our internal crisis is not resolved. Liberal policies are essential to avoid disaster. Neither a Socialist nor a Conservative Party will, at the risk of losing votes, advocate or follow a policy which will meet our needs; on major questions of economic policy, election platforms are degenerating into auctions.

By the inflationary policy of two Socialist Governments, continued in modified form by the Conservatives, pensioners and people living on small fixed incomes and the lowest wage scales have been most cruelly penalised. A constantly and rapidly depreciating pound strikes at the root of social justice. The Liberal Party, which made possible the Welfare Society by its early reforms, is maintaining its traditions by calling for a radical attack upon false economic policies which inevitably lead to ever-rising costs of living. Will either the Conservative or the Labour Party have the courage, on this side of disaster, to stem the tide of rising prices, subsidies and nominal wages?

Let us briefly consider what is required by our situation today – that of a debtor nation which must export much more than it imports or sink to the level of a second-rate power on a low standard of living.

Industry

First we must be able to compete with foreign manufacturers. We must, therefore, systematically reduce and finally abolish tariffs which 'protect' our home markets, which encourage price rings and monopolies, and which must, for that is their whole object, increase our prices and, as a result, weaken our power to compete. Conservatives want to protect employers who are economically inefficient against bankruptcy; Socialists want to protect workers against the loss of the particular jobs in which they happen to be working.

Monopolies

Both the big parties are vocal when out of office against monopolies, price rings and restrictive practices. Neither of them will make a fierce frontal attack when in power. Neither will so much as mention the necessity of a thorough examination of the place and functions of Trade Unions in a Britain which, in a generation, has industrially altered out of recognition. We Liberals have long advocated a Royal Commission to examine specific reforms which have been suggested.

Productivity

The maintenance of full employment, the improvement of our standard of living, and our ability to avoid a further devaluation of sterling depend essentially on productivity, which is the power to produce more goods and service with the same amount of labour and without an increase of hours. To obtain greater productivity we must give to capital both the reward of risk and the incentive to save – accepted in principle by Labour but fiercely resisted in practice – and we must give to workers the assurance of being partners in industry, entitled to their share in the fruits of prosperity. The Liberal Party alone has been advocating the general introduction of co-ownership schemes, desirable not only as incentives but as the foundation of industrial peace.

Taxation, expenditure and cost of living

This country will never be prosperous so long as some 40 per cent. of the national income is taken from the earner by the Government and Local Authorities. It has to be admitted that the scope for saving is limited; neither defence nor the social services must be whittled down at the expense of efficiency. That makes it all the more necessary that expenditure in other directions must be sharply scrutinised and waste avoided. Value for money must be the keynote.

One category of spending merits particular mention. We are spending some £300 million annually in subsidising agriculture alone in one form or another – nearly three-quarters of what we were spending on all food subsidies a few years ago. In Liberal eyes that policy, as a long-term policy, can only be regarded as short-sighted. The farmer desires to stand on his own feet. He cannot, however, be asked to sell in a free market and buy in a protected one. The time has come when the farmers' costs should be lowered by removing the tariffs on the imports of those materials he must use and by doing away with the monopolies and rings which raise the price of the equipment he needs. When this is done subsidies will no longer be necessary. Until this is done the need for some form of Government aid is fully recognised.

Devolution

If Parliament is to meet the external and internal challenges which face it, it must be relieved of the excessive burden of work which now falls upon it and stifles it. If there were no other reason than this Liberals would again, as in 1951, emphasise the necessity of instituting separate Parliamentary Assemblies for Scotland and Wales, and that practical reason is immensely fortified by the claims of those two countries to manage their own local affairs and legislate for them. Each of them, Scotland in the Highlands, and Wales in its scattered rural communities, has special problems with which the rest of the country is not faced.

Liberty

We exist as a Party to defend the rights of the individual, his liberty to live his own life subject to respect for the rights of others, to hold and express his own views, to associate with others of his own choice, to be granted all possible freedom of opportunity and to be subject to no penalty or discrimination by reason of his colour, race or creed.

Liberals see no sign that these fundamental freedoms, constantly open to assault, will be adequately defended without them. The colour bar has been here and there in evidence in this country. Crichel Down is of recent and odious memory; the powers of Government Departments to invade a man's privacy, and even to interfere with his livelihood, can today be abused without redress or appeal. The leaders of the two large Parties can decide on their own that discussion on the air of matters of great moment shall be forbidden for fourteen days before our masters in the House of Commons have told us what we ought to think and do. Trade Unions, who came into existence to defend freedom of association, are using a giant's strength to limit the freedom of workers to benefit from effort, to make life miserable for those they victimise – even to deprive them of their right to remain in their occupations.

The electoral system

If Liberalism is to play its part it requires its proper representation in the House of Commons. There are millions of Liberals in this country effectively disfranchised by our electoral system, which could secure rough justice when there were only two parties, but has for many years distorted the results of every General Election. The fate of a great country is entrusted to the chance result of what is one of the greatest of all gambles. It should be evident that if that democracy which we preach is to be a reality and not a farcical pretence we must have a more truly representative electoral system, in which no votes will be wasted, not even a Conservative vote in Durham nor a Socialist one in Bournemouth. The least we can and do ask is that the whole question be thoroughly investigated by a Royal Commission.

Your responsibility

Electors who believe in the need for a strengthened independent party to put forward Liberal policies will utterly waste their votes unless they support Liberal candidates where they have the opportunity.

The excessive over-privilege and the excessive poverty of fifty years ago are happily things of the past.

Today, the hardest working and the least vocal people are the vast middle-class who seek an opportunity to support a common-sense progressive policy, undeflected by any extremists exploiting or creating sectional interests.

Your responsibility in this new fast-moving world is to be a champion of constructive policies rather than a victim of negative apprehensions.

PEOPLE COUNT

THE LIBERAL
MANIFESTO 1959

Price 3d.

LIBERAL PARTY GENERAL ELECTION MANIFESTO 1959

People count

Date of Election	Thursday 8 October
Party Leader	Jo Grimond
Candidates	216
MPs	6
Votes	1,638,571
% of vote	5.9%

Foreword

People Count. . . and because more and more people are realising that Liberals believe that People count there has been the recent remarkable increase in public support for the Liberal Party. At this Election we hope to consolidate and improve that position as a first stage to the eventual formation of a Liberal Government which will be able to create a Liberal society in this country.

That is our ultimate aim and we appeal to all progressively minded people to start by working and voting for Liberal candidates at this vital Election.

Your Parliament

At the General Election the votes do not choose a Government, they choose a Parliament. The first task is for everyone to vote for a Member of Parliament and that Member should represent you and your neighbours.

You will get a Tory or Socialist Government after this Election, but the kind of Tory or Socialist Government you get will depend on the strength of Liberalism in the House of Commons and the strength of the Liberal vote in the country.

The House of Commons should be a strong influence on the Government. That is what it is for. Lately it has been far too much under the thumb of the Party machines and we must have more Liberals to save us from Tory or Labour reactionaries.

If the House of Commons is to be truly representative we must breathe new life into it to make it what you and I want. This has not been happening. First, most of the issues today are not between Conservatives and Socialists but between Liberals and the Government, whether it be Conservative or Socialist.

Workers' security

For instance, the question of how industry should be run is largely one of providing encouragement for efficient management, giving a greater stake in it, and a greater sense of security to the worker and recognising the important part which the Trade Unions must play, not against management but in close co-operation with it. We all depend on the industries of this country to produce a higher standard of living.

Liberals believe that they should not only be efficient but provide a friendly and secure atmosphere in which everyone involved can have a sense of useful purpose in serving the community. The only people who continually hammer away at this are the Liberals.

The need to bring the Social Services up to date and to sweep away out of date restrictions on the individual is a Liberal task.

Western unity

In Foreign Affairs, are we to put ourselves at the head of a great movement for greater Western Unity as Liberals want – a unity which is vital if the summit talks are to succeed in establishing a genuine peace? This is a Liberal issue.

On Defence, the issue for years has been 'Does Britain need to make its own A-Bombs.' On this Tories and Labour have been united in saying 'yes'. Only recently (and possibly too late) has Labour begun to see that if every country makes its own bombs the risk of war is increased. Liberals for years have been saying that the H-bomb ought to be held in trust for all the free peoples and we should all make a contribution to its production.

Partnership in Africa

Again in Africa, the issue is a fundamental Liberal one about how you treat human beings, in which the irresponsible desire for domination of black by white or white by black must be eradicated in favour of a system in which all races mix freely with full respect for one another.

The Conservative and Labour Parties are not united internally on many of the important issues such as Defence and financial policy. We have seen resignations from the Government, we know the fierce arguments which go on behind closed doors in Socialist Committees.

These arguments should not be hidden from the light of day. They should take place in the House of Commons and in the open Council Chamber, but the last thing either the Conservative or Labour Parties want is to air their disagreements in public.

Honest politics

We must have more Liberals in Parliament and Local Government for the sake of honest, aboveboard politics. We must have Liberals to raise these Liberal issues. The Conservative Party is clearly identified in the minds of the electors with employers and big business, and they cannot deal objectively or fairly with the problems continually arising between employer and employee. The Labour Party is in the hands of the Trade Union Leaders.

The return of a Socialist Government inevitably means that management is put on the defensive, for it does not know what is going to hit it next. The return of a Conservative Government means that the Trade Unions feel justified in going on to the offensive.

The whole nation is the loser from this crazy line up of power politics, and those who lose most in the struggle are those who live on fixed incomes, such as old age pensioners and a host of others who are solicited at Election time but are forgotten after the result is declared.

A Liberal vote is a protest against the British political system being divided up between two powerful Party machines, one largely financed by the employers and the other by the Trade Unions.

The Liberal task

There is a vital task to be done in building up a Progressive alternative Party. The Labour Party have failed to appeal to youth; they have lost their enthusiasm: and so long as they remain tied to nationalisation (which is part of their constitution) and financed by the vested interests of the Trade Union establishment, they will never broaden their appeal sufficiently to embrace all the people who want a progressive party in this country.

England is a democracy and that means there is a Government and an Opposition, and one takes the place of the other from time to time. After all, even Tories do not presumably envisage a Tory Government for ever, there must be an alternative and it should be Liberal, not Socialist.

As a result of the failure of the Labour Party to free itself from sectional interests or keep up its momentum, there seems at the moment to be every likelihood of another Tory Government. If it is not to slip under the influence of its reactionary wing we must demonstrate that there is a strong non-socialist block of opinion in the country which will not tolerate oppression in Africa, another Cyprus, or complacency over inflation, Government expenditure, and the set-up in the nationalised industries.

A big Liberal vote would show that there are people who share Labour's concern about poverty but who are opposed to nationalisation. This would make it harder for Labour leaders to carry through the nationalisation of steel and other industries.

Consumers all

There are millions of Liberals in this country. There are also millions of young people and uncommitted voters who simply do not see themselves mirrored in the image of Tory bigwigs or Labour bosses. There are all the consumers, small business owners, professional men and technicians, craftsmen and farmers, fishermen, shopkeepers and pensioners who have no interest in the Capital v Labour struggle and are greatly harmed by it. Now is their chance to make themselves felt in the New Liberal Party.

Below you can read some of the chief points in our policy but the immediate task is to build a non-Socialist Opposition whose arteries are not too hard to stand the flow of real blood of enthusiasm about the real issues of our time.

Jo Grimond

The British H-bomb

People Count . . . ordinary people, exceptional people. . . people who succeed – those not so successful, the rich, the poor, the young and the old age pensioners.

In the interest of all we must save to spend on the right things. The biggest item of government expenditure is Defence.

Stop the manufacture and testing of nuclear weapons by this country and offer to contribute to a general Western Nuclear Programme and aim, through strengthening the unity of the West, at having a greater say in the circumstances in which it might be used.

The West must be adequately defended by possession of the ultimate deterrent and with conventional weapons, but this must be done through the partnership of the Western Alliance. The fewer nations that manufacture the H-bomb, the more security there will be. This step more than any other would bring down taxes.

Cutting out waste in nationalised industries and government services would do this too. The Gas and Electricity industries should be allowed to settle their own charges and wages and should be made to raise their own capital in the market. The coal industry should be broken down into smaller administrative units and the miners given some share in running them.

Cut prices

Too much of your money is being wasted. You are also paying too much for many of the goods you buy. So – cut prices.

Housewives would pay less if tariffs were reduced step by step, distribution costs cut and price fixing agreements effectively banned.

Invest in education

People Count . . . and so do their children.

Britain's future as a nation lies with the children. More teachers and more schools are needed. Secondary schools come first. Then the primary schools must be improved. There is room for public, grammar, comprehensive and independent schools in our system. Remember Russia spends seven times as much per head on education as we do. America spends twice as much. A big extension of University education is needed. The means test on University education should be ended.

Opportunity in industry

Needed, too, for your children is opportunity in industry.

The 'bulge' years start in 1962 – when the large number of children born after the war will need jobs. Britain's production and productivity lag. It must expand so that jobs are waiting for them – Restrictive practices both by management and labour must go. The causes of crippling industrial disputes must be eliminated. It can be done if rank and file trade unionists are ready to fight for more industrial democracy.

Trade unions must be registered with the Registrar of Friendly Societies in such a way as to ensure fair elections and prevent victimisation.

Ownership for all

People Count ... This traditionally private-enterprise country must pull together to bring about ownership for all.

Liberals want co-ownership and co-partnership schemes encouraged through tax-reliefs. They want special tax-free employee savings accounts schemes brought in. They want more people to be able to buy their own homes. Schedule A income tax and Stamp duty must be abolished. To encourage mobility of labour, Liberals want temporary unemployment allowances increased.

The countryside

People Count ... Too many people have to live in crowded cities. In the Britain the Liberals want to create it is essential to revitalise the countryside.

This requires a new approach to agriculture. A land bank should be set up to provide cheap credit for farmers and rural industries. If this were done and tariffs on goods used by farmers cut, farmers will be made less dependent on the Government. Speed rural electrification and water supplies. Strengthen and improve the advisory services. Above all spend on the roads.

Double the present expenditure. The roads are dangerous, inefficient and uneconomic. Traffic jams are costing £150,000,000 a year in wasted time. Build more and better roads in the countryside. Then industry can be dispersed and people can move from the over-crowded cities. We must spend to save lives.

Aid the pensioner

People Count ... in the family of Britain.

The new Liberals share the concern of their forebears for the old, the sick, the needy, the disabled.

The poverty of the pensioner shames our wealth. Raise the pension to £3 for a single person and £4 16s. for a married couple. Tie it to a special cost-of-living index. Make private pension schemes transferable.

Help the sick

Make the Health Service more human and less 'Whitehall'. Provide effective out-patient and after-care facilities and special accommodation for the old. Invest more money on hospital building, pay and research.

Scotland and Wales

Liberals have long promised self-government for Scotland and Wales.

The Scots and Welsh are separate peoples, each with a great and distinctive tradition. Each country has special problems, including severe unemployment and depopulation, problems which cannot possibly be solved by a Government based on London.

Liberals would give Wales and Scotland Parliaments of their own. The United Kingdom Parliament would remain responsible for foreign and defence policy, but the Scottish and Welsh Parliaments would be elected to cope with their own countries' needs.

We should all benefit, because the Parliament at Westminster would have more time to give to wider issues. As an immediate step, Wales should have its own Secretary of State in the Cabinet.

Commonwealth partnership

The Commonwealth must be a really effective community of free nations. A Commonwealth Civil Service and a Commonwealth Development Fund should be set up to help the newer member states to build their economies. Set up a permanent Commonwealth Council of Ministers for closer consultations.

Britain must lead

People Count. . . Their first desire is peace.

It is against the background of the great heritage we possess in the field of civil liberties, a prudent economy with a freely convertible pound and the rule of law that Britain must lead.

Great Britain must demonstrate that what is morally right is economically right by giving aid to the newly developing countries, by leading a partnership in the Commonwealth, in Europe and through the United Nations. We must strengthen U.N.O. by establishing an international police force without delay. People count in Britain, in the Commonwealth, and throughout the world.

Liberals are determined to get on and get in

The new Liberal Party believes that the British people must stop being cynical about politics and politicians. People will show less apathy only if politicians give them a lead.

Youth is behind the new Liberal Party and is determined to send back more Liberal MPs to Parliament to lay the foundations of a future Liberal Government.

Fairer voting

The British people's sense of fair play should extend to the voting system. At the last election it took 120,000 votes to elect a Liberal to Parliament, 45,000 to elect a Socialist and 39,000 to elect a Conservative. Liberals urge fairer voting. This is part of the

Liberal programme for the Reform of Parliament and the Reform of Local Government to ensure that people count.

The vote does not belong to the Conservative and Labour parties. It belongs to the people.

People count

People count – in Britain – in the Commonwealth – throughout the world.

Abolish the earnings rule for pensioners; stop sending men to Coventry; give the small man a liberal deal; end hospital queues; slash taxes on goods in the family shopping basket; pay fair compensation for a land grab; do away with the Colour bar; trade with the peoples of the world – Exchange goods, not H-bombs; tell the Press, don't bar them from Councils; free the Police to do their proper job – their task is to prevent crime; help and encourage the Fine Arts.

THE LIBERAL
1964
M
MANIFESTO

Think
for
Yourself
vote
Liberal

LIBERAL PARTY GENERAL ELECTION MANIFESTO 1964

Think for yourself – vote Liberal

Date of Election	Thursday 15 October
Party Leader	Jo Grimond
Candidates	365
MPs	9
Votes	3,092,878
% of vote	11.2%

The Liberal Party offers the electorate a radical, non-Socialist alternative. In the long run, our objective is to form a government. In the short run, we seek sufficient support to send back a force of Liberal MPs which will hold a decisive position in the next Parliament.

Many thinking people in Britain dissociate themselves from politics today. A strong Liberal Party is essential to bring them into public life.

In the past five years we have brought new blood into local government by increasing the number of Liberal councillors from 500 to over 1,800. We have pioneered great issues of policy like the Common Market, regionalism and the need for national policies on redundancy and monopolies.

Liberal by-election successes forced the Prime Minister to sack seven Ministers and make the first hesitant Tory gestures towards modernization. We ask for your vote at this general election to bring about a more substantial and dramatic change in British politics.

A decisive Liberal influence is needed, in particular, to carry out three major aims. Modern technology provides the means of achieving a new age of abundance which could provide everyone with a richer life and great new opportunities. Since the war this country has lagged behind and failed to seize these opportunities. The vested interests in the Conservative and Labour parties have blocked the way. The Liberal Party seeks a decisive position in the next Parliament to make sure that change and growth are stimulated.

Our second aim is to ensure that individual people benefit from the new industrial revolution. The age of automation could be an age when the individual is trampled on and power is dangerously concentrated in the hands of big business and the state. Change must be humanised so that the new wealth within our reach is used to give the individual a richer life and protect the weak. Class consciousness in the factory, on the housing estate, or in politics, must give way to a new spirit of partnership.

The third Liberal objective is to apply the idea of partnership in international affairs.

In the nuclear age mankind cannot afford narrow nationalism. The economic benefits of modern science can only be achieved if there is a lavish flow of ideas, people and goods, amongst the nations. The giant risks of the nuclear age and the explosive problem of world poverty cannot be mastered until the nations act together. A strong force of Liberal MPs will ensure that Britain plays a new and greater part as a pioneer of the new international order that mankind so badly needs.

Creating the wealth

Britain has lagged behind since the war because the 'Establishment' in politics, in Whitehall, in industry, and the trade unions, has too often been unresponsive to the possibilities of the new age. To put this right, the way Britain is run must be drastically reformed; the new men and women who understand modern technology must be given wider opportunities to use their talents; economic growth must become a major aim through more skilful management of the nation.

A plan for expansion

To give economic expansion top priority, central government must be reorganised, and a Ministry of Expansion set up as the hub of economic government.

Parliament, the Ministry of Expansion and industry, would then draw up and implement a national plan for economic growth. It would be drafted by the Minister of Expansion in consultation with industry and the unions and then submitted to Parliament for debate and approval. Parliament would weigh up the implications and decide on a 4, 5 or 6 per cent rate of growth.

Expansion at home depends on selling more abroad. Britain should constantly take the initiative in the drive to bring down world tariffs. Cuts in our own high, outdated tariffs will help to expand world trade. They will also bring down our costs at home and thus make our exports more competitive abroad.

The Government must play a far more positive role in the export drive. Commercial staff in British embassies abroad, for instance, must help individual firms and work with them to get orders and expand their markets.

The sterling problem once more threatens our economic growth. Liberals will take the initiative to solve this deep-seated problem by the radical step of pooling international exchange reserves.

The international reserve pool could then develop a world strategy for expansion and prosperity, and seek in particular to build up the wealth and buying power of the impoverished southern continents where we must sell our goods.

Mobilising our skills

Britain's most valuable asset is skill. But restrictive practices, poor management, and lack of enterprise at the top mean that this is too often wasted. Three men are used on average in our industry to produce the output of one American worker. This need not be so.

The Liberal plan will set a target for the growth of national output so that every working man and woman can make full and satisfying use of his or her time at work.

Unions and management will be encouraged to bargain for higher basic rates, a shorter working week and longer holidays with pay, in return for the abandonment of out-of-date restrictive practices.

An incomes policy which penalises teachers and nurses, whilst speculators and company directors escape the net, is wrong. The Liberal incomes policy will aim at relating all incomes, including profits, to productivity, make allowances for groups that have been left behind, and see that social benefits like pensions, take their proper share of growing wealth.

Trade unions must be encouraged to adopt industrial unions and plant bargaining. Plant bargaining brings the shop stewards into the negotiations and cuts out the need to manipulate overtime, bonuses, and piece work rating, in order to get round the shortcomings of national rates. National agreements should fix adequate minimum rates and consolidate the position of groups who are getting left behind.

Partners in industry

Go-ahead companies have already realised that the alternative to negative control by the unofficial strike is real participation by the employee in the running of his firm.

The Companies Act must be amended to give all established employees in public limited companies a status comparable to shareholders. Employees must be given a share in the decisions and profits of the companies in which they work. Employees should be represented on the board of directors, or on a joint supervisory council. This is one way to ensure that ability gets to the top.

Public companies must be required to publish more information about their accounts. they should be published every six months; firms should be compelled to publish full accounts of subsidiary and associate companies, including contributions to political parties.

All pension rights must be made transferable. At present too many employers try to prevent key men changing their jobs. Experienced employees must have a right to periods of long leave which they can use to widen their background or train for an alternative job.

In an age of automation everyone must have the opportunity to learn fresh skills throughout his or her working life. There must be a massive expansion of education for management and government training centres, shorter and more flexible apprenticeships, and freedom of entry into skilled trades for qualified workers of any age.

To provide security against redundancy a national redundancy fund must be set up, financed by contributions from employers and the state. This would supplement unemployment benefit up to at least two-thirds of a worker's average earnings. Individual firms would be encouraged by tax rebates to provide even better benefits.

Reduce income tax

We will also simplify the tax system. The present complications foster tax avoidance and unfairly favour those who can afford a tax accountant or lawyer. The ownership of personal wealth must be spread more widely, estate duty will be replaced by a graded legacy duty and a tax on gifts paid by the recipients. The burden of tax on those who earn must be reduced by spreading the indirect tax net, taxing capital gains over a longer period and stopping tax dodges.

We will introduce equal pay for women for equal work and give women greater legal rights in marriage particularly in regard to property, the guardianship of children and the enforcement of maintenance orders.

We shall make it easier for married women to return to work without disrupting the home, by encouraging part-time work, improving training and retraining, removing tax disabilities and introducing an allowance for child minders.

Cost of living

A pound in 1951 is worth only 13s. 0d. today. The rising cost of living penalises people on fixed incomes, pensioners and many people in every walk of life.

Liberals will check the rise in prices by action against monopolies and price rings; tariff cuts and tax policy. These measures to spread the fruits of higher productivity to the consumer are the key to a just incomes policy. In particular we will outlaw certain restrictive practices and make take-over bids and mergers, subject to public scrutiny.

Fair trade legislation will protect the consumer against shoddy goods, misleading labels and markings up. It will also protect the shopkeeper against discrimination by suppliers who squeeze our retailers by withholding discounts which they give to their competitors.

The wrangle about nationalisation and denationalisation is irrelevant to most of the problems of modern industry.

Liberals want a truce in the dispute over steel which will take the industry out of politics and enable it to get on with the job. We press instead for modernisation of the industry, government help for redundancy, competitive marketing, and a world steel conference to cut tariffs and agree on world rules of competition.

In the past ten years more has been wasted by the Conservative Government on abandoned defence projects and other matters than the whole school building pro-gramme. Waste in government will not be cut out unless the best brains of the country are brought into administration from industry and the universities.

The House of Commons must also have better control over public spending and the formulation of policy on economic affairs, foreign policy and defence. Specialised par-liamentary committees on these matters, empowered to call on experts, should be set up to allow more time for broad debates in the House and permit MPs with specialised knowledge to share in framing policy.

Back bench MPs must be given more freedom to influence legislation. There must be more free voting, except on matters of confidence. to enliven debate and give it mean-ing. The House of Commons must be brought into closer contact with people, espe-cially young people. A royal commission should consider extending the franchise to those over 18.

A prosperous countryside

Increased earnings for farmers and farm workers are necessary to create a prosperous countryside.

Liberals will set up meat and grain commissions to manage the market for both home and imported produce so that the farmer gets the bulk of his income from the market and the housewife is assured regular supplies at reasonable prices.

We will allocate a larger share of Government money to stock improvement and projects for technical advance, capital aid to small farmers and schemes for group farming and co-operative marketing.

A Land Bank will be set up to make credit available to genuine farmers at low interest rates, thus creating conditions in which agricultural productivity can expand.

We will bring down the cost of farm materials through improved distribution, grading and marketing so that both the housewife and the farmer benefit.

The future face of Britain

The skills and potential wealth of Britain will not be fully used if people continue to drift to the south-east.

In order to establish a proper balance between the regions, there must be a broad national plan on the movement of population, the location of industry, new towns and transport.

Power from London

The key note of this national plan will be the decentralisation of power and wealth from London. In Wales, Scotland and the north and west of England, there are plenty of able men and women who could make a bigger contribution to the running of their own affairs. These untapped resources will not be released unless political power to make decisions is brought back to the people they concern.

A Scottish Parliament must be set up so that Scottish domestic affairs will receive the informed attention which Westminster cannot provide.

A Council for Wales will be established and a Secretary of State for Wales appointed. A Welsh development agency will be set up to plan, to lend money and to promote new industries. It will give special attention to the problem of mid-Wales. In Scotland a Highland development authority will be set up to arrest depopulation, and promote industrial and rural development.

Northern Ireland will also benefit from the policy of devolving power from London. The Liberal plan will provide broader regional tax advantages for Northern Ireland.

Liberals seek also to help the different religions and groups of Northern Ireland to live peaceably together without mutual discrimination or intolerance. A Bill of Rights should guarantee the citizen against discrimination.

Regional government

Throughout Britain regional authorities must be set up responsible, ultimately through elected regional councils, to the regions they represent. They must draw up regional plans and have the power to build new towns to counter the attraction of the congested areas. Today Whitehall ministries allocate school and hospital building funds or give permission for the siting of new factories. Such powers must be decentralised to the regional authorities so that the people who live in a region have responsibility for their homes, schools and jobs.

Regional planning also proves a key to transport policy. The Buchanan Report on 'Traffic in Towns' is at present no more than a scrap of paper. Regional authorities will have the powers and resources to help local authorities reshape our cities so that they can be pleasant places to live in. They must be empowered to provide specific subsidies to bus or rail services in rural areas to keep remote communities alive.

Transport shapes the future of our country, yet investment in roads, docks and railways, for decades, has lagged far behind the country's needs. A comprehensive national motorway network must be built. East long distance rail transport must be developed further and antiquated docks modernised within the framework of regional plans.

Homes for all

The chronic housing shortage can and must be ended and slums cleared within 10 years. This means progressively raising the building programme to at least 500,000 homes a year.

The regional authorities can once more provide the drive. Many of our 1,400 local housing authorities are tied to old-fashioned building methods because they can only build on a minute scale. Only regional authorities can help place orders on an industrial scale and make full use of modern techniques.

Vigorous action is needed to train more skilled men and eliminate restrictive practices and price rings in the building industry. Standards must be raised and jerry-building eliminated by the adoption of a national building code. The rate of slum clearance must be trebled to 180,000 dwellings a year, based on a national building survey. A land development corporation will provide capital funds and teams of experts to rebuild city centres.

More home ownership

House ownership must be brought within the reach of all. To bring down the cost of mortgages, profits and income tax on the surpluses of building societies must be abolished. Government guarantees for mortgages for periods of up to 30 or 35 years will help young married couples by spreading the period of repayment. Fuller use should be made by local authorities of their powers to grant 100 per cent home loans.

Rented homes in Britain tend either to be hopelessly expensive, derelict, or severely limited by a lengthy housing list. Here the only real answer is to build more houses and end the housing shortage. Non-profit-making housing associations could expand further if they are given more help by teams of architects and other experts which the regional authorities can afford to employ. The Rent Act must be modified to allow longer periods of notice and the reimposition of controls on landlords who demand extortionate rents.

Land prices

Liberals will check the rise in land prices by stimulating development away from the south-east; they will abolish the present unfair system of rating and replace it with a scheme based on site value rating. This would encourage development and better use of land, lower the burden of rates on the householder and ensure that the community shares in any rise in land values.

A social charter

Britain's social security system, pioneered by two great Liberals – Lloyd George and Beveridge – now needs bringing up to date. The old age pension must be high enough for people to live on without national assistance and linked to the national income so that pensioners share in the growing national wealth. The minimum state pension must be fixed at half the average national earnings – £8 10s. and £5 5s. respectively for the married and single pensioner today.

The National Assistance Board should ultimately be abolished when the need for it has disappeared, once the basic pension is raised. The earnings rule, which stops elderly people who draw a pension from earning a bit more, must also go. Widows' pensions must be brought into line with the nation's growing wealth.

Insurance stamps will be abolished. Social security should be financed by a social security tax levied in proportion to their pay roll, on employers two-thirds and employees one-third. Revenue for social security benefits would thus automatically rise with earnings.

Everyone must have the chance to supplement the basic state pension through an occupational scheme, paying a benefit of up to at least two-thirds of their own previous earnings, subject to a maximum and a minimum. Employers without a private scheme would contribute to a central fund to finance individual savings schemes.

The Liberal aim is to enable everyone in need or in old age to receive two-thirds of their previous pay through a combination of the basic benefit and an occupational scheme.

Better health services

The health services are crippled by a shortage of doctors, dentists and nurses. Hospital beds are empty for lack of staff. Liberals will encourage qualified doctors to practise by reforming methods of payment and introducing refresher courses; we will review the wage and career set-up of nursing and make it easier for married women to nurse part-time.

Prescription charges must be abolished. They create hardship for those least able to bear it, the old, the ill, the unemployed. Savings can be made in administration and through the bulk buying of drugs on a regional scale.

An expectant mother, or an elderly person, is often treated by several separate branches of the health and welfare services. We will end this wasteful duplication by setting up area health boards, which bring together the whole range of health and welfare services. The G.P. would have a leading position in this team, and thus recover the scope and opportunity he often lacks today.

Reform the law

Liberals will switch the emphasis in combating crime to prevention and rehabilitation. We will expand the police force and the probation service, improve pay and conditions to attract high quality recruits. To reduce the prison population, we will make greater use of alternatives to imprisonment; extend experiments in prison reform and remand procedure; improve after-care service, and appoint independent inspectors to visit prisons and investigate complaints.

Invest in people

Education decides the country's economic future and shapes our children's lives.

Here priorities are all important. The crux of our educational problem is the teacher shortage, and the first priority is to bring about a massive expansion of teacher training.

Liberals propose to double full time places in higher education in the next 10 years. Then the men and women will be available to reduce the size of classes and eliminate the slum schools. Special attention will be given to the primary and infant schools, where neglect has been worst.

Teaching as a career must be made more attractive by an improved salary structure, service conditions and pensions. New methods of teaching must be developed and financial rewards given to teachers who improve their skills. The setting up of new machinery for negotiating teachers' pay to replace the broken Burnham system is overdue.

The 11-plus exam must go. It is socially divisive and unfair in its results. We will encourage forms of non-selective secondary education, ranging from the campus system to the Leicestershire type schemes and the comprehensive school. This cannot be left to local authorities alone. The Government must help, especially with cash for buildings.

Partnership in the world

The Liberal aim is a true world order, based on controlled disarmament and a world-wide rule of law. This cannot come overnight. In the meantime Britain must work to build up a partnership between regional groups of nations consistent with the UN Charter.

Although the UN is not fully effective there is no alternative to accept a wider loyalty and this world institution gradually assumes new tasks and takes on real power. In particular we shall press for the establishment of a permanent UN force to maintain peace in areas of tension.

Britain is part of Europe and could have played a prominent part in the United Europe movement. Instead the Labour and Conservative parties dragged their feet. Today Britain is paying the price for these hesitations. Exports to the Common Market are faltering; the West as a whole suffers from growing political division.

In the course of the next Parliament, the chance to join a European Political and Economic Community may come again. This opportunity must not be thrown away. A strong force of Liberal MPs could decide this historic question.

Towards a welfare world

A joint Western programme of aid and trade is essential to defeat world poverty. The Freedom from Hunger campaign has shown the way. A world food plan must play a systematic part in development programmes. World commodity stabilisation schemes can steady prices of raw materials exported by developing countries and, incidentally, help to bring Britain into closer partnership with Europe. Britain must press for joint Western policies to lower trade barriers to manufacturers from the new nations.

In the second half of this century racial bitterness may be the gravest danger for mankind. Liberals reject racial discrimination for they believe fundamentally in the brotherhood of man. In Africa there can be no compromise with apartheid. Shipments of arms to South Africa should be stopped.

Commonwealth development

Britain has a special role to play in Commonwealth development. A Commonwealth Service must be set up, recruited from all the member countries, to cover the whole range of technical help needed by developing countries. An imaginative effort must be made to extend Voluntary Service Overseas. On immigration and race problems Liberals will take the initiative in setting up a system of Commonwealth consultation towards an agreed policy for immigration, exclusion and expulsion and the rights of political asylum.

World peace and security

No real progress will be made towards world peace and security until Governments accept that complete national independence is impossible in a world threatened by nuclear warfare. The attempt to maintain an independent British range of nuclear weapons has encouraged the proliferation of nuclear weapons, weakened our economy, and deprived our conventional forces of resources they desperately need.

Liberals will shift the emphasis to building up our conventional forces, so that Britain can fulfill its world-wide obligations until an effective UN force takes over. We will seek influence, not by buying American Polaris missiles at an eventual cost of some £600 m., but by pressing for new and effective NATO political institutions such as a powerful political–military secretariat to plan strategy based on a European Political Community within a true Atlantic partnership.

Collective control of nuclear weapons within NATO could be an important step towards disarmament.

Britain can best contribute by integrating TSR2 and our V bombers into the NATO structure.

We must also take the initiative in the disarmament discussions by pressing for a freeze on the development of nuclear strategic weapons; working to establish nuclear free zones; considering proposals for inspection against surprise attack; pressing for the admission of China to the disarmament discussions.

The Liberal challenge

This Liberal programme is designed to benefit the country as a whole.

At home Liberals have bold policies to reconstruct Britain and create a new spirit of partnership. Abroad they seek to apply the same spirit of partnership to world affairs.

A positive Liberal purpose in Westminster is required to ensure that the will of the people is done.

If all the people who vote negatively to keep the other side out, lend their support to this programme, a decisive Liberal influence will be certain in the next Parliament.

Think for yourself – Vote Liberal.

for All the people

THE LIBERAL PLAN OF 1966

LIBERAL PARTY GENERAL ELECTION MANIFESTO 1966

For all the people: the Liberal plan of 1966

Date of Election	Thursday 31 March
Party Leader	Jo Grimond
Candidates	311
MPs	12
Votes	2,327,533
% of vote	8.5%

Britain demands a new approach

Eighteen months ago many people had high hopes that a change of Government from Conservative to Labour would bring about a real change in the country's fortunes. They had watched the country drift from one economic crisis to another and seen how Britain's rate of expansion and industrial growth had continued to fall behind that of other countries.

Now events have shown that, for all their talk about modernisation, Labour too cannot find the answer to our problems. However admirable their intentions, they, like the Conservatives, have been unable to implement workable solutions.

There are very simple reasons for this. Both parties have their roots firmly in one section of the community or another. The Conservatives. both ideologically and financially, are still tied to the interests of capital. Equally Labour are tied to the interests of the Unions, often to the detriment of both.

Is it surprising that their actions are seldom acceptable or effective for the country as a whole?

Why are the Liberals different?

Today, more than ever, the unique position of the Liberal Party enables us to bring new thinking and a fresh, objective approach to Britain's economic and social problems and to put forward solutions that work. We can do this precisely because we have no vested interest in protecting one group or another. We are not a class party. We draw our support from all groups and classes and we are free to reconcile conflicting interests for the benefit of the whole community. We are the party of all individuals, no matter what their background.

What the Liberals have achieved

Already the three million votes polled at the last election in support of Liberal attitudes and Liberal policies have acted as a powerful brake and a positive influence on the policies of the Labour Government. Indeed the Liberal Party has provided the only effective opposition in curbing the wasteful excesses of Socialism and compelling Labour to give priority to at least some of the things that matter.

- Steel Nationalisation was shelved as a result of Liberal pressure and saved the country millions of pounds. Without that pressure it could still happen.
- Land Nationalisation was checked in response to Liberal pressure. The nationalisation of small plots of building land in private ownership has been dropped.
- Pensions and Rates. Although Labour's plans do not go far enough Liberal pressure has forced the Government to put these issues before further nationalisation plans.
- The Neglected Regions. For years Liberals have been calling for action to revitalise the depressed areas of Britain. Even the tentative moves now being made by Labour would not have been made but for Liberal pressure.
- The Highland Development Board. A clear example of a Liberal proposal being implemented by Labour in response to pressure from the Highland Liberal MPs.
- A Really Positive Vote. The effectiveness of Liberal pressure to date is only the beginning. An increased number of Liberal MPs and an increased Liberal vote in each constituency will bring about still more positive action in Parliament. And there is plenty to be done.

The most vital need is for a fresh and realistic approach to economic planning, defence and the machinery of government, because only then will the wealth be created that can bring about a real improvement in living standards, housing, education and the social services for all the people of Britain.

The policies outlined show the positive action that is needed. Consider them carefully and decide for yourself.

Three million people voted Liberal last time for what they knew was right. The 10 Liberal MPs have done the work of 30 times that many. Those votes have really counted. A higher vote. More MPs. The same drive. And a Liberal Government will be near.

HOW TO CREATE THE WEALTH

Britain must pay her way

Facing World Realities.

Britain today has the slowest rate of growth of any developed industrial economy. By 1980, if present trends continue, the only countries in Western Europe with a lower living standard will be Portugal and Spain. One reason for this pitiful performance is the attempt to carry world responsibilities far beyond our means.

In 1964 Britain's military spending overseas was £305 million, accounting for over half the country's debt. Expenditure of this kind hits us all.

The Labour Government is now trying to cut it down, but it has failed to cut the basic commitments, which made us spend the money, many of which are no longer realistic.

Britain is also still the centre of a world-wide currency system. Attempts to sustain the system have placed our economic policy in a strait-jacket and added a further restriction on our growth. In consequence we now have the largest debt in our history.

The Government must work for a radical reform of the world's financial system, in which we shall pool our exchange reserves with those of other Western powers and jointly assume responsibility for managing a new reserve currency.

While illusions of military and economic grandeur must be dropped, British industry needs the wider horizon of the Common Market. British exports to Europe have suffered badly from our exclusion. Waiting for something to turn up is not a policy. Britain must declare now her intention to join the European Community.

Growth comes first

The Labour Government has now set up a Department of Economic Affairs, but real power over economic policy still remains in the cautious hands of the Treasury. The Department of Economic Affairs can only become a real driving force for expansion if it has authority over short term as well as long term planning. It should work in partnership with a new Parliamentary standing committee on economic affairs in the formulation, execution and continuous modification of a new national economic plan.

Simplify the tax system

The tax system must be overhauled and simplified so that it encourages efficiency rather than evasion. A standing committee of experts from industry, finance and Government must be set up to fit successive budgetary measures into a sustained programme of tax reform.

Cut direct taxation

Direct taxation must be systematically cut and some of the burden shifted to inherited wealth and gifts. Death duties should be replaced by a legacy duty, to encourage the wider distribution of wealth.

Tax reliefs for industrial investment, even after the new grants, are less than they were two years ago. They should be restored to the previous level and increased as soon as possible to a level comparable with that of other industrial countries. Office machinery and services which earn foreign exchange should be allowed to benefit from investment grants.

Bring down prices

All people, but particularly the old and those living on fixed incomes, are hit by constantly rising prices. Between 1951 and 1964 the value of the £ dropped to 13s. 0d. Since the last Election the cost of living has risen by a further 13s. 0d in the pound.

The effective way to bring down prices is to increase competition by cutting tariffs.

Because this would hit monopolies and price rings it would increase efficiency, and prices would fall accordingly. If necessary the maintenance of price rings and gross restrictive practices should be made criminal offences.

A positive incomes policy

An Incomes Policy is a necessary aid, if we are to check inflation with a minimum of unemployment, and achieve a fair distribution of the wealth we have, but to succeed, an incomes policy must emphasise the need for greater productivity and efficiency before wages and incomes are increased.

In Western Germany reasonable price stability has been maintained, with only 1 per cent unemployment (less than in Britain today), thanks to planned immigration, generous redundancy arrangements and systematic training to induce people to change jobs. In Britain, an ambitious retraining programme is needed with payment of average national earnings during retraining. Longer periods of notice should be given to those who must change jobs. There must be a greater expansion in management training and shorter and more flexible apprenticeships.

Where there is direct confrontation with a large Union, Government intervention by tariff cuts or taxes may sometimes be necessary to prevent exorbitant wage increases in particular industries, but we would prefer wage increases to be restricted voluntarily. Labour's Prices and Incomes Bill can only undermine the confidence of the Unions.

Government pressure should be exerted to create strong unions covering whole industries and to rationalise the wage structure. Bargaining at individual plant level, in which higher earnings are negotiated in return for abandonment of restrictive practices, must be encouraged.

Partnership in industry pays

Getting both 'sides' together

Strikes, stoppages and demarcation disputes are three major causes of Britain's failure to pay her way. Too often they arise from class prejudices, the failure of employer and employee to understand each other's problems and the lack of any common purpose between them.

Each 'side's' distrust of the other's interests has led to inefficiency and prevented any lasting solution being reached. The Liberal Party, bound by no such interests, is in a unique position to bring the two 'sides' together and be accepted in doing so.

A 'say'

The first step must be to give employees more say in the running of the companies in which they work. Company law must be amended to require the setting up of Works Councils for regular consultation and negotiation between employee and management on all major issues affecting their company.

A Stake

Employees must be given the same status as shareholders and the consequent right to elect directors to the Board.

Management should be encouraged by tax incentives to increase employee shareholding, because a financial stake is an important part of a man's involvement with, and responsibility to, the company for which he works.

Industrial efficiency depends on partnership not conflict. Our proposals would bring about this partnership.

Contracts of service

A standard contract of service should be introduced covering the right to Union representation; an equal range of security benefits for wage and salary earners; holiday pay based on average earnings; a guaranteed opportunity for further education and training in employer's time; and equal rates of pay for men and women doing identical work. With such contracts it would be easier to gain the acceptance of arbitration rather than the immediate resort to industrial force and the contracts could be enforceable in the civil courts.

Harness technology

The establishment of the Ministry of Technology has not led to the 'white hot scientific revolution' promised by Labour before the last election. There have been small increases in government financed support for the National Research Development Corporation and for computers, but the machinery for science and technology is much the same as it was under the Tories.

Among Liberal proposals are expansion of the Atomic Energy Programme, reorganisation of the Council for Scientific Policy, with wider terms of reference, better co-ordination of the Work and Research Associations and full transferability of pensions for the Civil Service so as to ensure mobility of scientific manpower.

Expansion in farming pays

If you are a farmer or farm worker, today you can have little cause for satisfaction with Conservative and Labour farming policies. Both parties have allowed farming to drift. The farmer's life is hedged about with uncertainty. He never knows whether to expand or contract. His workers often leave the land. If you are a housewife, you too will have seen how this uncertainty has brought fluctuations and increases in the prices of meat, milk and dairy produce.

A few years ago only the Liberal Party recognised the need for selective expansion in food production. We called for a system of managed markets for home and imported produce under a Meat and Grain Commission, and a system of agricultural support that gave the farmer his return from the market rather than from subsidies, and one that guaranteed reasonable prices to the housewife.

The other parties now favour agricultural expansion, but the Labour proposals in the National Plan envisage a rate of growth in beef and pork production slower than that of the last five years. Only the dairy herd is set for expansion but the incentive to farmers is insufficient.

We welcome Labour's tentative scheme for easier farm credit, but we would extend it by a Land Banking system to help bona fide small farmers and ex-farm workers to make their farms efficient and modern.

Better prices for beef

If this country wants beef the Government must recognise the need to pay substantially more to the producer. Substantial price increases would in turn give the producer a higher price for calves and enable marginal milk producers to turn over to livestock. The confidence in expansion created would remove the need to raise milk prices to the housewife.

Cereals expansion

As long as subsidies remain at their present level, there will be uncertainty for both Government and farmer. With a managed cereal market the price could be gradually raised until the subsidy is eliminated.

Cost

These price adjustments would be self-balancing. The money saved on cereal subsidies and the levies collected on imports would provide sufficient funds for the increase

Livestock prices

Introduced over a period of years, this new system and increased technological investment in farming would create for the farmer the firm prospect of expansion, a real increase in income, and a decreasing dependence on imported produce.

Bring a new life to the neglected regions

A national physical plan

For too many people there is little incentive to stay in the area of their birth. Culturally and financially the draw is toward the South East.

While Britain has a national plan for the economy, there is no national physical plan to redress this balance. The drift to the South East continues. Only in the Highlands, where the Liberals swept the board at the last Election, has Labour, under pressure, set up a Development Board with money and real powers.

There must be a national plan for the future redistribution of population and development and the decentralisation of power and wealth from London.

Scotland and Wales

Greater power to run their own affairs must be given to the people of Scotland and Wales.

The Royal Commission on Scottish Local Government must be extended to examine particularly the devolution of power from Whitehall to Edinburgh with a view to establishing an elected Scottish Parliament.

A Council of Wales must be established and a Welsh Development Agency set up to plan, to lend money and to promote new industries.

There must be broader regional tax advantages to stimulate development in Northern Ireland.

Elected Regional Councils

Regional Councils nominated by the Central Government give those who live in the regions neither a say in their affairs nor a responsibility for them. Regional councillors must be elected – and paid. This is not a part-time job for amateurs.

Regional Councils throughout Britain must have full powers to co-ordinate all the industrial and cultural development within their regions. They must have their own financial resources and power to borrow, especially for physical re-development.

Power to plan

Regional Councils can only be effective if they have the executive power to plan for their areas. They should be responsible for the use of land, including new towns and new industries, public transport and hospital building, water supplies, regional resources and all facilities for leisure and the arts.

An effective regional policy also demands the decentralisation of Government offices and the nationalised industries, and the appointment of Regional Officers with status equivalent to the Civil Servant.

Reform Local Government

Our system of local government badly needs to become a more effective instrument of the electors' will. The aldermanic system in England and Wales should be abolished. All trading arrangements by Councillors with their Council should be disclosed in the minutes. The resources and functions of smaller local authorities should be merged to ensure that effective people are employed and efficient services provided at the most economic price.

A radical approach to transport

Whether we are private motorists, farmers or industrialists, poor road and rail communications affect us all, but particularly they strike at the root of exports, regional development, prices and agricultural expansion. Yet Britain's motorway network is smaller than that built in Germany thirty years ago, and under the National Plan investment in new roads gets a pitiful low priority.

A network of motorways can and must be constructed without throwing an additional burden on the taxpayer. Those who use roads want to see results. The new motorways should be Pay Roads. This would mean a small charge to the user, but it would be more than balanced by savings in fuel, delays, and wear and tear.

It would enable public loans to be raised, to build the roads quickly, and would provide a communication system to galvanise the economy.

British Rail's passenger and freight services must be rationalised, co-ordinated, and streamlined to meet the real demands of the customer.

In other countries, air shuttle services between cities are profitable. Why not here? Our provincial airports must be modernised and the number of inter-city services and airports increased as the regions of Britain are developed.

Non-racialist approach to immigration

We believe that immigrant entry to this country should be regulated by the availability of jobs or the possession of skills and not fixed at an arbitrary figure bearing no relation to vacancies.

The problems connected with immigration have aroused tremendous emotion. No one should minimise the social problems created. But clearly anyone who reflects upon the work of doctors and nurses in our hospitals, employees in our transport services, and many other industries, will recognise the significant contribution which immigrants are making to our society.

We appreciate that integration is not always easy and, in order that the full contribution of the immigrant may be realised, more steps must be taken at national and local level to provide facilities for non-English speaking immigrants to improve their knowledge of English and the British way of life. There must be a closer co-ordination of action at national and local level to promote racial harmony.

Above all the 'immigrant problem' is a problem of housing. Special subsidies must be made available to Local Authorities in areas of acute housing shortage.

Defence commitments must be cut

Too great a proportion of our national wealth is spent in pursuing a world peacekeeping role that in many areas is no longer realistic and that in any case is far beyond our financial resources to fulfil effectively.

We appreciate Labour's wish to limit defence expenditure but they envisage no equivalent cut in commitments as Mr Mayhew has so honestly pointed out.

Realistic priorities

We reject the idea that Britain still has an independent peacekeeping role East of Suez. The likelihood of our being required to act independently, in the defence of India and Pakistan for example, as the Tashkent Agreement demonstrates, grows more remote. We should cut our commitments East of Suez accordingly.

Apart from a temporary obligation to Malaysia our role is as a member of the United Nations and not as an independent peace-keeping force. We must therefore plan today for a gradual reduction of our bases in the Far East.

The Deterrent

Events have proved that only the Liberals were sincerely opposed to Britain's possession of an independent nuclear deterrent. Labour in office, despite all they said in Opposition, have in fact committed us to a nuclear role for the next 10 years. Thereby Labour have made their task of reducing the arms bill more difficult and encouraged the spread of nuclear weapons.

However, as we still have certain nuclear weapons under our control, steps must be taken to place these weapons under international control within the Western Alliance.

Select Committee on Defence

During the past 10 years millions of the taxpayers' money have been wasted on unrealistic commitments and abandoned prestige defence projects.

Never has the need for a Select Committee on Defence (quite apart from the other Parliamentary reforms which Liberals advocate) been made more obvious than when the Government issued their defence review on February 22nd. Here were policies, which will virtually affect the defence of the United Kingdom for the next decade, which had never been discussed in Parliament or by Parliament until the decisions had been taken and were irrevocable.

Our priority should be to ensure the security of the United Kingdom by retaining an effective defence force in Western Europe, which, by its very presence, will help to maintain our political influence in that area.

By cutting our Far East commitments we shall be able to do this and still bring defence expenditure into reasonable proportion.

Disarmament

We must call for a freeze in the development of nuclear weapons, work to establish nuclear free zones; and press for the admission of China to the UN and disarmament discussions.

Modernise the machinery of government

The prestige and influence of Parliament has declined. While the British electorate is often able to participate in the great formative debates of American democracy on television, too often major issues are discussed by Parliament only after the event.

The decline of Parliament must be arrested by radical reform of its procedures. Standing Committees on Foreign Affairs, Defence, Economics and Science and Technology must be set up so that Parliament shares from the beginning in the formulation of policy. Television, the medium of political debate, must be brought into the House of Commons.

Streamline administration

Labour has set up new Ministries, but this has not led to quicker decisions or more efficient planning. Indeed it has sometimes led to duplication and made problems worse. Administration must be streamlined to give value for money. Economics, Technology, and Social Security must each be the responsibility of a single Minister. The Housing and Local Government Ministries must be co-ordinated in a Ministry for Regional Planning and Development, within which Housing and Transport would become subordinated departments. Detailed planning would be decentralised to the Regional Councils.

The appointment of senior Ministers in charge of broad areas of policy would make possible a smaller and more efficient cabinet, comparable to Churchill's wartime machine.

Civil Service rules must be made more flexible to allow able people to be brought in from outside. But the test must be ability not political views. A small unit, set up by the Treasury, would ensure that recruitment of outsiders is fair and taps the best brains.

Electoral reform

The Electoral system must be reformed to ensure that membership of the House of Commons represents more accurately the will of the people. Through the Speaker's Conference we shall continue to press for changes in the method of voting. A system which allowed over three million voters only nine members of Parliament and which made it possible for a party with less than half the total vote to become the Government, is clearly in need of a radical overhaul.

The changes we propose would ensure that every vote cast really counted, and would dispel the present electoral apathy.

We shall press for votes for young people at 18. Today's youth is responsible and should be treated as such. At present, until they are 21 young people may not, without their parents' consent, travel abroad or enter into any legal contract including a mortgage, nor may they vote.

Full rights should be granted at 18.

HOW TO IMPROVE OUR WAY OF LIFE

Your home and your rates

Millions still live in slums or have no house of their own. Millions more have homes without lavatories and running water.

To rid the country of slums and shortage and build sufficient dwellings for all families to have their own homes, we must build at least five million homes within the next 10 years.

This can be done if we tackle the real causes of the problem.

Industrialised building techniques

System builders' factories run at a fraction of their capacity. Regional Planning Offices must be set up to co-ordinate these resources, guide the housing effort and speed the creation of housing consortia among Local Authorities. Only from large scale housing schemes can the full benefits of industrialised building be obtained. Building land is available but too little use is made of it.

Labour's Land Commission will do nothing to correct this. It will simply discourage owners from selling, and the badly devised levy will make land still dearer.

Site value rating, which would collect rates on the value of land instead of buildings, would encourage owners of vacant or underdeveloped land to sell instead of holding on for a better market price.

Homes to rent – help for buyers

Much new housing must go to cure the acute shortage of homes to rent at reasonable prices. Help from subsidies for Council Houses should be concentrated on those who cannot afford to pay the full economic rent and on Local Authorities with exceptional rehousing needs, particularly in areas where there has been a large increase in the immigrant population.

The Government must also encourage more capital to be invested in cheap privately built homes for rent. Tax reliefs should be given to landlords who build low rent houses, with rent controlled at a level which gives them a reasonable but not exorbitant return.

The present pattern of tax relief for home buyers, which helps a rich person taking out a mortgage and not those with little money, should be reversed, possibly by a straight interest rate subsidy, paid to the Building Societies on all mortgages up to £4,000. A Government fund should back one hundred per cent mortgages through Local Authorities and Building Societies.

Keeping the rates down

A complete change in the rate structure is urgently needed. The proposed Liberal tax on land values would spread the load and bring down the cost to the individual rate-payer. The transfer to the Exchequer of a higher proportion of Education and Road costs would reduce it further. The loss of income by Local Authorities should be guaranteed by an annual Government grant.

What price security and health

Security in old age, security in sickness, security in unemployment, these are our responsibilities to each other. The great Liberal concept of the Welfare State is threatened by its increasing failure to match real needs.

A long term plan linking benefits firmly to the general increase in national prosperity would ensure that all entitled to them share in the growing national wealth.

Security in retirement

Even after the 1965 increase in pensions, many old people are still forced to live on National Assistance and will be forced to still further as the cost of living rises; pensions should be raised high enough to make it unnecessary for them to ask for extra help. A reasonable level for a married couple would be half the level of average national earnings, rising accordingly.

These pensions should be paid to all old people, including those registered before 1948, the earnings rule which prevents pensioners from earning a little extra must be abolished.

Employees should be encouraged, through their unions and professional associations, to supplement the State pension with occupational schemes to a level not less than two-thirds of previous earnings; and pension rights must be fully transferable. Liberals oppose the idea of a monopolistic State Socialist Scheme.

At present an employee, as well as paying for his Insurance Stamp, has to contribute with his employer to the State Graduated Pension Scheme. The same money invested in a private insurance scheme would yield him a much higher pension. He should have the right to choose where he invests this extra money.

Security in sickness and unemployment

Sick pay and unemployment benefits must be raised to a realistic level. Two thirds of previous earnings should be the rule and full national average earnings for those undergoing retraining for a new job.

Security for wives, widows and children

The present system of family allowances which mainly benefit the better off, should be abolished. All children including the first should be eligible under a new system of allowances, graded from approximately £1 to £3 according to age. A widow with dependent children should receive from half to two-thirds of her husband's previous earnings, and others should receive sickness, unemployment or retraining benefits like anyone else. The present tax system discriminates against wives who, of necessity, have to stay at home, and it should be re-examined.

How will it all be paid for?

A closer partnership between State and private industry will help to rationalise the present wasteful contribution structure. A Social Security Tax, replacing National Insurance stamps and levied on employer (two thirds) and employee (one third) in proportion to the payroll would rationalise it still further. The tax should be varied regionally to encourage the creation of more jobs in areas of unemployment. Benefits on this scale will not be cheap and will take time to achieve, but would ensure maximum value for money contributed.

A Better Health Service. At present, unless you can afford to pay privately, your chances of obtaining a hospital bed at short notice are small. Even when you do you will find most of our hospitals crippled by shortages of doctors, nurses and modern facilities. And the same is true of dentists and GPs.

We must make better use of the qualified people we have by reforming methods of payment and encouraging, not penalising, married women who wish to return to work.

We must make the Service more efficient by co-ordinating the various branches of health and welfare under Area Health Boards in which the GP would play a vital part.

Funds must be made available to these Boards to provide better facilities for dentists and GPs, to improve existing hospital buildings, to build new hospitals and to provide new homes for old people.

What are your child's chances?

Although Conservative and Labour Governments have always expressed a desire to increase educational opportunity, in times of financial difficulty it is always education that they cut. Instead of setting up a proper building research group for Universities in order to bring down their costs, the Labour Government has simply imposed a six months' stop on building for Further and Higher Education thus throwing carefully phased plans into chaos.

We must get our plans and priorities right and then stick to them. Liberals recognise that education is the most important investment we can make.

Schools

Priority in school building must be given to bring our slum primary schools, urban and rural, up to a decent standard and to prepare for raising the school-leaving age. This means more generous support for minor works; special grants for depressed areas; and a willingness by Local Authorities to accept large scale industrial building.

Eleven plus

Liberals regard the abolition of all selection at eleven plus not as a dogmatic principle, but as a necessary and long overdue reform. We accept the need for detailed consultation at local level and we realise that not every area in the country can go 'fully comprehensive' immediately, nor do we regard the 'all-through, purpose-built eleven to nineteen comprehensive' as necessarily the best solution. We are fighting for reform in the interests of all the children, not in the interests of dogma or special privilege.

Higher education

We reject the Labour Government's long-term aim of two separate systems, one autonomous under the University Grants Committee and the other 'public' under the Local Authorities. The links between Universities and other institutions of higher education should be drawn closer together by exercising public control through Regional Councils rather than the 160 different Local Authorities.

If the teacher shortage is to be conquered, there must be new methods of part-time training and re-training for teachers. In this connection we regret the Government's failure in this Parliament to establish the University of the Air, proposed originally by the Liberals and promised in the last Labour Manifesto.

Teachers

All professional teachers should be professionally trained and their salaries, working conditions and pensions improved. This could be done if many sub-professional jobs in schools were taken over by ancillary staff.

Cost

The necessary improvements in our education cannot be made without expenditure of a higher proportion of the national income. We would oppose any plan to abolish all individual fee-paying schools although the role of the direct grant, grammar and independent schools must be re-examined.

A world we can make better

Liberals support the search for controlled disarmament. Meanwhile Britain must play her part in creating the conditions which will make the arms race unnecessary.

Strengthen the United Nations. The United Nations must be made to work. A permanent UN force is needed. Liberals want Britain to contribute to it. Any British Government should support the authority of the UN in settling disputes between States and policing scenes of international violence.

Liberals recognise that Britain is a European power. We cannot afford to carry responsibilities everywhere, and the East of Suez policy, persisted in by Labour, is as dubious politically as it is expensive militarily.

Join Europe

To play our part in Europe would not only be of great economic benefit it would make us a pioneer in the first supranational community where States have agreed to share some of their sovereignty. Liberals want the Government to declare its intention of joining the EEC at the earliest opportunity.

Once in Europe, Britain could be an effective Atlantic ally and with our fellow Europeans we could hope to influence American policy in places like Vietnam. Liberals believe in the late President Kennedy's concept of the Atlantic partnership between the USA and United Europe. Such a partnership would wield great power for progress.

Hunger and disease – the world's great enemies

Effective aid to the hungry millions of Asia, Africa and Latin-America means not only direct support but a co-operative effort by the rich States in the expansion of trade to the developing countries, through the reduction of tariffs and more credits and investment.

The Commonwealth

British aid is naturally largely directed to the Commonwealth countries. Although the Commonwealth consists of loosely linked and widely different nations it remains a valuable association bridging the gap between races. It will lose that value and the gap will widen if Britain compromises with racialism.

Rhodesia

The rebel regime in Rhodesia is not only defying the Crown and imposing an increasingly oppressive dictatorship. It is also poisoning race relations throughout Africa. Liberals therefore recognise the necessity of continuing pressure until the rebel regime can be replaced by an authority – representing all Rhodesians, willing to work for eventual independence based on majority rule and backed by effective British guarantees.

The challenges today are tough, but if they are met in Europe, and in United Nations as in Rhodesia, Britain can play a great part in the advance to peace.

CONCLUSION

Now it is up to you

Liberals are guided by principle not by doctrine. We are not frightened by change. We welcome it, provided that it is directed towards the real priorities.

If Britain is going to continue to play a significant part in the world there must be a radical change of attitude in Government. We can provide this because we are free to plan for the best interest of all individuals, not just for a few. And that means your interests. We want to see positive action to create a closer partnership between all sections of the community – State and private enterprise, employer and employee, business and union – Only we can bring about this partnership.

If you want to see positive actions based on Liberal ideas flourish, you know what you must do. It is up to you. For you. For all the people. Vote Liberal.

WHAT A LIFE!
Prices: Huge rise in grocery bills is
PRICES EXPLOSION IN THE HIGH-ST
Food prices expected to rise by at least 2 pc
Show 'em you care!
VOTE LIBERAL

LIBERAL PARTY GENERAL ELECTION MANIFESTO 1970

What a life! Show 'em you care!

Date of Election	Thursday 18 June
Party Leader	Jeremy Thorpe
Candidates	332
MPs	6
Votes	2,117,035
% of vote	7.5%

There must surely be a better way to run a country than the one we have used for the last twenty-five years. No wonder people are fed up with thirteen years of Tory rule and twelve years under Labour.

What have we achieved? What sort of society have we turned ourselves into materially and culturally?

The purchasing power of the pound today is only worth about 7/- compared with its value in 1945.

Wages keep going up but, owing to rising prices, many people are worse off.

Over 600,000 people are out of work and no one seems to mind. Up to half a million people are without a proper home. In the so-called Welfare State many thousands of disabled people get no help.

Parliament has become a slanging shop.

The precious right of free speech is in peril from hooligan anarchists.

Legitimate protests are regrettably too often the prelude to violence.

Strikes, official and unofficial, by a few, paralyse whole sectors of industry and make it daily more difficult to pay our way in the world.

The big labour unions use their power to take the biggest slice of the national wealth they can. The less powerful and the unorganised are left at the tail end of the pay claim queue. Inefficient monopolies pass on their price increases to the consumer.

The Hospital service is grossly overstrained because junior doctors and nurses are so badly paid.

We are only just waking up to the dangers of pollution and the damage we have done to the environment and the quality of life.

Crime increases at a dangerous rate, too often violent, and the forces of law and order are set an impossible and unnecessary task.

The election system bolsters up 'bigness'. The Big parties have totally unfair advantages against minorities. But the system is unfair even between the major parties.

The whole 'System' conspires against the individual, the unrepresented and the weak, in favour of the well-organised big battalions, and no one seems to care.

But unless someone does care and does something about it the 'System' will go on and on. It can only be broken by supporting something different and that something is the Liberal Party.

It may be true that Liberals cannot expect under the present system to jump overnight from a party of thirteen MPs and three million supporters to become the government of the day, but we can break the power of the big battalions if we can get a substantial increase in the number of Liberal MPs in the next House of Commons and show that enough people care and want to protest at the present political farce.

Politics is about power. It is about the sort of society we want to build and it must be a better one than we have now. Man has political power when he exercises a vote. A party has political power whether in government or opposition in so far as it influences and changes policy. Minority parties have political power when they influence policy or public opinion or successfully stand up against injustices or change the climate of politics.

The Liberal Party is the Party of power for the ordinary people. It is the Party for people who care.

The Liberal Party has political power but it needs more members in Parliament and a massive Liberal vote outside to strengthen and broaden that power and to use it to break the Tory/Labour stranglehold and create a really satisfying and worthwhile society to live in.

It is an old adage that he who pays the piper calls the tune. Who pays the Tory piper? In 1968/69 £752,086 was contributed to Tory funds by some 470 companies. Who pays the Labour piper? In March the TRADE UNIONS paid £350,000 to Labour's election fund. Big business tycoons and trade union bosses have a powerful say in British politics. We believe that millions of ordinary British people do not want our national politics to be dominated to the exclusion of all else by these two giant interests. Someone must speak for those whom big business and the big trade unions overlook. The Liberal election pledge is this: we will stand up to the big battalions on behalf of these people, where justice so demands. In what follows we show some of the ways in which we will do so.

The individual worker

The individual worker must have a say and a stake in the place where he works. In large-scale industry he is entitled to similar rights to those enjoyed by the shareholder. Industry must become a partnership between capital and labour, with management responsible to the partnership. Workers should participate in the election of directors.

Works Councils should be established in every plant. This will facilitate plant-bargaining and productivity deals. It will enable the aim of the Donovan Commission on Trade Unions to be realised by providing the proper machinery for negotiations at plant level between people who know, and are involved in, the local conditions. In this way industrial relations can be greatly improved and the causes of many strikes removed. This state of affairs cannot be brought about by using the power of the law as the Conservatives wish, and as the Labour Government at one time intended. Liberal plans for partnership in industry will give increased opportunities for profit-sharing. This will help to remove the suspicions entertained by labour about capital. Management and labour have to be moulded into one team, not a wrestling match.

The shopper faced by rising prices

The Liberals are not dominated by any sectional interest of producers. We are in a particularly strong position to defend the consumer. Stronger measures are needed to deal with monopoly conditions. All mergers over a certain size must go automatically to the Commission for Manpower and Industry. The linking of earnings to productivity is the way to deal with rising prices. Liberal industrial policy is designed to curb inflation. The Commission for Manpower and Industry should devote particular attention to the nationalised industries.

Those living in parts remote from London

Too much power is concentrated in Whitehall and Westminster. Genuine regional government must be established. Liberals propose twelve regional Assemblies in England, exercising many of the powers now exercised at the centre. This will allow the people of a region to have much more control over their own affairs than they have today. Labour has not put forward any proposals for regional government. They have, however, adopted a modified version of the Maud proposals for local government reform. These take local decisions further away from the individual than they are now.

Scotland and Wales are distinct national entities within the United Kingdom. We want them to have their own Parliaments for Scottish and Welsh affairs, united with England by a Federal Parliament. In Northern Ireland Liberals have introduced civil rights legislation only to be defeated by the forces of reaction.

Taxation reform

The tax system must be reformed and simplified so that it can be easily understood. There should be a permanent Parliamentary Committee on taxation, equipped to consult with experts, and able to assess foreign systems. We must have a more effective tax on transfers of wealth, through a progressive Gifts and Inheritance Tax. Selective employment tax should be replaced by a regionally variable pay-roll tax.

The small business

Very heavy burdens have been placed on the small businesses of this country. In the first three months of 1970, 1,039 companies failed. The equivalent figure for 1969 was 926, and for 1968 it was 762. Bureaucratic chores, selective employment tax, high interest rates, credit squeeze and taxation policies generally are taking their toll of small companies. Yet the smaller businesses are very important. They employ 50 per cent of the total manufacturing labour force and produce at least 42 per cent of the Gross National Product. Twenty-five per cent of all United Kingdom exports are made by several thousand companies in the medium-to small-size categories. It has often been the small firm which has been prepared to take the risks. The Chairman of the British National Council recently said, 'we are minimising the rewards and maximising the risks for small-scale enterprise'. Liberals want to reverse this trend. It is in the national interest to do so.

The farmer and grower

Agriculture is a major import saver. Yet over the last ten years real incomes have increased by 46 per cent while farmers' real incomes have increased by only 7 per cent. Constant under-recoupment at successive price reviews has brought this situation about. Liberals support the farmers' claim for more generous treatment. We want the present system of deficiency payments continued for all products except beef and cereals. For these we support the import levy system, which will be required if we join the Common Market. Small farmers and growers, who are efficient and whose holdings are viable, deserve to survive. Agricultural policy must be modified to give agriculture an assured future, and capital for improvements and expansion. Liberals call for the establishment of a Land Bank to provide capital at cheap rates of interest.

The independent trader

Even in these days of supermarkets and multiple stores there is still an important role for the independent trader with his tradition of personal service. We do not ask for any privileged position for him but we do demand that he is not discriminated against. Much of what we have already said about the small business also applies to him. In addition we believe it essential that the independent trader should have the same opportunities to secure sites in new development areas as his larger competitor.

The old

Pensioners have not the same organised power as those who are still working. The pension is inadequate. An adequate flat-rate pension for today's pensioner is much more important than elaborate schemes, like Mr Crossman's to provide earnings-related pensions in 1992! We want to move in stages to the position where the pension for a married couple is half average national earnings with a corresponding increase for the single person. Over and above the increased flat-rate pension we want to see special opportunity provided for those without a pension scheme where they work to save for their retirement with assistance from a Central Account financed by a levy on all employers without an adequate occupational scheme. We stand by our support for the principle of parity in public service pensions.

The young

Children are not a pressure group either. Everyone is agreed that they deserve the best possible start in life. The emphasis should be on the improvement of primary schools and the provision of nursery schools. Secondary education should be non-selective. Age eleven to eighteen comprehensive schools have an important part to play in this. But they are not the only means to a non-selective system. They should not be hastily imposed where the buildings, staff and facilities are not suitable. There should be greater opportunities for further education outside the Universities.

The low-income families

Five hundred thousand low-income families suffer severe poverty in this country. The system of family benefits must be altered to include one child families. A minimum statutory earnings level is essential.

The homeless and the slum-dweller

The shortage of homes causes misery for many. The continuing existence of city slums is a national disgrace. There must be a very great speed-up in the renovation of whole areas. The housing problem must be tackled on a regional basis. Talk of a surplus of homes in a few years time is nonsense. How many of these 'surplus' homes will be fit to live in?

Those paying rent

It is unfair that those who pay rent in the private sector should receive no help from the Government or local authority, whereas those who are buying a house through a mortgage or living in a council house do. Those in private rented accommodation should also be eligible for help.

The owner occupier

The percentage of the population owning their own homes is steadily increasing and Liberals welcome this. We want to see mortgage funds available for older, sound property as well as modern houses, at reasonable rates of interest. Every encouragement must be given to housing associations. Tax on building societies surpluses should be abolished. The obsolete rating system should be entirely reformed.

The voter

In order that all the votes cast at an election shall count we wish to reform the voting system by the introduction of proportional representation by the single transferable vote. This system would mean that Parties were represented in the House of Commons in proportion to the votes cast for them in the country. Nearly all voters could point to at least one MP whom they had helped to elect. The power of the Party Whips would be diminished. An important result of this reform would be that electors could choose between candidates representing different strands of opinion within the same Party, pro-Powell or anti-Powell Tories, for example, or pro-Common Market or anti-Common Market Labour candidates. Liberals were the first to advocate votes at eighteen.

The citizen against the bureaucrat

We have presented to the House of Commons a Bill of Rights which would safeguard the rights of the individual against the State. We shall continue to press for its adoption.

The citizen and crime

The upholding of civil rights is one side of the question of law and order. The other is the prevention of crime. We believe that the two basic causes of the increase in crime are the low detection rate and the fact that for many criminals crime pays. It is essential therefore to strengthen the police. Improvements in pay and conditions are required. Traffic control should be entrusted to a new Traffic Corps. The Courts should be able to adjudicate a convicted person bankrupt. The assets of a criminal could then be made available to repay his 'creditors'; those he has injured or robbed. Shotguns must be controlled as are other weapons.

The United Kingdom and the world

Liberals are determined to stand up for the individual against the big battalions. The need to check the powerful is the theme of Liberal policy at home. World co-operation is the theme of Liberal policy abroad.

The power and influence of the United Nations must be strengthened. The Middle East crisis should be settled along the lines of the Security Council resolution of November 1967. The continuance of NATO is essential until a genuine European security agreement takes its place. We look forward to the earliest possible withdrawal of United States forces from Vietnam and we regret the US invasion of Cambodia.

In Western Europe we want the closest possible political unity. We see Britain's joining the Common Market as a part of this unity. The Common Market is an exciting experiment in the pooling of national sovereignty in the economic sphere. It can be the forerunner of a similar unity in foreign policy and defence. Liberals advocated Britain's applying to join at a time when it would have been very much easier than now. The Labour and Conservative Parties would not listen though they both subsequently came round to this point of view when in office. Liberals continue to believe that satisfactory terms can be obtained for British entry. In any event we wish to see the breaking down of barriers to international trade.

Greater freedom in international trade will assist the underdeveloped countries who need markets for their products. We support the principle that in accordance with the Pearson Report Britain and other countries should contribute 1 per cent of Gross National Product of official aid to developing countries as soon as possible.

We are totally opposed to all forms of racial and religious discrimination.

Liberals care! We care for those the big battalions forget. We care for the poor and the oppressed. We care for those whose only crime is that they are not as big or as powerful as their competitors. We care for the citizen at the mercy of the bureaucratic machine. We care for those who feel that government is remote and hostile. We care for those struggling to make ends meet in the face of rising prices. We care for those who have no satisfactory place to live. We care for the old and the young who have no organisation to defend them. We care for those discriminated against on grounds of colour and religion. We care for those striving to raise their countries out of poverty. We care for co-operation between the nations. We care because we are Liberals and because the basic principle of Liberalism is a belief in the supreme value of individual human personality.

We appeal to Liberals to vote Liberal whenever there is a Liberal candidate. We appeal to others who sympathise with our views. We appeal to those who are dis-enchanted with the way things are run by Tories and Labour.

We appeal to voters not to waste their vote by piling up majorities behind Conservative and Labour candidates but use the vote positively and usefully to show how many millions of people in this country really care. You can do this by voting Liberal on June the 18th.

Change the face of Britain.

Take power.
VOTE
Liberal

15p

LIBERAL PARTY GENERAL ELECTION MANIFESTO FEBRUARY 1974

Change the face of Britain – Take power – Vote Liberal

Date of Election	Thursday 28 February
Party Leader	Jeremy Thorpe
Candidates	517
MPs	14
Votes	6,063,470
% of vote	19.3%

A personal message from Jeremy Thorpe

In this election, the paramount objectives of the Liberal Party, overriding all other considerations are to tell the people the truth about our country's situation and to secure a new approach to our problems in which sectional and partisan interests are set aside in favour of the general welfare of all.

We are faced with an immediate economic and social crisis, the seriousness of which it is impossible for anyone to calculate with assurance and for which no-one can offer easy remedies.

But the immediate crisis – desperate as it is – is only the culmination of a long process of deterioration in our ability, and the capacity of our political and social institutions, to manage our country's affairs efficiently and with tolerable sanity.

Moreover, the present crisis is but a symptom of a deeper underlying disorder afflicting not only ourselves but the whole of the so-called western world. The era of western affluence side by side with poverty, and largely at the expense, of the other World is at an end.

The situation is one which requires of all people – and all parties – a fundamental reappraisal of their attitudes and policies. Without such a reappraisal it is questionable whether our own or any democratic system can or will survive. Here at home, and at this election, no one and no party has a ready made prescription for the cure of our troubles either in the short term or the long run, and anyone who pretends to have such a cure is a quack.

But two basic requirements can be met. They might be called 'the essential conditions for democratic survival'.

The first is to recreate in our society and in our political institutions a loyalty to the 'general good', to which all sectional and partisan interests, however inherently worthy, must be subordinate. But all efforts towards such a consensus, towards finding this area of common ground, will be idle and fruitless unless accompanied by a recognition (and this is the second condition for survival) that our present society is grossly unfair in its distribution of privileges and material rewards between capital and labour, between class and class and between one individual and another. Only when it is manifest that the restructuring of our society is in hand and that a fairer society is in sight will the necessary political consensus be attainable.

People are now bewildered, frightened and often angry. The first business of any Government should be to draw the nation together and to chart the course towards a new society based on fairness and tolerance.

The role of the Liberal Party at this election is to act as a catalyst in bringing this about by securing the largest possible representation of the 'general interest'. And you, the elector, can help us in this task by rejecting the sterile class conflict of two discredited parties and voting in a new era of reconciliation. It will take courage, but the five Liberal by-election victories in the last fifteen months, during which period we have secured more votes than any other party, shows that it can be done.

Every Liberal vote cast at this election will be a nail in the coffin of the old two party system of confrontation and a step towards national unity and reconstruction.

Jeremy Thorpe

The crisis of Government

This country has seen two parties, Labour and Conservative, alternating in office during the last fifty years. For the last five years, both parties have had to deal with very similar problems; both have offered similar solutions; both, in Opposition have opposed the policies of their opponents and then adopted them on becoming the Government. In 1967 Labour in office introduced a compulsory policy of prices and incomes control which the Conservatives, in opposition, opposed vehemently. At the same time the Labour Party re-opened negotiations for Britain's entry into the Common Market and these negotiations concluded with the offer of terms of entry which were accepted by Labour in 1969. In 1969, the Labour Government also introduced its White Paper 'In Place of Strife' which advocated legislation to control Industrial Relations. The Conservative opposition opposed this measure. When the Conservatives returned to office in 1970 they immediately introduced the Industrial Relations Act which was bitterly opposed by Labour, despite the fact that many of the provisions for union registration and protection of employment had been in their own proposals. When the Conservative Government in early 1971 elected to join the Common Market on terms which Mr Roy Jenkins asserted were similar to those negotiated by the Labour Government, Labour opposed entry. Finally, having persistently opposed compulsory prices and incomes control, the Conservative Government did one more U-turn and introduced its own pay and price freeze in 1972 to be followed by Phase II and Phase III. Once more the Labour opposition stood on its head and opposed what had formerly been its own policy.

A crisis of confidence

Britain cannot be governed effectively when parties continuously change their policies and principles to make cheap political gains and without regard for their own principles or for public opinion. The crisis of inconsistent government has led to a crisis of public confidence in the two parties which have ruled this country for the last fifty years. Liberals refuse to accept that the present crisis is induced by any one political party, Tory or Labour. It is caused by the type of policies and politics which both parties espouse; policies which employ short term, instant cures, but which leave behind more problems than they solve; politics which are partisan, dividing and polarising the nation into confrontation between classes whether they be rich or poor, manager or worker, house owner or tenant. This country cannot be ruled from the extremes of right and left which set the people against each other – it must be run by a government whose neutrality is unquestioned, whose policies are fair-minded, and whose politics is not governed by vested interests.

A new type of politics

Politics has become sterile; the old two-party system has finally proved its inadequacy. Old political theories of unbridled free enterprise and undiluted socialism have been shown to be irrelevant. Even leading members of the Conservative and Labour Parties admit that their own administrations have failed to deal with our fundamental problems and yet they hang on limply to political power. Politics has gone away from the people and this, in a democracy, is the most dangerous development of recent years.

The Liberal Party's concern for the individual person expressed in our 'Community Politics' campaigns has been criticised by the old-fashioned politicians as the politics of the paving stone. Yet they forget that politics is fundamentally about people, and their problems – however trivial they may seem – should dominate the minds of all politicians. Liberals believe in the supremacy of the individual and that political institutions should serve, not enslave, the people. Fundamentally Community Politics is an attempt to involve people in the decisions that affect their daily lives at the time when the individual viewpoint can really be expressed effectively – not six months after the decision has been reached, through a futile protest or enquiry. Our policies to decentralise government; to democratise the vast bureaucracies which run our Education system, our Industrial Relations and our Health and Welfare services, are all designed to further the goal of 'people participation'.

A new party

But a party which seeks to transform the politics and administration of Britain must itself be organised in such a way as to avoid the pitfalls of compromise partisanship and inconsistency which have befallen parties in the past. The Liberal Party is a party of no vested interest – financial or individual. Opinion Polls have consistently shown that we draw our support almost equally from all sections of the population, whichever way it is divided up, and that between 40 and 50 per cent of the people at any given time would vote for the Liberal Party if they thought that a Liberal Government would be elected. Our five by-election victories have indicated that many people feel that the time has come for a Liberal Government.

Unlike the other two parties we draw on no permanent source of financial support, while the Conservative Party consistently draws on at least a million pounds per year from the vested interests of big business, and Labour relies on the vested interests of the Trade Unions for over 90 per cent of its election funds. Is it any wonder that the country is polarised by Tory–Labour confrontation?

The Liberal Party is tied to no sectional interest. That is why we can justly claim that we approach the problems of our country with no doctrinaire prejudices, no class inhibitions and no sectional interests.

New policies – a radical programme of reconstruction

Most of all, the present crisis demands fundamental changes in the policies which we adopt. The old values which have led to inequalities in wealth, property and power must go. Government must be seen to be acting fairly in the interests of all the people instead of the interests of the very few. We must set aside the sterile class conflicts, the debates about capitalism or socialism, and the policies that divide and weaken us as a nation. We must rigidly question any new initiative by asking the question: 'will it narrow the gulf between the classes; will it reduce conflict?' No policy will achieve any lasting progress without national acceptance. Until we achieve the ideal of national unity, any other policy aims to achieve economic growth or industrial efficiency, will be unattainable. What is therefore needed is a fearless programme of economic, social and industrial reconstruction and a clearout of the old values which have so dogged the progress of the nation.

Liberal policy aims

1 Establish the universal right to a minimum income balanced by a fairer distribution of wealth, through a credit income tax system and national minimum earnings guarantees.
2 Create an equal partnership between employers and employed in recognition of the equal importance of their contributions to the success of industry.
3 Decentralise government and bring political power to Scotland, Wales and the regions of England so as to ensure that decisions are taken as close to people as possible.
4 Involve people in exerting influence within their communities through participation; and encourage proper consultation in the exercise of national responsibilities for Health, Education and General Welfare.
5 Break-up monopolistic concentrations of political and economic power so that individual initiative is not suppressed.
6 Conserve and protect finite resources for the lasting benefit of the whole community.

All these aims have one end; to serve the individual and to create the conditions in which he can develop his personality to the full.

The long term crisis

Since the War, politicians, business leaders, trade unionists and journalists have all assumed that a high economic growth rate is desirable and have encouraged expectations that put a premium on the acquisition of more money to spend on material goods. But the pursuit of unlimited growth has been accompanied by soaring prices, high unemployment and high domestic demand which has led to recurring balance of payments crises. The usual remedy adopted by Tory and Labour Governments has been 'stop go' – boom followed by freeze and squeeze.

The Wilson and Heath Governments have even acted similarly – and mistakenly – in either holding out against devaluation of the pound until world pressure forced an uncontrolled devaluation, or holding on to a mistaken belief in the importance of maintaining our balance of payments at the expense of rising unemployment, which finally reached the million mark in early 1972.

The result of these policies has been the frustration of targets unreached and the deception of unfulfilled promises, as the following examples illustrate:

Value of the pound

Labour 1964–1970

'Devaluation does not mean of course that the £ here in Britain, in your pocket, or purse, or in your bank has been devalued.'

Harold Wilson TV Broadcast November 19, 1967

REALITY In six years of Labour Government the £ lost nearly 20 per cent of its value.

Conservative 1970–1974

'We have become resigned to the value of the Pound in our pockets or purses falling by at least a shilling a year.'

REALITY The £ of June 1970 dropped in value to 75p (or about 15/- in pre-decimal terms) in January 1974 (House of Commons Question/Answer), a drop of well over a shilling a year.

Unemployment

Labour 1964–1970

'We see no reason why unemployment should rise at all, apart from seasonal increases.'

Harold Wilson (Labour Party Press Conference March 29, 1966)

REALITY In six years of Labour Government Britain experienced the most prolonged period of high unemployment since 1940. For three-quarters of this period the number of unemployed was over half a million!

Conservative 1970–1974

'If we could get back to Tory policies, the unemployment position would be a great deal better than it is today.'

Robert Carr, May 6, 1971

'We accept absolutely the responsibility for the level of unemployment.'

Robert Carr, November 23, 1971

REALITY During 1971 and 1972 unemployed was running at record war levels. Unemployment averaged 758,000 (3.3 per cent of working population) in 1971, and 844,000 (3.7 per cent of working population) in 1972.

Cost of living

Labour 1964–1970

'The continual rise in the cost of living can, must, and will be halted to give the housewife relief and her family a genuine rise in their standard of living.'

George Brown, Swadlingcote September 27,1964

REALITY In just over five years under the Labour government prices rose by 25 per cent.

Conservative 1970–1974

'In implementing our policies we will give overriding priority to bringing the present inflation under control.'

Conservative Manifesto, June 1970

REALITY Retail prices have risen by over 33 per cent since the 1970 election. Food prices by nearly 50 per cent (Dept. of Employment index of retail prices, December, 1973).

Statutory wage control

Labour 1964–1970

'As to the idea of freezing all wage claims, salary claims . . . I think this would be monstrously unfair . . . I do not think you can ever legislate for wage increases, and no party is setting out to do that.'

Harold Wilson BBC Election Forum March 10, 1966

REALITY Four months later measures were taken to freeze wages and prices until the end of 1966, followed by 6 months of 'severe restraint'.

Conservative 1970–1974

'Labour's compulsory wage control was a failure and we will not repeat it.'
Conservative Manifesto June 1970

REALITY A compulsory price and wage freeze was introduced by the Conservatives in November 1972, followed quickly by Phase II and culminating in the crisis of Phase III.

Housing

Labour 1964–1970

'We have embarked on a massive expansion of the housing programme reaching by 1970 no less than 500,000 new dwellings. This is not a lightly given promise, it is a pledge.'
Harold Wilson (Election Speech) Bradford March 27, 1966

REALITY It was abandoned in January less than two years later. In 1970 less than 365,000 new houses were built, fewer than the 373,000 built in 1964.

Conservative 1970–1974

'It is scandalous that this year (1970), as last year, fewer houses will be completed than in 1964 when Labour took over. And far fewer are under construction.'
Conservative Manifesto June 1970

REALITY This Government completed only 293,000 in 1973, the lowest number since 1959, and on current trends they will again fail to achieve 300,000 in 1974.

The quality of life

In addition, the damage to the fabric of society and the environment as a result of the pursuit of unlimited growth has been enormous. To the extent that growth has been achieved, it has not increased human happiness. Instead there has been evidence of increased social disintegration to which the growth in crime, mental illness, drug taking and divorce all testify. Furthermore, the destruction of whole communities in the interest of 'redevelopment', the scarring of the landscape by motorways and the shattering noise of jets over rooftops near major airports are a few of the more obvious symptoms of incompatibility between unlimited material growth and the good life.

The Liberal strategy

Whether or not continued expansion is desirable, we now have to ask if it is indefinitely feasible. The Liberal Party believes that we now have to begin planning for an age of stability. The resources of this planet are limited and we shall not be able to go on increasing consumption of energy, raw materials and foodstuffs at current rates. The steep rises in world commodity prices and the restrictions imposed by the producer nations on oil supplies, are strong indications of a turning point in history, the significance of which has yet to be grasped by most politicians.

We must therefore act on two fronts to cut back on demand for our limited resources, firstly by effectively controlling domestic inflation which is causing intense pressure on our balance of payments and adding to the chaos of our industrial relations as well as preventing the development of long-term economic and social policies.

But secondly, we must now abandon the policy adopted by past Governments, based, almost entirely, on the crude maximisation of Gross National Product. GNP is not a measure of real benefit, including, as it does, outputs that are good, bad and indifferent, and to talk simply of unlimited increases in growth is to deprive people of the power to choose between the beneficial and the harmful.

Liberals advocate a policy of controlled economic growth, by which we mean the careful husbandry of resources and the limitation of private consumption by the few in favour of better public services for the majority of our citizens.

In terms of human resources a policy of controlled economic growth also recognises that the obligation to provide employment and a safe environment can no longer be sacrificed to the maximisation of industrial efficiency. People cannot be treated as 'lame ducks'.

Inflation – the present crisis

The major single problem facing the next Government will be that of inflation. Given the long-term crisis of resources which we face it is unlikely that inflation will ever be completely conquered but it can be controlled with determined and fair policies which have the support of the people. Conservatives and Labour Governments have pandered to vested interests to the detriment of the population as a whole. Both have been fearful of embarking on long-term policies to control the economy and attack inflation for fear of denting the profits of the big corporations and the wage packets of the strongest unions. Hence their timid attempts at controlling inflation have been under-cut by promises of an ultimate return to a free for all.

Liberals would control inflation through a combination of industrial reconstruction and a permanent prices and incomes policy enforced by penalties on those whose actions cause inflation. We propose that prices, dividends and average earnings within a company should be limited to an agreed annual rate of increase. Any company which increased prices faster than that rate would suffer an extra surcharge on its Corporation Tax payments equivalent to the amount by which its prices had exceeded the agreed norm. Excessive dividends and profits pay-outs would also be penalised by a tax surcharge, on a sliding scale according to the amount by which such increases exceed the norm.

If average earnings per person (including fringe benefits) within a company rose faster than the agreed annual rate, then both the employer and the employees concerned would have to pay an extra surcharge on their graduated National Insurance Contributions, again on a sliding scale according to the amount by which earnings had exceeded the norm.

Of course, there would have to be provision for appeal and this would be best achieved by the compilation of ad hoc reports on earnings levels and pricing policies in particular industries along the lines of the old National Board for Prices and Incomes. Such reports would also cover changes in relativities and wage differentials, which will have to be narrowed considerably, and Parliamentary consent would have to be obtained before reports could be implemented.

Thus instead of countering inflation by increasing everybody's taxes, as Mr Powell and the Labour Party advocate, Liberals would tax only those who cause inflation and would control the supply of money into the economy without having to resort to the blunt instrument of brutal cuts in expenditure on social services which once again hit the poor hardest of all.

A great merit of this policy is that it would enable wage bargaining to take place without direct government intervention and inevitable accusations of partisanship. Yet it would still enable the Government to maintain overall control of the economy. But no policy can hope to succeed unless it is accepted and seen as fair by the great majority of people. Two major defects in past policies must be remedied if this policy is to succeed: the unfairness of the present wage bargaining system which favours those who shout loudest must be ended, and a fairer pricing policy must be evolved to ensure that price increases do not merely contribute to increased profits.

Fair prices

Liberals would strengthen price controls by relating them to absolute rather than percentage margins. We would also insist that middle-sized companies were obliged to submit applications to increase prices, as are top companies. We would strengthen the powers of the Monopoly and Mergers Commission to investigate and regulate monopoly companies. The Government must stimulate competition where it can still be made to work, break up and control monopolies, prevent non-productive mergers and stamp out widespread restrictive practices. Nationalisation will not solve the problem of high prices or monopolies. As we have seen in so many nationalised industries, the public either has to suffer high prices or subsidise non-profit-making industries. Either way the consumer pays more.

But in the meantime, where there are rapid increases in prices which are beyond the Government's control, Liberals favour the incorporation of guaranteed wage increases into any agreed pay policy to allow compensation for any excessive rise in food prices which occurs. With food prices having risen by fifty per cent in three-and-a-half years such action is now required immediately.

A national minimum earnings level

We must work to narrow the differentials between the highest and lowest paid in our economy. At a time when average earnings have reached over £40 a week, six million working people still earn less than half of this sum. A Liberal Government would introduce a statutory minimum earnings level for a normal working week and no employer would be allowed to pay less than this amount.

The importance of such legislation has been starkly illustrated by the three-day week. Those who suffered most in reduced wages and redundancies have been the poor – precisely those who do not have earnings guarantees.

But we must also reform the wage bargaining free-for-all in which the poorest inevitably come off worst. To do this effectively we must reconstruct our framework of industrial relations to spread the monopoly power now vested in a few very powerful Unions.

A new charter for industrial relations

Britain lost more than 24 million working days last year – more than any other European country and almost double the amount lost in Italy, our nearest rival. Yet what have our opponents to offer as an antidote to industrial chaos? The Industrial Relations Act and the impotent Industrial Relations Court stand as monuments to attempted Tory repression, and a perpetual reminder to the Labour Party of its capitulation to Union pressure while in Government. Whatever the merits of the Act's provisions for contractual obligation and redundancy protection its practical effectiveness has foundered on Union opposition and Conservative folly. The dues which were expropriated from the AUEW political fund were drops in the ocean, but the action which confiscated money earmarked for the Government's opponents, was a devastating piece of party political warfare.

The Industrial Relations Act must be repealed and replaced by far-reaching legislation to introduce real democracy into industry. The Labour Party talks glibly about Industrial Democracy by which it means Union domination and the effective exclusion of over fifty per cent of our work force which does not belong to a union. The Liberal Party believes that all individuals should be involved in the industry in which they work and this has been the cornerstone of our policy for over fifty years. We believe that the two-party system in Britain based on a party of organised capital confronting a party of organised labour has helped to divide industry into two camps to the detriment of the community as a whole. We therefore advocate industrial partnership not merely as an aid in solving the economic problems of our country, but as a system which is right and just, and which will unite instead of dividing.

Liberal industrial policy has three objectives. Firstly, employees must become members of their companies just as shareholders are, with the same clearly defined rights. Secondly, it must be accepted that directors in public companies are equally responsible to shareholders and employees. Employees should be entitled to share in the election of the directors on equal terms with shareholders, and Works Councils representing all employees must be set up at plant level with wide powers to negotiate pay and conditions of work. Thirdly, employees should share in the profits of the company and the growth of its assets.

In the long term, the implementation of Liberal co-partnership policies will contribute to the solution of wage inflation, by ensuring that all employees benefit from wage increases and by including a measure of responsibility into wage bargaining. For in the day-to-day negotiations within each company, employees would realise that there is little to be gained by wage increases in excess of productivity. Such increases would simply reduce the amount available in which the workers would share. In short our policies would achieve the identification of employees' interests with those of the firm by providing a visible link between the immediate limitation of wage demands and the future prosperity which will be generated for both employees and shareholders as a result. We cannot believe that any reasonable employer would prefer an industrial strike and the loss of millions of pounds to the hope of industrial harmony and responsible wage bargaining through industrial partnership. Similarly, no responsible employee would refuse the opportunity to become an equal partner in his firm with an equal share in its profits in favour of continued confrontation, inequality and insecurity.

The energy crisis

The short-term problems caused by the miners' industrial action and the interruption of Middle East oil supplies demanded immediate action to reduce consumption, and in the main the Liberals supported Government restrictions in the use of energy and the three-day week, both of which we were convinced were necessary to avoid even more serious disruption of economic life as stocks would otherwise have fallen below the danger level. However, we have been critical of the inflexibility of the Government's anti-inflation policy, which prevented the National Coal Board from entering into proper negotiation on the miners' claim. Instead of being recognised as the life blood of a nation now deprived of a large portion of its energy supplies, the miners were made the scapegoat for the Government's obstinacy in clinging to out-dated policies. Any settlement with the miners must be permanent and ensure continuing reward for their contribution to the alleviation of the Energy Crisis. We believe that a settlement could have been reached if, in addition to the increases offered under Phase III, the NCB could have undertaken to make further rises available as the industry expands.

All political parties, including the Liberals, must share the blame for the decline in coal output since the middle sixties. In order to reverse the decline, the NCB should be encouraged to press ahead with the development of new coal reserves in Yorkshire and the Midlands.

The Government's policy of exploiting North Sea Oil and Gas must be done at a rate determined by a National Energy Policy so as to allow indigenous industries to acquire the necessary expertise and equipment. The policy must also have regard to the longer-term future when imports of hydrocarbons are likely to be even more expensive and difficult to obtain. Royalties from the production of North Sea oil should be used in part to encourage the development of other industries in Scotland and the North East – and later, if exploration in the Celtic Sea is successful, in Wales. We are not satisfied that the revenues accruing to the nation from our own oil are fair in relation to the latest assessments of the size and value of the fields, and Liberals will ensure that huge windfall profits are not made by the licensees, many of whom are foreign concerns who have been given licences on exorbitantly advantageous terms.

The Liberal Party advocates continuity of work on British nuclear reactor systems. The first advanced gas-cooled reactors will come into operation during 1974, and it would be a grave mistake to switch horses now to the American pressurised water reactor system, as it is suggested we are likely to do. The evidence from the United States shows that they are less safe. But energy policy should not consist solely of adjusting supply to meet whatever demand is created by existing market forces. Governments can influence demand as well as supply by pricing policy, incentives and capital projects. At a time when public spending on education, housing and health is being cut, it is not acceptable to press on with the £3,000 million projected expenditure on Concorde, Maplin and the Channel Tunnel simultaneously, quite apart from energy and environmental considerations. Since, however, air travel will become far more expensive as jet fuel increases in cost, Maplin is no longer necessary, and the airlines will not buy Concorde, the former should be scrapped and the latter severely curtailed. Similarly, fewer people will be able to afford Continental motoring holidays with petrol at £1 a gallon, as predicted by Lord Stokes, and the Channel Tunnel should therefore be rail only, saving £240 million. These are all complex problems, and it cannot be denied that we have been caught unprepared by recent changes in the energy situation. The importance of the matter has been recognised implicitly by the Government, in the creation of a separate Department responsible for energy, but there is still no authoritative body to give impartial advice to both Government and Parliament. We need a permanent Royal Commission, serviced by adequate professional staff and with funds to commission research by industry, universities and government research establishments. This body would be required to publish reports at regular intervals, the first of which should be on the long-term proposals in the coal industry. Such reports should then be debated in Parliament.

Finally, the Government's long-term plan to reorganise the steel industry and close some steelmaking plants should be reviewed in the light of the changed situation. Liberals believe that concentration on bigger and fewer plants, on the scale adopted by the Japanese, of which we have no experience, may prove detrimental, particularly if uncertainties over fuel supplies continue. In addition, the economic and social dislocation within traditional steelmaking communities affected by such closures provides a very powerful argument for a complete rethink of strategy by both the Government and the European Coal and Steel Community.

Social reconstruction

Underlying all our policies for social reconstruction are the twin themes of participation and individual freedom. Indeed the first is dependent on the second, for no person can play his full part in society unless he has the freedom to do so, and this must include freedom from discrimination, freedom from poverty and illness, the security of a roof over his head and the prospect of an equal start in life.

We are still a long way from achieving these goals even in 1974. Once again promises have been lightly made and cruelly broken because they have all been founded on assumptions of maximum production and economic growth. Only when we rid ourselves of the false logic that sees all social advancement as a product of economic efficiency will the well-being of society truly become a social service.

Health and social welfare

The reorganisation of the National Health Service has failed to unify the Health Service or to ensure adequate public participation in the decisions which affect them. Liberals would bring local authority welfare services into the main structure of a unified NHS by placing them under the financial and administrative control of the area Health Authorities. We also favour democratic election to Area Health Boards so as to ensure a strong voice for the community.

The Chronically Sick and Disabled Persons Act 1970, having been a Private Members Bill, has, in many areas, failed to give people the comprehensive services that were intended as it gives local authorities additional responsibilities without providing extra funds to discharge them. We would introduce a Bill encompassing the provisions of the 1970 Act, so that central finance can be made available for its implementation, and extending provision for the disabled to other fields such as education where urgent national provision is required in facilities and finance.

The Liberal Party opposed the increase in prescription charges, the abolition of free school milk in junior schools and increased school meal charges – all callously petty economies introduced by a Conservative Government and all hitting directly at the poor and needy in our society.

Security without means tests – a credit income tax scheme

Liberals have long advocated a system of credit income tax whereby social security payments would automatically be paid to those in need. The Government's tax credit scheme, however, falls well short of the Liberal ideal because it values administrative efficiency above adequate provision for social need, while the Labour Party still pins its faith in the paternalism and stigma of the old means tested welfare system.

The Liberal scheme represents a major onslaught on the Means Test Society and would replace most of the 44 means tests to which under-privileged and handicapped people are subjected.

The Liberal credit income tax scheme would sweep away existing tax allowances, family allowances, national insurance benefits, nearly all supplementary benefits, housing subsidies, rent and rate rebates, family income supplements and a wide variety of miscellaneous benefits. All income would be taxed according to a progressive scale from the very first pound, but everyone would be entitled to various 'credits' or allowances depending on circumstances. Where the liability to tax exceeded the value of credits there would be net tax to pay. Where the value of the credits exceeded the liability of tax the difference would be paid to the individual, automatically, through the tax system. Thus a redistribution of income could automatically be effected in favour of those needing help. There would be three types of credit – personal, housing and social. The most important would be the personal credit. This would be paid to every person and would be fixed at a level sufficient to guarantee a subsistence living to that individual. The credit for an adult would be greater than for a child. In the case of children under 16, the credit would be paid to the mother.

Then there would be a universal housing credit, paid regardless of whether the individual lived in rented or owner-occupied accommodation.

The third category of credits would correspond to national insurance benefits. There would be a credit for pensioners and for short- and long-term unemployment, sickness and disablement.

Whereas the Government scheme helps to tackle the poverty problem it has no intention of guaranteeing in every case that a family with no further help from the state would have enough to live on. The Liberal scheme does just this. It has estimated that a combined income and social security tax of 40 per cent (against the present 36 per cent) plus a recasting of VAT (but not on food) would be sufficient to operate the scheme. In the transitional period before the full introduction of our credit income tax scheme we propose that family allowances should be extended to the first child, and social security benefits proportionately increased with increases in average earnings. This is particularly urgent in the case of those such as widows whose circumstances can change so dramatically.

Provision for our pensioners

Pensioners have had a bad deal from both Tory and Labour Governments. Amid extravagant claims that they have kept pace with increases in the cost of living, pensioners have actually been left behind in the great wage race. Under the Labour Government pensions only rose marginally as a percentage of average earnings. The single pension represented 19 per cent of average earnings in 1964: and 21 per cent by the time Labour left office in 1970. Under the Conservatives the single pension has actually fallen back to 19 per cent of average earnings.

The Conservative Government's Occupational Pension Scheme incorporates a degree of compulsion which is anathema to Liberals in forcing everyone to contribute to a second pension scheme which will do nothing for today's pensioners. The last Labour Government had similar idealistic plans.

Liberals reaffirm the Beveridge commitment to introduce a basic pension which provides an adequate income irrespective of further financial provision. We would therefore increase the retirement pension in stages to 50 per cent of average earnings for a married couple and 33.5 per cent for a single person. Thus we would spread over a number of years a cost which if incurred immediately would amount to about £1,400 million. However, there would be a considerable saving in supplementary benefits which at present are claimed by a third of our 8 million pensioners, at a cost of £400 million.

This first phase of our pension plan would be a transitional stage, prior to the introduction of our full credit income tax scheme. Pensioners would be included in this scheme and would be entitled to a personal credit and housing credit as well as a pension credit resulting in an income of approximately two-thirds of average national earnings for a married couple. In addition we would reduce the retirement age for men to sixty. We would also abolish the earnings rule which penalises those who wish to go on doing a valuable job of work.

Education

Liberals have long recognised that resources for education are limited and across the board advance is impossible. We therefore took care to work out a ten-year development plan which would allocate clear priorities. In our view these should be:

1 The full implementation of the Plowden Committee's recommendations paying special attention to the need for pre-school education particularly in those areas of underprivilege and social deprivation, and the urgent reduction in the size of primary school classes to a maximum of 30 pupils.
2 The reorganisation of secondary school education on non-selective lines. There are more ways than one to organise a non-selective secondary school and we would allow local authorities maximum flexibility within minimum standards to adapt their system to local conditions.

3 A major reorganisation of curricula and school institutions to provide a more realistic last three years education for non-academic children.

4 The abolition of the binary system of further education and the closer integration of Universities, Polytechnics and Colleges of Education. In particular we would seek to establish Community Colleges open to all age groups, with the ultimate aim of providing further education to all who desire it. To this end an adequate student grant through our credit income tax scheme would be provided.

Homes for all

The Liberal Party opposes the present Government's housing priorities because it considers them socially divisive.

They have severely cut local authority house building at a time when rising house prices have hit those trying to buy their own home; rents have been raised under the Housing Finance Act while, at the same time, wages have been frozen and then reduced by the three-day week; finally, the Government has failed to reform the mortgage system and failed to act effectively to curb land hoarding and speculation.

Liberal policy would fundamentally change our system of housing finance and property taxation, providing help to householders and tenants on an equal basis and concentrating a two-pronged attack on the housing shortage by building more houses and preserving as many houses as are inhabitable. In particular, we would end the divisiveness and inefficiency in the national housing programme by encouraging more flexible and enterprising policies which will allow for greater co-operation between local authorities, particularly in respect of the homeless, and an enhanced role for self-build organisations, possibly through the establishment of Government-approved consortia.

These are our proposals:

1 Freeze all rents during the period of economic restraint.

2 Repeal the Housing Finance Act and replace it with a genuinely fair rents system geared to true housing costs and pay a single housing allowance to tenants and householders on an equal basis automatically through the tax credit system.

3 Make all new urban office building contingent on the grant of a certificate of social need and concentrate the resources of the building industry on the housing programme.

4 Institute a crash programme of house-building in both public and private sectors with full use being made of industrialised building techniques.

5 Concentrate on housing renovation and repairs wherever possible, rather than on wholesale demolition.

6 Oblige Building Societies to stabilise interest rates by drawing on their reserves. Introduce new types of mortgage for first home buyers with low level initial repayments which rise with increased incomes and the cost of living.

7 Withdraw tax concessions and improvement grants for second home purchasers.

8 Give greater financial encouragement and responsibility to Tenants' Co-operatives and Housing Associations.

9 Give local authorities power to acquire at cost price those properties which have stood unoccupied for three years.

Paying for security – a radical redistribution of wealth

To finance all these proposals, there must be a radical redistribution of income and inherited wealth, the credit income tax proposals being the principal instrument for the former, and the Liberal proposal for a Gifts and Inheritance Tax, to replace Estate Duty and related in its incidence and rate to the gift or legacy and the wealth of the recipient, for the latter.

Site Value Rating

We must also ensure that a proper contribution is made by those who own property and land.

As a means of reforming the present rating system which penalises those who improve their property while subsidising those who let it decay, Liberals have long advocated that rates should be levied on the value of the site only, and not on the value of the site and buildings as now. This would enable much of the present burden of rates to be shifted from householders.

The rating of site values would also be levied on land which, after proper inquiry, had been zoned for development but which had not been developed within a reasonable period. This would be an effective punitive measure against land hoarders and speculators.

Site value rating also recognises the undisputed fact that today a major source of wealth resides in development land and property rather than in income. Over a period of years there is no doubt that the rating of land values could gradually replace income tax as a main source of revenue. It would also recover for the community a proportion of the increased value of land created by mere assignment of planning consent.

The status of women

Liberals will put particular emphasis on securing equality of opportunity and equal treatment for women. As a nation we can no longer afford to ignore the talent and energies of half our population as we have done so often in the past. We would legislate to ensure equal opportunities for women in all spheres of activity particularly in regard to employment, remuneration and social interaction. In particular we advocate the establishment of an independent Sex Discrimination Board, establishment of the principle of equal pay for work of equal value, tougher legislation to outlaw restrictive and discriminatory practices in industry and equal social security benefits for men and women, with adequate provision for maternity leave. Our aim is to provide the opportunity for women who so wish freely to seek satisfying goals other than a lifetime of childbearing.

Civil liberties – a bill of rights

Every person is entitled to protection from arbitrary interference in his personal and private affairs. Liberals are concerned that in our increasingly complex and bureaucratic society, fundamental freedoms should not be impaired or the individual citizen put at a disadvantage in his dealings with authority. Hence we have long advocated that minority and individual liberties should be guaranteed through a Bill of Rights effect-ive in all parts of the United Kingdom and at all levels of Government and administra-tion. Among protected guarantees should be the freedom of speech and assembly, the right to a fair trial, and protection against discrimination on the grounds of race, religion, sex or national or social origin. We would establish a small Claims Court where redress for minor injustices could be sought without recourse to the complexity and delay of the court circuit. Finally, we oppose any laws which penalise people retrospectively for actions done in the past, when through lapse of time they have become immune from prosecution or administrative action.

Immigration and race relations

The Liberal Party regards freedom of movement as an important basic principle. However, since 1965 we have accepted that a densely-populated country such as ours cannot, at present, adequately cater for all those people who wish to come here. Accordingly we have supported a system of regulation whereby would-be immigrants are allowed to enter the United Kingdom only if they possess a work voucher showing that they have an actual job waiting for them or they possess particular skills which are needed in this country. While opposing illegal entry we strongly oppose the retro-spective provisions of the 1971 Immigration Act and would take immediate action to remove these and other discriminatory clauses in that legislation.

We believe that we have a primary obligation to citizens of the United Kingdom and colonies, and also to Commonwealth citizens whose right to register as UK citizens after five years' residence in this country was removed by the 1971 Act and should be reinstated. We believe that a Royal Commission should urgently examine and clarify the rights of UK and Commonwealth citizens on the lines outlined above. In the meantime husbands and children from Uganda should be allowed to join refugees who have settled here. We are opposed to all forms of racial discrimination. The goal of integration is of critical importance and there should be a separate Minister for Com-munity Relations and greater financial support for the Community Relations Commission.

The future of our community

The environment

Liberals recognise the need for an urgent re-appraisal of the use man is making of his material environment. We are concerned that in the present economic crisis panic measures should not be taken for the sake of short-sighted expediency, that might cause irreversible damage

The Liberal Party was the first to adopt a National Population Policy which includes free family planning advice as part of the NHS and a programme of education stress-ing the need for responsible parenthood in this era of scarce resources.

We insist on stringent controls on the use of all potential pollutants and in particular the establishment of a regionalised Pollution Inspectorate with investigatory and puni-tive powers over the use of noxious substances. In particular we are concerned that there should be the maximum recycling of all materials and that individuals and communities should have the legal means to resist, where necessary, threats to their environment from Government or commercial agencies.

The protection of our environment must be extended to the preservation of natural resources including our sources of energy, our landscape and our countryside. We strongly support the principles of nature conservation and assert that the co-ordination of policies in other fields such as agriculture and transport must be pursued urgently.

Finally, the global environment, of which Britain is only a small part, can only be permanently preserved through international co-operation and support for United Nations environmental agencies.

Transport

Transport is inextricably bound up with overall development and must be integrated with national, regional and town and country planning. Our main priority must be to provide for integrated policies which acknowledge the changed roles of our various modes of transport. Conservative and Labour Governments have consistently worked on a piece-meal basis, Liberals assert that it is time to work out an overall strategy. In particular we advocate the prohibition of any further closures of railways and water-ways until a study group has reported on the possibilities of further transferring freight carriage to rail and water. A new attitude must be taken to our railways which takes into account social and environmental factors as well as capital expenditure.

Transport has become a social service in many cases, particularly the regions and rural areas. We believe that County Councils should collaborate with the Ministry of Transport in promoting research studies into rural transport needs and preparing schemes for meeting them. Liberals hold the view that there must be a limitation of access for private vehicles to designated areas of city and town centres. Adequate parking facilities on the outskirts must be complemented by free, reliable public trans-port within these areas. Liberals would also establish Regional Transport Authorities to determine priorities of investment in all forms of transport, co-ordinate long-term planning of main roads, ports, airports, railways and inland waterways. Immediate attention must be given to assess the impact of increased oil prices upon our transport infrastructure.

Agriculture and the Common Market

Liberals are well aware of the grave difficulties being experienced at the present time in many sections of the agricultural community. The Government, so far, has been deaf to the Liberal warnings and appeals concerning the plight of the dairy farming and livestock sections of agriculture. This could result in a actual food shortage in this country, particularly with regard to fresh foods arising from the excessive slaughter of breeding animals by farmers who, overwhelmed by the high cost of feeding stuffs and the very high interest rates, believe that their future is extremely insecure.

Help should be given to these sections of agriculture immediately, for the sake of both the farmer and the consumer. To build up to a sufficient level of profitability for the farmer and maintain a decent basic price for the consumer can be achieved in a variety of ways. One way which is capable of instant implementation is to compensate the consumer by raising pensions, and increasing family allowances which should also be extended to the oldest child. In our view it is necessary to create a farm structure which will encourage young men to enter agriculture as a career, with a possibility of achieving management and ownership. In the immediate term an improved wage structure for the industry must be established. The Agricultural Credit Corporation must also be swiftly expanded into a Land Bank. Loans would be available at a fixed rate of interest for projects which might properly be regarded as medium-term, in particular for the purchase of livestock and for projects now covered by Government grants, but should not be available for the purchase of farms or of land. In the present climate, it is essential that United Kingdom Marketing Boards should be retained and voluntary co-operatives encouraged. The Annual Price Review should certainly be retained but be coupled with a five-year strategic review.

In order to help keep down the price of land and make farms more readily available to genuine farmers, agricultural losses should no longer, in any circumstances, be allowable against profits from other businesses. Furthermore, Estate Duty relief should be restricted to bona fide agriculturalists. This would help prevent the major transference at the present time of city assets into agricultural land. Agricultural land in productive use would be zero-rated under our policy for Site Value Rating.

The Common Agricultural Policy of the European Economic Community must represent a just balance between the interests of consumers, efficient producers and international trading. The widening of the Community has already resulted in a less protectionist attitude but Britain must make an all-out effort to broaden and deepen this attitude. In the UK we do not have the problem, which has existed in the Community, of uneconomic farming units and we accept the need for measures to reduce their number. Finally, Liberals believe that there should be a rapid expansion of domestic production and an energetic drive by this country to secure allies in the Common Market for a major modification of the Common Agricultural Policy, so as to secure reasonably-priced food for the consumer and an acceptable return for the farmer.

Power, people and the community

The Liberal Party believes in devolution, decentralisation and electoral reform. We favour the immediate implementation of the Kilbrandon recommendation to establish elected Parliaments in Scotland and Wales and to this effect a Bill has already been introduced into the House of Commons by Liberal MP, Jo Grimond.

In the long term we would establish a federal system of Government for the United Kingdom with power in domestic matters transferred to Parliaments in Scotland, Wales and Northern Ireland and Provincial Assemblies in England. The Westminster Parliament would then become a Federal Parliament with a reformed second chamber in which the majority of members would be elected on a regional basis. If Britain is to have effective and successful centres of commerce and finance outside London there must be a real devolution of political and economic power to the regions. Recent Local Government reform has removed decision-making even further from the people. We advocate the setting up of Neighbourhood Councils below the District Councils to act as efficient transmitters of protest and suggestion from the community.

Liberals would introduce proportional representation by the single transferable vote for all elections. The present electoral system buttresses the discredited 'two-party system' of confrontation. Electoral Reform, while giving fairer representation to different sections, will make co-operation between them easier. The success of proportional representation in Northern Ireland in uniting a divided community through a power-sharing executive is strong testimony for its introduction in Britain as a whole to heal the rifts in our society.

Parliament has lost touch with the country. It must be brought back to the people and its proceedings opened up to the broadcasting media. Its formality must not deter improvements in the organisation of business to make Parliament more efficient and effective, with really full-time members elected for fixed five-year periods.

Liberals urge the establishment of direct elections to a European Parliament which would give full democratic power of control over Community activities.

Maximum opportunity must be offered at all levels for involving citizens in the process of Government, through the fullest possible provision of information.

Europe and the world

We must not allow our present national crisis to let us forget the immense problems of instability in the world, that have loomed and threatened in the last few months. The need for international co-operation and understanding has never been more pressing and the contribution of Britain to building a better world as well as our hopes of a better life in these islands depend on partnership with our democratic neighbours.

The European Economic Community

Liberals have always insisted on the duty of Britain to play a leading role in transforming Western Europe from warring rivalry into a united community, hence our consistent support for British membership of the Common Market. Further more, it is only as a full participant in the world's largest trading entity that we can hope to solve our chronic balance of payments problem and at the same time develop the political unity that will guarantee peace and free us from the spectre of domination by the super powers.

We deplore the delay in joining the Common Market for which Conservative and Labour Governments were equally to blame, but we are even more critical of the narrow-minded nationalism of many so-called 'internationalists' in the Labour Party who still shun their responsibility to represent their constituents in the European Parliament. We also condemn the Conservative Government for abdicating their great opportunity to develop the Community in a democratic and outward-looking manner in favour of meek compliance with the interests of the French Government. The present Common Market structure is not what we voted for and the Liberal representatives in the European Parliament have lost no opportunity to point the way in which we feel the Community should develop. Liberals are thus effective but constructive critics of the policies of the Common Market. We want to reform its institutions to see real power exercised by an elected European Parliament. We want to see the progressive reduction of the protectionist aspects of the Common Agriculture Policy, an imaginative and effective regional policy and the harmonisation, not bureaucratisation, of economic and social policies, for the benefit of all members. Finally, we want to see the adoption of an outward-looking trade policy towards the rest of the world and particularly the developing countries. We believe that the great purposes of the Community can be achieved with far-sightedness and vision.

Foreign affairs and defence

Looking beyond the EEC we are in favour of the maintenance of NATO until such time as a new European security system based on mutual withdrawal and the mutual reduction of forces in the East and West has been successfully negotiated. Within this limit we support efforts at détente and in particular the Ostpolitik of the West German Government. We are opposed to the admission to the European Community of any country which has not a democratic form of government, and are unhappy about the association with NATO of countries like Portugal and Greece which are not democratic. The purpose of NATO should be to defend democracy.

But the maintenance of our traditional alliances is also of critical importance if we are to return stability to world commodity and money markets and absorb the massive disruption that has and will continue to be caused by the quadrupling of oil prices. Positive international agreements are vital to bring a new radical world monetary framework that could save the world from damaging economic recession and exacerbated racial tension. Finally, it is essential that through a new monetary framework Britain and the developed world recognise the plight of the Third World and begin to grant realistic exchanges for raw materials and commodities that will raise the Third World from starvation and deprivation.

Conclusion

This is the Liberal Party's programme for national reconstruction. It is fundamental because we believe that the crisis which faces us as a nation is deep-seated and requires a fundamental response. It is ambitious because the multiple crisis that faces us offers the opportunity to put the past behind us and embark on a new era of reconstruction. Above all it is idealistic because we must raise our sights beyond selfish personal concerns, we must stop internal feuds which weaken and divide us and look to a future without class conflicts, partisan bitterness and excessive self-criticism.

WHY BRITAIN NEEDS LIBERAL GOVERNMENT

10p

LIBERAL PARTY GENERAL ELECTION MANIFESTO OCTOBER 1974

Why Britain needs Liberal government

Date of Election	Thursday 10 October
Party Leader	Jeremy Thorpe
Candidates	619
MPs	13
Votes	5,346,754
% of vote	18.3%

A personal message from The Rt. Hon. Jeremy Thorpe

'This election will make or break Britain. It is already certain that the Government which takes office after the election will face the greatest peace-time crisis we have known since the dark days of 1931.

The fact that we are committed to two elections in one year highlights the uncertainties and divisions of British politics. Mr Heath called the first election back in February because his industrial and economic strategy had totally collapsed and he had no alternative. He lost, and relations between the Conservative Party and the Trade Union Movement will take many years to restore.

Mr Wilson has called the second election because he is not prepared to accept the disciplines of a minority Government. So long as a minority Government governs on behalf of the whole nation it can command a majority in Parliament. At the last election, the electorate clearly refused to give him a mandate for those divisive parts of his programme such as further nationalisation and clearly in calling for an election he has shown he is not prepared to accept that verdict.

Liberals are unashamedly committed to breaking the two-Party system in which the Party of Management alternates with the Party of Trade Unionism, each committed to the reversal of their predecessors' policies. Both interest groups represent vital elements in our society. Neither should ever be allowed to dominate the thinking of the government of the day. Instant reversal has brought uncertainty over Europe, over pensions, in the future of industry and has undermined confidence and stability.

As the leader of a national political party it is my duty to warn the nation of the consequences if we fail to overcome this crisis. It is also my duty clearly and firmly to point the way out of our desperate situation.

The first priority must be to promote a sense of common endeavour and national purpose in government. We must persuade all people to lay aside the differences which divide and weaken us as a nation and to unite in pursuit of a solution to our difficulties. We must persuade ourselves that the survival of Britain is far more important than the advancement of any single individual or party and that we have far more in common as British citizens than the artificial divisions which society inflicts on us.

But this unity will not be enough unless we can also isolate and deal with the fundamental defects – economic, political and social – which have led us to the brink of disaster. The next Government will have, without prejudice or precondition, to set itself to reconstruct Britain on a much fairer basis. It will have to attack poverty at source, redistribute wealth and income so that the rewards of endeavour correspond more closely to the value of the effort involved. It will have to remove the class divisions inherent in our society, particularly in our industrial relations and in the way we allocate national resources between rich and poor.

I do not claim that it can be done overnight but I do say that unless a start is made – and very soon – the new endeavour, which is needed to rescue us, will not be forthcoming.

Now is the time to decide whether we are to continue the steady decline in our national life, or whether we are going to pull ourselves back from the brink. Only with the necessary political will coupled with the concerted efforts of us all can we rescue ourselves. In asking for your commitment to the Liberal cause at this election, I am inviting you to join 6 million voters who support a party untainted by failure in government and unprejudiced by vested interests. The Liberal Party can attract the support of all people drawn from every spectrum of our society who want to see a fair and tolerant society in Britain. With 6 million voters on which to build, and 600 candidates in the field, the opportunities open to us are unlimited.

The sort of policies which we are putting forward are fair – they are realistic – they are tough. I claim that they represent a programme which can unite Britain and can achieve the success which as a nation we have so long been denied.

Our greatest asset is that we could become the first post war Government which owed nothing to any sectional group or interest. In the February election, 2 million traditional Liberals were joined by 2 million previous Tory and 2 million previous Labour voters giving us a total of 6 million votes. It only needs to do this again, and we have united the centre in British politics.

In short, I believe that Liberals can become the catalyst to bind the country together in a new spirit of common endeavour and I ask for your support in this great undertaking.'

Jeremy Thorpe

Britain in danger

This country faces two immediate crises. The first is potential economic catastrophe caused partly by world events and partly because of our own stagnating economy. The second is a crisis of national disunity in which there is a distinct lack of faith in government at the very time when it is most needed.

Unless the next Government deals immediately with these problems any long term aims for the future will be quite unattainable. This Manifesto unashamedly concentrates on the immediate situation and outlines policies to deal with it. We have deliberately refrained from restating our full programme of policies which were set out in last February's Manifesto 'Change the face of Britain' and in the document 'Forward with the Liberals'. Nevertheless they are an integral part of Liberal thinking and our aims and principles remain valid.

The basic principle of Liberalism is a concern for the individual. We do not think in terms of bosses or masses or classes. We start with the individual men and women who make up these vast conglomerations of people.

The great issue facing all nations in this century is how to combine the collective activity of the state, necessary for the welfare of the people with democratic freedoms and an opportunity for individual initiative in economic enterprise. The Liberal Party's great claim is that it approaches this problem with no doctrinaire prejudices, no class inhibitions and no sectional interests.

We seek to redistribute so that all may own and so that none may be impoverished. We seek to create an individual partnership between capital and labour. We seek to devolve power to Scotland, Wales and the regions of England. We seek to decentralise by ensuring that every act of government is carried out at the lowest level consistent with intelligent administration.

Through participation we want to see ordinary men and women having a say in all that goes on around them. And just as we seek to break down concentrations of political power, we seek in the same way to break down monopolistic concentrations of economic power.

In the world sphere we are essentially internationalist. We oppose narrow, self-interested policies by nations or power blocs. We welcome the opportunity to transform the European Economic Community into a Liberal, outward looking federation of free people with sovereignty, pooled in respect of vital political and economic tasks, but with equally clearly defined powers and responsibilities for the constituent states and regions.

All these themes have one end. To serve the individual and to create the conditions in which he can develop his personality to the full. But these aims are endangered by the immediate problems which we now face.

Unless the British people unite to overcome our common difficulties our future prosperity as a democracy will be in grave jeopardy. The remainder of this Manifesto examines the immediate crisis and outlines the Liberal solution.

The economic crisis

This Election is being fought against the threat of economic disaster, caused by stagnation and high inflation. The rapid upsurge in world commodity prices has resulted in balance of payments deficits for almost the entire Western World.

Britain has been particularly hard hit. Our cost of living soared by 16 per cent in 1973 alone and is currently rising at the rate of 20 per cent. a year, which means that our money will buy only four-fifths of what it could buy a year ago.

Unemployment is again increasing rapidly. Thousands of people are losing their jobs every month – 35,000 in August alone. If present trends continue, three-quarters of a million people could be out of work by the end of this year.

We are borrowing astronomical sums of money abroad. This year alone, our balance of payments is in deficit by £4,500 million. Our share of world trade is steadily declining and no amount of North Sea Oil, or any other panacea, will repay these debts in the foreseeable future.

In short, we are living beyond our means and this unpalatable truth must he communicated to the people, whatever the political consequences. As Jeremy Thorpe has said: 'It is time for Britain to wake up and realise that only a total change of course in our politics, our economy and our national aspirations can save us from disaster'.

The political crisis

Before any Government can begin to get to grips with the economic situation, it must regain the confidence and respect of the electorate.

Our present electoral system is a fraud. Far from ensuring representative government, it polarises power between two extremist parties representing opposed classes and prevents a proper representation of alternative view-points. At every Election less than half the voters get the candidate of their choice returned to Parliament.

Many people are frustrated by the lack of success which is apparent, regardless of the party in office. The prospects for success are continually undermined by the fact that, once a party becomes the Government it feels obliged to cancel much of what its opponents had previously done in office. Time and time again it is ultimately obliged by events to readopt these policies. This constant vacillation causes the most devastating uncertainty in our political and economic life.

The class war produces deep and irreconcilable differences between the Conservative and Labour Parties, but these differences stem, not from a substantial issue of principle, but from preconceived dogma which has no relevance today. Class-based parties, above all, are responsible for the partisan nature of British politics and the divisions in society between rich and poor, manager and worker, householder and tenant.

It is impossible to conceive of a Labour Party dependent on the trade unions for 90 per cent. of its funds being able to operate an effective incomes policy, when its paymasters, the union leaders, object to wage control.

Conversely, how can a Conservative Government take effective action to control prices and stamp out restrictive practices in industry when it is dependent on big business for over a million pounds a year?

Yet these are precisely the policies we need at the moment if we are to overcome inflation.

Nor will any policy achieve lasting progress without the consent of a large majority of the population. Since the war, neither of the other two parties has won the support of more than half of the electorate. Neither can achieve the necessary degree of unity because each is incapable of appealing to any significant number of the other's traditional supporters. A Labour Government instinctively raises the suspicions of business; a Conservative Government immediately alienates the Trade Unions.

The time has come for stability in Government and an end to class confrontation based on fear and mistrust. This country can no longer be ruled from the extremes of right and left, setting people against each other; it must be run by a Government whose integrity is not in doubt, whose policies are fair minded and whose politics are not governed by vested interests. It is the unique characteristic of the Liberal Party that it can provide such a Government because it is without doctrinaire prejudices, class inhibitions or sectional interests.

Inflation – the immediate crisis

The major single problem facing the next Government will be that of inflation. This Election will solve nothing unless we decide now that we are to make a conscious and concentrated effort to get on top of inflation. On the contrary, it will do positive harm if, as has happened so often in the past, the nation is left bitterly divided as a result.

The next Government must be honest with the public and admit that in the present circumstances a statutory prices and incomes policy is absolutely necessary as an essential weapon against inflation.

The Liberal Party has consistently advocated statutory controls; the other parties have studiously avoided them until forced into action by an adverse situation. When they have taken action both have pandered to vested interests to the detriment of the population as a whole. They have been fearful of embarking on long-term policies to control inflation for fear of denting the profits of the big corporations or the wage packets of the strongest unions. Their timid attempts at controlling inflation have been undercut by promises of an ultimate return to a free-for-all. As a result, their policies have failed because the nation was unprepared for such measures and the necessary restraint was not forthcoming.

No policy will gain acceptance unless it is seen to be both effective in its operation and fair to all concerned. Inflation divides society; it punishes and deprives the weak and protects and rewards the strong. It encourages a situation where the rich get more and the poor go to the wall, where wealth is illusory but poverty is real. Therefore, it is dangerous to attack inflation without at the same time protecting those who are most vulnerable to its effects.

The Liberal Party believes that this can only be done by means of a fundamental redistribution of wealth and resources. We understand the fear of inflation that motivates moderate – and not so moderate – men to press for higher and higher wages. We are prepared to resist these claims when we feel they are unjustified and against the national interest. But we also recognise that even the most efficient policy will be breached unless the causes of inequality are removed.

We therefore advocate, as an essential prerequisite to the introduction of statutory prices and incomes control, a programme of social reform.

In effect, this would be an agreement between the people of this country and the Government of the day. In return for immediate measures to alleviate poverty and industrial uncertainty and unrest, the next Government could count on positive acceptance for a measure of restraint. Such a programme should contain four minimum proposals:

- First, a policy for creating and redistributing national wealth.
- Second, measures to encourage true competition and power-sharing in industry.
- Third, a review of our public expenditure programme with priority being given to maintaining and expanding social welfare provision.
- Fourth, the reform of our electoral and governmental structures to reflect more accurately the will of the electorate.

Creating and sharing wealth

Our primary task in the immediate aftermath of the Election will be to establish an agreed attitude towards managing the economy. This must include a statutory policy for prices and incomes, which will only allow personal wealth to expand at a rate which the nation can afford. At the same time it must effect a redistribution of incomes and a far greater degree of social justice. The present grossly inequitable distribution of incomes is starkly illustrated by the plight of those engaged in the health, social and public services, many of whom are women. The next Government should legislate immediately to introduce a statutory minimum earnings level, corresponding to two-thirds of the average wage, for a normal 40-hour working week. This would mean guaranteed earnings of £27, at current rates, for the 44 million working people who earn less than this amount, the figure automatically increasing with rises in average earnings. If phased in over a three-year period it would add 3 per cent per annum to the national wage bill, and would necessitate a corresponding cut-back in the expectation of above-average wage earners. Such people will have to be content with pay increases which cover only rises in the cost of living.

At the same time the Government should undertake to implement in full the principle of parity with equivalent jobs in the private sector for those working in the nationalised industries and public services.

A similar selective policy for prices must be evolved to protect the family from excessive price increases at a time of wage restraint. The present supervision of prices, dividends and profit margins should be continued and middle-sized companies should be obliged to submit applications for price increases in the same way as top companies. More positive efforts must be made to break up monopolies and price fixing and to recreate a genuinely competitive economy. The Monopoly and Mergers Commission should be given powers to investigate and regulate monopoly companies. The Government should stimulate competition where it can still be made to work, break up and control monopolies, prevent non-productive mergers and stamp out restrictive trade practices, so that profits are made fairly, in truly competitive circumstances.

Industrial development

Our immediate aim is to restore confidence and stability in industry, to encourage an even flow of investment and to distribute wealth more widely. Policies for nationalisation are irrelevant to the problems of industry. As the Court Line disaster has shown, the merest hint of nationalisation is sufficient to drive away private investment, leaving the long-suffering general public to foot the bill. There is a role for private and public enterprise but a clear line of demarcation should be drawn between them. And both must change their mode of operation if confidence and stability in industry is to return.

A national programme for industrial development ought therefore to contain four basic objectives, namely: The reform of Company Law to induce a far greater degree of public responsibility in industry and make the management of companies responsible to shareholders and employees on an equal basis. Then there must be a concentrated attack on monopolies on the lines of the American anti-trust laws. Nationalisation will not solve the problems of high prices or monopolies. As we have seen in so many nationalised industries, the public either has to suffer high prices or subsidise non-profit making industries. Either way the consumer pays more.

Next, the Government should consult with industry to establish the prospects for investment. Where the economic advantages to the nation would be enhanced by investment in certain industries, the Government should also be prepared to under-write the necessary finance for a limited period of time, if necessary. An essential prerequisite to this policy must be a commitment by Government to refrain from further nationalisation except where there is no other viable alternative, and liquidation would be detrimental to the nation, as, for example, in the case of Rolls-Royce.

Finally, a phased introduction of worker-participation and co-partnership schemes at all levels of industry from the shop-floor upwards, should involve union and non-union workers in the exercise of power. We would require legislation to set up works councils in all industries above a certain size and to establish the principle of worker representation at board level. The introduction of approved profit-sharing schemes (or, in the case of the nationalised industries, a dividend for each industry, based on prod-uctivity) is also essential if the necessary co-operation is to be achieved at plant level.

The key to a successful programme of industrial development lies in a continuous flow of investment capital, a stable and contented work force and a steady increase in output. These must be our objectives.

Public expenditure and family needs

The most vital provisions any Government can make for its people are to ensure that they have a decent roof over their heads and an adequate income. In the immediate period of low or non-existent economic growth, we cannot assume that our expend-iture on these programmes will be paid for by greater production and economic expan-sion. Therefore we must find the money from other sources. We must now learn to live within our means. Strict economies in non-essential expenditure must now be made if our public services are even to be maintained at their current standards, let alone expanded.

The indexation of savings against inflation would protect those dependent on their savings and encourage greater investment. This should be accompanied by a far greater degree of austerity and care in the deployment of public money.

At local level there must be a radical overhaul of the rating system as quickly as possible, so as to redistribute the burden fairly between ratepayers and to raise the finance necessary to ensure the continuation of essential services. Liberals would intro-duce site value rating to replace the current rating of property by a rate geared to the value of the land on which the building stands. This would redistribute the burden of rates more fairly between domestic and industrial rate payers.

To reduce the burden on local authority expenditure, teachers' salaries should be paid through the Exchequer, thereby saving local authorities £570 million a year. Local authorities should also be given limited scope for raising revenue independently through appropriate local taxes.

Our priorities in the field of social welfare must be twofold; to reform and expand the provision of family welfare and to stabilise the chaotic system of housing finance. In general, the aim must be to recast existing programmes as far as possible rather than incurring further expenditure. In the case of the National Health Service, however, only a massive injection of capital can save it from imminent collapse and this will have to be done almost immediately.

The other major exception to this rule must be old age pensioners. In spite of the recent increase, the basic State pension is still pitifully inadequate, and over two million pensioners are forced to draw Supplementary Benefit in order to exist. The next Government should give an immediate commitment to tie the pension to a stated percentage of national average earnings. This would provide an automatic index against inflation and ensure that pensioners are not left behind in the wage race. The target to be met, over a three-year period, ought to be 50 per cent of average earnings for a married couple and a third for a single person. At present wage rates this would work out at £21 and £14 respectively. The total cost would be £1,400 million, which can be raised by transforming the present contributory National Insurance system into a fully graduated Social Security Tax. This would be paid by employer and employee on a ratio of two-thirds to one-third, and would be much fairer on the low paid and self-employed. At present they pay a higher percentage of their earnings in National Insurance contributions than the above average wage earner. In addition Liberals will take the initiative in seeking all-party agreement on the creation of a second pension structure for all those in full-time employment. This would end the uncertainty and instability in the Occupational Pensions field caused by the changes in policy of successive governments.

In the field of housing, we must accept that we cannot continue indefinitely to subsidise the Building Societies in a vain attempt to keep interest rates down. If subsidies are necessary, they should be paid to individuals on the basis of need. In the short-term, our immediate priority should be to enable those who wish to buy their homes to overcome the twin barriers of inflated house prices and high interest rates. In ten years the price of an average new house has risen three times, the cost of a mortgage has risen five times whilst the proportion of an average family's income spent on mortgage repayments has increased from 25 per cent to 50 per cent. The average price of a new house at over £10,900 is well beyond the reach of over half the population and unless steps are taken soon to alleviate the situation, home ownership will become a thing of the past.

This problem can be overcome without any extra governmental expenditure by the introduction of flexible mortgage schemes for all those buying their own home.

The Liberal proposals were discussed with the Building Societies prior to being incorporated in a recent pamphlet, and provide for three new schemes:

For those whose earnings are linked to the cost of living, through, for example, threshold agreements, an index linked mortgage would be appropriate. Under this scheme repayments begin at a lower initial value but rise automatically with increases in the cost of living index.

For those who are near retirement and wish to buy their first, and probably their last, home, the equity mortgage scheme would enable them to do so. Here the Building Society would buy a share of the house by contributing an interest-free grant, thus reducing the cost of the mortgage, in return for a share of the capital value when the house is sold. These schemes have already been discussed with representatives of the Building Societies and there is no practical reason why an enterprising Government could not introduce them immediately.

We must make far better use of existing accommodation. Wherever possible local authorities should purchase unsold properties for use as council houses, rather than leaving them to lie empty. If builders could be sure of selling their houses, there would be much greater incentive to press ahead with new contracts. Our proposals would achieve this at minimal cost to the Government.

In making adequate provision for low income families, the next Government ought to take steps to ensure that financial aid goes to those in need and is not wasted. This can be achieved in two ways. Firstly, the wasteful and indiscriminate food subsidies should be scrapped and the £700 million thus saved spent on increasing family allowances and extending them to the first child. This would cost £340 million in a full year and would be far more effective than reducing the millionaire's loaf of bread by 2p. The remainder of the money saved could be put towards implementing the Finer Committee's recommendation, that an adequate allowance should be available to single parents with families to support, and assisting the disabled and other needy people.

Secondly, the first steps should be taken towards overhauling the entire Social Security system, eliminating most of the 44 means tests and replacing the unnecessary duplication between the Inland Revenue and the Department of Health and Social Security. Liberals would introduce a full scale tax-credit scheme which would encompass all existing allowances and welfare benefits. It would also replace all tax reliefs on mortgages, rent allowances and rent rebates by a single housing allowance paid to tenants and house buyers alike. The essence of the scheme is simple and was set out in our Manifesto last February. A Government commitment to phase in such a scheme over a five-year period is essential if the necessary agreement from those on low pay for a statutory prices and incomes policy is to emerge.

Implicit in all our objectives in the field of social policy is a commitment to ensure full and equal rights for women in every sphere. Liberals were the first to initiate legislation against sex-discrimination and there will be no let up in our campaign for equality between the sexes.

Controlling inflation

Once a minimum programme of social reform is agreed, we believe that any Government has the moral authority to ask the nation to exercise restraint in its economic aspirations in order to control inflation. But experience has shown that voluntary restraint is inadequate; there are always those who will break the rules either through force of habit or because they have the economic power to get what they want. Therefore, a statutory policy with tough sanctions on those who break it is essential. Liberals would control inflation through a combination of industrial reconstruction and a prices and incomes policy enforced by penalties on those whose actions cause inflation. We propose that prices and average earnings within a company should be limited to an agreed annual rate of increase. Any company which increased prices faster than that rate would suffer an extra surcharge on its Corporation Tax payments equivalent to the amount by which its prices had exceeded the agreed norm.

If average earnings per person (including fringe benefits) within a company rose faster than the agreed annual rate, then both the employer and the employees concerned would have to pay an extra surcharge on their graduated National Insurance Contributions, again on a sliding scale according to the amount by which earnings had exceeded the norm.

Of course, there must be provision for appeal if confrontation with those who have a special case is to be avoided. This would be best achieved by the compilation of ad hoc reports on earnings levels and pricing policies in particular industries, along the lines of the old National Board for Prices and Incomes. Such reports would also cover changes in relativities and wage differentials, which will have to be narrowed considerably, and Parliamentary consent would have to be obtained before reports could be implemented. The Relativities Board would be retained for this purpose. Thus instead of countering inflation by increasing everybody's taxes, as Mr Powell and the Labour Party advocate, our policy would tax only those who cause inflation and control the supply of money into the economy without having to resort to the blunt instrument of brutal cuts in expenditure on social services which, once again, hit the poor hardest of all.

A great merit of this policy is that it would enable wage bargaining to take place without direct government intervention and inevitable accusations of partisanship. Yet it would still enable the Government to maintain overall control of the economy.

The next Government must face up to the problem of domestic inflation immediately on assuming office if we are to avoid the perils of bankruptcy, poverty and unemployment. We believe that this programme is the minimum that will generate the necessary consent for a tough anti-inflation policy.

The need for agricultural expansion

As long as our agriculture industry is allowed to decline we shall become increasingly dependent on the vicissitudes of the world market. Therefore we must become more self sufficient through greater domestic food production.

Farmers have had a raw deal recently and badly need an injection of confidence. The next government should undertake to introduce a temporary guaranteed price for beef and an increase in the milk subsidy. The pig subsidy should also be extended through the winter.

The Government should also seek a radical change in the Common Agriculture Policy of the Common Market in order to secure a reasonable return for the farmer and more stable prices for the consumer. This can only he done from within the community by a government committed to our continued membership. World food prices now exceed those pertaining in Europe and it would he totally against our economic interests to withdraw, regardless of the political considerations involved.

There remains the political crisis; this must also be faced now if our democracy is to survive and our government to is regain the confidence of the electorate.

Power to the people

The two-party system began to crumble at the last Election. Alienation and cynicism with conventional politics is particularly felt in Scotland and Wales where the Westminster Parliament is a distant and inadequate form of representation.

Two major reforms must be introduced by the next Government. First it must replace the present antiquated electoral system, in which 19 million people have no influence on the choice of government. Liberals favour a fully proportional system using the single transferable vote in multi-member constituencies. Second, there must be a substantial devolution of power from Westminster, initially to Parliaments in Scotland and Wales, along the lines advocated by the Kilbrandon Commission on the Constitution. These Parliaments should have substantial legislative and budgetary powers – nothing less will satisfy the aspirations of the people of Scotland and Wales for full self-government, which Liberals support. Ultimately, Liberals want a Federal system of Government in Britain with Assemblies established in the regions of England.

Unless these reforms are carried out very soon the process of alienation from Government will become so deep seated as to be beyond redress.

A similar feeling of antipathy will soon be felt towards the European Communities unless there are direct elections to the European Parliament. This has been part of Liberal policy for a very long time and a government led initiative would help restore confidence in the European idea as well as being an indication of continued faith in our membership of the Community.

The above measures constitute the minimum social, economic and political programme which can save this country from the immediate crisis. We cannot afford another five-year period in which major problems are swept under the carpet while politicians pretend that inflation does not exist. The next Government must be prepared to implement substantial radical changes in policy which will lay the groundwork for future economic prosperity. In doing so it must have regard for the long term, as well as the immediate, future. For only if we build on the foundations laid will we reap the rewards that economic self-restraint can produce.

The Liberal challenge

The Liberal Party challenges the people of this country at this Election to break away from the class-based politics of the past in favour of a party without vested interests to consider, which is free to act on behalf of the individual person. Politics should be about people in their own communities but, in spite of so many elections in recent years, ordinary people feel that government is too distant and no longer heeds what they say. The re-organisation of Local Government and the restructuring of our health and social services has resulted in larger, more distant units of administration. The Liberal Party believes in self-government at every level, so that ordinary people can take and use power to influence their daily lives. All our policies, from the reform of government, and co-partnership in industry, to democracy in education, are designed to ensure that the individual viewpoint can be expressed effectively. Without the active participation of the great majority of people, our ability to overcome the economic problems which we face will be greatly impaired.

Only a new political alignment can provide the momentum for economic stability. At the last Election, 6 million people supported the Liberal Party as the vehicle for this new momentum. Many others stood on the brink but their traditional allegiances and the understandable fear of breaking with the past prevented them from committing themselves fully. Yet the seeds have been sown, and after the election a strong Liberal Party in Parliament could break up the confrontation of the two class parties and create the conditions for a broad based radical alliance led by Liberals. Over 47 per cent. of the electorate would like to see a Liberal Government. If this support is translated into votes there will be a Liberal Government.

THE REAL FIGHT IS FOR BRITAIN

The Liberal Manifesto

25p

LIBERAL PARTY GENERAL ELECTION MANIFESTO 1979

The real fight is for Britain

Date of Election	Thursday 3 May
Party Leader	David Steel
Candidates	577
MPs	11
Votes	4,313,811
% of vote	13.8%

Introduction by the Rt. Hon. David Steel

With your support this election could be about something more important than a change of government. It could be a chance to change a failed political system.

Britain is deadlocked and that deadlock has meant economic and social decline. There can be very few voters, even among the keenest adherents of the Conservative or Labour cause, who really believe that our problems can all be solved just by yet another change of government. Oppositions promise grandiosely to generate 'the white hot heat of technological revolution' or to 'roll back the frontiers of the state'. It takes at least a year or two of government for them to come to terms with reality and discard their doctrinaire programmes. Each time the country is weakened further.

We have tried confrontation politics for long enough. In 1964, in 1970, in 1974, incoming governments promised that they held the key to Britain's industrial and social problems, if only they could undo the achievements of their predecessors and push their own prescriptions through Parliament. The hopes they raised have all been cruelly disappointed. It is high time to try a different pattern of government, which is based upon the consent and support of the broad majority of the electorate. That alone can now provide the basis for the long term programme of reform which Britain so desperately needs.

The Liberal Party has taken the first step towards breaking the deadlock during the past Parliament, by proving that co-operation among different parties is possible, practical and good for Britain. Unavoidably in this first experiment in a new style of government, our achievements were relatively limited. Many of the reforms which we wish to see implemented have had to wait.

But during the 18 months of the Liberal Agreement with the Labour Government the stability and consistency provided by co-operation among parties which represented a clear majority of the electorate, and the requirement that the Labour Government respect the views of that majority, helped to bring down the annual rate of inflation to 8 per cent. The Tories had raised it from 5.9 per cent to 13.2 per cent.

Labour raised it further to a peak of 26.9 per cent, now it is rising again. The Lib-Lab Agreement also reduced Interest Rates to 10 per cent (Minimum Lending Rate). The Tories left it at 12.5 per cent under Labour it reached a peak of 15 per cent in October 1976. It is now back up again.

Industrial confidence began to return during the agreement. The divisive policies promoted by Labour's lunatic left-wing were effectively held in check. On Liberal insistence the law was changed to encourage profit-sharing, to help bridge the gulf of mistrust between the two sides of industry – which has so far led 48 companies to adopt new profit-sharing schemes.

Sadly, much of what was achieved for Britain during those 18 months has been thrown away since last October, as Labour clung on to office without secure and agreed majority support. If either of the two establishment parties grabs an exclusive hold on office after this election, Britain will slip even deeper into industrial confrontation and economic decay. The truth is, the Labour and Conservatives parties share a vested interest in the preservation of Britain's divided society. The unrepresentative nature of our electoral system protects them from the full effects of public disillusionment. Continuing industrial and social confrontation reinforces their links with the opposing sides of industry. Britain's secretive and centralised structure of government protects them, turn and turn about, from Parliament and the public.

Many, on both front benches, would rather see Britain's economy drift further behind our continental neighbours, would rather accept another cycle of industrial conflict and popular discontent, than touch the pattern of adversary politics which supports their alternating hold on political power.

I appeal to you, as a voter concerned with what is best for Britain, to throw your support behind the fresh approach which the Liberal Party represents – and which we have now demonstrated can work for Britain. The effectiveness of whatever government emerges after this election, the whole style of British government, will depend less upon which big/dinosaur Party returns with the largest number of parliamentary seats, than upon the size of the Liberal wedge in the House of Commons. A mass Liberal vote throughout the country and many more Liberal seats will call the final whistle on a discredited Tory/Labour game.

Part Two of this manifesto sets out the Liberal Party's detailed electoral programme. I want here to stress four underlying themes: our commitment to fundamental political and constitutional reform; our proposals for economic and industrial reform; our plans to change and to simplify our overburdened tax system and our concern to bring to bear an environmental perspective across the whole range of government policies.

Political reform is the starting point. Until we break the two-party stranglehold, until we get away from the adversary class politics which are embedded in our parliamentary structure, we cannot successfully tackle the problems of economic weakness and industrial mistrust, of misspent resources in housing, of uncertain management of the public sector and of mishandled relations with our neighbours abroad. Electoral reform is the key to the lock. A democratic electoral system would deprive the Conservative and Labour parties of their ability to maintain electoral support by frightening wavering voters with the spectre of a single, unacceptable alternative. It would force them to face up to their own internal contradictions: the unstable coalition within a weakened Labour Party between its nationalising left and its conservative centre; the tensions within the Conservative Party between moderate Tories and doctrinaire free-marketeers. A democratic electoral system is needed, too, to generate the popular consent which is essential to support a long-term programme of economic and social reform.

The reluctant and unsatisfactory compromises which recent governments have offered in response to demands for the reform of Parliament, for an end to official secrecy, above all for devolution and decentralisation, also demonstrate the need for more thorough-going change and the inability of the establishment front benches to meet that need. Privately, many MPs from both the Labour and Conservative parties accept the case for far-reaching changes, but they are unwilling publicly to challenge their own leadership. A powerful wedge of Liberal MPs in the next Parliament could start a chain reaction of political change.

Economic and industrial reform must accompany and follow from political reform. Hardly surprisingly, the owner party and the union party have resisted the extension of democracy to industry, seeing a transformation of the pattern of industrial relations as a threat to their entrenched interests. Labour's preferred approach would only strengthen the position of trade unions, which are already one of the most conservative forces in our society. They do not want to involve the workforce as a whole. The Conservative alternative of lightly-disguised confrontation is even more dangerous in 1979 than their Selsdon Park proposals were in 1970, and would no doubt lead again after a painful two years in office to another expensive U-turn.

We Liberals seek instead to alter fundamentally the framework within which economic policy is made, to bring the different sides of industry together to work constructively to increase the well being of Britain – not to battle destructively over each other's share of a dwindling national cake.

The two-party confrontation has also wrought havoc with our tax system. Successive governments have tacked on new additions to an already unwieldy structure. It is too complex for most taxpayers to understand or to be sure of their rights and obligations. Many changes have been rushed through Parliament without adequate debate or consideration of their implications, at the behest of some vested interest or in the service of some outdated ideology. As a result tax avoidance has become our fastest growing industry. Liberals are concerned to simplify the personal tax system and reduce its burden to create a tax structure which encourages initiative and promotes a wider distribution of wealth, and above all to establish principles for a stable tax system which can command the respect of the electorate as a whole: wealthy, poor and average earners.

Neither of the two established parties has paid any serious attention to the long-term conservation of Britain's environment and resources. The argument over North Sea oil has been conducted in terms of immediate benefits rather than long term needs. The necessity to grow more of our own food and the conservation of man's natural habitat, including its flora and fauna, have been wrongly regarded as low priorities in politics. The debate over Britain's future dependence on nuclear power has hardly touched Parliament, conducted instead by environmental groups through the limited forum of the Windscale inquiry. Yet conservation and recycling of our limited and often finite resources is a vital issue for Britain's future, and an issue which concerns a growing section of our electorate. We Liberals have used our influence to force Parliament to pay more attention to the ecological perspective.

But Parliament as at present constructed does not find it easy to focus on questions like this, which do not fall conveniently into the categories established by the conventions of two-Party politics or the Left/Right dog-fight. Here is a key issue for Britain as the new Parliament takes us into the 1980s, too complicated for the current ritual of debate but too important to ignore.

It may seem paradoxical that Liberals call at once for more stable government and for radical change. Our concern is for long-term change, as opposed to the twists and turns of short-term policies which have characterised British government since the end of the Second World War. Worthwhile reforms for Britain's economy, for its industrial relations, its tax structure, its social services, its political system itself, can only be achieved after thorough examination and open debate – and can only be made to last if they command the respect and acceptance of the majority of the electorate.

That is why we are prepared to co-operate with other parties, even as we insist on the need for a fundamental break in Britain's political habits. Of course we want in time to see Britain led by a Liberal Government, implementing a coherent radical programme with the support of a clear majority of voters. But meanwhile we are prepared to co-operate with whichever party will go with us some way along the same road. It would, after all, be a profound and radical change for Britain to benefit from stability in economic policy, to gain a new consensus in pay policy and industrial relations, to achieve a wider agreement on the structure of taxation, or to open up a searching debate on the best use of Britain's limited resources.

It would be a radical change in itself for the next government to have to base its policies upon the support of the representatives of a genuine majority of the electorate. With your support, and the support of millions of voters like you, we can ensure that those changes take place.

David Steel

The Liberal programme

Economic and industrial recovery can only follow from a radical programme of political and social reform. In a liberal society in Britain, power and wealth will be distributed more widely, and government subjected to open democratic control. Participation and self-management will be encouraged, in government and in industry; public and private power will be, where possible, dispersed: individual initiative and independence will be rewarded; and a sense of partnership and community strengthened. But UK action alone cannot provide the stimulus for these major political and social changes. Many of our problems have to be tackled at the European level; action is also needed in the regions and nations of the United Kingdom, and within local communities through the efforts of voluntary bodies and community groups. But in an over-centralised Britain the process of reform is most urgently needed at the centre, in Westminster and Whitehall.

Political reform

Britain has a grossly undemocratic voting system, over-centralised government and an ineffective Parliament. Piecemeal changes have failed to introduce the necessary constitutional reforms. Bureaucracy and powerful organisations triumph at the expense of individuals who feel powerless to influence decisions that affect them. Liberals believe:

1 That electoral reform is the essential first step to representative parliament and government.
2 In open government accountable to a reformed parliament.
3 That decisions must be taken at the most local level practicable.
4 People and their communities must take part in decisions that affect them.

Reform of the voting system

Our first priority is electoral reform, because Britain's voting system is a root cause of our troubles:

- It damages living standards by preventing consistent economic and social policies.
- It leads to governments claiming a false mandate in favour of policies which have been decisively rejected by a majority of the voters.
- It encourages native voting, frustrates the intelligent elector and leads to increasing alienation from the whole political system.
- It rewards parties based on class distinctions and reinforces class divisions. Without reform our whole democracy is at risk.

Liberals demand proportional representation at all levels of government:

- At Westminster, to give us representative parliaments and genuine majority government.
- For future elections to the European Parliament, to avoid the disgrace of being the only member of the EEC not to use a fair voting system.
- In local government, where the present system can often produce one-party dominance with its dangers of corruption.

The system adopted must ensure that every vote is of equal value and affects the result. It must also ensure that parties win roughly the same proportion of seats as their proportion of votes, allow voters a choice between candidates in each party, and reflect minority interest and viewpoints. Liberals believe that of available PR systems, the single transferable vote (STV) best achieves these results.

The main opposition to the overwhelming popular demand for electoral reform comes from political machines exercising unjustified privilege, and from those MPs who fear that if voters had a real choice they would not be re-elected. Liberals support the people in their fight against electoral privilege, and will give first priority in the new Parliament to obtaining a cast-iron commitment to the early introduction of electoral reform.

Reform of Parliament and Government

Parliament should take control of its own business out of the hands of Government, and set up powerful Select Committees, to assert vigorous democratic control over the Executive. Section 2 of the Official Secrets Act should be repealed. We would introduce a Freedom of Information Bill similar to that of the Liberal MP Clement Freud in the last Parliament. This would give a right of public access to all official information except for certain listed categories (e.g. defence, economic and commercially sensitive information, and individual records). A National Efficiency Audit should be set up to scrutinise public expenditure plans and reduce waste. We need fixed dates for parliamentary elections to avoid the uncertainty which Prime Ministerial privilege imposes on the country.

The House of Lords should be replaced by a new, democratically chosen, second chamber which includes representatives of the nations and regions of the United Kingdom, and UK members of the European Parliament.

Reform of the Constitution – a federal solution

Liberals supported the Scotland and Wales Acts, for all their defects, because we believed they offered a step in the right direction. These deficiencies – the weakness of the proposed Welsh Assembly and the constitutional contradictions in the Scotland Act – were exposed in the referendum debates and contributed to the results. This experience has reinforced our belief that the massive decentralisation of power from Westminster and Whitehall to Scotland, Wales and the major regions of England – for which we have long called – must involve legislative, executive and fiscal powers taken together. It has also demonstrated the need for a federal approach, which will involve a written constitution and a Supreme Court, as the only approach which can achieve legislative devolution within a workable framework of government for the United Kingdom.

Whatever the outcome of the election, Liberals will press for the widest possible consultations among the parties on constitutional reform.

Local Government

The Tory reorganisation of local government proved an expensive disaster. In due course, the district and county councils must be replaced by one tier of multi-purpose authorities, whose boundaries match local needs and circumstances.

We support the establishment of parish councils in urban areas and the extension of the powers of existing parish councils. These councils should have a statutory right 'to be consulted' by local government and other bodies and a duty to stimulate local democracy.

Northern Ireland

Progress towards peace ought to come from within the Province but if outside help is required Great Britain must be prepared to contribute.

As an interim measure we propose that a 15 to 20 member Advisory Council be elected by the people of Northern Ireland using PR(STV). Such a council would be large enough to let every significant viewpoint have a voice but small enough for all its members to have real discussion with each other as well as with the Secretary of State and other political representatives.

The Council would:

1   Represent the views of the people of Northern Ireland to the Secretary of State and advise him accordingly, and

2   discuss how a constitutional conference should be set up to consider the means by which a generally acceptable form of government for the Province should be developed.

There must be no capitulation to violence. Direct rule must continue for the time being. The civil power must be given military assistance for as long as required. Britain will not force Northern Ireland to unite with the Republic of Ireland. All elections, including those for Westminster, must be by PR(STV). Continuing emphasis must be placed on the achievement of full human rights.

Reforms to strengthen citizens' rights

The liberty of the individual requires constant vigilance. Restrictions can only be justified if they protect the freedom of others. Liberals emphasise:

1   Legislation to protect individual rights.
2   A clear definition of citizenship.
3   Equal opportunities for men and women in all spheres, especially equal pay for work of equal value.
4   Protection for minority groups.

Individual freedom

We need a Bill of Rights – as a first step, Britain should incorporate the European Convention of Human Rights into United Kingdom law. Individual rights protected by law should include:

- The right to see, correct and add comments to one's personal records held by public and private bodies.
- The right of individual privacy.
- The right of free association with others, including the right to be represented through a Trade Union.
- The right to work without having to be a member of a Trade Union and the right to cross a picket line without intimidation.
- The rights of those in police custody, by means of revised Judges' Rules.

Reduction of crime

The steady increase in crime can only be checked in the short run by:

- Recruiting many more police, by improving working conditions.
- Strengthening the links between the police and the communities that they serve. Having the greatest practicable number of policemen 'on the beat' by day and night.
- Making more resources and facilities (including secure accommodation) available to magistrates and others concerned with juvenile offenders, to curb juvenile crime and rehabilitate juvenile offenders.

- Prisons must be modernised and further experiments made with non-custodial treatment, except for those whose imprisonment is necessary for the protection of society.

At the same time, we must realise that the long term solution is to attack vigorously the social, environmental and economic seedbeds of crime such as broken homes, bad schools, drink and drugs, decaying cities, bad housing, unemployment, and the boredom of mass production society.

Nationality and entry to the UK

There should be only one class of citizenship for citizens of the UK and colonies. We would abolish the discrimination against non-patrials which creates second-class citizens. Citizens of the UK and colonies, including residents of Commonwealth countries who accepted the offer of remaining UK citizens when independence was granted, should have a right of entry. Spouses, children and other dependents of UK residents should be allowed to join their families in Britain and all children who have been born abroad of British mothers must have automatic right of citizenship.

Liberals deplore the Tory policy of inflaming people's fears about unrestricted immigration when the numbers of immigrants are actually falling. We should, wherever practicable, accept bona fide refugees.

Equal opportunities for women and men

In order to ensure equal opportunities and rewards for women and men, we propose:

- Changes in the patterns of work to allow for greater flexibility, part-time and weekend work, so that men and women can better meet their social and family needs.
- Legislation to ensure that job evaluation schemes give adequate weight to factors found predominantly in work customarily done by women.
- Removal of anomalies in National Insurance benefits which are based on outdated assumptions about the roles of men and women in contributing to family income. Reshaping the Equal Opportunities Commission to create an effective instrument against discrimination.

Minority rights

Britain is a diverse and multicultural society and Liberals rejoice in its richness, which owes much to the peoples of many different ethnic origins and cultures who have chosen to live here. We defend their right to maintain and develop their own traditions. Minority groups must be allowed to practise and advocate their beliefs, provided this does not reduce the freedom of others. We will protect and defend the rights of minorities by:

- A comprehensive law out-lawing discrimination on grounds of race, sex or political belief with enforcement through a single Anti-Discrimination Board.

- Providing a legal right for nomadic people to live according to their life-style so long as this does not harm others.
- Removing all legal discrimination based on sexual orientation.

Economic and industrial reform

The failures of our political system are reflected in our economic and industrial system. Confrontation is used instead of co-operation, resistance to change obstructs innovation, and frequent changes of government policy weaken our economy still further. Inflation has started to rise again, unemployment is unacceptably high and we are becoming increasingly uncompetitive in world markets. We have an unjust industrial society in which most workers are pitted against management and are denied any share in decision-taking or in profits.

We need a radical long-term programme of reforms to restore Britain's economy and industrial prosperity. Liberals believe in:

1 Controlled and steady economic growth (in co-operation with our European partners), with greater attention to conservation of scarce resources, especially energy and land.
2 Harnessing the potential of all at work to improve enterprise and productivity.
3 Providing opportunities of useful work for all.
4 Protecting the citizen from inflation by reconciling rises in incomes with the real rate of growth of the economy.
5 Ensuring that the primary aim of government intervention in industry should be the promotion of viable market enterprises.

We see a revolution in attitudes amongst all at work through the introduction of Democracy in Industry as the key to reversing Britain's economic decline. This means employees sharing control and profits with shareholders. We would achieve this by giving all employees (irrespective of trade union membership) legal rights as individual members of their company; a direct vote in electing the board of directors jointly with the shareholders; rights to information about its plans and prospects; to participate in decisions through elected works councils; and to share in the profits. Liberals would encourage producer co-operatives by establishing a Cooperative Development Bank.

Efficient use of resources means reducing Britain's consumption of non-renewable raw materials, through government support (including tax incentives and penalties) for conservation, energy saving and recycling schemes. Whilst public expenditure already takes too large a share of our present national income, our health services, the schools and other essential public services cry out for more resources and the armed services remain underpaid. Economic recovery is essential to provide in the long run extra funds needed to continue the fight against poverty and deprivation. But in the immediate future, they can be found only by a relentless war against bureaucratic waste in central and local government.

More jobs in new industries, as well as in agriculture and in the service sector, must be created to replace those being lost through international competition and technological change. Further positive discrimination in favour of small businesses and producer co-operatives, through changes in the tax system and in planning controls, will help to provide the catalyst for industrial renewal. This will build upon the success of the Liberals in getting the Government to appoint a senior Cabinet minister for the small business field, which has already led to major tax concessions and other reliefs.

Employers, unions and public authorities must not be allowed to obstruct retraining. Liberals also challenge the belief in bigness for its own sake and concentration of control at the centre in both the private and public sectors. We aim at decentralisation, with greater autonomy for individual working units to encourage initiative and participation.

We would introduce a sustained prices and incomes policy based on wide consultation and enforceable at law. Our incomes policy would be supported by tax measures and a national minimum income. It would reward increases in value-added. We support attempts to synchronise annual wage settlements.

Liberal proposals for reducing personal taxation, introducing industrial democracy and profit-sharing are essential elements of an incomes policy since they would transform the industrial climate, restore incentive and reduce inflationary expectations.

The role of government is to provide a stable political and economic framework, not to dominate the economy. But it is dangerous to pretend that government can be taken out of economic and industrial planning, given the unavoidable importance of public spending and the active involvement of governments of competitor countries in supporting their industries and promoting their own economic interests. There is no case for further large-scale nationalisation in Britain; but attempts to denationalise at present would further disrupt the industries affected. The National Enterprise Board provides a valuable mechanism for assisting new industries and for aiding companies temporarily in difficulty, but it should disengage from them when they regain commercial viability.

The framework of government economic and industrial policy should be made more open and more subject to parliamentary control, by including Opposition parties on the National Economic Development Council and by establishing a Select Committee for Economic Affairs to consider its reports. Economic recovery is too vital to be subjected to all the twists and turns of partisan tactics, with Opposition parties glorying in their ignorance of facts which face government, and promising to reverse central decisions. Consistent economic policy requires a transformation of the way in which policies are debated and decided.

Reform of the tax system

The British tax system frustrates initiative, inhibits new enterprises and discourages the wider spread of wealth. Penal rates of taxation encourage successful avoidance and evasion; whilst the poor and disadvantaged face a bewildering array of means tests and often fail to receive an adequate income.

Liberals believe in:

1 Providing an adequate minimum income for all.
2 Treating men and woman as equals for tax purposes, whether married or single.
3 Providing greater incentives for earning, productivity and enterprise.
4 Encouraging employees to build up a stake in their enterprise.
5 Widening the distribution and individual ownership of wealth.

The central reform needed is the introduction of Credit Income Tax which should:

- Abolish the means test.
- Introduce cash credits in place of personal allowances, social security payments and national insurance benefits.
- Provide credits for students of all ages, for rate relief and housing.

We also need a major switch from taxes on income to taxes on wealth and expenditure and propose:

- Income Tax starting at 20 per cent with a top rate of 50 per cent.
- A substantial increase in the level of income at which people first pay income tax.
- A gifts and legacies tax paid by the recipient in place of Capital Transfer Tax.
- A wealth tax on very large capital accumulations in place of the Investment Income Surcharge which would be repealed.
- Tax incentives for profit-sharing and employee share ownership.
- Self assessment of tax liability with spot-checks by the Inland Revenue.

The changeover would be introduced over several years and be matched by indexation of taxes on drinks and tobacco, a single rate of VAT and the replacement of the employer's National Insurance contribution with a regionally varied payroll tax.

In a Federal Britain, regional and local government would have powers to raise the revenue they need for the services they provide. Income tax would be the main source of revenue at regional level with a tax on all land values (except agricultural land which would be zero-rated) being the main source of revenue for local government, which would also have powers to levy its own taxes. These would replace domestic rates.

A caring society

Liberals laid the foundations of the modern welfare state, but the original vision has been lost in a jungle of complex rules, means tests and decisions taken by remote officials. Those most in need often fail to get help or are caught by the poverty trap, whilst others fall through the gaps.

Liberals believe in:

- Recreating services which recognise and respond to human needs, without excessive bureaucracy.
- Making a reality of democratic control.
- Providing greater choice for the individual.
- Renewing inner city life.

The change to Credit Income Tax

Tax credits would meet the needs of the unemployed, retired, disabled and disadvantaged, and provide for maternity, children and students of all ages. All income would be taxable and where tax liability exceeds cash credits, the difference would be paid as tax; where credits exceed tax, individuals would receive cash regularly.

It would take several years to introduce a full tax credit scheme and in the meantime, we would give priority to:

- Further increases in child benefit and the progressive conversion of other allowances against income tax into positive cash credits.
- The introduction of a supplementary pension for all pensioners not qualifying for a full earnings-related pension under the new state pension scheme, reducing the number of pensioners needing to apply for supplementary benefit.
- The introduction of a disablement allowance to help offset the additional expenditure caused by disablement.
- The early introduction of housing credits based on average local rents. An increase in the mobility allowance and its extension to those over retirement age.
- The implementation of the Finer recommendations for one-parent families. The removal of the anomalies affecting widows and others through the application of the rule about overlapping benefits.

Care in the community

Liberals seek to make the welfare state more effective and democratic. Providers and receivers of care should participate in running the services. The elderly (especially the over 75s), single-parent families, the disabled, the mentally handicapped and the mentally ill should have priority for additional resources.

We propose to tackle the mushrooming bureaucracy created by the Tories reorganisation of the health service by abolishing the area health authorities and bringing power back to the level of the local health district, and by placing the regional health authorities under the control of elected Scottish, Welsh and Regional assemblies.

We would give a greater role for voluntary organisations in partnership with official services. We oppose widespread closure of cottage hospitals and encourage the retention of local pharmacies.

Housing

Housing policy should retain existing communities and help build new ones. Priority must be given to improvement of existing houses instead of wholesale clearance and rebuilding. Everyone must have access to adequate housing with a wide choice of tenure and type of home – within the price they can afford. Private and council tenants should have reasonable security of tenure, and help control the management of housing and its immediate environment. We would introduce an Occupiers' and Owners' Charter which safeguards the rights of both tenants and owners of rented housing.

Housing co-operatives and smaller locally-based housing associations, which should be run democratically, should be encouraged. Councils should be required to build more homes for sale, and adequate resources should be provided for the full implementation of the Housing (Homeless Persons) Act, a measure introduced by Liberals.

Liberals would concentrate resources on inner cities by positive planning for community based jobs, schools, housing and entertainment.

Education and training

We see education and training as a lifelong process that must be as widely available as possible to people of all ages. Secondary education must be non-selective with schools and colleges matched to local needs and working together to give maximum choice to students. Post-school education must be integrated with closer links between universities, polytechnics and further education.

We want to see:

- Nursery education for all children whose parents want it.
- The immediate right of rising-fives to enter primary school.
- Use of successfully qualified teachers now unemployed to reduce class sizes and improve literacy and numeracy.
- The involvement of all staff, parents and pupils in the running of schools through elected governing boards, and elected schools councils for secondary schools.
- Improved links between schools and industry to ensure preparation for the world. Expansion of adult education and a major expansion of training and retraining facilities in which Britain still lags far behind its industrial competitors.
- Education for retirement from employment.

Conservation of resources and environment

The industrial world consumes far too much of the world's non-renewable resources and is becoming increasingly dependent on imports of energy. Many of man's activities threaten the natural environment. Few recognise that after the year 2,000, shortages of food, raw materials and energy will mean drastic changes to our lifestyles. The bonanza of North Sea oil must not blind us to the dangers facing us when the oil runs out. We must start to change our attitudes now. Liberals believe in:

1 Conservation and wiser use of scarce resources, especially land and energy.
2 War on waste and pollution.
3 The need to preserve the natural environment for future generations.
4 A re-ordering of our economic and social priorities to put them on a sound basis.

Energy and North Sea oil

Liberals have repeatedly expressed doubts about a massive commitment to nuclear power and questioned the decision to expand the Windscale reprocessing plant. We must spread the extraction of North Sea oil over a longer period and use the revenues for long term investment with high priority for widespread energy conservation and developing alternative energy sources. We must:

- Substantially increase research and development on fusion, wave, solar and other sustainable sources of energy.
- Make greater use of combined heat and power systems which use waste heat.
- Promote maximum efficiency in the production and use of coal and the use of primary fuels.

- Set up a permanent Energy Commission to discuss in public future energy options. Not build any more nuclear power stations, at least until the problems of safe and permanent disposal of radioactive waste have been solved.

Transport

We would legislate to improve the standards of public transport in both towns and rural areas by making it more responsive to local needs and subject to democratic control. We would:

- Encourage self-help and other schemes which improve freight and personal mobility in rural areas.
- Amend the licensing laws governing stage carriage services to encourage local operators.
- Plan jobs and homes closer together, discourage the private motor-car in city centres and provide better facilities for pedestrians and cyclists.
- Limit expenditure on new road-building to socially desirable projects. Increase emphasis on road safety and therefore support the early introduction of tachographs in lorries.
- Oppose further nationalisation of the ports and reject implementation of the Dock Work Regulations Scheme.
- Retain the British Waters Board and increase expenditure on canal maintenance. Retain the British Rail network – and, where necessary, treat it as a social service. Support a rail-only Channel Tunnel financed with the aid of EEC finances. Improve the international communications of the regions by dispersing more international air traffic outside London.

Food and agriculture

Liberal policy aims at providing a fair return for the farmer and reasonably priced food for the consumer. We also need a co-ordinated approach to the needs of food production and conservation of natural wild life which recognises their interdependence. We therefore propose:

- Fundamental reform of the Common Agricultural Policy to produce competitive prices, avoid structural food surpluses and encourage efficient farming; the creation of a Land Bank to help new entrants to farming, and the expansion of co-operatives.
- More land for small-holdings.
- To raise the guaranteed minimum earnings for farmworkers.
- Radical reform of the Common Fisheries Policy, conservation of fish stocks and a fifty mile exclusive limit for each member state within the EEC.
- Increase the number of abattoirs to EEC standards to discourage the export of live animals.

Safeguarding the environment

Land is a finite resource and we need careful planning to ensure an adequate supply of land for housing without using valuable farm land. Resources should be concentrated on inner city renewal and rural regeneration so that all parts of Britain are fit to live in. We have a duty to preserve in trust for future generations that which we inherit from the past. We would:

- Make polluters pay the cost of their pollution. Drastically amend the Community Land Act.
- Introduce taxation of the unimproved value of land, in its optimum permitted use (agricultural land to be zero-rated).
- Introduced fiscal incentives for conservation, reclamation of industrial wasteland and recycling.
- Encourage rurally based crafts and appropriate industries in rural areas. Support the demand of the General Election Co-ordinating Committee for Animal Protection for a Royal Commission on Animal Welfare.
- Ban the importation and manufacture of any product derived from any species whose survival is threatened, and work for a total ban on commercial whaling. Expedite the work of the Commons Commissioners and legislate to implement the recommendations of the Royal Commission on Common Land with regard to access and management.
- Preserve moors, scrub woodland, wetlands and other wildlife 'reservoirs'.

Europe and the world

Liberals believe in:

1 Opposing all forms of aggression and imperialism.
2 Emphasising the protection of political and human rights as a basis for foreign policy.
3 Fostering closer co-operation within the European Community as the most constructive means of promoting Britain's best interests.
4 Supporting closer integration of defence, security and weapons procurement policies within the Atlantic Alliance as the most effective way of utilizing scarce resources.
5 Working for a more equitable distribution of power and wealth throughout the world. Liberals support positive co-operation with the developing countries.

Economic weakness and political failure have reduced Britain's standing and influence in the world and strained the friendship of our partners in Western Europe and beyond.

In Europe, we support a stronger and more democratic Community. Our long-term aim is a federal Europe based upon democratic institutions and an equitable sharing of economic and social burdens. This involves working towards economic and monetary union and more effective regional and social policies to overcome unemployment and deprivation. It also means commitment to the strengthening of the European Parliament. Only such a Parliament, elected by Proportional Representation, can provide democratic political solutions to Europe's problems and make nationalist solutions as irrelevant as they are dangerous.

Both Labour and Conservative Governments have been short-sighted and inward-looking in their attitudes to Europe. The Labour Government's nationalistic stance has harmed Britain's interests by blocking avenues for wider agreement. Britain's foreign policy should become increasingly concerted with our European partners, and our aim must therefore be the evolution of common European policies, not to pursue the nostalgic illusion of independent power.

Europe's foreign policies must include continued close relations with the United States. We firmly support a peaceful settlement of the Middle East conflict within the framework of the relevant United Nations Resolutions. In Southern Africa, Britain has a special historic responsibility, and we must continue to work with our allies and with the United Nations to promote peaceful change. We support the Anglo-American efforts being made to end bloodshed and to establish an independent Zimbabwe with a Government elected under international supervision. We believe that sanctions should not be lifted nor recognition accorded until such a government is established.

Europe's defence must be a common defence, based on integrated forces and an integrated command within the Atlantic Alliance. Co-operation in armaments should be accompanied by ending British arms sales except in the context of a treaty of mutual defence. The fundamental solution to the problem depends on the establishment of a credible system of international controls of arms sales under the aegis of the United Nations. Arms control negotiations with the Soviet Union and its allies should be vigorously pursued to promote a basis for the mutual and balanced reduction of forces and armaments.

It is one of the most important duties of Europe to help those peoples of the Third World who still lack effective influence in the international economy. In this context, Britain, because of our links with the Commonwealth, has a distinctive contribution to make. Liberals want to see reductions in the barriers to world trade, and support current negotiations to give the developing countries stable prices for their raw materials. UK official aid should be increased to achieve the targets agreed by the United Nations.

The work of the UN specialised agencies and of voluntary organisations should be generously supported. Aid should be directed wherever possible through multi-lateral channels, but there is no justice in assisting governments which systematically deny basic human rights to their own citizens.

Conclusion

The Liberal programme offers a coherent framework for a series of reforms which will need years of intensive effort. This requires for its success the support of an informed public, co-operation in industry, and a new spirit of mutual understanding among the democratic political parties. The vital choice at this election is whether Britain will start along this new path, or continue to shuffle down the slope of economic and political decline. The contents of the first Queen's Speech are less important than the membership, composition and spirit of the new Parliament. A stronger Liberal presence, backed by a powerful Liberal vote throughout the country, will ensure that the door is opened to fundamental change, not slammed shut again by the negative reactions of the old two-party game which has failed the nation.

Working together
for Britain

Programme for Government

THE SDP/LIBERAL ALLIANCE GENERAL ELECTION MANIFESTO 1983

Working together for Britain

Date of Election	Thursday 9 June
Party Leader	SDP – Roy Jenkins, Liberal Party – David Steel
Candidates	SDP 311, Liberal Party 322
MPs	SDP 6, Liberal Party 17
Votes	SDP 3,570,834 – Liberal Party 4,210,115
% of vote	SDP 11.6%, Liberal Party 13.7%

Programme for government

The General Election on June 9th 1983 will be seen as a watershed in British politics. It may be recalled as the fateful day when depression became hopelessness and the slide of the post-war years accelerated into the depths of decline. Alternatively it may be remembered as the turning point when the people of this country, at the eleventh hour, decided to turn their backs on dogma and bitterness and chose a new road of partnership and progress.

It is to offer real hope of a fresh start for Britain that the Alliance between our two parties has been created. What we have done is unique in the history of British parliamentary democracy. Two parties, one with a proud history, and one born only two years ago out of a frustration with the old system of politics, have come together to offer an alternative government pledged to bring the country together again.

The Conservative and Labour parties between them have made an industrial wasteland out of a country which was once the workshop of the world. Manufacturing output from Britain is back to the level of nearly 20 years ago. Unemployment is still rising and there are now generations of school-leavers who no longer even hope for work. Mrs Thatcher's government stands idly by, hoping that the blind forces of the marketplace will restore the jobs and factories that its indifference has destroyed. The Labour Party's response is massive further nationalisation, a centralised state, socialist economy and rigid controls over enterprise. The choice which Tories and Socialists offer at this election is one between neglect and interference. Neither of them understands that it is only by working together in the companies and communities of Britain that we can overcome the economic problems which beset us.

Meanwhile the very fabric of our common life together deteriorates. The record wave of violence and crime and increased personal stress are all signs of a society at war with itself. Rundown cities and declining rural services alike tell a story of a

205

warped sense of priorities by successive governments. Our social services have become bureaucratic and remote from the people they are supposed to serve. Mrs Thatcher promised 'to bring harmony where there is discord'. Instead her own example of confrontation has inflamed the bitterness so many people feel at what has happened to their own lives and local communities.

Our Alliance wants to call a halt to confrontation politics. We believe we have set an example by working together as two separate parties within an alliance of principle. Our whole approach is based on co-operation: not just between our parties but between management and workers, between people of different races and above all between government and people. Because we are not the prisoners of ideology we shall listen to the people we represent and ensure that the good sense of the voters is allowed to illuminate the corridors of Westminster and Whitehall. The TUC and CBI, each paying the bills for the party it supports, have been too much listened to and ordinary people have been heard too little.

We do not believe that all wisdom resides in one party, or even in the two parties of the Alliance. There are men and women of sense and goodwill in both the other parties. But they have opted out and allowed the demands of the old party politics to make the House of Commons the most noisily partisan assembly in the Western World.

Our concern is for the long-term, not just for tomorrow. We do not want to solve our immediate problems by piling up new crises for future generations. So when we plan for industrial recovery, we are not simply seeking growth for growth's sake. We want an increase in the sort of economic activity which will provide real jobs, which will rebuild our decaying infrastructure, which will conserve energy, and which will re-use and recycle materials rather than wasting them. We want to invest in education and housing since our long-term future depends upon the skill and maturity of the next generation. The lavish promises and the class-war rhetoric of the Conservative and Labour manifestos have no place in our Programme for Government. We offer instead a sober assessment of the first steps back to economic health and social well-being. But the vision which unites us is of a nation of free people working together in harmony, respecting each other's rights and freedom and sharing in each other's success. To achieve these hopes, we must not only change failed policies. We must reform the institutions which produced them.

When we advocate a fairer voting system we are therefore talking neither about a constitutional abstraction nor the self-interest of a new political force. Of course we want fairness for ourselves, but even more do we demand a change in the interests of the majority, whose wishes are increasingly distorted by the pull of the extremes. This is in the interests of the cohesion of the country, for it is wrong and dangerous that one big party should be a stranger to the areas of prosperity and the other an incomprehending alien in the areas of deprivation. It is also in the interests of a more stable political and economic direction, without which those who work in industry, public or private, or in the community services, will not have the framework within which to plan for the future.

We believe that Britain needs the fresh start of the Alliance even more in 1983 than it did in the heady days of our birth in 1981. The Labour Party has not become more moderate. The extremists have been taken out of the shop window; they have not been removed from the shop. The policies of nationalisation, attacks on private enterprise, withdrawal from Europe, with its devastating effect upon our exports and investment prospects, and alienation of our international friends and allies, are all enthroned and inviolate. Jobs and national safety would be at risk.

Mrs Thatcher offers no alternative of hope or of long-term stability. Some of her objectives were good. Britain needed a shake-up: lower inflation, more competitive industry and a prospect of industrial growth to catch back the ground we had lost over the years. But the Government has not succeeded. After a bad start it has got lower inflation, but the prospects even for the end of this year are not good. And the price paid has been appalling. British industry has seen record bankruptcies and liquidations. Unemployment has increased on twice the scale of the world recession.

Prospects for the future are more important than arguing about the failures of the past. The last four years could be forgiven if we now had a springboard for the future. We do not. At best we have a prospect of bumping along the bottom. On present policies the 80's will be a worse decade for unemployment than the 30's. Nearly a half of those without a job in 1933 got one by 1937. By 1987, if we continue as we are, unemployment will be at least as bad as in 1983. As a reaction, if the old two-party system is allowed to continue, we shall then lurch into the most extreme left-wing Government we have ever known.

The Alliance can rescue us from this. There is no need for hopelessness. By giving a moderate and well-directed stimulus to the economy, accompanied by a firm and fair incomes policy, we can change the trend and begin to get people back to work. Unlike the Labour Party, we would do it in a way which encouraged private business. We believe in enterprise and profit, and in sharing the fruits of these.

Beyond that, further success will depend upon the international climate. That is not wholly ours to command. But it does not intimidate us. The world is looking for a lead. Concerted expansion, greater currency stability, a recognition of interdependence between poorer and richer countries are all possible and necessary. We need the vision and sense of enlightened self-interest which produced the Marshall Plan and pulled post-war Europe together.

It is an opportunity for Britain. We yearn for a world role and are qualified by our history and experience to perform one.

The Alliance is unashamedly internationalist. We cannot live in a bunker. We are for a British lead in Europe, for multilateral disarmament and for a new drive to increase our own prosperity by co-operating with others to reduce poverty and squalor throughout the world. We offer reconciliation at home and constructive leadership abroad. We are not ashamed to set our sights high.

David Steel, Leader of the Liberal Party
Roy Jenkins, Leader of the Social Democratic Party

The immediate crisis: jobs and prices

Our economic crisis demands tough immediate action. It also requires a Government with the courage to implement those strategic and structural reforms which alone can end the civil war between the two sides of industry.

The immediate priority is to reduce unemployment. Why?

To the Alliance unemployment is a scandal; robbing men and women of their careers, blighting the prospects for a quarter of all our young people, wasting our national resources, aborting our chances of industrial recovery, dividing our nation and fuelling hopelessness and crime.

Much of the present unemployment is a direct result of the civil war in British industry, of restrictive practices and low investment. But in addition Conservative Government policies have caused unemployment to rise. An Alliance Government would cause unemployment to fall. How? Can it be done without releasing a fresh wave of inflation?

We believe it can. We propose a carefully devised and costed jobs programme aimed at reducing unemployment by 1 million over two years. This programme will be supported by immediate measures to help those hardest hit by the slump – the disadvantaged, the pensioners, the poor.

Ours is a programme of mind, heart and will, it is a programme that will work!

The Programme has three points:

- Fiscal and Financial Policies for Growth
- Direct Action to provide jobs
- An Incomes Strategy that will stick.

Sustained policies for growth

These will be based on carefully selected increases in public spending and reductions in taxation. Despite the impression Mrs Thatcher gives, the Conservative Government is borrowing £8 billion a year. It is costing us £17 billion to keep over 3 million people on the dole. In view of the depth of the slump, we think it right to increase public borrowing to around £11 billion and to use this money in two basic ways:

- to reverse the reduction in public investment which over the last decade has been little short of catastrophic, through a selective programme of capital investment in the water and sewerage systems, electrification of railways, building and repairing roads, rebuilding and refurbishing hospitals, investing in housing, improving transport services and developing energy conservation schemes.

- to concentrate the funds available for tax reductions in areas where tax cuts have a direct impact on prices such as the abolition of the National Insurance Surcharge (the 'tax on jobs') and in this way keep prices down as growth is stepped up. We will stop the nationalised industries being forced to raise prices for gas and electricity merely to increase Government revenue.

Such action to rekindle growth without inflation, buttressed by a less restrictive monetary policy and management of the exchange rate to keep our exports competitive, will be pursued so as to reduce unemployment by 400,000 over our first two years.

Direct action to provide jobs

The immediate action we propose is targeted on those among the unemployed in greatest need, the long-term unemployed and the young. It does not throw money wildly about, but has been carefully drawn up to achieve the biggest early fall in unemployment we can manage at the lowest practicable cost. Our main proposals are:

- to provide jobs for the long-term unemployed in a programme of housing and environmental improvement – house renovation and insulation, land improvements; these jobs are real jobs crying out to be done. There will also be a major expansion of the Community Programme. We will back programmes of this kind with great determination to ensure that they generate at least 250,000 jobs over two years;

- to extend the Youth Training Scheme so that it is available to all 16 and 17 year olds and give real help to those who want to stay on at school after 16 or go to college or take a training course. Our long term aim is to see all 16–19 year olds either as students with access to work experience, or as employed people with access to education and training. But the extension of training proposed here would alone reduce youth unemployment by 100,000;

- to create more jobs in labour-intensive social services. There is a great need for extra support staff in the NHS and the personal social services. These services are highly labour-intensive and their greatest need for extra people is in regions of high unemployment. We propose the establishment of a special £500 million Fund for the health and social services in order to create an additional 100,000 jobs of this kind over two years;

- to give a financial incentive to private firms to take on those longest out of work – To boost jobs in the private sector, we propose to pay a grant to companies for every extra job they provide and fill with someone unemployed for over six months. The scheme will be for employment pay, not unemployment pay. The Government loses about £100 per week (in unemployment benefit and lost tax revenues) for every person unemployed, so it is not extravagant to pay £80 a week for each additional job. According to the best estimates this incentive could increase employment by around 175,000 jobs within two years of its introduction.

In sum, our immediate programme of direct action would reduce unemployment by well over 600,000 in two years. What is more, it will do so in a highly cost-effective way by switching the money which is now paid to people to do nothing, into payment for useful jobs instead, and it therefore will not involve irresponsible increases in public spending or borrowing.

Taken together these proposals should reduce unemployment by 1 million by the end of our second year in government.

An incomes strategy that will stick

We do not pretend that a lasting return to high levels of employment can be achieved painlessly, or without a reemergence of the inflationary pressures which record unemployment has temporarily damped down. We are convinced there is not hope of a lasting return to full employment unless we can develop ways of keeping prices down which do not involve keeping unemployment up. And unlike either of the two old parties, we are prepared to face up to this by pursuing a fair and effective pay and prices policy that will stick. It is Labour's refusal to face up to the need to restrain incomes, at the dictates of its union paymasters, which above all makes Labour's claim to have a solution to unemployment so utterly bogus, and it is Mrs Thatcher's refusal to contemplate anything other than unemployment as an incomes policy which condemns the country to permanently high unemployment if she wins another term.

In drawing up its counter-inflation programme, the Alliance has faced the question of pay and prices policy head on. Unlike other parties, the Alliance will seek a specific mandate from the electorate in support of an incomes policy. We shall campaign for a series of arrangements to keep price rises in check whilst unemployment comes down. Specifically we propose:

- to establish a range for pay settlements. The Government will discuss with representatives of commerce and industry, trade unions and consumers, the prospects for the economy as a whole, and will establish the desirable range within which pay settlements should be negotiated given the outlook for unemployment. The Government will provide forecasts of the implications for unemployment, inflation and growth, of pay settlements at different levels, and the objective will be to arrive each year at an agreed norm or range for pay settlements. In the absence of agreement the government will announce its own view and tailor its policies accordingly, but every effort will be made to minimise disagreement and establish a common view.

- a fair deal for pay in the public services. The agreed norm or range will provide the background to a fair and systematic approach to pay in the public services. A single, independent Assessment Board for public service pay will be set up to provide fair comparisons. Agreed arrangements for arbitration will be needed. As a result, public service sector pay will grow at broadly similar rates to that of comparable groups in the private sector.

- new arrangements to discourage excessive pay settlements in the private sector. Pay settlements in the private sector will be negotiated with no direct interference in settlements made by small and medium sized businesses. We intend to set up a Pay and Prices Commission to monitor pay settlements in large companies, with powers to restrict price increases caused by wage settlements which exceed the agreed range. At the same time, we shall legislate to introduce a Counter Inflation Tax, giving the Government the power to impose the tax if it becomes necessary. The tax will be levied by the Inland Revenue on companies paying above the pay range. It will be open to successful companies where productivity increases have been high to pay above the agreed range if they do so through the distribution of shares which are not immediately marketable.

- the nationalised industries will be subject to similar restraints on excessive wage settlements and will not be permitted to evade the consequences of excessive wage settlements and counter-inflation tax payments simply by raising prices.

We would, if we were convinced it was necessary in the prevailing circumstances, be prepared to introduce a fully statutory incomes policy to cover the interim period whilst these new arrangements are being introduced.

Previous incomes policies have been short term reactions to crisis. They have been reversals of earlier policies. They have had no mandate from the electorate. The Alliance presents its policy now because that is both honest and necessary. To work, a pay and prices framework must be understood and supported. The framework we propose can last. It is flexible. It will encourage growth and reward productivity and initiative. It offers the only way of regaining growth without refuelling inflation.

Strategy for industrial success

The Alliance is alone in recognising that Britain's industrial crisis cannot be solved by short term measures such as import controls or money supply targets. Our crisis goes deep. Its roots lie in the class divisions of our society, in the vested interests of the Tory and Labour parties, in the refusal of management and unions to widen democracy in industry, in the way profits and risks are shared.

The policies offered by the two class-based parties will further divide the nation North v South, Management v Labour. Our greatest need is to build a sense of belonging to one community. We are all in it together. It is impossible for one side or the other in Britain to 'win'. Conflict in industrial relations means that we all lose.

But how do we reduce conflict? How do we end class war in industry? Not by intimidating the unions through unemployment. Not by nationalising, de-nationalising, re-nationalising. Not by pretending the problem doesn't exist.

The Alliance is committed to policies which will invest resources in the high-technology industries of the future. We are committed to a major new effort in education and training. We are pledged to trade union reform, to tough anti-monopoly measures. Above all we will act to share profits and responsibility in industry far wider than ever before.

We need to do these things to ensure Britain's economic success in a brutally competitive world. But the aim is not merely economic growth for its own sake. To live fulfilled and meaningful lives we each need challenge, reward and responsibility. In British industry far too many feel they have no stake in success, no role to play, nothing to contribute. It is that feeling which leads to bitterness, and conflict. The time has come to change these things – now, before it is too late.

Partnership in industry

Britain has made little progress towards industrial democracy, yet several of our European partners have long traditions of participation and co-operation backed by legislation. They do not face the obstacles to progress with which our divisive industrial relations present us. To be fully effective, proposals for participation in industry need to be buttressed by action on two fronts: a major extension of profit sharing and worker share-ownership to give people a real stake where they work as well as the ability to participate in decision making, and reform of the trades unions to make them genuinely representative institutions.

Participation at work

We propose enabling legislation that will offer a flexible and sensible approach:

- An Industrial Democracy Act to provide for the introduction of employee participation at all levels, incentives for employee share-ownership, employee rights to information, and an Industrial Democracy Agency (IDA) to advise on and monitor the introduction of these measures;
- Employee Councils covering each place of work (subject to exemption for small units) for all companies employing over 1,000 people. Smaller companies would also be encouraged to introduce Employee Councils;
- Top level representation will, for example, be through directors elected jointly by employees and shareholders, or a Representative Council with rights to codetermination on a range of issues;
- No 'single channel' appointments by trade unions: every employee must have a vote and be able to exercise it secretly.

Profit-sharing and employee share-ownership

We propose:

- through the Industrial Democracy Act to encourage companies to develop collective share ownership schemes based on profit sharing as an essential component of industrial democracy. We will also increase the exemption limit for Corporation Tax relief on Inland Revenue approved profit-sharing and share-ownership schemes to £3,000 per employee;

- to give specific encouragement to co-operatives through increased funding for the Co operative Development Agency – to provide advice and financial support for those setting up co-operatives.

Giving the unions back to their members

Employee democracy in industry can only be extended if trade unions are made genuinely representative of their members since they are bound to have an important role in participation. It is for that reason, and not in any spirit of 'union bashing' that we propose further democratisation of the unions themselves. We want to see effective, representative and responsible trade unions playing their full part in industry, and in this we stand apart from the Conservative Party, which has no interest in participation, and which wants to reform the unions only in order to weaken them.

We will legislate to provide for:

- compulsory secret individual ballots, normally on a postal basis, for the election of the national executives of unions and, where appropriate, union general secretaries;
- the right for a certain proportion – 10 per cent – of the relevant bargaining unit to require a ballot before an official strike can be called;
- maximum encouragement of arbitration, as a fair and constructive means of

settling disputes, including a legal requirement in essential public services that any dispute be taken to impartial arbitration operating on common principles for all public service groups, before industrial action shall commence;

- measures to provide for a more efficient and more effective trade union movement:
- tax exemption for union contributions to encourage a better level of funding, a Trade Union Development Fund to assist union mergers and rationalisation, statutory rights to recognition for unions that have won majority support from the relevant workforce; adequate facilities at the workplace and reasonable time off for union representatives to perform their duties; and increased support for education and training for shop stewards and representatives. We propose an Employees' Charter clearly safeguarding trade union and workers' rights.

We favour a careful balance of collective and individual rights on existing closed shops, with action against the pre-entry closed shop matched by retention of legal provision for union membership agreements on condition the latter rests on substantial workforce support and that exemption from union membership is available on grounds of conscience.

Government and industry

Prioity for industry

We cannot restore employment or achieve the standards we want in our social services unless we first reverse our industrial decline. So the rebuilding of our industry and commerce must be given priority in the formulation of government policies.

Government and private industry

The role of an Alliance government in relation to private industry will be to provide selective assistance taking a number of forms:

- an industrial credit scheme, to provide low-interest, long-term finance for projects directed at modernising industry;
- a national innovation policy, to provide selective assistance for high-risk projects, particularly involving the development of new technologies and for research and development in potential growth industries (with a corresponding reduction in R and D spending on defence);
- public purchasing policies to stimulate innovation, encourage the introduction of crucial technologies and aid small businesses;
- Government assistance in export promotion, with increased efforts to reduce non-tariff barriers to trade;
- we will establish a Cabinet Committee chaired by the Prime Minister at the centre of decision-taking on all policies with a bearing on the performance of industry.

The Alliance will strengthen the Monopolies and Mergers Commission to ensure its ability to prevent monopoly and unhealthy concentrations of industrial and commercial power. The aim is to guarantee fair competition and to protect the interests of employees, consumers and shareholders.

Government and public industry

We must get away from the incessant and damaging warfare over the ownership of industry and switch the emphasis to how well it performs. Thus we will retain the present position of British Aerospace but will not privatise British Telecom's main network nor sell off British Airways. But we will make the nationalised industries successful and efficient as well as properly responsible to their consumers. Specifically, we propose that:

- where nationalised industries are operating viably in competitive conditions, Government regulation and control should largely be removed. Their borrowing on the market should not be subject to external financing limits (EFLs), and they should effectively be run as independent enterprises;
- where public industries are not subject to market forces – e.g. the public utilities – or where they are dependent on public finance – e.g. the railways – alternative means of exerting pressure to ensure operational efficiency are required, and we will set up an Efficiency Audit Commission to report regularly and publicly to a Select Committee of Parliament on the overall management and discharge of their responsibilities by the industries concerned;
- we will seek to distance the Government from direct involvement in nationalised industries. They must be free to run their industries according to the criteria laid down for them, without political interference.

New and small businesses

To encourage the growth of new and small businesses, we will attack red tape and provide further financial and management assistance by:

- extending the Loan Guarantee Scheme, in the first instance raising the maximum permitted loan to £150,000; and the Business Start-Up Scheme, raising the upper limit for investment to £75,000; and introducing Small Firm Investment Companies to provide financial and management help;
- zero-rating building repairs and maintenance for VAT purposes and reducing commercial rates by 10 per cent;
- making sure the Department of Industry co-ordinates and publicises schemes for small businesses and that government aid ceases to discriminate against small businesses;
- tailoring national legislation such as the Health and Safety Regulations to the needs of small businesses and amending the statutory sick pay scheme to exclude small businesses.

Agriculture and fisheries

Agriculture is an important industry and employer. To encourage its further development we will:

- increase Government support for effective agricultural marketing at home and abroad and continue support for 'Food from Britain';
- ensure that agriculture has access like other industries to the industrial credit scheme we propose;
- encourage greater access to farming, especially by young entrants.

We believe that the provision of alternative sources of employment is the key to many other problems of the rural areas. To this end, we will promote moves at local level to establish rural development agencies.

The Alliance is determined to safeguard the future of our fishing industry which needs help to re-build after years of uncertainty and the drastic consequences for the deep-sea fleet of 200-mile limits in the waters they used to fish. We believe:

- that in order to conserve stocks for the future, EEC inspection must be strengthened to ensure that conservation measures are fairly enforced on the fleets of all member states;
- that better marketing and promotion, better vocational training, and reasonable credit terms would all help the future of the industry;
- that government measures must take account of the special importance of our inshore industry to rural communities.

Energy

The first priority of the Alliance energy policy is the conservation and efficient use of energy. A programme of house insulation is part of our jobs plan and a programme to encourage increased energy efficiency in industry will lead to a substantial increase in employment and savings to the economy.

For the foreseeable future, coal will continue to supply a large part of our major energy needs. To ensure the continued prosperity of the coal industry we will make substantial investments in the modernisation of techniques and capacity. This does not mean a dramatic schedule of pit closures. There will be some employment problems – where the oldest deep pits are coming to the end of their economic life. The Alliance plans for jobs and industry are designed to give particular help to areas like these where new employment is needed.

The North Sea currently produces the oil and gas we need. But we want to make sure that there are enough reserves to keep up British oil and gas production. So we will encourage the exploration for and development of new reserves. We want to link Britain up by pipeline with the rest of the North Sea gas-fields so that, together with our European partners, we can make the best use of the gas that is there.

We will invest as a matter of urgent priority in different types of energy and new technologies, especially the use of sources of energy like the sun, wind, waves and the heat below the earth's surface and the development of combined heat and power systems. We are determined to maintain a British power plant industry.

The power stations we have and are currently building will be enough for our needs for some considerable time to come. We see no evidence including anything yet submitted to the Enquiry to justify the building of Sizewell or other PWR generating stations. However research into nuclear waste disposal must be continued in order to cater for existing needs and we would develop Britain's research programme and expertise in the field of nuclear power and the possibilities presented by fast-breeder technology and fusion.

Education and training

The third basic condition for industrial success is a people with the skills and self-confidence that will be needed for the challenges of new technology. The education and training systems are not providing enough people with the skills necessary to make them employable and the country successful in competition with its rivals. We are falling further behind. Japan on present plans will be educating all its young people to the age of 18 by 1990. More than 90 per cent of the 16–19 age group in Germany gain recognised technical qualifications. And it is not just a matter of school-leavers. Our managers are less professionally qualified than our main competitors'. From the bottom to top we are underskilled, and this has to be put right if we are to prosper in future. To do this, to raise standards in education and training and to improve their effectiveness, is the object of proposals set out in the next Section.

Creating one community

A fundamental purpose of the Alliance is to reduce the divisions which over the last two decades have been fragmenting our society, and restore our sense of being one community.

The gap between rich and poor is as wide today as it was forty years ago when the Beveridge Report was written. There has been a big increase in poverty and urban squalor as a result of the present slump. The pressures of the recession have placed an increasing burden on women in particular. The trend towards two nations in health, education and the social services is accelerating as those who can pay increasingly opt for private provision.

To combat these trends will require determined action across a wide front:

- immediate help for those bearing the burden of unemployment;
- a determined attack on poverty, aimed at releasing those locked in the poverty trap, by raising the living standards of the hardest-pressed families;
- action to raise standards in education and the quality of health care provided by the NHS and remove the inadequacies in the state services which lie behind the trend to private provision;
- increased investment in housing, drawing on wider sources of finance to build new communities of mixed ownership, together with urgent attention to the rehabilitation of existing council estates, the decentralisation of housing management and tenants' rights;

216

- giving serious priority to the environmental aspects of actions and policy changes at the earliest possible stage;
- creating one nation will also require positive action to tilt the balance more in favour of disadvantaged and depressed minority groups and to focus assistance on inner city areas.

This must be backed by firm action to strengthen the rule of law, with support for an effective police force commanding the confidence of the community in the fight against vandalism and crime.

Immediate help for those in need

The burden of the slump is being borne quite disproportionately by those now in long-term unemployment and by the poor, especially poor families with children. We propose to take the following measures straight away:

(a) help for families with children by increasing Child Benefit by £1.50 per week; increasing the Child Allowance in Supplementary Benefit by £1.50 per week; increasing the extra child allowance of one-parent families;
(b) help for pensioners. We will up-rate the pension twice a year because the present system gives rise to serious injustices. We will make sure pensioners can earn money without losing pension; we will increase the death grant to £250 for those of lesser means; standing charges for gas, electricity and basic telephone services will be abolished;
(c) help for the unemployed and sick by increasing Unemployment Benefit, Sickness Benefit and sick pay by 5 per cent; giving long-term Supplementary Benefit to the long-term unemployed; changing the rules so people are not forced to spend their redundancy money before they can get Supplementary Benefit;
(d) help for the disabled by spending an extra £200 million a year to make a start on many reforms which will help disabled people. These will include the extension of the invalid care allowance and full rights under the non-contributory invalidity pension to married women and the abolition of the age limit on the mobility allowance;
(e) finance. The total cost of these proposals is approximately £1,750m. This will be financed by: raising the upper limit at which National Insurance contributions are paid to £315 per week; reversing the recent increases in the high rate tax bands; and by the first stage of phasing out the married man's tax allowance. Therefore this programme does not require an increase in public borrowing.

Attacking poverty

The Alliance proposes to carry through a major overhaul of the welfare system. The original grand design of the liberal reformer, William Beveridge, has been mutilated over the years. Instead of a basic benefit, which was to secure for the old, the sick and the unemployed, a tolerable minimum standard of living as of right, we have a complex network of benefits dependent on 44 different means tests. Many people are dependent on benefits which are woefully inadequate. Millions are in poverty because they fail to apply for benefits to which they are entitled. Others find that they are worse off if they earn more.

Mass unemployment has made the scale of our problems greater than at any time since the war. We believe that we can offer a better, simpler structure of social security which would be the most important reform since Beveridge.

In the long term, we plan a complete integration of the tax and benefit systems. We aim in the next Parliament to bring together all the major benefits – Family Income Supplement, housing benefits, free school meals, Supplementary Benefit, and to replace them with a simpler, single benefit, the size of which for each family will depend basically on the number of children and their housing costs.

The levels of benefit we propose mean that:

- a working family with two children, currently earning £100 per week, will be around £24 per week better off;
- single parents with two children, currently helped by Supplementary Benefit, will be around £10 per week better off;
- single pensioners only getting the state pension will be £5.50 per week better off, and pensioner couples in the same position £10 per week better off;
- help will especially be concentrated on poor families with children since these are the real centres of hardship.

The benefit will be used to supplement people's income – whether from a job, unemployment or sickness benefit or a pension – and the amount people actually get will depend on their income. The benefit will be gradually withdrawn as incomes rise – but in a steady way so that as people earn more they do end up better off despite the reduction of benefit – and the overall effect will be a substantial boost to the incomes of those suffering most hardship.

The additional spending which the new welfare system will involve will be paid for from three sources. First by the continued phasing out of the married man's extra tax allowance (over at least three years). This is part of the removal of sex discrimination in taxation and will allow us to introduce the principle of separate taxation of earned income for all men and women. Second, by not fully indexing personal tax allowances, and third, by a relatively small increase in public borrowing – around £600–£700 million over the final programme.

This attack on poverty is basic to the Alliance strategy for creating in Britain a more united and caring community. The Conservatives speak only of an efficient and competitive society. We seek a civilised community using the resources provided by a revived economy to guarantee to all the security and self-respect that are every citizen's right.

Education, health and housing

Building a united, civilised community requires decent standards in education, health and housing for everyone. The Tories have imposed savage cuts in the social services and an Alliance Government would increase spending to restore and improve standards.

But it will not be enough just to spend money. The social services are too centralised, too bureaucratic. They are often insensitive and unaccountable. We will aim to make the social services more democratic, attuned to the needs of the individual. In this way, also, they will become more efficient.

Education and training

The principal need in education and training is to release the full potential of the individual. It is on the skills and energies of our people that our survival depends. An increasingly complex and technical society places great demands on the educational system and as falling school numbers continue to release resources these must not be withdrawn but invested to create better education opportunities.

The needs of the under-fives have to be met by both education and the social services.

- We will ensure that at least one year of pre-school educational experience is available for all children under five;
- We will act to raise standards in the primary and secondary schools in three ways:

  (i) by involving parents, teachers and local people more in the running of schools – these are the people who really care about standards;
  (ii) by ensuring that children study a broader range of subjects than they do now right through to eighteen, putting more stress on maths, science and technical subjects as well as practical skills to make them better equipped for life in today's world. It is especially important to ensure that these opportunities are equally available to girls as well as boys;
  (iii) by improving the in-service training of primary teachers and of others with specialist skills e.g. in maths.

- we will develop a broader bridge between school and work including more part-time schooling, and more work experience and better technical education for all pupils;
- we will undertake a major re-organisation of education and training for the 16–19s, so that school leavers are not faced with the dole but can opt for either education and training or employment or a combination of the two. Present arrangements are disjointed. Britain is well behind its competitors, resources have been devoted to ad hoc schemes not necessarily leading to employment, and many young people are unable to acquire skills and qualifications. So we propose:

  (i) a single Ministry of Education and Training combining the youth training functions of the MSC and the responsibilities of the Education Departments,
  (ii) full-time vocational courses offering sustained and properly planned periods of work experience, and the replacement of the time-served apprenticeship with training to set national standards,
  (iii) greater access to work experience for all 16–19 year old students and a right to further education and training for those of this age-group in work,
  (iv) expansion of the YTS to enable all 17 year olds not covered by the above to participate in a Government training scheme,
  (v) a new system of educational maintenance allowances to ensure that help is

available to those who stay on at school, those who opt for further education and those who opt for further training.

- we will increase access to Higher and Further Education. We shall also review the structure of higher education to see that people who are keen to work in industry are provided with the right range of skills at this level. This may mean for example students typically taking a wider range of courses before moving on to a job or more specialist education;
- we will actively support Adult and Continuing Education. Initial education alone cannot prepare people adequately for life. It must be made easier for them as part of their normal development to acquire new skills and to retrain as technology advances.
- we will ensure further public support for the voluntary and statutory sectors of the youth service.

Improvement in training facilities provided by the State will be accompanied by fiscal and other incentives to companies to increase their training efforts.

Health and social services

The Alliance is wholly committed to sustaining and strengthening the NHS. The Health Service must be funded to ensure that extra help goes to those most in need and that sufficient resources are available to meet the needs of our ageing population. The Alliance is committed to the steady increase in the real level of funding for the health and personal social services required to maintain standards in the face of demographic changes such as the increasing numbers of old people.

In addition, the Alliance will set up a special Fund with £500 million each year to pay for new schemes and ideas submitted by area health authorities, local authorities and other voluntary organisations to help the poorest areas and the neediest people. The funding of this scheme will count as part of the Alliance's immediate employment programme, and employment as well as other criteria will govern the choice of projects by the fund. The areas of greatest need in the health and social services are also high unemployment areas, so that such a special fund is an ideal use of available money.

Within the health programme, action will be taken to make better use of the health budget by:

- increased emphasis on primary care, health education and preventive medicine;
- emphasising community care, not as a cheap option but because of the improved quality of care this brings;
- re-allocating funds between areas and between users to increase equality of access to services for people in need whatever their means or wherever they happen to live. Particular attention will be given to the traditionally under-funded services such as those for the elderly, the chronically disabled and the mentally handicapped;
- encouraging local experiments and plans to improve services;
- reducing the drugs bill by extending the practice of generic prescribing, saving over one hundred million pounds.

The quality of care will also be improved by our policies in three related areas. First, the continuing commitment of all NHS staff is vital if the health service is to deliver the best care it can. This means NHS staff must be properly and fairly treated. We gave our commitment in Section II to determine pay in the public services by a new system based on fair comparison with other groups and a fair arbitration procedure which will also apply to NHS staff. Second, we will pay far more attention to prevention of accidents, illness and stress, making sure that health and safety legislation is properly applied and reducing environmental risks, for example by removing lead in petrol. Third, we will work for much closer co-operation between public and private services, to maximise the amount and coverage of health care available to the community as a whole. As with private schools, we have no wish to ban private health services, but nor will we subsidise them.

In the personal social services, the Alliance is determined to make the welfare state less bureaucratic and more responsive to people's needs, charting a more imaginative way forward by creating community-orientated services, incorporating a much greater degree of voluntary effort, and making much better use of the dedication and enthusiasm of professional staff, working with and through voluntary groups. We favour caring for people in the community for example, helping the elderly to live among family, friends and neighbours. We will support and sustain the family, in particular by helping those, especially women, who carry the burden of this care. We will encourage the development of supportive care in the community for children through a wide range of facilities including pre-school play schemes and nursery centres, and will support training for child-minders. Imaginative grants can produce value for money and high community involvement.

Housing

Housing standards have fallen under the Tory Government, and fewer houses have been built. Council tenants have been able to buy their own houses but face almost impossible financial difficulties if trying to move out of council estates into private housing.

Alliance housing policy has three basic aims: to restore the housing stock where this is needed, to provide wider genuine choice for consumers and to allocate available funds with greater fairness.

This will mean increased investment. Britain's building industry has been one of the worst hit by the recession, 1 in 8 of the unemployed are in construction. Higher investment here will not only help the tenant, the home buyer and the home-owner: it will help the whole country by creating jobs and boosting the economy.

Investment. There is an urgent need for increased investment in housing. The Housing Programme has suffered more than any other under this government, falling in cash terms from £4,514m in 1979–80 to £2,792m now which represents a fall of almost two-thirds in real terms. The all-party Environment Select Committee predicts a shortage of nearly half a million houses by 1985. And not enough is being spent even to maintain the standard of existing houses. More than 2 million houses are now 'unfit for habitation' or 'in serious disrepair', and the figure is rising.

We propose:

- a steady expansion of local Council and housing association building programmes, particularly for the single and the elderly, local council programmes to be in low density, human scale developments;

- vigorous programmes of repair, improvement and rehabilitation of existing Council estates;
- scrapping VAT on repairs;
- maximum use of improvement grants to the private sector with particular help for elderly owner-occupiers who face difficulties in maintaining their houses;
- attracting institutional investment in a new type of non-profit making rented housing to be managed by housing associations;
- encouraging partnership schemes between local councils and private builders to provide houses to rent; and low cost house ownership opportunities on the same estates.

The last two proposals will involve new non-public money in housing, and cut down the public expenditure costs of increasing housing investment.

Widening choice in housing. We propose:

- changing council allocation and transfer procedures to give tenants far more choice about where they live;
- encouraging shared purchase and other schemes which bring owner occupation within the reach of lower income families;
- providing new sources of rented housing to compete with local councils;
- breaking up the large monolithic council housing departments into Neighbourhood Housing Trusts run jointly by tenants and Council representatives;
- decentralising the management of the remaining Council housing to local offices responsible to local boards composed of Councillors and tenants;
- introducing a new Tenants Charter to define standards of repairs, maintenance and amenities to which tenants are entitled;
- giving tenants the right to call in an outside contractor from an approved list when they are dissatisfied with the Council's performance on repairs and sending the bill to the Council;
- establishing a single national scheme to help tenants wanting to move from one area to another.

The Right to Buy should be retained. After the introduction of proportional representation and hence greater accountability, Councils could be given more discretion to decide their housing policy. However, there should be a right of appeal in which Councils would justify to the Local Government Ombudsman any proposed restriction on the individual's right to buy, such as in areas of housing need or in certain rural areas where cheap rented housing is necessary to keep an adequate proportion of young people in the community.

Major extension of the capital home loan scheme. At present this scheme to help first time buyers is a paltry thing adding at most £110 capital for £1,000 saved by the buyer. The Alliance wants to give far more substantial aid to those determined to buy their own homes but without the means to do so under present arrangements.

We will extend the scheme so that anyone saving £1,000 over 2 years will receive an extra £1,000 at the end of that period. Rents paid over more than five years by Council tenants will count as equivalent to £1,000 savings and will also qualify for the additional £1,000. Ten years rent will entitle the tenant to £1,500 and 15 years to £2,000. We will seek to devise similar arrangements for private tenants.

Of course the present limits on the maximum value of properties which can qualify for such assistance will be maintained. The scheme is to help those who cannot otherwise become home-owners, not to benefit those with adequate resources. This will be strictly enforced.

This measure is imaginative and bold. It opens up new prospects and hope for many who are determined to save and work for a better way of life.

Greater fairness. Housing subsidies must be distributed more according to need. Council tenants have been particularly hard hit by the government's policy of deliberately forcing up rents far faster than the rate of inflation. Central government subsidies to local authority housing fell from £1,274m in 1980/81 to £370m in 1983/84 with the result that in most parts of the country, housing accounts are now moving into surplus. The Alliance says this process must stop. Council rents should be fixed so that housing accounts balance. Any surplus should be reinvested in improved management and maintenance, and not used to subsidise the general rates.

For owner-occupiers, the Alliance's long-term policy is to reform mortgage tax relief so that it relates to individual income rather than the size of the loan. In the meantime, tax relief will be limited to the standard rate of income tax. The Alliance also intends to encourage 'low start' mortgages and other schemes to bring home-ownership within the reach of more people.

The environment

There can be no healthy economy without a healthy environment. For far too long we have been wasting irreplaceable resources and amenities, both natural and manmade on which our community's prosperity and well-being depend. In all public decision-making the environmental aspects of changes should be assessed and taken into account from the beginning.

Pollution

We endorse the 'Polluter Pays' principle – that those responsible for pollution should pay for the resultant environmental damage. Existing pollution control legislation must be enforced and extended as recommended by the Royal Commission on Environmental Pollution.

Limiting waste

We will encourage the manufacture of products to last longer than at present and the manufacture of those goods which cannot be re-used from materials which can be re-cycled. We will provide financial incentives for authorities with responsibility for waste disposal to construct new plants to re-cycle waste material.

Transport

Without an effective public transport system the environment will suffer serious damage and energy resources will be wasted. We believe that new investment should be linked with modernised operating practices to ensure a future for our railways, and we therefore reject the negative philosophy of the Serpell Report. Careful planning and co-ordination is required to meet the different public transport needs of both the cities and the countryside.

Land use

We need a fundamental change in the way in which we plan our cities, towns and villages to develop greater participation by those directly affected, to protect, create and develop living communities.

Farming and conservation

We will give increased responsibility to local bodies representative of farming and environmental interests which would be based on the present Farming and Wildlife Advisory Groups, in the award of agricultural grants and subsidies, and which would seek to reconcile different interests in the use of land.

Animal welfare

Cruelty to animals and unnecessary suffering by animals demean our society and the Alliance would, as a matter of priority, establish an advisory Standing Commission on Animal Welfare. This would keep under constant and rigorous examination all issues of animal welfare including experimentation on live animals, the treatment of farm animals, the transportation of animals and the regulations covering the use of animals for entertainment. A caring community must care for animals as well as for human beings.

Transforming the political system

Electoral reform

The introduction of Proportional Representation is the linchpin of our entire programme of radical reform. Alone of the political parties the Liberal Party and the SDP recognise that our economic crisis is rooted in our political system. As class based parties, Labour and Conservative represent and intensify our divisions. The 'first-past-the-post' voting system ensures the under-representation of all those who reject class as the basis of politics. Electoral reform is thus a pre-condition of healing Britain's divisions and creating a sense of community. It is also a change we must make if we are, in the full sense of the word, to be a democracy.

The national interest demands electoral reform. The Alliance will not hesitate to use its strength in the next Parliament to ensure the introduction of a system which will strengthen the power of the voters.

A system based on proportional representation will provide a stable political framework in two ways. First, in order to form a government, political parties combining together will need to command the support of about half the voters. The policies such a government will pursue can only be less dogmatic and extreme than those likely to be followed under our present system where governments can be elected with the support of no more than one quarter of the electorate. Secondly, the political parties will have to aim much more for the centre ground and will be much more reluctant to adopt the divisive policies we see at present.

Specifically we propose to:

- replace the existing electoral system with a system of Community Proportional Representation. It will be based on multi-member constituencies which correspond to natural communities. It will use a system of preferential voting under which people list candidates in the order of their choice. The outcome will be that the share of seats gained by the parties in Parliament will reflect their support among the voters.

Thus natural communities like cities (e.g. Hull, Plymouth, Leeds, Edinburgh), and counties (e.g. Somerset, Northumberland) will be single multi-member constituencies of different size, represented by different numbers of MPs. Preferential voting by single transferable vote (STV) will enable the voter to distinguish between candidates of a particular party and thus to affect the character of that Party in Parliament. A single Party will not be able to gain a parliamentary majority unless it secures nearly 50 per cent of the votes. There will be a spread of representation in every part of the country and we will see the end of the increasing political polarisation between North and South.

Electoral reform is no academic matter. While this is our preferred system it is not the only acceptable system of fairer voting. It is necessary to strengthen and restore faith in our democratic process, under which the relationship between seats and votes is becoming entirely arbitrary. A switch to proportional representation will transform the character of our politics, producing a more constructive political dialogue, and it will change the nature of the policies pursued by successive governments. As the fundamental reform required for continuity of policy – crucial if we are gradually and steadily to overcome our basic economic problems – it is no less than the precondition for economic recovery and future prosperity.

Decentralising Government

In addition to electoral reform, the Alliance is committed to two further constitutional reforms: decentralisation to make government more accountable to the electorate, and basic legislation to protect fundamental human rights and freedoms.

Our system of government is inefficient because it is over-centralised. Departments, Ministers and Parliament are hopelessly overloaded and Parliament cannot adequately control the executive; there is great reliance on non-elected quangos, particularly at regional level – such as Regional Health Authorities, and Regional Water Authorities which together with the regional 'outposts' of central government departments now constitute an undemocratic regional tier of government; local government is too dependent on and dominated by central government – which has eroded not only its independence but also its sense of responsibility – and the Tories have made the spending of individual local authorities subject to central control. The overall result is lack of efficiency and lack of accountability, and the concentration of political power in London leads to a concentration of economic power there too, accentuating the trend to two nations – a relatively prosperous South, and a relatively deprived North. We need to disperse power in order to help spread prosperity.

In the light of these deficiencies in the structure of government, we propose:

- to transfer substantial powers and responsibilities, currently exercised by the centre, to the nations and regions of Britain. The demand for devolution is clearly stronger in Scotland than in Wales or in some of the English regions, and we do not believe that devolution should be imposed on nations or regions which do not wish it. But there is a strong practical case, especially in terms of regional development, for relevant public expenditure to be allocated between and within regions in line with regional needs. We therefore propose:

    (a) immediate action to set up a Scottish Parliament with a full range of devolved powers, including powers to assist economic development and powers to tax, but not to run a Budget deficit;

    (b) to enact Scottish devolution in an Act which would also provide the framework for decentralisation to assemblies in Wales and the English regions as demand develops;

    (c) in the English regions to set up economic development agencies with substantial powers. To make these development agencies, and other nominated regional authorities which already exist, accountable in the first instance to regional committees of a reformed Second Chamber.

    (d) in Northern Ireland to encourage a non-sectarian approach to the problems of the province. We support the present Northern Ireland Assembly and will work towards a return to devolved power in place of direct rule from Westminster. We favour the early establishment of an Anglo-Irish consultative body at parliamentary level representing all parties at Westminster, Belfast and Dublin.

- to revitalise local government, restoring its independence and its accountability to the local electorate by:

    (a) introducing proportional representation at local level to make local government representative of its electorate and responsive to currents of opinion in that electorate;

    (b) simplifying the structure of local government to make it more effective by abolishing one of the existing tiers of local government. This will be done by stages against the background of our proposals for the development of regional government. It would inevitably involve the eventual abolition of the Metropolitan Counties, and the GLC (but not ILEA) and would also allow for the restoration of powers to some of the former County boroughs;

    (c) paving the way to the abolition of domestic rates and reducing local government's dependence on central grant, by introducing a local income tax. This change in the structure of local government finance will increase the independence of local government;

(d) extending the right of local communities to have statutory Parish or Neighbourhood Councils.

- to increase the accountability of Government to Parliament by reforming the operation and procedures of the House of Commons, to make its control of the executive more effective and to reform the powers and composition of the House of Lords, which must include a significant elected element representative of the nations and regions of Britain.

This set of proposals amounts to an extensive decentralisation of power from the centre, both to the nations and regions and to local government, and to considerable strengthening of democratic accountability at all levels of government.

Promoting individual rights

Resting on our laurels as the oldest modern democracy, we have become smug and complacent with the result that the rights we have taken for granted are being increasingly threatened. The third major area of constitutional reform therefore includes a series of measures to buttress our now shaky structure of liberties and rights and guarantee them by law. Changes in the power of the State, the media and in technology require specific protection of rights by statute. Such action will be coupled with determined action to strengthen the rule of law, giving full backing to the police subject to a proper system of accountability.

Individual Rights

The following are our proposals:

- a new Bill of Rights. It is shaming that our citizens have so frequently had to go to the European Court to have basic rights enforced. We shall incorporate the rights and freedoms of the European Convention of Human Rights into English, Scottish and Northern Ireland law by means of a new Bill of Rights Act which will be paramount over all inconsistent statutes and common law.

- we shall create a UK Commission of Human Rights to help people bring proceedings under the Bill of Rights to secure compliance with its provisions. This will incorporate the existing Equal Opportunities Commission and Commission for Racial Equality and will deal with discrimination on grounds of sex or race;

- the Alliance believes that sex and race equality are fundamental to our society. They will be promoted by positive action in relation e.g. to public employment policies which will be monitored in central and local government. Anti-discrimination legislation will be actively enforced;

- nationality and immigration: we believe the British Nationality Act 1981 to be offensive and discriminatory. We will revert to the simple concept that all those born in Britain are entitled to British Citizenship. There should be objective tests for citizenship and a right of appeal against refusal. Immigration controls will be applied without discrimination on grounds of sex, race or colour, and rules on dependents will be revised to promote family unity;

- we shall legislate for public access to official information, including the right of individuals to have access to information on themselves, subject to a Code of Practice defining exceptions and limitations;

- we support state financing of political parties. Trade Union members must have the right to 'contract-in' on the political levy and to determine their union's party political affiliation by secret postal ballot. There should be equivalent action to regulate company donations to political parties.

The Rule of Law

We are dedicated to extending individual rights but rights also carry responsibilities. We need to restore our traditions of responsible citizenship. There is great concern about rising crime. The number of serious cases has this year risen above 3 million for the first time in our history. The rise in the crime rate has accompanied the rise in unemployment. As the Conservative Government has put more and more men and women out of work, the family has been undermined, whole communities have lost their self-respect and good and neighbourly values have been forgotten. Many citizens now live in terror of the vandal, the mugger and the thief. Old people in particular are cruelly exposed to violence and abuse. The causes of crime are complex but we all have an obligation to resist the dangerous slide to lawlessness that has brought fear to our streets. The Alliance believes that it is vital to support and reinforce the police in their efforts to prevent and detect crime.

But policing can only be effective if it is responsive to and carries the support and confidence of local communities. We therefore propose:

- to support community policing with local policemen on the beat and living locally, small local police stations and reforms to police recruitment and training policy;
- support for local liaison committees which will involve people in helping the police to do their job;
- to enhance confidence in the police by introducing a conciliation service and an independent system for the investigation of serious complaints. We will establish a new police disciplinary offence of racially prejudiced behaviour and introduce lay visitors into police stations;
- to improve police accountability outside London by strengthening the community element on Police Authorities and encouraging community representation at the level of police divisions. For the Metropolitan Police, we shall as an interim measure establish a Select Committee drawn from London MPs.

Action to protect and promote individual and minority rights is an essential part of the Alliance's determination to heal division and enhance Britain's awareness of being one, inter dependent Community. Prejudice against racial and other minorities, discrimination against them and against women in job opportunities and in pay, all threaten the creation of this community. The Alliance is born of Liberal and Social Democratic values. In government it would be true to those values.

The Alliance recognises that the expansion of television technology through cable, video cassettes and satellite offers great opportunities in the creation of a better informed society and provides new opportunities for the Arts.

However these technologies also carry dangers to our society if they become vehicles for pornography and violence. This must not be allowed to happen, and the State must have particular regard to its responsibilities for the young.

Peace and security

Alliance policies in the field of foreign policy and defence are uncompromisingly internationalist. They are based on the view that Britain must play a full and leading role in the community of nations.

The Alliance holds that Britain's security as a country depends on the cohesion and effectiveness of the NATO alliance; that our political and economic interests require us to play our full part in the European Community, and that the poorest countries of the world can best be helped if the industrial nations pursue more expansionary economic policies in concert.

The Alliance's commitment to internationalism and its recognition of the inter dependence of nations clearly differentiates its approach from that of both the Labour and Tory parties. In a dangerous and complex world there is a temptation to withdraw into narrow and nationalistic attitudes. This is what both the class-based parties have done.

Labour is now pledged to policies which would isolate and weaken Britain – import controls, unilateral withdrawal from the EEC, one-sided disarmament. If these policies were enacted our Allies would lose all confidence in us, the Western Alliance would be badly undermined and as an economically debilitated and less influential country we would be quite unable to launch the international initiatives now desperately needed to help the poor of the world through concerted economic expansion and aid.

The Conservative Party specifically refuses to recognise the true inter-dependence of nations in its approach to both development and peace. It has failed utterly to respond to the challenge of the Brandt Report. Their refusal to countenance the inclusion of Britain's nuclear systems in any disarmament negotiations displays their lack of real commitment to multilateral disarmament; their determination to spend vast sums on Trident betrays their lack of confidence in any commitment to our alliance with the United States.

The Alliance sees little prospect for progress towards a more peaceful, prosperous and just world unless inter-dependence is accepted as the basis of international relations. This leads us to radically different policies from those advocated by the class based parties in three key areas:

Defence and disarmament

The Alliance believes Britain must be properly defended and our forces equipped for that task. We pay tribute to the courage and determination of our armed forces in the Falklands and in Northern Ireland. Our defence policies reject both Labour's one-sided disarmament and the Conservatives' escalation of the nuclear arms race. The main points of our policies for defence are:

- to adhere firmly to the principles of collective security. Britain cannot defend herself alone, and the NATO Alliance has made a decisive contribution to the maintenance of peace in Europe. Participation in NATO must be the cornerstone of the country's defence policy, and in order to consolidate the NATO Alliance we reaffirm our commitment to the NATO target for strengthening conventional forces in Europe;

- we accept the need for a nuclear component in the NATO deterrent whilst the USSR has nuclear weapons. NATO should however move away from its present excessive dependence on the early use of nuclear weapons. We therefore support raising the nuclear threshold in Europe and moving towards a 'no first use' policy by strengthening NATO's conventional forces and establishing a 150km Battlefield Nuclear Weapon-Free Zone at the central front. An Alliance Government would regard such a zone as the basis for negotiations with the Russians on a wider verifiable nuclear weapon-free zone;

- we strongly back multilateral disarmament and arms control efforts, in particular the Geneva negotiations for reduction in both sides' strategic (START) and the intermediate range (INF) nuclear weapons. More specifically, the START and INF talks should be merged or at least closely linked so that trade-offs can be made across weapons systems: Trident should be cancelled to avoid a new and provocative contribution to the nuclear arms race and demonstrate our commitment to arms control; Polaris should be included in the merged START and INF talks as a further contribution to the prospects of multilateral disarmament.

- the Geneva negotiations should be pursued to a successful conclusion. Before deciding whether or not to oppose the deployment of Cruise missiles in Britain, an Alliance Government will take account in particular, of the negotiating position of the Soviet Union and the United States; the attitude of our NATO partners in Europe; and whether arrangements for a double safety-catch system have been agreed;

- if successful progress in nuclear weapons reductions has not been achieved in the negotiations at Geneva, an Alliance Government will explore the opportunities for a verifiable, mutual freeze on the production and deployment of all nuclear weapons;

- we strongly support an agreement between East and West to ban the production and possession of chemical weapons and we would work for mutual and balanced force reductions in Europe and a comprehensive test ban to strengthen the Non-Proliferation Treaty;

- on international security, we support the recommendations in the Palme Report, and wish to see the UN's peace-keeping role strengthened, and increased powers given to the UN Secretary-General. An Alliance Government will press for a European initiative to register the sale of arms to Third World countries, and will act to end sales of British arms to regimes which persistently and brutally violate human rights.

This set of policies – stressing disarmament on both sides, a nuclear weapon-free zone in Europe, strengthened conventional forces for NATO and reduced NATO reliance on nuclear weapons, the cancellation of Trident and the inclusion of Polaris in disarmament negotiations – will reduce the danger of nuclear conflict and increase Britain's security.

Membership of the European Community

The Alliance is wholly committed to continuing UK membership of the European Community. Membership has increased our political influence with our European neighbours and in the world beyond. Continued membership is also unequivocally to our economic advantage. The community is by far Britain's largest trading partner, with over half of our exports going to community countries or countries with whom they have Free Trade Agreements. It also provides an influential framework for the discussion of the Irish problem between two member states, ourselves and the Irish Republic. Withdrawal, to which Labour is committed, would have a highly destructive effect on exports and hence on jobs. We would also lose a great deal of foreign, particularly US investment which has come here because we are in the Community.

The Alliance advocates further development of the Community and new common policies. At the same time however, there is a great deal wrong with the structure of existing policies, and we will take the lead in putting things right.

First, we support political development of the Community through adoption of the common electoral system for the 1984 direct elections to the European Parliament; more majority voting in the Council of Ministers; and greater involvement of the European Parliament in the appointment of the Commission.

Second, to correct the imbalance in existing activities, an Alliance Government will press for expansion of Community activity on regional and social policies, industrial innovation, energy conservation and the development of renewable sources of energy. To develop new policies we accept the need for an increase in community revenues on a more diversified and fairer basis. We will work for some reduction in the agriculture budget first by holding back intervention prices for agricultural products in surplus and if need be by setting a limit on the quantities of production eligible for intervention support.

These are important policies which will help to solve the British budget problem, help solve some of Europe's most chronic difficulties such as the imbalance of wealth and development between regions, and switch the balance of Community activities more directly in line with Britain's needs.

Third, we will take the lead in advocating the development of new policies where Europe has everything to gain from standing together. We must increasingly stand together in trade talks, following the pattern of the recent Multi-Fibre Arrangement talks and GATT talks in which the Commission spoke for the Community. We must increase political co-operation to reach consensus on foreign policy questions and be prepared to move into new areas such as a common procurement policy for defence. We need to develop a Community industrial policy to spend money on easing the pain for areas dependent on declining industries and also in encouraging new, high technology investment. And we need to develop and back initiatives at European level through the Social Fund aimed at reducing youth unemployment from 25 per cent to the level of general unemployment. There is great scope for launching joint economic policies and an Alliance government will take the lead in advocating them. Fourth, an Alliance government will make Britain a full member of the European Monetary System in order to iron out the wild fluctuations in the exchange rate which have done such damage to exports and jobs over the last few years.

Helping the world's poor

Conservative policy towards the poor countries of the world has been mean and short sighted, reducing the level of British aid and effectively excluding Third World students from our higher education system. The widespread pursuit of restrictive policies has plunged the world into the worst slump for 50 years, and the poor countries have suffered most. On the other hand, Labour's restrictive trade policies would be extremely damaging to the developing world. There is no hope for them or for the rest of the world if protection leads on to waves of retaliation and countries destroy each other's markets, sending the world economy spiralling further downwards.

We want to do two things. First, to advocate joint policies, to be developed and implemented by the major industrial countries, to take the world out of slump. We advocate co-ordinated action:

(a) joint expansionary measures following the example of the 1978 Bonn Economic Summit, so that the main countries expand together, so managing to avoid balance of payments difficulties and the inflationary consequences of collapsing currencies;

(b) monetary stability. Co-operation between the three main currency blocs – the US, Japan and the EMS (including Britain) – to keep their currencies stable;

(c) Additional finance for the developing world so that general expansion is not frustrated by credit constraints – increased resources for the IMF and World Bank, and fresh issues of international money (Special Drawing Rights).

International policies of this kind could chart the way out of recession. In so doing they would help developing countries – and, indeed, the developed countries alike – than any foreseeable increases in levels of aid. However, Britain has a significant individual contribution to make to Third World development through its own aid programme. An Alliance government would:

- increase the proportion of GNP spent on aid over 5 years to 0.7 per cent;
- concentrate aid on the poorest countries and on the poorest people in those countries;
- increase financial support for the work of voluntary agencies, stressing urgent projects;
- promote more generous funding for overseas students, especially those from the poorest countries and the poorest students from other countries;

- support the principles of the Brandt Report, and in particular the proposals for increased credit through the international institutions.

The programme of reform set out in this document rivals in scope and imagination that of the liberal reforming government of 1906–11 or the Attlee administration of 1945–51. It is a formidable challenge to the nation to opt for a decisive change of course to put things right. There is no chance that either of the two old class parties will carry out any of the fundamental reforms – to the system of pay determination, or the structure of industrial relations, or the welfare state or the political system – advocated in this document, all of which are now desperately needed. The Alliance alone provides the opportunity to decide against the failures of the past and offers new hope for the renewal and rejuvenation of our country.

The SDP/Liberal Alliance Programme for Government

Britain United

—— The time has come ——

SDP/LIBERAL ALLIANCE GENERAL ELECTION MANIFESTO 1987

Britain united: the time has come

Date of Election	Thursday 11 June
Party Leader	SDP – David Owen, Liberal Party – David Steel
Candidates	SDP 306, Liberal Party 327
MPs	SDP 5, Liberal Party 17
Votes	SDP 3,168,183 – Liberal Party 4,173,450
% of vote	SDP 9.7%, Liberal Party 12.8%

Foreword: Britain united

The Alliance's vision is of a Britain united, a Britain confident, compassionate and competitive. We know that it is possible to unite our country. We know the British people want greater unity. But we also know the task of drawing Britain together again can only be achieved through political, economic and social reform on a scale not contemplated in our country for over forty years.

At the last election, about a third of the nation's voters didn't even both to turn out.

It's hard to think of a more damning condemnation of politics in this country.

But it's not difficult to understand why so many people feel cynical and uninterested.

Since the last war the Tories and Labour have each had six turns at Government.

Many honourable men and women on both sides have worked hard for the nation but the system has defeated all but a few.

Rigid dogmas, the overriding need for party unity, and indiscriminate three-line whips have all helped to create a climate of conflict and rancour.

Listen to Parliamentary question time and count how many times the Speaker has to call for order. We've had forty years of yah-boo politics and where has it got us?

We live in a country that is patently unfair to many of its citizens. While politicians brandish statistics at each other on TV chat shows, we can all see with our own eyes what is happening to our schools, hospitals and inner cities.

We know there is more crime because our own homes have been broken into, our own neighbours have been mugged, our own children have been offered drugs.

We know that unemployment remains a huge problem because few families haven't been touched by its shadow.

For many, the situation seems hopeless. Unable to contemplate five more years of uncaring government under Mrs Thatcher, they still do not trust the Labour Party.

Mr Kinnock tries hard but for how long can he keep the lid on the extremists of the Left?

They already dominate some of the Town Halls. When the election is over, will they emerge again to claim the rewards of their silence?

Many of these people feel that the Alliance is the answer – but they ask what chance does it have of changing things? The answer is – every chance.

At the last election, the Alliance won nearly 8 million votes, little less than the Labour Party.

If just 72 more people in every 700 vote for the Alliance this time, we will be the single largest party in Parliament. If just 5 more people in every 700 support us, we would have over 70 seats and almost certainly hold the balance of power.

Think of it. Issues would be judged on their merits. We would curb the Tories' divisive policies and stop the destructive antics of the Labour Left.

Politicians would be forced to listen to each other and work together. The two-party, two-class pantomime would finally be over.

It's not an impossible dream. It's closer now than at any time in our history. All you have to do to make it happen is to vote Alliance on June 17th.

David Steel
David Owen

Introduction

There has never been an election like this in modern times. All the evidence and all the commentators confirm that it is a three-way contest which the Alliance enters from a position of unprecedented strength and promise. The Official Opposition is falling apart and is now quite unable to present itself as a realistic alternative to a Government which presides over the worst unemployment ever known in the lifetime of those who are of working age. The two-party system has broken down because it is rooted in outdated battles of class and ideology, and provides no outlet for the vast numbers of people who want individual freedom to go hand-in-hand with social justice, who want the state to back industry without trying to take it over, who want power to be given back to communities instead of concentrated in Whitehall and who want a nation which is soundly defended but takes the lead in the quest for negotiated disarmament and a fairer world.

In any Government the policies which have been set out in the election programme can only tell part of the story of how they will behave in office. It is at least as important to know and trust the values and principles for which they stand, and which will guide their response to the new events and new problems with which governments have to deal. These values, we believe, are embodied in this Joint Programme. They are our guide-book for government:

- Governments are there to protect and preserve the freedom of citizens, to whom they should be accountable and open;
- Freedom must extend to all the people, and Governments must therefore widen the opportunities of those whose liberty is limited by lack of employment, education, health care, housing or help in dealing with disability;
- Governments should not try to do what can be better done by individuals, by communities, by voluntary organisations or by private enterprise, but should set about enabling people to help themselves; however governments should be ready to enter into partnership with these organisations to tackle the problems that neither it nor they can solve alone;
- Decisions of Government should be taken democratically at the most local level compatible with effective action;
- Governments should learn to listen to the people to whom they are accountable;
- Governments should exercise the creative leadership to enable society as a whole to match its needs and resources with the work to be done – of which there is an abundance in Britain today;
- Government must challenge and curb all those who threaten individual freedom by the abuse of monopoly power, by the denial of rights or by crime and violence;
- It is the business of Government to act fairly in the pursuit of a united society, not to identify itself solely with any one section of society or region of the country;
- Government should take positive steps to ensure equal opportunities for women – who make up 52% of the population – and for minority groups such as the ethnic communities.
- Government must enable society to take the longer view, setting the right balance between present consumption and future investment and ensuring that economic development is sustainable and environmentally responsible.

These values must also guide foreign policy, where the defence of the nation goes hand-in-hand with the promotion of peace and fairness in a world marked by severe inequality and injustice.

We believe that Government at all levels can be more open, more accountable, more fair and more in tune with the wishes of the people of this country if it is allowed to break free of the two-party system and the old class conflict which that system feeds. Our country and its people deserve better, and here is how we believe it can be done.

Better government

Most of the problems facing our country cannot be solved unless we get better government. That means government which can carry the people with it in its major policies, and it means government which the citizens can call to account. Our system is currently failing in both respects, and it is getting worse. Under our proposals no government will be able to ride roughshod over the rights of its citizens.

First, we insist that the voting system should be reformed so that no minority which is what Mrs Thatcher's Party was at the last election – is given an inflated

Parliamentary majority. Fewer people voted Conservative at the last election than the one before, yet the system gave the absolute power of a massively increased majority to Mrs Thatcher, and ensured that the House of Commons could be little more than a talking shop. No wonder Labour leaders join with the present Conservative leadership in wanting to keep the old system – they can see that it offers the only hope of inflicting on the nation policies which the majority of the people reject. The Alliance will introduce community proportional representation, using the well-tried single transferable vote system with constituencies based on local communities. This system also gives the voters the chance to show which candidates they prefer and would increase the opportunities for women to be elected to Parliament, and make the election of representatives of ethnic minorities more likely. We will reform the voting system for local government on a similar basis, which is the real answer to the abuse of power by the Town Hall extremists. Fairly elected local councils can and should be entrusted with important responsibilities because they are not run as one party states. We will end the scandal whereby England, Scotland and Wales are denied fair representation in the European Parliament; we will introduce a new Great Reform Charter covering a range of specific legislation, all aimed at strengthening our democracy both locally and nationally.

We will open the doors of government so that incompetence and deceit cannot be hidden behind them. We will repeal Section Two of the Official Secrets Act and introduce a Freedom of Information Act so that the public have access to government information, to give people access to their personal files, including medical files, held about them by public bodies and to build on the foundation laid by the Access to Personal Files Act, which was introduced as a private members bill by a Liberal MP. We hope to strengthen data protection laws. In areas of government where secrecy is needed, we will introduce new safeguards including a committee of Privy Counsellors to oversee the security services.

We do not believe that Whitehall knows best. British government has never been more centralised than it has become under Mrs Thatcher. In education, health and every aspect of local government, power has been taken over by Ministers. As a result of what the Conservatives have done, an extremist government would have far more opportunities than ever before to control people's lives. This centralisation is inefficient as well as dangerous. How on earth can the man or woman in Whitehall know the needs, the problems and the potential of every community from Shetland to the Scillies? The Alliance will reverse this trend.

We will introduce a code for the public service and reassert the safeguards of ministerial responsibility and civil service impartiality which have been severely eroded under Mrs Thatcher's Government, as the handling of the Westland affair showed.

We will devolve power to the nations and regions of Britain. We aim to establish an elected Scottish Parliament, Welsh Senedd and elected regional assemblies throughout England. Public support is essential for progress to be made within the framework of an initial Devolution Act. The devolved structure will require a step-by-step process starting with establishing a Scottish Legislative Assembly with wide powers and self-government in her domestic affairs. This would be created within an overall framework in a devolution bill which sets out the objectives and principles for devolution of powers within the UK. Wales already has a well established, but unaccountable, layer of devolved administration; we therefore aim to create a Welsh Senedd and would publish an early Green Paper on its powers and responsibilities. The abolition of the Greater London Council and the six metropolitan county councils has created a vacuum. London is now the only major capital city in the democratic world without a democratically elected local authority. Greater London is of sufficient size and importance to be a region in itself and there is already widespread support for such a regional assembly, which should be established as soon as possible. We shall publish an early Green Paper with proposals for an elected Greater London regional assembly and setting out the proposals, as the need and demand is established, for the creation of democratically elected regional governments in England.

Local government needs a fair system of local finance which the rates no longer provide. The Government's alternative of a poll tax is unacceptable because it is grossly unfair: it does not relate taxation to the ability to pay. We are committed to the planned introduction of a local income tax as the main source of local government revenue in place of domestic rates. We believe that business rates should be related to ability to pay and we will consult with industry and commerce as to how this can be achieved.

Parliament itself needs a shake-up. A fair electoral system will have that effect but even under the present system many existing Parliamentary practices will not survive for long after this election, because three major political forces will be strongly represented. It will no longer be possible for two political parties to run the House of Commons to suit their own convenience. We intend to put the control of parliamentary time in the hands of an All-Party Business Committee and to make much more use of select committees: we want widely-supported private members bills to have sufficient time to be debated and decided upon. In recent years the House of Lords has proved the value of a second chamber by its careful scrutiny of bills which got little attention in the Commons and by its willingness to defeat the government on issues of national concern. But there can be no justification for basing the membership of the second chamber so largely on heredity and on the whim of Prime Ministers. The Alliance will work towards a reform of the second chamber linked with our devolution proposals so that it will include members elected from the regions and nations of Britain and will phase out the rights of hereditary peers to vote in the Lords.

We will greatly strengthen the rights of the individual. British Governments have sought to lull citizens into a false sense of security by claiming that our rights are protected by an unwritten constitution. Hundreds of British people find out every year that these protections are inadequate and they have to go to Strasbourg to seek protection from the European Convention on Human Rights. We will enact the European Convention into British law, so that the citizen can secure redress in the British courts.

We will establish a Human Rights Commission, which will take over the work of the Equal Opportunities and Racial Equality Commissions, and counter all discrimination on grounds of race, sex, creed, class, disability or sexual orientation. The Commission would be able to initiate action in the courts.

We will open up opportunities for women at work and in public life. Today, fewer than one in five of Government appointees on public bodies are women. We will secure equal representation of women on all appointed public bodies within a decade; our social and tax policies aim to give women equal rights and freedom to choose their way of life.

The Alliance accepts the need for immigration controls and for clear legal definition of British nationality, but also accepts that the law in this area is fundamental to individual rights and should be fair to everyone regardless of race and regardless of whether they are men or women. There should be effective rights of appeal against refusal of citizenship and referral to an independent body in cases of deportation, and immigration procedures should be revised so as to promote family unity without significantly affecting immigration totals, which remain lower than rates of emigration from Britain.

We will combat discrimination against black people in housing and employment and take positive steps through such measures as contract compliance to secure equal opportunities for racial minorities, and we will devote more police resources to dealing with racial harassment.

We will combat prejudice against and misunderstanding of people with disabilities, to improve their quality of life, and to extend educational opportunities for disabled young people.

We will restore the principle that anyone born in Britain is entitled to British citizenship. We are adamantly opposed to discrimination and we will repeal the sexist and racist aspects of the British Nationality Act 1981.

The Great Reform Charter

Democracy in Britain did not just happen. It was the product of reform – reform against vested interests of both left and right. In 1832 Britain took the first step with the Great Reform Act. Further instalments of reform followed in 1867, 1884, 1918 and 1928 before all men and women had gained the vote. Yet, since then, our democracy has stood still despite the tremendous changes in the economy and society. The Alliance believes that it is time for a new era of reform. For, without getting the structure of our democracy right, we will get nothing right.

The Alliance, if empowered by the British people, will:

- Replace the undemocratic 'first past the post' electoral system with proportional representation based on a single transferable vote for all Westminster and local authority elections;
- Introduce PR for elections to the European Parliament. We support a common system for all member states;
- Repeal the Official Secrets Act and replace it with Freedom of Information legislation providing for a public right of access to all official information, subject to limited and specific exemptions to protect national security and proper law enforcement and privacy;
- Reform the law of confidentiality to ensure that freedom of expression on matters of public interest is not unnecessarily restricted;
- Incorporate the European Convention on Human Rights and its protocols into British law in a Bill of Rights;
- Remove the right of the Prime Minister to determine the date of general elections and replace it with fixed-term parliaments;
- Devolve power to a legislative Scottish Assembly, establish a Welsh Senedd and decentralise decision-making to the English regions in accordance with the wishes of their electors;

- Extensively reform Whitehall procedures in order to make the governmental system more responsive to the wishes and needs of the people;
- Reform the House of Commons procedures;
- Reform the House of Lords.

Opportunities for women

The Alliance is committed to the principle that women should have equal opportunities and in government we will take positive steps to ensure this ideal becomes a reality.

- We will open up opportunities for women in public life by securing equal representation of women on all appointed bodies within a decade.
- We will strengthen the rights of women at work through equal pay for work of equal value, equal treatment, ensuring that all public authorities and private contractors are equal opportunity employers. We will restore the maternity grant and improve benefits for families.
- We will offer a tax allowance to help with the costs of childcare and remove the tax on the use of workplace nurseries.
- We will ensure that girls and women have equal opportunities in education and training.
- We will promote measures that give employees with family responsibilities rights to parental and family leave.

The Alliance wants to see more women in Westminster. Changing the electoral system to a form of proportional representation will increase the opportunities for women to be elected to Parliament.

Northern Ireland

We intend to secure progress towards a peaceful and secure life for the people of Northern Ireland. That depends on the acceptance of three fundamental principles:

- Rejection of violence;
- Recognition that both Unionist and Nationalist traditions have their legitimate place;
- Acceptance that Northern Ireland should not cease to be a part of the UK unless a majority of the people of Northern Ireland so wish.

The government of Northern Ireland must be based on a partnership between the two traditions. The Alliance welcomes the Anglo-Irish agreement as a genuine attempt to achieve the objectives we set out. We wish to see a UK/Irish Parliamentary Council, and a devolved assembly where responsibilities and power will be shared. We would improve arrangements for considering Northern Ireland legislation at Westminster.

Our commitment to incorporate the European Convention on Human Rights into UK law will strengthen individual rights in Northern Ireland and we would reform the Diplock courts so that three judges preside over non-jury trials; in this and other respects we believe that the passing of identical anti-terrorist measures in Northern

Ireland and the Republic can increase the authority those measures carry in a divided community. We also support the establishment of a joint security commission.

We would encourage the participation of people from the minority tradition in the RUC and believe that a totally independent police complaints procedure should be established. We would introduce the 110-day limit on the time in which a prisoner may be held in custody before appearing in court, as we propose for England and Wales.

We would encourage those who are working for reconciliation in Northern Ireland and who are seeking to eliminate sectarianism and discrimination in religious life, education, housing and politics.

We believe that the membership of the EEC offers not only practical help to Northern Ireland, but also prospects for the long-term development of a confederal relationship between UK and the Republic of Ireland which could offer a solution to a problem which has claimed over 2,500 lives in the last 18 years.

Fighting crime

Crime rates have soared in this Government's last eight years. Overall, crime is up by over 60%, burglaries have almost doubled, while robberies have increased two and a half times over. People, particularly elderly people, live in fear in their homes and in the streets and women feel increasingly unable to go out at night.

Detection rates have dropped from over two-fifths in 1979 to under a third in 1986. Increases in police numbers have been largely offset by special duties like policing strikes and demonstrations, and by a drop in the working week. There are few extra bobbies on the beat.

The Alliance would tackle both crime and the causes of crime. Some Labour-controlled boroughs refuse to co-operate with the police in combating crime. The Conservative Government refuses to recognise that homelessness, unemployment and aimless bed-and-breakfast regimes are breeding-grounds of delinquency. Both are wrong.

The police

The Alliance firmly supports the police in the battle against crime; that fight can only be effective if the police get the support of the whole community, through community policing and policemen on the beat. Many police forces are still under strength: yet more officers are needed to provide the kind of local policing which we believe is essential. An Alliance Government will finance a further 4,000 police officers over and above the present Government plans and 1,000 more civilians, so releasing police officers for patrol duties.

Proportional representation for local government would stop unrepresentative extremists from controlling police authorities. It would mean more sensible police authorities and make possible a democratically accountable police authority for London. We oppose the police monitoring units by which some Labour councils attempt to undermine the police. The Alliance fully accepts the need for chief officers to have full operational control of their force. The Alliance supports a fully independent system for investigating complaints against the police. We reject moves towards a national police force. We would appoint a Royal Commission to review the question of police accountability.

Upholding the law

We will create a new Ministry of Justice. Its responsibilities will include the strengthening of the rights of the citizen to legal aid and advice and improving court and tribunal procedures. We will establish a family court system and set up a new legal services council.

Sentencing Policy. Sentencing is often seen as arbitrary, with the same crime attracting widely divergent punishments. For the criminals, sentences become more of a lottery than a deterring force. We will strengthen the role of the Judicial Studies Board in setting guidelines for sentencing. This will mean that any judge stepping outside the Board's recommendations would be asked to explain the reason and any special circumstances. This would maintain a judge's flexibility, while keeping sentencing broadly consistent. It would also limit the ever-increasing upward trend in sentencing.

A Royal Commission on the Presentation of Violence in the Media. We will establish a Royal Commission to report within a year on the public presentation of violence on TV and the reporting of crime in newspapers, to make recommendations on the possible link between these and violent crime on the streets.

Crime Prevention Units. There would be a duty on all local authorities to establish Crime Prevention Units, and to work closely with the police to help in setting up Neighbourhood Watch schemes. They would advise on security in all new planning and building.

Insuring Against Crime. We aim to make insurance available to all council tenants, who are twice as likely to be burgled as home owners and far less likely to be insured.

Curbing the Sale of Offensive Weapons. We will curb the sale of knuckle dusters, battle knives, spiked shoe straps, cross-bows and catapults.

Lifeline

Too many elderly people suffer from isolation, fear and cold.

We intend to give them the safety, security and warmth they deserve. Britain has 6 million people aged 70 or over. For them our 'Lifeline' programme will:

- include free installation of a telephone;
- protect them against the criminal by free installation of secure locks;
- cut their heating bills by free home insulation;
- abolish standing charges on electricity, gas and telephones.

These 6 million people live in 4.5 million households and this will cost £180 million. 'Lifeline' will build on present schemes and will also be part of our long-term job guarantee.

Crime Crisis Areas

An Alliance Government will target 'Crime Crisis Areas', those with the highest rates of crime, for special anti-crime measures. Chief Constables, in consultation with Community/Police Liaison Committees and police authorities, would define these areas. They will have:

- More police on the streets;
- Local police stations re-opened. Police Posts should be established where no station is close by;
- Security grants to pay for entry phones and security locks;
- Projects to make crime danger spots safe and to provide effective street lighting and more caretakers on estates;
- New housing estates designed to minimise opportunities for crime, and hazardous public areas will be redesigned;
- A legal obligation imposed on British Telecom to keep all public telephones in constant repair. In London up to half our public telephones are broken at any one time – many of them the only lifeline in high crime areas.

Dealing with offenders

The prison scandal

The prisons are bursting at the seams, yet Home Office projections show numbers increasing until the end of the decade 1985–1995. Of the 13,000 increase, 5,000 people will be untried and unsentenced.

The Alliance believes drastic action is needed to reduce the prison population, while ensuring that those responsible for violent and serious crime are kept out of society for as long as the Courts think necessary. Imprisonment rarely rehabilitates the prisoner. Three-fifths of all men who receive a prison sentence re-offend within two years of being released.

The minimum standards for prisons proposed by NACRO, and accepted in principle by the then Home Secretary as long ago as 1981, should be adopted as a target to be achieved within two years. A limit of 110 days should be laid down as soon as possible for remand prisoners. If not prosecuted within that period, they would be released. This system operates successfully in Scotland. Probation authorities should be required to provide bail hostels adequate to accommodate their own needs. The Home Office should make a special 100% grant for the purpose.

The 'short, sharp, shock' has failed. As the Magistrates' Association has recommended there should be a single youth custody sentence. Detention centres, already under-used by the Courts, should be abolished, and the accommodation released to be used for remand centres.

Alternatives to prison

Every effort should be made to ensure that fine defaulters, elderly shoplifters and drunks are not sent to prison.

- Police cautions and intermediate treatment should be more widely used. Where punishment is appropriate, it should normally be community service rather than prison; but many of these offenders are more appropriately dealt with by rehabilitation or medical treatment.
- The probation service must be expanded to enable bail and non custodial sentences to be supervised where necessary under appropriate supervision.

- The Home Office should consider extending the period of automatic remission for less serious offences.
- We strongly support victim support schemes.
- Offenders should recompense their victims, either directly or indirectly. Community service orders oblige offenders to undertake work for the community. They should be more widely used.

These changes should ease the frustration that threatens to erupt in the prisons, and enable prison officers to do the professional job they want to do. We welcome 'Fresh Start', which proposes shorter hours and less reliance on overtime, but recognise that unless overcrowding is tackled, this reform may not work.

Building the future

A generation ago, Britain was among Europe's richest countries. Today Britain is falling down the league of industrialised nations. Real income per head is well below that of Sweden, Germany or France. Our manufacturing trade has gone into the red. In every year since 1983 we have imported more goods than we exported, the first time that has happened since the Industrial Revolution.

Worst of all is unemployment. Many more than the three million people registered as unemployed have no jobs. The Government has juggled the figures and brought in cosmetic devices to hide the truth. But the facts won't go away. The dole queue is three times what it was in 1979. Unemployment has been a low priority for this Government, used to keep down inflation. Tax cuts have had a higher priority than job creation. The cost in human misery and hardship, loss of confidence and self-respect, not least among young people, has been incalculable.

Britain, like other industrial countries, has to cross the gulf between the first industrial revolution, based on steel, engineering and railways, and the second, based on the sunrise technologies of micro-electronics, bio-technology and new materials. To cross that gulf demands investment in new buildings, plant and machinery, and above all in the research and development on which new products and new processes are based. Yet under Mrs Thatcher's Government, investment in manufacturing industry and in R&D has fallen substantially. We must give a much higher priority to training and education. There has been a huge decline in apprenticeships and skill training in Britain in the last eight years, although the new technologies demand much higher qualifications and regular updating of knowledge.

The Government has failed to use the once-in-a-lifetime opportunity North Sea oil gave us to invest in our industry and in our people. High interest rates have crippled businesses of all sizes; sudden ups and downs in the sterling exchange rate have handicapped exports. Even the proceeds from selling-off state assets – our assets – have gone into cutting taxes to buy votes.

These are our objectives:

- to reduce unemployment, first amongst those unemployed for a year or more, and amongst young people; in three years we will reduce unemployment by one million;
- to bridge the gap between the older industrial areas and the areas of prosperity. The older industrial areas have lost a million jobs. We would encourage regional

development agencies and local employment initiatives to harness the energy and enthusiasm of the local people in these hard-hit areas. The South-East would benefit too, for house prices are now soaring far beyond the ability of most families to pay, and attractive countryside is besieged by developers;

- to build a new partnership between business and government, to re-equip our factories, tackle the blight of our inner cities, and draw up a strategy for a competitive and successful industry;

- to abolish class division in the workplace by encouraging a single status for white collar and blue collar workers, and creating opportunities for all employees to share in the profits, decisions and ownership of firms;

- to strengthen the rights of women at work including equal pay for work of equal value and equal treatment. We will ensure that all public authorities and private contractors are equal opportunity employers and we will promote changes to enable those with domestic responsibilities to secure access to employment. We would restore maternity grants and give a tax allowance to help with child-care costs. We would remove the tax on the use of workplace nurseries and encourage wider provision of child-care facilities.

Unemployment

Unemployment at present levels is not the inevitable result of new technology or world recession – Japan has only 2.5% unemployment and US unemployment has fallen by two million since 1983. It can be reduced in Britain. The key is to ensure that in creating new jobs the nation does not embark on another round of severe inflation which will damage competitiveness and cost us jobs in the long run. Labour ignores this danger and the Conservatives use it as an excuse for allowing unemployment to remain high. The Alliance is prepared to take the difficult steps necessary to create jobs and control inflation at the same time.

Therefore we will expand the economy by targeting resources to increase output and exports rather than consumption and imports. New capital investment building up to £1.5 billion per annum will support the framework of services on which industry and society depend, like transport, homes, schools, hospitals and drainage. We will give more spending power to the poorest people in our society, which will itself generate more economic activity with much less impact on imports than general cuts in income tax.

We will control inflation by winning the support of the British people for our incomes strategy; as a back-up we will legislate for reserve powers for a counter-inflation tax on companies under which inflationary increases would be unattractive because they would go in extra tax: profit-sharing would be exempted. We would introduce fairer arrangements for public sector pay, with an independent pay and information board whose findings would inform and assist negotiations, arbitration procedures and incentives to negotiate no-strike agreements in essential services.

We will join the exchange rate mechanism of the European Monetary System, enabling us to make our currency more stable and to reduce current interest rates by as much as 2%. We would also seek to develop the role of the EMS within the world economy.

For the long-term unemployed we will provide a guarantee of a job through:

- a building and investment programme aimed at providing 200,000 jobs in such essential areas as transport, housing, insulation, urban renewal and new technologies;
- a new recruitment incentive to encourage companies to take on over 270,000 job-less people;
- a crash programme of education and training, offering new skills to the unskilled unemployed, with 200,000 places;
- 60,000 extra jobs in the health and social services to improve care in the community and more jobs in nursery education;
- an expanded job release scheme, opening up 30,000 jobs by allowing men to benefit from the scheme at 62 years of age.

Rebuilding British industry

Manufacturing and services go hand in hand, but only a quarter of services are trad-able and two thirds of our exports depend on manufacturing. Britain cannot survive on a basis of low-tech service jobs. Nor can business flourish without a thriving indus-try to buy their products. Manufacturing industry is the driving force at the core of our economy. Its decline must be reversed.

Therefore:

- We will introduce Industrial Investment Bonds to attract investors into industry, a new industrial credit scheme to provide medium-term finance for manufacturing companies and a tax allowance for investment in new technologies;

- We will work in partnership with industry and put industry first. There will be a new Cabinet Industrial Policy Committee responsible for overseeing the develop-ment and implementation, in co-operation with industry, of a broad industrial strategy with long-term priorities;

- We will encourage employers to take on more staff by a 25% cut in their National Insurance Contribution payments targeted on assisted areas and areas of high unemployment;

- We will introduce a training incentive with rebates for companies who spend more money on training and contributions from those who do not provide it themselves; our new Department of Education and Training will monitor standards and turn youth training into a fully comprehensive, high quality vocational and educational programme for 16–19 year olds;

- We will increase the lamentably low funding of civil research and development, placing emphasis both on commercial exploitation of new technology using the British Technology Group, and on boosting basic scientific research; we would give greater support to European Community joint research programmes;

- We will give more backing to exports using the Export Credit Guarantee Depart-ment and the Aid and Trade Provision (funded from the DTI) more effectively than the present Government has done in recent years because of its ambivalent attitude towards public sector support.

- We will press the European Community to take stern action against dumping. We will launch a more determined attack on unfair restrictions on our trade, including those imposed by Japan on a wide range of products and services and by the US on our high-technology exports;

- We will insist on a strong competition policy to promote efficiency and give consumers a fair deal: the Office of Fair Trading will be strengthened and will take on the responsibilities of the Monopolies and Mergers Commission and companies seeking mergers will have to justify them; individuals and institutions will have power to seek redress in court against anti-competitive practices;

- We will continue to judge whether industries should be in the public or private sector on objective criteria related to competition and efficiency. We opposed the privatisation of British Gas and British Telecom although we would not reverse it but instead concentrate on improving consumer choice and protection. We supported the privatisation of Rolls Royce. We would not privatise water authorities and the Central Electricity Generating Board on grounds of public policy relating to safety standards and care for the environment. We welcome the fact that British Steel is now operating profitably. We believe it should be retained as a single entity to withstand international competition and should be considered for privatisation providing its success can be maintained;

- We will work with the people of the hard-hit regions to stimulate new economic activity and new prospects for jobs through regional development agencies. We will encourage the setting up of local venture capital funds to finance new enterprise. We do not believe that government always knows best, so we will support local initiatives through appropriate fiscal and financial means.

Backing small business

- We will build a partnership between government, entrepreneurs and investors to encourage new businesses and create new jobs. We will especially encourage small businesses, which will be a major motor of growth and employment in the 1990s.
- We will reduce the tax and administrative burdens on small businesses.
- We will promote the establishment of Small Firms Investment Companies to provide equity and loan finance.
- We will introduce a Bill to enable business to charge interest on overdue payment of bills, if they so wish.
- We will ensure that there are business start-up schemes and expansion schemes specifically geared to encouraging enterprise by women.
- We will ensure small businesses get their fair share of public contracts from both central and local government.
- We will encourage local public/private initiatives, such as the Enterprise Agencies, which we identified in our Worksearch Campaign.

Industrial Investment Bonds

We will introduce Industrial Investment Bonds to liberate many new and small businesses from the high cost of borrowing start-up capital.

These bonds will help bridge the gap between the new businessman who needs access to low-cost funds and the investor, including individuals, who would like to back him or her provided the balance between risk and reward is reasonable. We will accordingly allow new and growing companies to raise funds through the issue of Industrial Investment Bonds which will pay interest free of tax to investors.

A similar scheme is already providing a valuable kick-start for many new companies in the United States. Together with the Business Expansion Scheme, our Industrial Investment Bonds will give the next generation of businesses the most favourable climate ever to build up employment for the community and profits for themselves and their investors.

We will promote partnership

For too long the industrial sector has been a battleground between opposing forces of capital and labour, instead of a mutually beneficial and equal partnership.

- We will legislate for employee participation but believe that flexibility must be allowed in working out the detail for employee councils at the place of work. These councils should have the information and the rights to enable them to contribute to strategic decisions; opportunity must be provided for participation at top level – for example by employee directors or a representative or supervisory council, or by directors elected by shareholders and employees jointly.
- We will encourage other forms of industrial participation, including co-operatives in which it is workers who hire capital and management skill; we will establish an Industrial Partnership Agency incorporating the Co-operative Development Agency to take a lead in this field.
- We will strengthen the law in relation to Directors' statutory obligation to have regard to the interests of their employees as well as their shareholders; this should include a requirement to consult employees before making a recommendation in response to any take-over bids.
- We will extend incentives to employees' share-ownership and profit-sharing which were introduced at Liberal insistence in 1987.
- We will encourage wider share ownership by a scheme which gives more people a direct tax incentive to become small investors;
- We have long been committed to trade union reform aimed at giving unions back to their members and we have taken the lead in promoting the extension of postal ballots and internal elections and have vigorously opposed pre-entry closed shops. Trades unions are an essential element in the protection of the employees' interests, which is why we would return union recognition to GCHQ members. Our central aim is to make unions democratic and accountable and therefore entitled to positive rights including the right to recognition and the right to strike balanced by the acceptance of their responsibilities to their members, their industries and to the wider community.

- To reduce industrial conflict we support a system of referring disputes to independent arbitration prior to any industrial action. We will also encourage the establishment of freely negotiated strike-free agreements especially in the provision of essential public services.
- We will take action through equal opportunity and contract compliance policies to eliminate discrimination against ethnic minorities and women.
- We will actively promote measures that give employees with family responsibilities minimum rights to parental and family leave.

Agriculture

The Alliance will promote a healthy farming industry. We must arrest the precipitous decline in farm incomes of recent years. Our policies for aligning supply and demand of agricultural produce are designed to secure fair returns for farmers' efforts. Adequate price and income support is required to enable necessary farming adjustments to be made.

We will join the exchange rate mechanism of the European Monetary System to lower interest rates, promote financial stability and prevent unfair discrimination against British farmers through over-valuation of the green pound.

The Alliance will work to reform the CAP; the policy has achieved secure food supplies but has gone on unchecked to produce wasteful and hugely expensive surpluses. Many farmers who borrowed heavily on inflated land prices to meet production demands are now threatened with bankruptcy. The Alliance will secure the income of British family farms by negotiating adequate guaranteed prices for determined quantities of production, with additional quantities disposed at much lower floor intervention prices: a two-tier pricing system. An eligible tonnage for each member-state will be agreed to take into account the differing farm structures in the Community.

We will seek a fairer share of milk quota for British producers and the retention of the right to quota transfer and leasing. Transfer of quotas through an agency would create a pool of quota to be administered by the Milk Marketing Board and would help small family farms.

We are committed to supporting the less favoured areas, and ensuring that the upland beef and sheep industries are safeguarded through differential premia and retention of the sheepmeat regime.

We shall increase Government support for effective marketing schemes for farm produce at home and abroad. Farm-based processing and marketing co-operatives will be assisted to retain more of the selling price of foodstuffs in rural communities.

We will encourage conservation, the reduced use of chemical inputs, organic farming and less intensive methods of livestock production. The Government's cuts in agricultural research, education and advice will be reversed. Special efforts will be devoted to lowering input costs. The Alliance will sponsor partnership between Government and industry to promote both research into new uses for farm produce which will help to sustain incomes and into the improvement of animal welfare.

We will encourage farmers to diversify taking account of the needs of tenant farmers and other small family farms. We will make annual payments for the upkeep of important amenities such as walls, hedges, footpaths and meadows. We will provide further support for the custodianship of areas of environmental importance, and the encouragement of mixed forestry on the farm with establishment grants and annual payments for growers. We will propose clear guidelines for land use to assist diversification and to protect the countryside.

The Alliance rejects proposals to rate farm land or buildings. We also reject the Government's proposals for a poll tax which will apply to farmers and farm workers and, unlike Alliance proposals for local government income tax, is not based on the ability to pay.

The Alliance wishes to support new entrants to the farming industry, and therefore proposes the retention of County Council smallholdings and the promotion of tax incentives to encourage landlords to let more land.

We would promote local rural employment, including farm-based tourism, through properly funded rural development agencies and by means of a credit scheme which would provide working capital at low rates of interest to agricultural and rural industries.

We will also encourage the establishment of a Credit Union (or Farm Bank) designed to help farmers secure finance at fair and reasonable rates.

Fishing

The Alliance in government will act to strengthen the contribution the fishing industry can make to the livelihood of rural communities.

After many years of turmoil from the loss of traditional distant water fishing grounds and the protracted negotiations for a fair Common Fishing Policy, what British fishermen now need above all is stability to plan and invest for the future. We will:

- Improve the conservation of fish stocks by the use of licensing and technical means that will safeguard stocks and decentralise the administration of quantitative controls so as to give fishermen greater responsibility for the management of necessary conservation measures with the flexibility to recognise regional differences.
- Strengthen the European Community Inspectorate so as to achieve fair enforcement by all member-states.
- We will support better vocational training, fish processing and marketing and export promotion under the co-ordination of the Seafish Industry Authority.
- We would not impose light dues on fishing vessels.

The Alliance believes that these policies will help to secure jobs, greater prosperity, greater fairness, and a sense of pride in the industries upon which our future depends.

Health and community care

The National Health Service is in a state of fundamental crisis and malaise. It is suffering shortages and declining standards. Our people are seeing their services cut, their waiting lists lengthened, and more and more needs going unmet. Unless a Government is elected again which is committed to the ideas and ideals of a National Health Service, one of the great achievements of 20th century civilised society could be in irreversible decline.

We will back the National Health Service by increasing its budget so that by year five it will be £1 billion per annum higher than that planned by the Conservatives. Our Health Service was once the envy of the world: now the strains under which it is working are well known, and we are losing some of the best health professionals who can no longer do the job they were trained to do because of inadequate resources. We aim to restore a sense of pride in the Health Service and to give it a new sense of direction. Our priorities for change are:

- to provide prompt medical treatment for those who need it, regardless of who they are or where they live. There are huge inequalities between and within regions of the country in availability of hospital treatment and family doctor services. We would set aside special funds – building on the recently introduced funds to cut waiting lists – to back good practice. The Conservative Government has increased prescription charges by 240% over the last eight years which is much higher than inflation. We will not increase prescription charges beyond the inflation rate;

- to promote good health, not merely to treat illness. This means targeting resources in health education, promoting healthy eating, tightening up food labelling and facing up to the problems presented by smoking and alcohol abuse. We will ban advertising of tobacco products. Our policies to deal with unemployment, poverty and poor housing are crucial in reducing ill-health. The primary health care team working with family doctors must be built up and their preventive work expanded. There should be more screening, including well-women clinics, with efficient follow-up for known risk groups;

- to create a new innovation fund, to tackle inequalities in health care, improve the 'cinderella services', and to fund new developments and new priorities in health care; this will have an initial life of five years, with a budget which will total £250 million in the first three years. This will be in addition to money spent on creating new jobs caring in the community;

- to make 'care in the community' a reality. We are not prepared to see patients turned out of the old institutional hospitals without adequate facilities to care for them in the community. We want to support 'carers' who look after elderly and handicapped people in their own families and their own homes. We intend to introduce a carers' benefit, and we want carers to have more opportunities for a break from their responsibilities.

However, we recognise that for some people good institutional care remains the best solution;

- to strengthen patients' rights, through statutory access for the individual to his or her own medical files, through more opportunities for patients to participate in decisions and through stronger community health councils;
- to give real independence to the Health Education Authority;
- to restructure the nursing profession along the lines proposed in Project 2000.

In the longer term we want to see health authorities brought under democratic control at local level, but the NHS has suffered so many bouts of reorganisation under successive governments that for the moment the priority must be to let those running the service get on with the job.

We would remove the centralising pressure to make all authorities do things in the same way, and we would leave authorities with more freedom to decide, for example, whether privatisation of services was likely to improve patient care or not; we would give these authorities more direct control over their budgets.

We uphold the right of individuals to use their own resources to obtain private medical care, but we will not allow private medicine to exploit the NHS by using facilities at subsidised cost and we will work to end the delays which give rise to 'queue-jumping' through private medicine.

Right to treatment

No client of the NHS should have to wait longer than six months for hospital treatment. No-one should be kept waiting for years in pain, with unnecessary crippling disabilities for lack of a hospital bed. Patients should have the right to treatment in other authorities where there is spare capacity.

The Alliance will work to ensure that every patient receives hospital treatment for routine operations within six months of referral by a GP. The backlog of people waiting is now of crisis proportions. We estimate it will take two years to reduce the maximum waiting time to one year. We aim to reduce this to within six months during our first term of office.

To end long waiting lists District Health Authorities and Health Boards will be empowered to:

- Buy and sell hospital treatment from each other to obtain the best and quickest service;
- Buy services from other Districts with surpluses. Selling services between DHAs would be a new incentive for good management practice rather than penalise success;
- Pay travelling costs for patients who cannot afford transport out of their districts;
- Appoint more hospital doctors and negotiate with consultants so that they give priority to their NHS waiting lists rather than on private practice;
- Ensure an increased number of places in local hospitals for convalescence and community care to release beds for acute treatment.

GPs will need to have full computerised information on waiting lists when they make their first referrals. There are already substantial funds within the NHS for computerisation and the Alliance will ensure all GPs can be linked to hospitals nation-wide.

In consultation with the medical profession, we will draw up and regularly review a list of routine operations such as hip replacement for which all patients should expect treatment within our six-month target.

In consultation with District Health Authorities, we will agree allocations of extra resources, taking into account the numbers of patients from outside their area that Districts are already treating.

The vital role of the voluntary sector

In health and in many other fields of service the work of volunteers and voluntary organisations is vital: the Alliance sees no benefit in state monopoly, and welcomes the dedication, innovation and diversity which the voluntary sector can bring. We want a more stable framework for the voluntary organisations making them less dependent on short-term funding which can be misused by local councils and government departments as a means of exerting political control in the voluntary sector. We will:

- Expand opportunities for individual voluntary effort, giving young people, for example, the chance to volunteer full-time for a year without losing their social security entitlements and by linking existing voluntary groups with new initiatives;
- Ensure that experience gained by volunteers is given proper accreditation to enable those without traditional qualifications to gain access to further and higher education;
- Ensure adequate public core funding to enable voluntary organisations to take full advantage of tax concessions on payroll giving and individual donors;
- Support services which advise voluntary organisations on how to develop their management skills and structures to ensure staff development and better service delivery;
- Support and help to widen the network of Citizens Advice Bureaux, Law Centres and other legal advice services.

Ending poverty

We can and will relieve many thousands of people from the burden of poverty.

Poverty in Britain is getting worse. The Conservatives' taxation and benefit policies have redistributed income from the poor to the rich, from people with dependent children to single people and childless couples, and from one group of the poor to another group of the poor. This is unjust and unacceptable. The Alliance will tackle poverty by targeting much higher benefits to those with the lowest incomes in relation to their needs. We will help families with children. We will improve benefits for the disabled and those caring for elderly and disabled relatives at home.

Our proposals fall into two parts:

- First, we will, over the first two years, improve the incomes of pensioners, families with children, the unemployed, disabled and carers. These improvements will be paid for in part from increasing public expenditure by a net £1.75 billion by the second year. The remainder will be paid for from increased tax revenues and from changes which will make the tax system fairer.
- The second phase of our proposals will be a restructuring of the tax and benefits systems to create one integrated system which will be simpler and fairer.

The Immediate Package

Pensioners

We intend to concentrate the bulk of extra spending on helping poorer pensioners with incomes on and just above the state retirement pension. We will increase the basic state retirement pension by £2.30 a week for a single person and £3.65 for a married couple. This will include the forecast update of the pension in 1988. For poorer pensioners we will introduce an additional benefit of £3.70 a week for single people and £5.75 for couples. This will increase the incomes of poorer pensioners in total by £6 per week (single person) and £9.40 per week (couple).

- We will introduce a Death Grant of £400, recoverable from the estate of the deceased, specifically designed to help pensioners with a small amount of savings feel confident that most of their, or their spouse's, funeral costs will be covered by the Grant;
- We will require standing charges for gas, electricity and telephones to be abolished for everyone;
- The £10 Christmas bonus has became hopelessly inadequate to meet the extra spending pensioners and widows face at Christmas.
- We will increase the bonus by paying a double pension in the first week of December. A single person will receive £39.50 and a married couple £63.25. The net cost will be £268 million.

Child benefit

We will increase child benefit by £1 per child a week in the first year and by a further £1 per child a week in the second year.

Maternity grant

We will introduce a maternity grant of £150 for the first child born in every family and of £75 for the births of each subsequent child;

Families in work

We will add £5 per week to the family credit due to be introduced in April 1968 as a replacement to family income supplement. These families will also gain from the extra child benefit. Unlike the Conservatives we will retain at this stage free school meals and milk for family credit recipients regardless of whether the families are in work or not; this will ensure equal treatment with families dependent on benefits.

Families out of work

We will increase the family premium under the income support scheme by £5 per week and, in this first phase, we will increase the net amount per child received by income support families by £2 per child per week;

Single parents

We will increase the single parent premium for income support recipients by £1.10 a week, single parents will also benefit from the increased child benefit and, if their earnings are low, from the extra £5 on family credit. If they are not in paid employment they will benefit from higher family premium and the child additions.

Young people

The Conservatives' benefit changes include setting a new low personal allowance for unemployed 18–24 year olds with a higher Personal Allowance for single people 25 and over. We do not support this discrimination based on age and we will abolish the 18–24 income support rate to ensure that all single people receive the same amount of benefit.

Long-term unemployed

We will establish a new premium under the income support scheme for the long-term unemployed without dependent children of £3.50 a week for a single person and £5 for a couple.

Social fund

We will not place cash limits on the Social Fund and we will replace loans with grants. We will establish clear criteria of eligibility for special payments and a right of independent appeal and will ensure that the very poor receive extra money to cover heating costs.

Housing benefit

We will not impose a 20% rates charge on those with very low incomes as the Conservatives plan to do from April 1988. We will not implement the Conservatives' proposed cuts in the funding of Housing Benefit.

The total gross cost of this immediate package over two years is £3.6 billion and the net cost is £1.75 billion, which will be met from our planned expansion of the economy. Part of the cost of the package will be met by changes to the tax system, and by starting to phase in independent taxation for married women.

We will change the current personal tax allowances into a standard allowance worth the same value for all taxpayers and will not uprate the Married Man's Tax Allowance. Pensioners', Single Person's and Wife's Earned Income Allowances will continue to be uprated with inflation. We will confine Mortgage Tax Relief to the basic rate of tax, so that all taxpayers benefit equally from it at the same rate.

People with disabilities

The biggest handicap faced by people with disabilities is the barriers put up by the rest of us to their participation in society. The Alliance therefore supports measures which reduce the physical and attitudinal obstacles faced by those with disabilities and which enable all to enjoy as many as possible of the opportunities which are often taken for granted by the able-bodied.

We believe that the majority of people with disabilities wish to live an independent life in the community and in their own home. In support of this we will:

- speed up the full implementation of the Disabled Persons Act 1986;
- increase the income of people with disabilities who are dependent on benefits by £3.50 per week and provide additional financial support through our tax and benefit proposals;
- ensure that 'care in the community', policies are properly co-ordinated and funded, unlike the current situation which has been described by the Audit Commission as resulting in 'poor value for money and unnecessary suffering';
- tackle discrimination against disabled people through our proposed new Bill of Rights and the Human Rights Commission;
- support the voluntary organisations of and for disabled people and ensure that they are properly consulted on matters which affect them;
- ensure that the needs of disabled people are taken into account in housing, public buildings and by public transport operators. We would expand support for the specialised transport which can often be the key to independent living for people with limited mobility;
- improve the provision of education for those with special needs, in colleges as well as schools, backed by a National Advisory Committee.

People caring for dependent relatives

We will legislate through the Carers' Charter for carers' needs. We will replace Invalid Care Allowance by a more generous Carers' Benefit.

We will seek to improve the position of people with disabilities in our society.

The second stage

The next stage will be to implement our structural changes to the tax and benefit systems. We will replace income support and family credit by a new basic benefit for those in or out of work. Basic benefit entitlement will be gradually reduced as income rises. Child benefit will be payable to all alike, whether they are in or out of work.

We will introduce legislation to merge the tax and benefits systems, and employees' NICs with income tax at a high threshold. These structural changes will not come into effect until the second Parliament.

In the meantime we will continue to freeze the Married Man's Tax Allowance, and this extra revenue will enable us further to improve benefits for families with children, people with disabilities and carers.

Our longer-term objectives

- We will reform capital taxation to encourage wider distribution of gifts and legacies;
- Wider tax relief for savings, including savings directly invested in small businesses,

ending the artificial distinction between income from earning and income from investment;

- We would move towards an equal and flexible retirement age for men and women giving everyone the right to retire at any age from 60 to 70, with a reduced pension for those retiring below 65 but protection for women currently approaching retirement at 60;
- We will aim to restore the link between pensions and average earnings, broken by the present Government, which will become more feasible if our plans to achieve growth while restraining inflation are given the chance to succeed.

Education: the essential investment

We will increase investment in education and training by an additional £2 billion per annum beyond that planned by the Conservatives by the fifth year.

Britain lags far behind our main industrial competitors in the proportion of our people who receive higher education, further education and skill training. Basic research is seriously underfunded. As a result, industry lacks the qualified and skilled people it needs, and individuals are not given the chance to develop their potential.

We aim:

- To widen access to education;
- To raise standards in schools;
- To increase research;
- To provide more effective training and skills.

Our schools are in turmoil. The decision of the two largest teachers unions to conduct a series of strikes in protest at the removal of their bargaining rights by the Teachers Pay and Conditions Act, means another term of disrupted education for the children of England and Wales, with especially serious consequences for those taking public examinations this summer. Many of these pupils have suffered repeated disruption of their schooling over the past three years; they are innocent victims of other people's actions.

To continue with the current Government's present policy, which would deny to the teachers negotiating rights for the next three years, cannot create the mutual trust between the teachers, the local education authorities and the Secretary of State that is essential to improved morale in the profession. Without an improvement in morale, pledges of higher standards are in vain; higher standards in the schools can only be achieved by a committed self-respecting teaching profession.

The teachers unions have been divided among themselves on pay and conditions. That is why the Alliance urged earlier this year in the House of Lords that an independent review body should put forward recommendations as a basis for negotiation. That was done by the Main Committee in Scotland; after an agreed settlement, disruption ceased in Scottish schools.

The Alliance believes that the Government should make it clear that teachers pay and conditions would be imposed for the current settlement only; and that an independent review body would be established to make proposals on teachers' pay and conditions as a basis of negotiation. We understand and sympathise with the teachers' anger at the removal of their negotiating rights. We would restore them. But the action by the teachers unions should cease. It does nothing to achieve their aims. It is damaging pupils' education, is alienating public opinion and undermining the standing of teachers in the community. It is in no-one's interest that it continues.

Investing in Quality

A national programme for raising educational standards
The Alliance TEN POINT PLAN

- ENCOURAGING PROGRESS

We will require all schools, both maintained and independent, to publish indicators showing progress in academic results related to intake and social factors such as community involvement, truancy, and delinquency.

- SETTING GOALS

We will ask each school to set targets for improvement – in the case of maintained schools, in consultation with their local education authority.

- ASSISTING IMPROVEMENT

We will institute 'special inspections' of all schools which regularly fall below a certain level in terms of progress achieved.

- REWARDING EXCELLENCE

We will institute an annual 'Queen's Award' for schools, to be judged by an independent panel of experts, for outstanding progress, teaching and curriculum innovation and success.

- PROMOTING PROFESSIONALISM

We will establish 'teacher fellowships' as one year awards to outstanding teachers.

- SPREADING TECHNOLOGY

We will develop Information Technology Centres as resources of technological expertise in collaboration with local colleges, polytechnics and universities and computing.

- ENRICHING EXPERIENCE

We will initiate a pilot project of summer schools, targeted on inner city children, to enhance performance across the curriculum; we will approach independent schools to participate and make their facilities available for these summer schools.

- BOOSTING NUMERACY

We will inaugurate a national numeracy campaign, backed by advertising and television.

- INVOLVING PARENTS

We will launch pilot projects for parental involvement in schools.

- EMPOWERING PARENTS

We will establish a 'code of good practice' for local education authorities including:

- Parents having a voice on education committees;
- LEAs publishing their policies on home/school links;
- LEAs appointing an advisory officer with special responsibility for developing a closer partnership with parents;
- The training of parent governors.

The Alliance plans

- To create a united Department of Education, Training and Science, and put local education authorities in charge of much of the local training work of the MSC;
- To restore negotiating rights to teachers and to create a General Teaching Council to enhance professional standards, which will also be supported by more in-service training and appraisal to ensure that good teachers do not have to leave the classroom to become administrators in order to achieve adequate rewards and status;
- To raise standards in schools through increased resources for books and materials, doubling teacher training in shortage subjects such as maths, science and computing, through special funds for innovation, through a stronger Inspectorate and through a broad and balanced curriculum established by consensus providing for a core range of subjects to be studied by all pupils but allowing for local needs to be reflected and innovation to be tried.
- To make available one year's pre-school educational experience for all children;
- To develop the potential of each young person by the wider use of profiles and records of achievement, by discouraging early specialisation, by reforming the A-level examination so that it covers a wide range of subjects over the arts–science divide, by positive action to encourage girls to take up subjects previously dominated by boys, and by seeking to build on achievements rather than merely penalising failure;
- To enable schools to have full charge of their own budgets, as the Alliance has done in Cambridgeshire, ensuring that a fully representative governing body is accountable for making the most effective use of the available money;
- To get rid of artificial divisions at 16 by taking steps towards a single system of education and training allowances, replacing the present arrangements which make YTS schemes more financially attractive than further study;

- To develop tertiary colleges where local conditions are appropriate;
- A crash programme to overcome skills shortages, with an expansion of training and re-training facilities under the guidance of local education authorities, giving representation to trainees in the management of schemes;
- A training incentive scheme to encourage employers to increase their commitment to training; companies spending above a certain quota on training would receive a rebate;
- To enable the long term unemployed to take up vacant places in further and higher education courses without losing benefit, with the student able to leave the course immediately a job becomes available;
- To widen access to further and higher education by an immediate restoration of benefits taken away by the Tories, plus a 15% phased real improvement in student support.
- To recognise that education is a life-long process, and that more people need to return to it at different stages of life either to learn new skills or to acquire basic skills; we will seek to make access to higher and further education for mature students easier and to strengthen those institutions which are specifically geared to their needs; the European Social Fund should be widened to help in this area;
- To guarantee a period of free further education based on Open University levels of funding for everyone over 16 to be taken at a time of their choice;
- To restore confidence in our Universities, Polytechnics and Colleges by according proper recognition to their value and increasing so far as possible the resources available to them, by expanding scientific research, which has been severely cut, and widening access. We will increase the number of students by 20% over five years as a step towards our goal of doubling the proportion of our young people going in to higher education by the year 2000. The higher education sector would have a major part to play in our crash programme to overcome skill shortages; we intend to create a Higher Education Council to co-ordinate the planning of both sectors of higher education; we support corporate status for Polytechnics but oppose the Government's plans to bring them under national control;
- Improved education provision for those with special needs, in colleges as well as in schools, backed by a National Advisory Committee;
- We recognise and would uphold the rights of those who wish to pay for independent education in the private sector. We would phase out the Assisted Places scheme without affecting pupils already in the scheme, so that money which has been diverted from the state system can once again be used to raise the standards in state schools. We believe that charitable tax reliefs in private education should only go to genuinely philanthropic activities, and would review the workings of charity law with that object in view. We will encourage greater co-operation between state and independent schools.

An Alliance for young people

The Alliance seeks to give young people the opportunity to shape their own lives and play a full part in their community. Our policies are designed to provide a platform for young people to speak out and to increase their financial independence.

- We will build on the YTS to turn youth training into a fully comprehensive, high quality vocational and educational programme for 16–19 year olds;
- We will offer a job guarantee for our young people who have been unemployed for over a year;
- Our 'Rent-a-Room' scheme will help satisfy the need, particularly among single, young people, for rented accommodation and will make it easier for them to travel to seek work;
- We will abolish the 18–24 income support rate so that all single people will receive the same rate of personal allowance;
- We will review the duties of local authorities to house the homeless and in the first instance will aim to give 16–18 year olds leaving local authority care, a statutory right to be housed;
- We will get rid of artificial divisions at 16 by taking steps towards a single system of education and training allowances, replacing the present arrangements which discourage young people from continuing in full time education;
- We will restore student benefit entitlements, make a 15% phased real improvement in student support, increase the number of full time equivalent students by 140,000 (20%) in five years and double the number by the end of the century;
- We will reduce the age of candidature to eighteen to enable young people to take a full part in local and central government.

Green growth

There cannot be a healthy economy without a healthy environment. We will take proper care of our environment. Under an Alliance government every aspect of policy would be examined for its effect on our environment, which we hold in trust for future generations. We will ensure Britain takes the lead in promoting sustainable economic growth and investment in new technologies designed to remove pollution and thereby create new job opportunities.

The Alliance will set up a new Department of Environmental Protection headed by a Cabinet Minister who will be responsible for environmental management, planning, conservation and pollution control, and promoting environmental policies throughout government. Among the priorities of this department will be:

- Powerful disincentives to polluters based on tougher penalties and implementation of a 'polluter pays' principle for cleaning up the damage backed by support for good practice;
- The safest possible containment and disposal for industrial waste, with recycling wherever feasible;
- Clean Air legislation setting new standards, with tough measures to deal with acid rain and an acceleration of the phasing out of lead in petrol;
- Introducing a statutory duty for both private and public sector companies to publish annual statements on the impact of their activities on the environment and of the measures they have taken to prevent, to reduce and eliminate their impact;
- Protection of the green belt round our cities.

The Alliance is opposed to privatisation of the water authorities, which would hand over vital environmental responsibilities affecting rivers, sewerage, water quality, pollution control and fisheries to private hands. These functions should be restored to democratic control.

Energy and the environment

We will institute an energy policy which meets the needs of industry and the domestic consumer and has full regard to the environment. Britain is in a better position than many other countries to do this because of the natural assets we have. Alliance energy policy avoids dependence on any single source of supply and is based on:

- More prudent use of our oil and gas resources so that they are not depleted too quickly;

- Continued modernisation and development of the coal industry, including new coal-fired power stations with measures to prevent acid rain and more help to areas affected by pit closures; the power to license coal mines would be transferred from British Coal to the Department of Energy to prevent abuse of monopoly;

- Much more research and development work on renewable energy sources, including wind, solar, wave and geothermal energy; we will vigorously pursue proposals for tidal barrages such as those suggested for the Severn and the Mersey, subject to taking the environmental impact into account;

- Far more effort into energy efficiency and conservation, including higher standards of insulation in homes and encouragement of Combined Heat and Power schemes; nevertheless there will need to be a programme of replacement and decommissioning for power stations which are reaching or have reached the end of their design lives.
  Existing capacity and planned coal-fired power stations are enough to meet our needs for some time to come and we see no case for proceeding with a PWR at Sizewell or other nuclear power stations at the present time. Safety must come first and after Chernobyl there is clearly a need for a wider investigation into the safety of nuclear power, and there is also a need for a thorough and independent review of the economics of nuclear power generation.

We will continue research into nuclear fission power including research into the fast breeder reactor which may be needed if renewable resources prove to be less viable than we believe. We remain committed to the Joint European Torus (Jet) nuclear fission project.

There is a serious problem concerning the disposal of nuclear waste, and further studies will be commissioned to solve the problem as satisfactorily as possible. We do not believe that this critical matter should be rushed and therefore advocate on-site storage until suitable methods which have proved to be safe are available.

We would abide by the international convention (the London convention) which prohibits marine dumping of nuclear waste.

The environment is under particular stress in two areas: the cities and the countryside. The Alliance is determined to protect and improve the quality of life in both.

Improving the quality of life in the inner cities

Our cities are in danger of changing from having been centres of initiative and activity in the past into industrial deserts, pessimistic about their future. The division and bitterness in Britain that Conservative neglect in central government and Labour control in local government have brought about are seen at their worst in our major cities.

Urban neighbourhoods need to be no less distinct and individual than rural communities but the Labour and Conservative attitude has been to regard the city and particularly the inner city as one huge problem area and as a battleground for the class struggle. Those who live there know better and are appalled at the damage inflicted on the close, caring communities of the past.

The Alliance believes that the strong city cannot survive without strong neighbourhoods. We have confidence in the ability of those who live in the inner city to renew their own communities, but they must be given the political and economic tools to do the job. Too many of the people who serve the inner cities in professional jobs live in suburbs remote from local problems.

- Through a partnership of the public and private sectors we would invest in housing, schools and the infrastructure to encourage those who work in the inner cities to live there.
- We will make attractive residential accommodation available and closer to the city centre to end the twilight ghettos that assist the mugger and the burglar.
- We will support opportunities for local people to work in their own community, to establish new businesses through local enterprise agencies and to train for needed skills.
- The Alliance will use the Urban Programme to establish community centres, enhance voluntary groups and assist tenants to manage their own estates.
- We will promote the establishment of elected Neighbourhood Councils with statutory parish status, where there is clear demand.

Genuine law and order depends on communities supporting the police in preventing crime and being confident enough to end the anonymity on which criminal activity thrives. Renewing our cities and enabling urban communities to develop a real sense of stability and security is the only sound way of preventing and detecting crime.

Protecting and enhancing our countryside

The Alliance seeks to provide better opportunities for those who live and work in the countryside, to check decline and depopulation (especially of young people), to support small businesses and to encourage self-help solutions to rural problems.

Our agricultural policies are designed to allow farmland to remain in use rather than being set aside. However, our planning strategy will allow for alternative land use which is in keeping with, and makes a sensitive contribution to the local rural economy.

- We will give strong support to the Development Commission and COSIRA, in their efforts to promote local enterprise and to re-use existing buildings for these purposes. In regions where Development Agencies are set up they will promote a co-ordinated approach to the rural economy. Rural areas with severe economic problems should be designated to receive aid from the European Community regional fund;

- We will encourage imaginative schemes to maintain essential facilities in the countryside such as rural transport, village schools, call boxes and sub-post offices, all of which have been threatened under the Conservatives; nationalised industries and privatised monopolies such as British Telecom should be placed under stronger obligations to recognise rural needs;
- We will conserve our heritage of buildings;
- National Parks, areas of outstanding natural beauty and green belts should be fully protected, with those who live and work in these areas having a full, democratic voice in planning policies and recognition given of the added problems they face;
- Forestry policy should place more emphasis on broad-leaved species, and larger scale afforestation should be subject to a special system of planning controls;
- We oppose the privatisation of the Forestry Commission.

Better housing

Home start

Owning a home of one's own is most people's dream but not everyone can afford the high cost of taking the first step. We will open the door to home-ownership for thousands more the young and the not-so-young – to enable them to cope with the initial problem, buying a home, when their resources are most stretched.

We will build on and considerably improve the existing Capital Home Loan Scheme with a tax credit of up to £1,000 for every new buyer. This will give first time buyers the benefit of lower monthly repayments at the start of their mortgages.

All those eligible will have average incomes for the two previous years not exceeding £20,000 (joint) or £10,000 (single). A ceiling will be worked out, region by region, on the price of the home purchased, so as to exclude people rich enough to buy very expensive homes. We estimate this will cost around £50 million per annum once the scheme is fully underway.

We will abolish Stamp Duty on house purchases for everyone participating in 'Home Start'. Stamp Duty now stands at 1% on purchases priced at above £30,000. Abolition would be worth at least £300 and could in the south-east be worth £500 to a first-time buyer.

We will take action to deal with homelessness and bad housing. Housing is a vivid example of the Conservatives' cynicism. The Government decided the narrow rules restricting local housing powers, cut back the capital sums available and is now blaming the local housing authorities for the housing crisis such national decisions cause. In particular the restriction of spending on housing to only 20% of the money coming to local authorities from capital sales makes no financial or social sense. We will remove the restriction.

- We will tackle the problem of homelessness;
- We will give tenants more control over their environment and more choice;
- We will provide more choices for private tenants;

- We will give the elderly and disabled more opportunities to move to more suitable housing or to adapt their present homes;
- We will stop housing problems from restricting economic opportunities – it is no use getting 'on your bike' to find work if the only available jobs are in places where there is no affordable housing accommodation;
- We will require each housing authority to draw up a housing strategy to determine what are the areas of need and how they can best be met working with voluntary organisations, housing associations, building societies and the private sector, as Alliance groups on local councils are already doing;
- We will open up a new 'partnership' sector of rented housing funded by building societies and institutions with a central government contribution to keep rents at reasonable levels; these schemes would be run by their tenants as co-operatives with the support of local councils and Housing Associations. In the long run we want public support for housing costs to be even-handed between those who rent and those who buy;
- We will target our housing assistance on those who most need it. We will promote mortgage schemes which can open up home ownership to a wider variety of people, such as index-linked mortgages and shared ownership; we will improve the availability of home improvement grants to homeowners to maintain the fabric of their properties for the benefit of the whole community;
- We will retain the right to buy. We also wish to give local authorities enough discretion to deal with local housing shortages. Parliament must ensure that limits are set on such discretion to ensure that it is not used to deny the right to buy to tenants in general, and that anyone who is precluded from buying his or her present home is given the opportunity to buy another property on comparable terms through portable discounts;
- We would restore to councils the right to spend the proceeds of council house sales on replacing and repairing housing stock;
- We will insist on higher design standards in public housing, more and greater recognition of the contribution that good community architecture can make to the quality of life and we want investment directed at improving existing properties wherever justified rather than demolition;
- We will incorporate rights for council tenants to control and improve their houses in a statutory tenants' charter;
- We will set up a national mobility scheme covering all sectors of housing;
- Once more homes are available because of the Alliance's housing strategy, we will extend the statutory duty of local authorities to provide for the homeless, phasing in extensions to the 1977 Act beginning with single people over 40 and young aged 16–18 leaving care or who are otherwise homeless.

Rent-a-room

There is a desperate need for rented accommodation, particularly for single people and couples. There are millions of owner-occupied houses and council houses in Britain with spare rooms.

Many are deterred from renting by the present rentals red tape. Another crucial factor is to make it easier for people to travel to seek work. We will act to enable owner-occupiers and council tenants wishing to let a room in their own home to do so more easily, and to their financial advantage.

- Rental income up to £60 per week will not be subject to income tax or capital gains tax.
- We will legislate to invalidate clauses in mortgage contracts or local authority letting contracts that prohibit such lettings.
- Re-possession of such rooms will be made easier.
- The 'Rent-a-Room' scheme will be restricted to owner-occupier, council tenants, or tenants of housing associations, letting a maximum of two rooms in their home.
- The rent will be determined by the market, but only rental income up to a total of £60 per week will be disregarded by the Inland Revenue.

We will legislate to impose a duty on local authorities to issue and regularly review licences to approved agencies, such as housing associations, housing aid centres, or commercial agencies, in their area to operate the scheme. Such agencies will enter into contracts with both landlord and tenant, and will be responsible to the landlord for ending any tenancy arrangement within a fortnight. Court procedures will be speeded up to ensure that possession in all genuine cases is obtainable in that time.

The 'Rent-a-Room' scheme will benefit many people. First, it will help single people and couples, particularly the young, and those moving in order to get work to find suitable accommodation, where at the moment it is both scarce and expensive. Second, it will help owner-occupiers, including elderly people, to increase their income, to assist with mortgage repayments or with the maintenance for their homes; it should help some young families to be able to afford to become home owners for the first time.

Home income plan

For many elderly people their only capital is their home and they do not have a regular income. Elderly home owners on low incomes, in fact, are becoming one of the most deprived sections of the community. The proportion in low standard homes is double that of the population as a whole and many others in good homes are short of spending money.

To enable Britain's elderly home owners to live more comfortable, independent and happier lives we will introduce a tax-assisted Home Income Plan. It will significantly increase their income or provide money for essential house expenses and repairs.

The Home Income Plan will enable them, if they choose, to unlock the capital value of their homes to meet their need for more income now.

They will be able to take out a mortgage on part of the value of the house and use it to buy an annuity providing regular income. The interest on the loan will be added to the capital sum so that neither interest nor capital need be repaid during the borrower's lifetime.

Although several leading building societies and life assurance companies offer home income plans at present, they are of limited value because the interest has to be paid gross after the death of the borrower. Yet tax relief is allowed if the borrowers reduce their income by repaying the interest during their lifetime. Neither method gives really fair value and so only 25,000 home income plans have been taken out.

We will make Home Income Plans a really worthwhile benefit for older people by allowing them to postpone the interest payments and qualify for tax relief when the interest is finally repaid. This could, on life assurance industry calculations give an 80% boost to the income of a woman in her 70's.

Tax relief for pensioners aged 70 or over who take out Home Income Plans would cost less than £40 million, assuming a 70% take-up. The cost would take time to build up and would not be incurred all at once.

Transport

We will maintain public transport.

Wider car ownership has improved the quality of life and enhanced the freedom of millions of people, which we welcome; at the same time, transport policy has to deal with the problems of congestion and road safety, which arise from busier roads, and has to ensure adequate public transport for those who do not have access to a car, including many women, young people and the elderly. While so many people have greater freedom of travel than ever before, significant minorities now have significantly less opportunity to travel than previously, especially in rural areas and some outlying housing estates.

The Alliance believes that:

- Deregulation of bus services under the Conservatives was botched. Bus services could only survive if they paid for themselves, leaving many elderly people and single-parent families isolated in their own homes. The Alliance supports comprehensive competitive tendering for a network of necessary bus services, with local councils involved in planning and financing them. This combines greater enterprise and new ideas with more care for deprived groups and areas. Local councils and transport authorities should use their subsidy powers to ensure that essential services are maintained and that public transport in cities is attractive enough to reduce congestion resulting from commuting by car;
- We will undertake a major renewal of road, rail and port infrastructure as part of our programme of measures to tackle unemployment; we will build more by-passes and a designated national heavy lorry network to get more of the vehicles out of the towns, villages and residential areas;
- We will support investment in our rail network both to encourage the transfer of freight from road to rail and to ensure that the nations and regions of Britain all share in the economic advantages of the Channel fixed link.

The Conservative Government has presided over a decline in our merchant fleet which threatens our national economic and security interest. We would entrust the lead role in co-ordinating maritime policy to a senior member of the Cabinet; and we would seek to help the industry through the present crisis by positive financial support and a determination to ensure fair play in world shipping markets.

Arts, broadcasting and recreation

- We will ensure that people have the opportunity to enjoy the arts and physical recreation and to develop their own potential through these activities. To help achieve this aim we will double arts funding within the lifetime of one Parliament.
- The Alliance will set up a unified Ministry, headed by a Cabinet Minister, to have responsibility for the arts, broadcasting, films, publishing, leisure and recreation – these activities are at present scattered amongst Ministries within which they are of minor significance and are subject to control rather than enhancement;
- We will further decentralise funding for the arts, channelling it through enhanced regional arts associations and the Scottish and Welsh Arts Councils;
- Wherever possible we will replace grants with endowment trusts providing greater stability and independence for the arts with a mix of public and private funding;
- We will co-operate with artists to achieve better deals through stronger copyright and public lending right laws;
- We regard the BBC World Service, the British Council and the provision of educational facilities for overseas students as very effective cultural ambassadors and we will ensure that increased funds are available to carry out that task;
- We will secure the maximum access to sports facilities for the whole community.

Animals

We will strengthen the protection of animals.

A civilised society treats animals with care and compassion. An Alliance Government will therefore set up an Animal Protection Commission which will considerably improve control over the welfare of animals in laboratories, farms, zoos, slaughter houses and circuses, as well as domestic and wild animals, and at a reduced cost, by unifying all existing Government responsibilities in this field. The Commission will be given extensive powers to advise, inspect and enforce legislation, and to review the effectiveness of existing legislation to deal with cruelty, in particular police entry powers and the power of the courts. The Commission will include fair representation from animal welfare organisations as well as users.

Britain, Europe and the world

The Alliance will ensure that Britain's foreign and defence policies help to bring a fairer and safer world. The things we want to achieve in our own country will not be possible unless we co-operate with other countries to achieve a fairer and safer world. Our concern that people should have basic human rights and a decent life cannot stop at the Channel. The huge public support for famine relief, the vigorous public debates on peace and defence and the public compassion for those suffering from oppression in many parts of the world refute the narrow-minded view that world affairs are not an election issue in Britain.

Our aims

The Alliance is firmly internationalist. Opportunities for international co-operation have been thrown away by the Governments of the post-war years, when Britain needed to develop a new role and new relationships in a changed world.

We see the future of the United Kingdom as being bound up with the future of the European Community. As an enthusiastic and committed member of that Community Britain can significantly influence political and economic decisions.

Britain is also a member of the Commonwealth and should be using that position to develop concerted policies on eradicating hunger and on issues such as South Africa and Namibia, yet Mrs Thatcher has made such agreement impossible and treats respected Commonwealth leaders with disdain.

Britain should take the lead in seeking international agreement on selective, targeted sanctions, backed by help for the Front Line States, as a means of increasing the pressure for an end to apartheid in South Africa.

Britain should have a sufficiently mature relationship with the United States for the British Prime Minister to make clear where British foreign policy departs from that of the President of the day. The British Prime Minister should disavow such ventures as the bombing of Libya and support for the Contras, as so many Americans do, rather than allying with the most conservative forces in the White House.

On defence and disarmament, Britain should be firmly committed to the achievement of multilateral disarmament and firm in our acceptance of our responsibility towards collective security through NATO: the Alliance rejects the one-sided approach which characterises both the escalation of our present nuclear capacity through Trident and Labour's decision to remove all nuclear weapons from British soil without securing the removal of those weapons which could threaten us.

The Alliance believes that Britain should take a lead in seeking international efforts to tackle the basic problems of the poorest countries of the world, particularly the burden of debt which is crippling their efforts to feed their own people and the need to get a fairer system of international trade which is not biased against the poorer countries.

Europe

The European Community must be the basis of a united Europe which has common policies on trade, technology and social policy, and encourages Europe's scientific and industrial development. We believe Labour's negative attitude to the European Community, and the obstructiveness of Mrs Thatcher's Government, not least in vetoing the proposed European Community programme for co-ordinated research and development, is short-sighted and unconstructive. In a world of super-powers, Europe has to speak with a united voice.

The Alliance would:

- Ensure fair elections to the European Parliament by proportional representation to give proper rights to the people of this country;
- Seek reform of the Community's political institutions so that the bureaucracy is properly accountable to the European Parliament, and that the Council of Ministers shares power effectively with the Parliament;

- Work for reform of the Common Agricultural Policy so that it no longer dominates the Community budget, and to develop Community policies on regional development, social and employment issues;
- Support European initiatives to put effort and resources into developing advanced technology; we would accept the negotiated European Community co-ordinated research and development programme;
- Make it easier for companies to sell throughout Europe;
- Extend the common rights of citizenship in Europe.

Global co-operation

An Alliance Government will:

- Increase British support for the United Nations, develop its capacity for peacekeeping, restore Britain's membership of UNESCO and increase British backing for the UN agencies such as the High Commission for Refugees;
- Develop Commonwealth and European co-operation on a wide range of issues, including sanctions against South Africa designed to increase pressure for an end to apartheid and peaceful change before war becomes inevitable; we are also determined to end South Africa's illegal occupation of Namibia;
- Increase efforts through international co-operation to deal with the threat of terrorism.

Peace and security

We will promote disarmament while maintaining sound defence.

Everything we prize most highly could be threatened by the destruction of our freedom through armed intervention or threat, or by the destruction of a world which now contains a massive arsenal of nuclear weapons. But at long last there is now an opportunity to halt the arms race. The Alliance is determined to combine sound defence against any possible threat with determined efforts to reduce and even remove the massive nuclear stockpile, which causes increasing anxiety to the peoples of the world. New opportunities for arms agreements are being opened up by the changed priorities of a new Soviet leadership: we cannot afford to assume that this new and welcome trend in Moscow will continue unchecked, but at this delicate and hopeful stage it is vital that we have a British Government determined to seize the opportunity to drive sensible bargains on arms control which are secure because they are seen on each side as being realistic. Britain cannot defend itself or the values of western democracy alone, just as it cannot achieve international disarmament solely by its own actions: both the other Parties have chosen in different ways to ignore the reality that our defence and disarmament efforts are interdependent with those of other countries.

The Alliance is committed to NATO, and we accept the obligations of NATO, including the presence of Allied bases and nuclear weapons on British soil on the basis of clear arrangements for a British veto over their operations including where appropriate, dual-key systems; we believe it is essential to strengthen the European contribution to NATO.

The Alliance welcomed the outline agreement discussed at Reykjavik to remove all intermediate nuclear weapons from Europe, and Mr Gorbachev's later acceptance that such a deal should not be linked to the future of the US Strategic Defence Initiative; The Alliance believes that this must be only the first, vital step in a continuing process which will include both shorter-range nuclear weapons and conventional forces.

The Alliance would withdraw UK support for President Reagan's Strategic Defence Initiative, which clearly involves breaching the ABM Treaty, is destabilising and is likely to lead to further escalation.

- We will seek to revive negotiations on a Comprehensive Test Ban. In the meantime Britain should itself ban nuclear weapons testing and should encourage the US to do likewise.
- We would seek a battlefield-nuclear-weapon-free zone in Central Europe extending 150km in each direction from the East–West divide.
- We believe that NATO relies too heavily on nuclear weapons at all levels for deterrence. A strengthened European pillar, involving effective defence co-operation and improved conventional strength would better enable Western Europe to move towards the elimination of dependence on first use of nuclear weapons. NATO should adopt strategies and weapons which are more self-evidently defensive in intent and which are concerned with minimum deterrence.
- We want to see a new initiative achieve Mutual and Balanced Force Reductions and we would be prepared to include Britain's nuclear weapons in disarmament negotiations.
- We would continue Britain's efforts to achieve a multilateral treaty prohibiting the manufacture, development and possession of chemical weapons. In the meantime, we would oppose any manufacture of fresh stocks of chemical or biological weapons.

In government we would maintain, with whatever necessary modernisation, our minimum nuclear deterrent until it can be negotiated away, as part of a global arms negotiation process, in return for worthwhile concessions by the USSR which would enhance British and European security. In any such modernisation we would maintain our capability in the sense of freezing our capacity at a level no greater than that of the Polaris system. We would cancel Trident because of its excessive number of warheads and megatonnage, high cost and continued dependence on US technology. We would assign our minimum deterrent to NATO and seek every opportunity to improve European co-operation on procurement and strategic questions.

We would seek to reduce the flow of arms to areas of conflict and to ensure that arms from Britain are not supplied to repressive regimes, particularly for their internal security operations.

Shared earth

The Alliance will:

- Increase the share of Britain's GNP which goes in development aid, which has gone down from 0.52% to 0.33% under the Conservatives, so that we reach the UN target of 0.7% by the end of a five-year Parliament;

- Concentrate aid on raising the living standards of the poorest through more rural development, environmentally sustainable resource use, promotion of self-sufficiency, recognition of the role of women, appropriate technology, training and education, making full use of experience and expert voluntary agencies;
- Seek to increase awareness of development issues through more resources being devoted to development education;
- Change the situation in which many poor countries pay more in debt repayments to rich countries than they receive in aid by seeking international agreement on debt rescheduling and cancellation;
- Combine the Aid-Trade Provision and the Overseas Development Administration's 'soft-loan' facility with the Overseas Projects division of the Department of Trade and Industry and the Export Credit Guarantee Department into one division of the DTI – help to British industry will no longer be taken from the aid budget.

Conclusion

The Alliance came into being to achieve these things. From three sources came the political ideas and momentum which are now carrying the Alliance forward. One was Liberalism, a long and honoured political tradition from which we draw not only the philosophy of individual freedom but also a record of achievement in the establishment of the modern welfare state and the championing of local communities. The SDP combines a commitment to social justice and ending poverty with a dynamic approach to wealth creation and its leaders have extensive experience of government. A third element, which has ensured that the strength of the Alliance is infinitely greater than the sum of its parts, is the support of those who have never before been members of a political party, because no party seemed to offer them the chance to realise their aims. Their numbers continue to grow.

The Alliance is therefore different. It involves two political parties working together, and taking along with them the great mass of people who are dissatisfied with the politics of recent years, the kind of politics which is so dismally displayed in the shouting match of the House of Commons at Prime Minister's Question Time. All political parties involve compromises between different views and different strands of opinion – the Labour and Conservative parties each embrace an enormously wide range of opinion. But for them the spirit of compromise, if it operates at all, has to be concealed, kept within the party and denied in public. We make no secret of the fact that our programme draws on the ideas of our two parties and that we are keen to work together to achieve shared goals. Like the others we seek to put our entire programme forward for endorsement and to form a majority Alliance Government, but unlike the others the whole approach of the Alliance underlines our belief that if we are in a balanced Parliament we must heed the message of the voters and work with the other parties to seek an agreed programme which commands the widest possible support.

The Alliance is different also because it is not the voice of any one section or interest. It is not paid for and controlled by the trade union movement, as is the Labour party, and it does not have the massive dependence which the Conservatives have on the City and big business. These links make each of the other parties powerless to reform their own institutional backers and incapable of understanding or winning the confidence of their institutional opponents. The Alliance has a capacity to be fair which is based on its independence and on the breadth of its support, typified by the fact that we have been able to win by-elections in the heart of the countryside in a former Conservative stronghold in Ryedale and in a former Labour stronghold in Greenwich, both seats now held by Liberal and SDP women MPs.

The Alliance is different in another respect. It is not merely seeking to become the elected government of the country, but to overhaul the system of government so that all future governments, of whatever party, are based on real public consent and full participation in an open society. Our intention is not simply to get into the driving seat but to re-design the vehicle. Once the Alliance has reformed the voting system, no future government will be awarded the power of a majority without the support of a majority of the people, and no kind of extremism, whether of the left or of the right, will be able to get in through the back door. Not only that – if we find ourselves exercising power in a Parliament with no overall majority, we guarantee that we will use that power to block extremism and to fight for the kind of reforms which make sure that governments cannot push people around and individuals have the opportunity and the means to achieve their full potential.

The Alliance is different too, in its belief about the nature of society. Our aim is a civilised society in which individual freedom goes hand-in-hand with care for others. Individual freedom is central to our beliefs, but if it is not accompanied by social responsibility it becomes freedom only for those who can afford it, or the survival of the fittest. But when society as a whole tries to meet human needs it must respect individual choice and be aware of the dangers and limitations of state provision, otherwise there will be no freedom, and public services will be both inhuman and inefficient. Declining public services and the inhuman scale of organisations like the DHSS and the big council housing departments have contributed to a widespread feeling of apathy and despair, and many young people in particular feel that this society has no place for them and does not want to listen to them. Government must work in partnership with people, enabling them to use their own organisations, their own local communities and their own skills, and giving them effective democratic control over those services which can only be provided by the community as a whole. Our society is one that recognises that the arts are not an optional extra, to be grudgingly afforded when the economy is booming, but play an essential part in meeting the wider needs of individuals and in broadening the vision of communities. Our aim is a society in which values other than the purely economic are recognised and valued. Our society is one that recognises the importance of the environment in which we live – even those who are successful do not want to live in a shoddy society whose values are dominated by greed and selfishness. We recognise the crucial need to live in harmony with our environment and we will support those developments in our industrial and social activities which are environmentally enhancing and benign. We aim to join the nations which lead the field in environmental protection instead of trailing amongst the last.

The Alliance is also different in being concerned about both unemployment and inflation. The Conservative Party concentrates all its attention on inflation and ignores unemployment and its consequences. The Labour Party concentrates all its attention on unemployment and ignores the fact that increased inflation undermines expansion and inevitably puts brakes on efforts to get people back to work. We must have sustainable growth. That is why our proposals for expanding the economy are accompanied by plans for an incomes strategy and for a firm monetary and exchange rate discipline through entry to the exchange rate mechanism of the European Monetary System. But in the long term we will only succeed if we give the top priority to industry. The service and manufacturing sectors of industry are mutually dependent, but manufacturing industry has been devastated in recent years. We believe it is the engine of growth and our competitors in Japan, in Germany and in the US demonstrate that only too well.

Much of what the Alliance wants to do to ensure basic standards in the public services and to encourage people to find new ways of caring for one another depend on achieving success through our economic and industrial policies, which are designed to enable us to achieve greater prosperity. Some of what we want to do will have to wait until we have earned the resources with which to do it. We are not prepared to enter an electoral auction seeing who can make the largest bids to spend money which is not there and will not be there unless taxes and borrowing are increased to unreasonable and imprudent levels. Investment in industry and particularly in new and high technology industry is the key to creating the wealth we all want. We deplore the way in which windfall benefits such as oil revenues and the proceeds from privatisation have been frittered away instead of being used to enhance the basic fabric of our society.

The other parties know that the Alliance is different, and they fear it, even to the extent of burying their own fundamental disagreements with each other so as to co-operate against us. In the House of Commons they have voted together against elect-oral reform, and against some of the measures designed to put trades unions fully under the control of their members. They work with each other in an attempt to preserve the appearance of a two-party system long after it is dead: Conservatives carefully protect Labour's privileges in the House of Commons to ensure that latterly only Labour and Conservative working peers have been appointed to the Lords, in vain hope of silencing the Alliance voice. We do not rule out the possibility that after the next election there could be an informal 'Lab-Con pact' to keep the Alliance out, as there has been on several local councils: it would be the old parties' way of attempting to stagger on as if nothing had happened after the two-party system had suffered a shattering defeat. Indeed we believe that Labour and Conservative supporters should now be asking their candidates 'In a balanced Parliament will you work with the Alliance or with our traditional opponents?'

That is why our prime aim is an Alliance majority government, an aim that can certainly be realised at this election. Indeed, such are the absurdities of the voting system that quite small increases in Alliance support can make the difference between fifty Alliance seats and three hundred. If we get that majority we will at once set out to reform the system which produced it. Our commitment to fair elections is clear. We are the only political grouping who, if given a majority, would use that majority power forthwith to reform the system under which we gained it. But we will also be able to get on with the job of bringing down unemployment while managing the economy on a sound basis so as to prevent inflation from increasing dramatically again. We will be able to embark on immediate improvements in basic services like education and health, while we open the way to the longer-term proposals in these and other fields which will give people more chance to realise their full potential and build a caring community. We will be able through our tax and benefit proposals to improve the lot of those who now find themselves on or near the poverty line. We will be able to make the conservation of the environment a priority of government, and pay special attention to the needs of cities and countryside. We will be able to house many of the homeless through more imaginative housing policies involving partnership between public and private housing. We will pursue policies on defence and foreign affairs which will make Britain a force for good in the world, recognising our interdependence with other nations.

All this is possible, and our Joint Programme sets out the main steps we will take. These aims and values are also a clear guide to the way we would use the power we had if no party had an overall majority. We would insist that the views of the substantial section of the electorate who had voted for us went into the process by which the programme of a new government was decided. If other parties seek to cheat the electorate of that right, we shall seek to bring the matter back before the voters as soon as possible. We are not prepared to see the views of so many voters ignored any longer.

An election of opportunity

We believe that our priorities are right, that our proposals are practical and that our values are those which are most urgently needed in the government of this country. We make no claim to have a monopoly on good ideas. We seek from the voters the chance to give back to them the power and the opportunities which are rightly theirs. Their time has come.

Changing
Britain
for good

**The Liberal Democrat
Manifesto 1992**

LIBERAL DEMOCRAT GENERAL ELECTION MANIFESTO 1992

Changing Britain for good

Date of Election	Thursday 9 April
Party Leader	Paddy Ashdown
Candidates	632
MPs	20
Votes	5,999,384
% of vote	18.3%

Be warned: this manifesto may not be what you expect.

This manifesto does not promise good times just around the corner. It does not avoid difficult questions out of fear of unpopularity. It simply tells the truth; the truth about what Liberal Democrats believe has to be done in order for Britain to succeed.

If you want Britain to stay the same then you probably won't like this manifesto. But if you want real change, if you long for a better future for yourself, your family, your community and your country, then read on.

Britain has a clear choice at this election. We can stay much as we are, in the same old muddle, with difficult decisions postponed.

Our failure to adjust to the modern world will then become ever more serious. We will lag further behind in creating and sharing wealth. More and more people will lose their jobs and homes. Our environment will go on deteriorating. Our public services, already second rate, will become even worse.

We shall fail to get the best out of the European Community, because our leaders will continue to be afraid to tell us that shared success in the Community means sharing sovereignty too.

Our system of politics will continue to foster confrontation and short-term thinking, and exclude ordinary citizens from the business of government.

This manifesto offers a different choice for Britain.

Liberal Democrats do *not* believe that our country's under-performance has to be accepted. Another forty years of failed government is *not* inevitable. Britain has many advantages: a wealth of natural resources; a long history of engagement with the rest of the world; a mature and inventive people who value tolerance and freedom.

But Britain will only succeed when its political leaders start treating voters as informed citizens with shared concerns, not as ignorant consumers to be manipulated. Now is the time for change.

That is why in this manifesto we set out a clear analysis of Britain's problems and our proposals for putting them right. Above all, Liberal Democrats will trust our fellow citizens with the truth.

So this manifesto is different from others you may read.

We do not shrink from the real choices for our country.

We are not afraid to say what needs to be said.

We are not afraid to do what needs to be done.

And we are clear that if we want to make a modern Britain, we must first *change* Britain.

What Liberal Democrats stand for

Liberal Democrats put people first. We aim to create a society in which all men and women can realise their full potential and shape their own successes. We believe that if we could liberate this wealth of talent we would transform our economy and create a shared society of which we should all be proud. Liberal Democrats know that this cannot be achieved without fundamental reform.

We must change our political system to give the citizen more power and the government less; our economic system to confer power on consumers and to provide employees with a share in the wealth they create; our public services to guarantee choice and dignity to each of us; and our education system to equip us better for the modern world.

Liberal Democrats recognise the importance of the things we own in private but we also know the value of what we hold in common. We believe that people are at their best as members of communities, where they care about each other and for those less fortunate than themselves. So our policies are designed to strengthen communities, tackle crime and poverty, build up the common wealth and improve the shared quality of life.

In the economic sphere we know that the free market is the best guarantee of responsiveness to choice and change. But we believe the market should be our servant not our master. So we see the role of government as crucial in making the market work properly, by creating the conditions for success, promoting competition, breaking up monopolies and spreading information. And government has to be ready to make the investments which private enterprise will not, whether in transport, education or public works.

Liberal Democrats know that we have a duty, not only to each other but to the generations which follow us, to protect the environment. We believe that this is best achieved not by making people poorer or less free but by building true environmental costs into the market so as to reward those who conserve and penalise those who pollute.

Liberal Democrats are uncompromisingly internationalist. We know that there is a limit to what Britain can achieve alone and we are committed to building in the wider world the sort of society we strive for at home, founded on mutual cooperation, political liberty and shared prosperity. We have long been committed Europeans, believing that Britain can only be secure, successful and environmentally safe if we play our full part in building a more united and democratic Europe.

Globally, Liberal Democrats will work to strengthen international cooperation. We reject outdated notions of national sovereignty, believing that they now stand in the way of common action to deal with the scourges of disease and hunger, the deterioration of the Earth's environment and the continuing dangers of the post-Cold War world.

We believe that all government, whether local, national, or increasingly European, should be bound by the rights of the individual and should be fully accountable.

Because Liberal Democrats alone understand that we shall not change Britain's future unless and until we change Britain's electoral system, we are committed to electoral and constitutional reform. We shall not rest until the government of Britain fully belongs to the citizens it is there to serve.

Britain's balance sheet

In drawing up this manifesto, we have begun from where Britain is today. Like any good auditor, we have been realistic about national achievements and failures, about opportunities and problems. The result is a balance sheet which shows our country's strengths and weaknesses.

Despite some points of promise and potential, Britain's balance sheet shows how much still needs to be done. The following pages reveal the extent to which, in the economy, in the environment, in education, and in local services, successive British governments have failed to realise the opportunities of the past decades. Although there are bright spots, the general picture is one of relative decline in relation to other advanced democracies.

Forty years of failure are the result not only of misjudged policies from both Conservative and Labour Governments. Even more crucially, they are the product of an outdated political system which has consistently sacrificed the long term to the short term and abandoned principles for expediency.

The economic balance sheet

Positives

1   In some ways, British industry is thriving. In 1991, UK exports climbed to a record level of £103,804 million.
2   Industrial relations have improved markedly since the 1970s. Trade unions have become more responsible and democratic. Days lost through strikes fell from more than 29 million in 1979 to under a million in the year to October 1991.
3   The excessively high income-tax rates inherited from the last Labour Government have been brought down – from a top rate of 83% in 1979 to 40% in 1992.

Negatives

1   Unemployment has been the most obvious cost of the current recession. The latest figures show 2,604,100 out of work. The number unemployed for more than six months has doubled in the past year.
2   The recession is biting deeply into industry. Business bankruptcies have jumped from 28,935 in 1990 to 47,777 in 1991.
3   High interest rates are throttling the chances of economic recovery. British three-month rates stood at 10.7% in February, compared to 9.5% in Germany, 5.3% in Japan and 4.3% in the US.
4   Britain is failing to invest for the long term. Investment in manufacturing industry fell from £3.1 billion in the first quarter of 1990 to £2.5 billion in the last quarter of 1991.
5   This failure to invest for the long term can be seen also in innovation, the development of new ideas and products. In 1984–88 only 3.4% of patents granted in the US to other nationals went to Britons (3.7% in 1979–83). By comparison, France had grown from 3.3% to 3.4%, and Japan managed 18.8% (against 12.9% in the earlier period).
6   Britain's record of economic growth is very poor. The UK economy contracted by 2.2% in 1991 – the biggest annual fall since the 1930s – while Italy's grew by 1.3% and Germany's by 1.9%.
7   Conservative management of the economy has stoked the biggest credit boom in Britain's history. Average personal debt as a proportion of disposable household income mushroomed from 57% in 1980 to 114% in 1990.
8   Conservative taxation policies may have reduced high marginal income-tax rates, but it was the rich who benefited, not the country as a whole. From the beginning to the end of the 1980s, take-home pay rose by 41.4% for those on 1½ times the national average, by 37% for those on the national average and by only 32% for those on half the average.

The environmental balance sheet

Positives

1   Britain has a massive advantage in natural resources that give it the potential to be at the forefront of renewable energy generation. Government estimates show that up to 45% of electricity demand could be met from wind power.
2   Government action can significantly affect standards of environmental protection. The market share of unleaded petrol rose from 1.1% to 43.0% between August 1988 and November 1991, due to widening tax differentials.
3   Britain has a positive record on protecting its countryside. More of our land is protected in National Parks than any other EC member, and one more has recently been announced, in the New Forest.

Negatives

1   In too many ways Britain unfortunately deserves its nickname of The Dirty Man of Europe. Carbon dioxide emissions – the main source of global warming – increased in the UK from 525 million tonnes in 1986 to 530 million in 1989.

2 The UK produces more sulphur dioxide, the main cause of acid rain, than any other EC member, but is only now beginning to install pollution-control devices to power stations. Germany started in 1984.

3 Prosecutions for water pollution more than doubled between 1981 and 1988, while an additional 40 beaches were found not to be complying with EC standards in 1990 – making a total of 20% of all British beaches.

4 The Government has failed to invest in the development of renewable energy sources – despite the fact that they avoid the pollution problems associated with coal, oil and gas. Currently, just over £20 million is spent annually on renewable energy research and development, compared to more than £200 million a year on nuclear power.

5 Even worse, the Government has cut the budget of the Energy Efficiency Office, while investment in energy conservation would save money *and* reduce pollution. The 1990–91 level of funding, a meagre £23 million, is lower than it was four years before.

6 Pollution from road transport has risen from 884 million tonnes of nitrogen oxides in 1980 to 1,298 million tonnes in 1989.

7 At the same time, the proportion of freight carried on the railways between 1980 and 1990 dropped from 9% to 7%, while the proportion using road transport rose to 83%.

8 Rail transport is placed at a disadvantage in Britain. Levels of government support for the railways fell throughout the 1980s, from £1262 million in 1980–81 to £462 million in 1990–91.

The educational balance sheet

Positives

1 In some ways educational standards are improving. The number of teachers in nursery and primary education grew from 176,228 in 1986 to 193,516 in 1991.

2 Similarly, pupil–teacher ratios fell from 18.2 in 1980–81 to 16.9 in 1990–91.

3 Some of the Government's changes have been for the better. The idea of Local Management of Schools has, in some places, produced school management of imagination and quality.

Negatives

1 Overall, government funding of education is inadequate. The proportion of Britain's gross domestic product devoted to education fell from 5.6% in 1981–82 to 5.0% in 1990–91.

2 The number of secondary school teachers fell from 224,618 in 1986 to 198,030 in 1991.

3 There has been a serious decline in the number of people qualifying as teachers, down from 25,000 in 1980 to 18,500 in 1988. The Government is planning further cuts in teacher-training facilities.

4 British children lose out in critical areas of education. The proportion of children

in pre-compulsory education in 1987–88 was a mere 3.6%, compared to 13.5% in Germany, 17.0% in Belgium and 18.4% in France.

5 Compared to our competitors, not enough of our young people stay on to post-compulsory education. The proportion of 16–18 year olds in full-time education or training was 35% in Britain in 1988, compared to 47% in Germany, 66% in France and 79% in the USA.

6 Investment in scientific research and development has fallen from 0.35% to 0.28% of GDP (while in Germany it stands at 0.40%), not only affecting our higher education system but creating a knock-on effect throughout the British economy.

The social balance sheet

Positives

1 Overall, British standards of health are improving. Life expectancy for men rose from 70.8 years in 1981 to 73.2 years in 1991, and for women from 76.8 to 78.8 years.

2 Home ownership in Britain rose from 55.8% of households in 1981 to 67.3% in 1991.

3 The size of the police establishment has increased by 15% since 1978–79. Expenditure on the police rose by 55% in real terms over the same period, and police pay showed a 29% real rise.

Negatives

1 While the NHS hospital sector's real purchasing power grew by 15.6% between 1980–81 and 1990–91, expenditure requirements (due to demographic change and the rising costs of medical technology) in fact increased by 21.3%.

2 The total number of people waiting for NHS treatment in the UK rose to more than one million in March 1990. 25% of inpatients wait for longer than a year for treatment.

3 The number of sight tests has fallen by 21% since the introduction of charges in 1988.

4 The Government has withdrawn funding for new house building, and refused to allow councils to spend the receipts they have gained from new home owners. As a result, the amount of local authority housing built has fallen from more than 65,300 homes in 1979 to a mere 8,600 in 1990.

5 The number of people accepted by local authorities as homeless rose from 70,000 in 1979 to almost 170,000 in 1990 – and this does not include the single homeless.

6 With the massive expansion of mortgage lending and the subsequent use of interest rates to bring down inflation, the number of mortgages over 12 months in arrears rose from 59,690 in June 1991 to 91,740 by the end of the year. The number of properties repossessed rose by 74% over the 1990 figure to 75,540 in 1991.

7 Outcomes have failed disastrously to match the input of additional resources to law and order. Recorded rates of notified crime have increased year on year by 5.5% on average, and by a massive 16% in 1990–91.

8 At the same time, crime clear-up rates have declined by 32%.
9 Britain has proportionately the largest prison population of any Community country – and we also have more prisoners serving life sentences than the rest of the EC combined.

Policies for the new century

It is clear from our analysis of Britain's balance sheet that Britain needs change. Here are our first steps, the key measures which we believe must be taken straight away if we are to break the cycle of Britain's decline, unlock the full scope of Britain's potential and pave the way to future success.

The first steps

- Britain's political institutions need thorough-going reform: stable and representative government, elected Parliaments in Scotland and Wales, decentralisation of power to the English regions and to local government, freedom of information and a Bill of Rights. As the essential measure to secure and entrench lasting reform **we will introduce fair votes by proportional representation for Parliamentary elections.**

- In the middle of the recession, the economy needs new impetus not a tax cut. **We will immediately introduce an emergency programme of investment in the infrastructure and in public works in order to get companies and people back to work, thus reducing unemployment by 600,000 over the next two years.**

- Lower inflation and a stable climate for industry to plan and prosper will lead to long-term prosperity. **We will give the Bank of England independent responsibility for monetary policy, with a requirement to promote price stability. We will put the pound into the narrow band of the Exchange Rate Mechanism.**

- Environmental priorities must be built into all economic decision-making, ensuring that economic success goes hand in hand with environmental responsibility. **We will introduce new environmental incentives.**

- The skills and capabilities of the British people must be adequate to meet the challenges of the new century. **We will increase investment in education by £2 billion, funding this by an increase of 1p on income tax.**

- Older people deserve greater security. **We will protect private pensions, and increase the basic state pension, making it payable as of right without means testing.**

- Britain's future must be safeguarded by active membership of a European Community which is united and democratic and in which decisions are taken as close to the people as possible. **We will take decisive steps towards the economic, monetary and political union of a democratic Europe.**

Only when these key steps have been taken will government and individuals alike be able to plan for the long term, instead of focusing on the short term and the next election.

The balance of this manifesto sets out the Liberal Democrat vision of the future: our long-term programme for government. The detailed costing and revenue-raising effects of our proposals are contained in a separate supplement.

1. BRITAIN'S PROSPERITY: PUBLIC INVESTMENT; PRIVATE ENTERPRISE

Liberal Democrats aim to encourage a competitive and enterprising economy which is environmentally sustainable, founded on partnership and advanced skills and closely integrated with Europe.

What the economy needs is a new impetus. The Government's proposed tax cut will not achieve this. Only new investment will provide the kick-start needed to escape from recession and reduce the waste of talent and energy which results from unemployment.

But Liberal Democrats also recognise Britain's long-term needs. We are committed to the free market, to free trade and to the creation of a competitive and enterprising economy. We do not believe it is government's job to run business – people do that much better. We see government's role as enabling firms and entrepreneurs to have the best possible chance. That means encouraging competition, investing in skills, involving employees in the success of their companies, nurturing small businesses, playing a positive part in the construction of the new European economy and, above all, bringing greater stability to national economic management.

Our long-term aim is to shift the burden of taxation away from the things the country needs more of – income, savings and value added – and on to the things we want less of, such as pollution and resource depletion.

Turning Britain round

The current recession is undermining Britain's competitiveness and future success. Unemployment and business closures lead to a wastage of talent and a loss of resources. At the same time, essential investment in our country's future, in infrastructure, in education and training and in innovation, is being neglected.

Liberal Democrats will introduce an emergency programme of investment to end the slump. We will immediately put in hand a major programme of public capital investment, funded by reversing the Tory tax cut together with a prudent increase in borrowing. This, combined with a freeze in business rates and new investment in education to increase the nation's skills, will kick-start recovery and create jobs.

We will:

- Attack unemployment by creating new employment opportunities. Our emergency programme should reduce unemployment by at least 600,000 over two years. We will increase spending on public transport, housing, hospitals and schools, on energy efficiency and conservation projects and on education and training – all sensible investments for the country's future. We will aim to guarantee everyone out of work for six months or more a place on either a high quality training programme or on a work programme with a strong element of training.

- Invest in infrastructure. We will provide support for transport infrastructure, including a dedicated high-speed rail link from the Channel Tunnel to connect with the major routes to the North and West of Britain, and the extension of electrification throughout the country. We will encourage the expansion of airports outside the South East.

- Freeze business rates this year, thus effectively reducing them in real terms, a larger reduction than that promised by the Government.

- Create a training incentive for firms through the introduction of a levy equal to 2% of payroll, from which they would deduct their expenditure on training. We will require employers to release their employees aged under 19 for a minimum of two days a week further education and/or training for nationally recognised qualifications. We will establish a fully integrated system of skills training, leading to recognised qualifications for a broad range of skills. We will increase 'access' courses for mature students and retraining for women returners and those in mid-career. We will fund crash courses in the main areas of skill shortage, aimed in particular at the long-term unemployed.

- Invest in local economies. We will set up and fund new regional development and local enterprise agencies. We will encourage TECs to become strong, locally based, employer-led organisations providing business services, acting as an effective voice for business at local level, and overseeing training of those in employment. We will encourage decentralisation of banks and other financial institutions. We will end the present Government's policy of clawing back from local authorities, amounts equivalent to those they receive from the European Community's regional development fund.

- Invest in research, innovation and design. We will increase immediately the government science budget to 0.35% of GDP and raise it steadily thereafter. We will establish regional technology transfer centres to bring together the resources of industry, colleges, and government labs. We will encourage industry to invest in innovation and to improve the provision of seedcorn capital. We will reverse cuts in design consultancy schemes and provide additional funding for the Design Council.

Making Britain competitive

A climate of enterprise and competition is vital if British industry and products are to compete effectively in overseas markets. Yet the current Government has concentrated instead on converting public into private monopolies. We will:

- Stimulate competition. We will take tough action against monopolies, mergers and financial raids. The Monopolies and Mergers Commission will be combined with the Office of Fair Trading and made independent of government, increasing its effectiveness. We will introduce a Restrictive Practices Act to penalise anti-competitive behaviour and end price-fixing by cartels. We will encourage greater competition in the banking sector.

- Break up monopolies. We will break up the monopoly providers of services such as British Telecom and British Gas. We will permit access by private operators to the British Rail track network. We will liberalise the coal industry by transferring ownership of coal reserves to the Crown (in line with other minerals), and issuing licences to operate pits to other groups, as well as British Coal.

- Promote consumer rights. We will take the lead within the EC to ensure that all products come with accurate, full and simple product and service information. We will give consumer watchdogs, including the regulators and trading standards departments, greater powers, and improve redress for inadequate goods and services.

- Encourage decentralised wage bargaining. Our plans to spread employee owner-ship and participation will encourage wages to be set according to the profitability of individual firms rather than to some national 'going rate'. In addition, we will encourage moves towards greater decentralisation of wage bargaining at company level and, in the longer term as national and regional government develops, in the public sector.

Promoting enterprise

Government needs to provide an immediate impetus to get the economy moving. But long-term private investment in the production of high-quality tradable goods and services is essential for long-term success. This will only be possible if we encourage a climate of investment, enterprise and partnership.

We will:

- Reform taxation to increase investment. We will increase investment substantially in schemes such as SMART to encourage innovation in industry, particularly in small and medium-sized enterprises, especially those involved in manufacturing. We will reform corporation tax and the taxation of savings to achieve even treat-ment for different forms of savings. This will reduce the current tax penalties on investment in industry.

- Encourage a long-term approach to private investment. We will reverse the burden of proof for acquisitions away from the target company towards the predator, and require companies to ballot their shareholders on bid plans. We will reform com-pany law to require greater disclosure of information such as expenditure on research and development. We will define the responsibilities of non-executive dir-ectors and insist that all publicly quoted companies have them on their boards.

- Encourage small businesses and the self-employed, and ensure a 'level playing field' for them in competing with their larger counterparts. This will include relieving the administrative burden on small businesses, legislating to make interest payable on overdue debt, and encouraging TECs, chambers of commerce and local enterprise agencies to reorganise to form a network of business-led 'one-stop shops'. We will encourage, and if necessary legislate for, banks to treat small businesses fairly by agreeing contracts for services.

- Encourage flexibility in working patterns, including part-time and flexi-time work, job-sharing and homeworking, adequate backup for carers of the young or old, and access to appropriate training. We will encourage a new system of tax-free child-care vouchers for parents of children under five, given by employers and usable in workplace, local authority and private nurseries and for individual quali-fied carers.

- Share success in industry. We will legislate to establish the right of every private sector employee in a substantial company to have access to a share in ownership and/or in the profits they help to create. We will encourage profit-related pay, employee share-ownership schemes and employee buy-outs. We will relaunch the Cooperative Development Agency.

- Build partnership in industry. We will ensure that every employee has a right to participate in decision-making in their enterprise. We will set up a new Industrial Partnership Agency to help companies and their employees find the precise forms of partnership which best suit them.

Serving customers

Many financial institutions, and particularly some of the high-street banks, have a poor record of customer service, for individuals and businesses. It is still far too common to see charges applied to accounts, or interest rates changed, without customers being fully informed, and to see new types of accounts opened without existing customers being told that they could benefit from them.

Banks which are responsive to their customers will be good for the economy. We will ensure that commercial borrowers are entitled to a full contract specifying the terms, conditions and duration of the services provided. We will introduce rights for customers of all financial institutions, ensuring they are fully informed when changes are made which do or might affect them.

Child care vouchers

Britain seriously lags behind its continental neighbours in provision for child care for working parents. This not only unfairly impedes opportunity for the people concerned. It holds back the contribution to the economy of many highly skilled workers.

We will encourage the introduction of a system of child care vouchers, provided by employers to parents with children under school age. They will be usable to pay for child care in a range of places – workplace, local authority or private nurseries, play groups or by individual qualified carers. The parent will choose, topping up the value if they wish. Child care vouchers will be deductible expenses for the employers and tax free for the parents. Self-employed people will be able to purchase vouchers and receive similar tax advantages. In due course the principle could be extended to cover child care for older children.

Creating long-term prosperity

We will change the ways in which economic policy is made and implemented, to bring greater stability and a sensible framework to economic management – ending the present 'boom, bust' approach. This requires fuller integration with the European Community. Our key changes are:

- Establishing an operationally independent Bank of England to become the Central Bank of the UK, to ensure disciplined economic management, to end political manipulation of the economy and to form the rock upon which a long-term anti-inflationary strategy can be built. This will also help progress towards an independent European Central Bank.

- Moving sterling to the narrow band of the European Exchange Rate Mechanism as soon as possible, helping stable progress towards lower interest rates.

- Taxes and public spending to be set to reach a 'savings target' for the nation over a period of years. We will set a target as a total of private- and public-sector savings, and adjust fiscal policy to achieve the target over the medium term. If the country does not save enough to achieve the target, we will alter taxes and public spending accordingly, to ensure adequate long-term investment and keep the economy developing in a non-inflationary way. We will encourage individual savings by giving tax relief on all income paid into new Registered Savings Accounts.

- Reform of the annual Budget. We will publish a draft Budget four months before the final version, to promote open discussion of economic and taxation policy. This will facilitate the integration of spending and revenue-raising, a measure we have long advocated. This will also make it easier to measure the impact of economic policy on the environment. We will establish an independent National Statistical Commission to collect and publish statistics and improve their quality.

- Working towards European economic and monetary union, including the estab- lishment of an independent European Central Bank and a single European cur- rency. We will renounce the Conservatives' Maastricht 'opt-out' clause, accept the timetabled approach to EMU, and renegotiate the Social Chapter with a positive British input.

Changing the economy for good

Liberal Democrats recognise that if we are to improve Britain's disappointing eco- nomic performance we have to change the governmental system which produces it. Our proposals for electoral and constitutional reform are a prerequisite for better economic performance.

Proportional representation will produce greater stability in government, ending the economic disruption caused by sudden sharp swings in government policies before and after elections. Home rule and decentralisation will ensure that economic power and prosperity is spread throughout Britain. Integration within Europe will create the framework for long-term economic strength. Freedom of information legislation and open government will improve competition and encourage informed debate. A written constitution will ensure that politicians can no longer ignore long-term priorities for short-term expediency and political advantage.

2. BRITAIN'S ENVIRONMENT: ENVIRONMENTAL PROTECTION AND CONSERVATION

Liberal Democrats are determined to ensure that Britain changes its ways so that it become a leader, not a laggard, in facing the environmental challenge. Polluters will pay and conservers will be rewarded. Taxation will be gradually shifted from the things we want more of – income, savings and value added – to the things we want less of: pollution and resource depletion.

The accelerating destruction of the environment is one of the most serious challenges we face today. Its symptoms are becoming clearer with every year, from global warming and holes in the ozone layer to poisoned rivers and polluted air at home. They threaten not just our ability to enjoy our towns and countryside but our health and our children's future. Liberal Democrats aim to cut pollution and clean up the local environment.

We aim to build a society that does not create wealth at the expense of the environment. Our economy currently functions unsustainably, producing unacceptable levels of pollution and rates of resource depletion. We will create new incentives to follow environmentally sensitive strategies and behaviour.

Protecting our heritage

Conserving and enhancing the physical environment, countryside and townscape alike, is of crucial importance to everyone's quality of life. Liberal Democrats will:

- Improve countryside protection policies for National Parks, heritage coasts, areas of outstanding natural beauty, and sites of special scientific interest. We will tighten controls against exploitation, we will create more National Parks and we will improve access to the countryside.
- Introduce Countryside Management Agreements for farmers and landowners who wish to take them up. These will be drawn up in conjunction with local planning authorities with the aim of managing the countryside to develop sustainable agriculture, safeguard plant and animal wildlife, and preserve traditional landscape features, such as woods, hedgerows and dry-stone walls.
- Reform land use planning so that the protection of the natural environment becomes a major feature of the planning system. We will decentralise planning decisions as much as possible, giving a key role to the local plan drawn up by the local authority.
- Clean up the cities. We will improve public transport, reduce traffic congestion, and

encourage pedestrianisation and cycling schemes. We will encourage more parks, gardens and green spaces. We will provide more resources for councils to deal with noise complaints and make compensation for excessive commercial noise more widely available.

- Promote better waste management. We will provide grants for recycling schemes, introduce regulations on the use of packaging materials, and encourage local authorities to clean up litter. We will clean up beaches and coastlines by ensuring full treatment of sewage.
- Improve standards of animal protection. We will set up an Animal Protection Commission to enforce and recommend changes to legislation. We will phase out battery cages and unacceptable systems of factory farming, tighten controls on the export of live animals for slaughter, and establish a dog registration scheme. We will prohibit experiments involving pain or distress for non-medical and non-veterinary purposes, promote alternatives to the use of animals in research and education, and ensure that laws against badger-baiting and dog-fighting are enforced. On hunting with hounds, Liberal Democrats as a party have declared their opposition, but recognise, like the Conservative and Labour parties, that legislation is a matter of conscience for each individual MP.
- We aim to build a society that does not create wealth at the expense of the environment. We will create new incentives to follow environmentally sensitive strategies and behaviour.
- We will issue factories and power stations with licences setting a ceiling on permitted emissions of pollutants.

Air pollution index

Air pollution threatens the health of millions of people – particularly children, elderly people and anyone with a respiratory problem such as asthma. Government monitoring stations measure levels of pollutants such as nitrogen oxides or low-level ozone but fail to publicise them widely. When levels exceed World Health Organisation guidelines, the result is described as 'good' – in other countries it would be called 'poor'.

We will increase the number of monitoring stations, ensuring that all major urban areas are covered. We will publish a regular air pollution index and encourage newspapers and TV and radio weather forecasts to use it. This will increase public consciousness of the pollution issue and prove of real benefit to the health of vulnerable people.

Controlling pollution

We will use market mechanisms, where feasible, to reduce pollution by ensuring that environmental costs and benefits are fed into the economy. Direct controls will still be needed in some cases. We will:

- Set targets for cutting pollution. These include a 30% reduction in carbon dioxide emissions from the UK by the year 2005; our energy policy is geared to this target. We will ban the use of CFCs and halons by 1994.
- Introduce a system of tradable emission licences. We will issue factories and power

stations with licences setting a ceiling on permitted emissions of pollutants such as sulphur dioxide. These will be tradable: those who are most efficient at reducing pollution would have surplus licences which they could then sell either to those less efficient, or back to government. The targets for emissions – and therefore number of licences available – will be reduced year by year, leading to a steady fall in pollution.

- Create a new Department of Natural Resources with sole responsibility for environmental protection, leaving the Department of the Environment to cover local government and housing. We will set up an independent and powerful Environmental Protection Agency to work with the new European Environment Agency.
- Put forward plans for a powerful United Nations Environment Programme to lead global efforts to protect the environment, operating within the framework of an 'Earth Charter'. We wish to see a world market in tradable emission licences for carbon dioxide and other pollutants. This would not only provide incentives to cut pollution but also act as a channel for transferring resources to developing countries.

Conserving energy

Without an effective energy policy, government cannot have an effective environment policy. Britain's national energy strategy must be set within an overall European framework, with the aim of reducing pollution, improving energy efficiency and boosting the use of renewables.

We will:

- Support a Community-wide Energy Tax on all energy sources. This will be related to levels of carbon dioxide emitted and will provide a strong incentive for saving energy and investing in cleaner sources. Extra revenue raised through the tax will be fed back into the economy by reducing other taxes such as VAT and by protecting those least able to adapt to the higher price of energy.
- Invest in energy conservation and efficiency. We will set new energy efficiency standards for homes, offices and factories, and for products such as light bulbs, fridges and cookers. We will give grants for home insulation and the installation of solar panels, and introduce energy audits of buildings. We will encourage combined heat and power and district heating schemes.
- Double government spending on renewable energy research. We will establish a Renewable Energy Office to promote research, development and application, in particular of wave power, hot rocks geothermal energy, passive solar design of buildings, small-scale hydropower schemes and wind energy. We will complete the study on the construction of a Severn Barrage.
- Start to phase out nuclear fission power stations, which are prohibitively expensive and potentially hazardous. We aim to complete the phase-out at the latest by the year 2020 (and earlier if feasible), and we will not proceed further with the construction of the Sizewell B PWR. We will continue nuclear research, but at a lower cost. Reprocessing spent nuclear fuel rods increases the volume of waste and should be undertaken only when necessary for safety reasons.

Water District Discount

According to the Government, water bills will rise by 50% within the next few years. For many households (in, for example, Wales), water bills are now higher than bills for all local government services put together. Since 1989 nearly a million summonses have been issued to people who could not pay their water bills.

At present water companies have a Bulk Supply Discount for commercial customers – a 'wholesale price' for their water. Liberal Democrats will alter the licensing conditions for water companies to extend this to groups of domestic consumers who live on large estates and in sheltered housing complexes. This District Discount will keep down bills for elderly people and many low-income inner-city residents living on large estates.

Making transport clean and efficient

By expanding the provision and quality of public transport and reducing society's dependence on the private car, we will improve travel efficiency and protect the environment. We will achieve this by:

- Investment in public transport, increasing its frequency of service, speed and safety, and reducing its cost to the individual – especially in isolated rural areas where the need is greatest. We will encourage new schemes, using light railways and trams in cities. We will require local authorities to define minimum standards of accessibility in their areas and draw up transport plans which meet them.
- Immediate improvements in the rail network, allowing more movement of goods and passengers by rail and less environmental damage. We will construct a high-speed link from the Channel Tunnel to connect with the major rail routes to the North and West, and extend electrification throughout the country. We oppose the privatisation of British Rail, but will allow private operators access to the rail network, while giving BR the freedom to raise investment capital on the open market.
- A reduction in fuel consumption. All political parties accept that long-term increases in petrol prices are not only environmentally necessary but unavoidable. We will phase these in gradually by applying our Energy Tax to petrol, while at the same time graduating Vehicle Excise Duty and Car Tax according to fuel efficiency – so that the most efficient vehicles pay least. These price increases will not be brought in unless and until compensation schemes for individuals and rural communities which have no alternative to the use of cars are ready to be introduced. We will scrap the remaining tax breaks for company cars and apply tougher limits to permitted emissions.
- Assisting people in rural areas by making concessionary fares on local public transport widely available. We will encourage the use of village minibuses, 'post and passenger' buses and taxi services. People who have no alternatives to private cars will be helped by our plans to graduate Vehicle Excise Duty and by specific target measures to help isolated communities.
- Action against traffic congestion in urban areas. We will encourage local authorities to introduce peak-hour bans on cars, traffic calming measures, car-sharing schemes and further pedestrianisation. We will introduce a variety of road-pricing

schemes, in which motorists pay a premium to use highly congested roads at busy times of the day.

- New priorities for road building. We will approve major motorway or trunk road investments only where it can be demonstrated that alternative transport provision cannot meet the need at lower economic and environmental cost. Essential new roads and improvements will still proceed, but the creation of a 'level playing field' in decision-making between rail and road will ensure some switch of passenger and freight transport to the railways.
- The expansion of airports outside the South East, while at the same time freezing further development at Heathrow, Gatwick and Stansted.
- Reversing the decline in the Merchant Fleet. For economic and defence reasons, we will boost British shipping and promote recruitment and training for the Merchant Navy.
- Environmental planning policies. We will introduce planning policies which will encourage the building of homes near workplaces, leisure facilities, shops and other services. Where this is not possible, public transport routes must be easily accessible. We will encourage the use of information technology to decentralise work.

Building a sustainable economy

Liberal Democrats aim to build an economy which is not only competitive and enter-prising but also environmentally sustainable, leaving future generations a wealth inheritance – of knowledge, technology, capital and environmental assets – at least as great as that inherited by the current generation. Our proposals are:

- A better method of measuring economic progress. The conventional target of growth in GDP is a poor indicator of progress. We will modify GDP by incorporat-ing measurements of pollution and resource depletion to create a figure for sus-tainable national income. We will also use indicators of social and personal quality of life such as changes in life expectancy, literacy rates and educational attainments to give a better measure of progress. The Prime Minister will present an annual report on changes in these indicators to Parliament.
- A system of environmental incentives and penalties. We will make available, grants and subsidies for environmentally friendly activities, such as home insulation, and to help individuals and industry adjust to our new stricter standards for pollution control. We will penalise activities which harm the environment or deplete stocks of raw materials through taxation, so that prices reflect the damage they do. Our new Energy Tax is this manifesto's key proposal in this area. The revenue raised will be used to reduce other taxes such as VAT.
- Enable consumers to identify and choose sustainable products. We will introduce new product labels, showing information such as energy consumption during use and the environmental impact of the production process. We will introduce strict standards of life expectancy for consumer durables and encourage deposit-refund schemes. We will improve recycling and waste-disposal systems. We will encourage environmental audits for companies, showing the environmental impact of their activities.

Reviving rural communities

Our policy for the countryside aims both to protect Britain's natural environment and to recreate success in one of Britain's greatest industries, agriculture. The farming industry is passing through a period of profound change; most farmers recognise that the industry must achieve a better balance with the market and the environment. We will help this transition by:

- Working for fundamental reform of the Common Agricultural Policy. We want to ease the adjustment from the present price support mechanism towards market prices and direct support aimed at assisting the farming industry in transition and at environmental and social goals. These will be funded by savings made out of the present intervention mechanisms of the CAP.
- New incentive payments for environmental objectives, in particular for extensifying food production (using land less intensively), and reduced-input and organic farming. Countryside Management Agreements, described above, will be a key feature in this shift of CAP resources from price support to environmental goals.
- Reformed systems of direct support, aimed in particular at helping family farms and crofts.
- Introducing renewable limited-term tenancies for agricultural land, encouraging new entrants to farming. We will encourage local councils to continue to provide smallholdings and to introduce part-time holdings for new entrants.
- Expanding forestry. We support the long-term aim of doubling the area of the UK under forestry, but this must include a higher proportion of broad-leafed hardwoods. We oppose the privatisation of the Forestry Commission. We will create more community forests near large towns.
- Encouraging fishing and fish farming. We will improve the Government's decommissioning proposals and appraise, with the industry, effective technical conservation measures. We should move towards fisheries licensing and management on a more regional basis to help traditional fishing communities and protect those who fish sustainably, such as mackerel handliners. We will transfer full planning responsibility for fish farming to local authorities, and we will increase research into the environmental aspects of fish farming and diversification. We will work with the EC to counter the dumping of stocks into the Community.
- The extension of Rural Development Agencies. These will be responsible for coordinating development and diversification, in partnership with local authorities, the private and voluntary sectors and local communities.
- Tougher action on food safety. We will transfer responsibility for food standards from the Ministry of Agriculture to a new Food and Drugs Commission. We will bring in much tighter labelling requirements for all foods, and make funding available for food research and scientific establishments. We will improve consumer representation on government advisory committees.

3. BRITAIN'S SKILLS: EXCELLENCE FOR ALL

Britain's citizens are our greatest asset. Liberal Democrats will invest in people to enable every individual to fulfil their potential, and, in so doing, build the nation's economic and social strength. We aim to create a first-class education system for all, not just by providing adequate public funding, but also through reforms which increase choice and opportunity for each citizen.

Liberal Democrats start from the belief that every individual, whatever their age, sex, background or ability, possesses a unique potential and a valuable contribution to offer society. Our target is excellence for all. This requires more relevant courses, higher standards and improved provision. Excellence also has a cost. We will guarantee that Liberal Democrats will increase investment in education by £2 billion in the first year, even though this will require an extra penny in the pound on income tax. Our priorities for investment are preschool education, education and training for 16–19 year olds, and adult education.

Aiming high: raising standards

Our aim is simple – to give Britain a world-class education system, in which high quality is the key, by the year 2000. We will:

- Create the framework for high standards by establishing a single Department of Education and Training with oversight of all education and training. We will set up a National Qualifications Council to coordinate a single system of academic and vocational courses for 14–19 year olds, and a new Higher Education Standards Council to monitor quality in higher education.
- Improve inspections. We will ensure that a fully independent HM Inspectorate of Education and Training, properly staffed and funded, reports on the entire range of public and private provision from preschool education to universities. Local inspectors of schools will be answerable to the Inspectorate, which will also have a new role as Education Ombudsman. We will carry out a School Buildings Audit alongside the regular four-yearly local school inspection, to assess the physical state of schools and equipment. We will reinstate the buildings standards suspended in 1989.
- Support teachers. We will set up a statutory General Teaching Council to improve professional qualifications and set standards for teacher training and retraining. We will improve provision for in-service training and career breaks for women teachers with children. We supported the introduction of the Teachers' Pay Review Body and believe it will ensure that teachers are properly rewarded.

Putting education at the heart of the community

Liberal Democrats pioneered Local Management of Schools. Now we aim to increase further the day-to-day independence of schools and colleges within a democratically accountable framework of local education authorities. This includes:

- A new independence for schools and further education colleges. We will give schools increased administrative support in return for the wider opening of their facilities to the local community. We will fully fund individual teacher costs. We will encourage every school to enhance its character, ethos and areas of special interest within a more flexible National Curriculum framework. Within this context of greater freedom for all schools, we will end the two-tier system created by Grant Maintained Schools and City Technology Colleges by returning them to the strategic planning framework of the local elected education authority. Strategic responsibility for adult and further education will remain with the LEA. LEA representatives on school governing bodies will reflect fairly the political balance of the authority.

- A new role for local democracy. We will require LEAs to guarantee a suitable place, with proper support, for every child in education and training up to the age of 19. This will include responsibility for ensuring that schools and colleges meet the highest standards of academic performance, discipline and behaviour, and for providing special services for schools, such as peripatetic music, language development, or behaviour support. Published information about schools and colleges will recognise achievement on the basis of 'education value added' – progress made by pupils – rather than crude 'league tables' of results.

- Independent schools. We recognise the contribution to excellence which the best of these schools make, and the right of those who wish to pay for private education to do so, but this should not be subsidised from public resources. We will phase out the Assisted Places Scheme without affecting those already in it, and restore the money saved to state schools. We will review the charitable status of independent schools with the intention of ensuring that the benefits of charitable status are only awarded to those institutions that make a genuine contribution to the wider community.

Opening schools to the community

Schools should be seen as a valuable resource, not just for their pupils but for the communities around them. Access to their libraries, computers, meetings rooms, sports halls, playing fields and swimming pools could make a big contribution to community life.

We will encourage all schools to open up these facilities to local people in the evenings, at weekends and in school holidays. Some of our proposed expansion of adult education will be organised in this way. Local authorities – particularly community councils where they exist – will help to provide the administrative support needed to manage such open access.

Educating the individual

Liberal Democrats will ensure that every individual can receive high-quality education and training throughout their life from before school to retirement. But the current system places too little emphasis on vocational achievements.

We will:

- Guarantee preschool education for every child. We will guarantee every child access to two years' preschool education with a choice of preschool provision.

- Introduce a National Record of Achievement. We will ensure that every pupil has a National Record of Achievement so that progress is properly documented and shared between parents and schools. Supplemented by individual diagnostic testing, this will replace the current Standard Assessment Tasks in order to raise standards.
- Reduce class sizes. We aim to reduce maximum class sizes so that no registration class in the country need have more than 30 pupils.
- Reward academic and vocational achievements. Our new National Qualifications Council will develop a modular, credit-based course and examination structure for the 14–19 age group, covering both vocational and academic courses. This will build on a simpler, more flexible National Curriculum and a revised and extended system of National Curriculum levels. Pupils from the age of 14 will study a balanced curriculum around a core of maths, English, science and a foreign language, adding specialisms in academic, vocational or technical courses, some delivered by employers in the workplace. We will ensure that all 14–19 year olds have a personal tutor and careers advice, helping them build the foundations for personal fulfilment and success.
- Broaden post-16 education. We will give all 16–19 year olds in work the equivalent of at least two days a week education or training. Courses will be selected by both the employer and the individual and will be accredited as part of our new 14–19 system. Those studying full time will study up to three major and two subsidiary subjects, adding work experience, parenting and citizenship to build a baccalaureate-style programme.
- Improve Special Educational Needs provision. We will give every LEA a separate Special Educational Needs service with its own budget for which schools will bid for funding. We will require schools to prepare, for every child with special needs who is not currently covered, an indicative statement to identify needs, set targets and report progress. The service will be monitored by specialists in the local inspection team and in HMI.
- Enable education for life. We will give every citizen an entitlement to a period of retraining or education at a time of their choice during their adult lives, based on distance learning costs. We will start by giving this guarantee to those groups most in need, including the long-term unemployed and single parents.
- We will guarantee that Liberal Democrats will increase investment in education by £2 billion in the first year. Our priorities for investment are preschool education, education and training for 16–19 year olds and adult education.

Opening the doors to higher education

Britain's higher education system still provides excellent standards of education, but does so for too few people. Liberal Democrats aim to increase both participation and flexibility in studying for degrees, because not all students want to follow traditional three-year courses. We will:

- Increase the number of students in higher education to two million by the year 2000. As well as more young people, we will particularly encourage the participation of women, people from minority ethnic and poorer backgrounds, and people with disabilities.

- Increase flexibility in courses. We will introduce a credit-based system, enabling students to achieve a diploma after the equivalent of two years, with the option of a further one or two years' study leading to a degree. We will make financial assistance available for part-time study.
- Open up new opportunities for study. We will develop distance learning opportunities and extend the franchising of higher education courses so that courses can start at local colleges – helping people who wish or need to study from home.
- Fund students properly. We will abolish student loans and restore student entitlement to housing benefit and income support. As our plans for the reform of tax and benefits are implemented, we will establish a Student Income Entitlement and a Student Allowance to which all students, both full- and part-time, will be eligible.
- Guarantee quality. Our new Higher Education Standards Council will ensure that as numbers rise, quality does not suffer. We will establish a proper career structure for research fellows and set up a Pay Review Body for academic and non-academic staff to halt the brain drain.
- Invest in research. We will immediately increase the science budget to 0.35% of GDP, and raise it steadily thereafter. We will establish a new Humanities Research Council.

4. BRITAIN'S PEOPLE: HEALTHIER, SAFER AND BETTER HOUSED

Liberal Democrats will invest in local services to enable communities to thrive. Our aim is to ensure that individuals of all backgrounds and means can live free of the fear of sickness, poverty and crime.

The steps we outline in this paper are necessary to create a fair, democratic and prosperous society, in which individuals are able to make their voice heard and develop their talents and skills to the full. But we believe that people can realise their potential best not as isolated individuals, but as members of thriving and responsible communities. We will invest in the network of community services – health, housing, crime prevention, social security, arts and sport – to improve quality, choice and opportunity for everyone.

Guaranteeing high-quality health care

Liberal Democrats remain steadfastly committed to the original aims of the NHS: to enable everyone to live free of the fear of illness, injury and disability; to provide health care free at the point of delivery and regardless of ability to pay. The Government's 'reforms' mean that patients are made to follow the money; under our proposals, money will follow the patients. We especially oppose the two-tier Health Service which the Government is creating. Our priorities are:

- A decent level of health service funding, including an annual real increase to match the costs of new technology and the growing number of elderly people. We will start to replace the underfunding suffered by the Health Service under the Conservatives, invest more in renovating and constructing new health service buildings, and increase spending in the priority areas listed below. We will abolish tax relief for private health insurance, whilst protecting the rights of existing policy-holders.

- Health promotion – keeping people healthy, and treating the root causes of ill health. We will provide resources for preventive medicine, health education and occupational health, invest in screening programmes for the prevention of disease, tackle the problems of drug abuse, ban tobacco promotion, remove charges for eye tests and dental checkups, and both freeze and extend exemptions from prescription charges. We will increase resources for primary care. We will restore a comprehensive dental screening service in schools and improve the dentists' NHS contract. We will require all government departments to take account of the impact on health of their decisions – of crucial importance in areas such as industrial investment, housing, social security and environmental protection.

- Real choice in health care. We will introduce an effective Patient's Charter, including rights to hospital treatment within a specified time, a choice of GP, guaranteed access to health records, and a comprehensive no-fault compensation scheme. We will require health authorities to publish a Charter of Services, defining basic entitlements, and provide redress where these are not satisfied. We will establish a new National Inspectorate for Health to guarantee a quality service.

- Better health care for women. We will ensure access to clinics providing health promotion, counselling, family planning and screening services, particularly for cervical and breast cancer, and advice on maternity and child care. We will increase the availability both of treatment by women health professionals and of home birth.

- High-quality community care, available through voluntary, private and local authority services to people unable to care for themselves. We will give users control over the options for care and provide services in a way which guarantees individuals maximum independence while retaining existing community links. We will provide bridging finance for local authorities for the transition to the new legislative arrangements on community care.

- Investment in NHS staff, including in-service training, especially in areas of significant shortage and changing roles. We will reform medical staffing and training to replace the consultant-led hierarchy with teams of accredited specialists.

- A health service for all. We will ensure that the assessment of health-care needs and the strategic planning of all services are the responsibility of democratically accountable health authorities. We will replace the so-called 'internal market' with service agreements between authorities and hospitals and other health units. We will replace GP fundholding with a system which guarantees GPs freedom to refer patients outside the service agreements negotiated by health authorities. We will create a common structure of Local Management of Hospitals and community units, ending the ability of NHS Trusts to dispose of their capital assets, to set their own terms and conditions of service for staff, and to withdraw from local planning of health services.

Providing good housing

Decent, affordable and safe housing is vital to personal happiness and family life. We will encourage home ownership, but we recognise that the housing market has been distorted by mortgage tax relief, and we believe that choice in housing means providing more rented accommodation in both public and private sectors. We will:

- Introduce housing cost relief weighted towards those most in need and available to house buyers and renters. This will replace mortgage tax relief for future home buyers, which often helps most those who need it least, and causes enormous distortions in the savings and housing markets. People holding mortgages will be protected: they will have the choice of moving to housing cost relief or continuing to receive mortgage interest tax relief.

- Boost house building and renovation. We will relax controls on local authority capital receipts, especially for new council building, for houses built in cooperation with housing associations, and for renovation and repair work. We recognise that the urgent need for homes can only be met by mobilising both private investment and public spending. We will therefore create a new Partnership Housing sector to ensure high-quality affordable rented housing.

- Improve tenants' rights to better standards of repair and maintenance in the public and private sectors. We will encourage councils to create more tenants' cooperatives. We will retain the right of council tenants to opt for a change of landlord, but only after a fair ballot.

- Take urgent action on homelessness. We will pay income support to claimants in advance and assist with initial deposits, extend the duty of local authorities to provide accommodation for 16–18 year olds, and encourage councils to assist each other with housing needs. We will fund the provision of short-term rented housing to reduce the use of bed and breakfast accommodation. We will legislate to bring into use dwellings left empty without reasonable cause for more than a year.

- Adopt new environmental standards for all buildings, commercial and domestic. We will introduce a requirement for energy audits on all new buildings as a pre-condition of grants for home insulation, solar heating and other energy-saving measures. Homes which meet the new standards will be exempt from stamp duty on house purchase. We will encourage shared combined heat and power schemes, and encourage those planning new houses to take into account the scope for passive solar heating.

Home energy efficiency discount

Saving energy in the home makes good environmental sense, and will save money on electricity and gas bills. We will make houses which meet high standards of energy efficiency exempt from the first £1000 of stamp duty when they are sold. Their energy standard will be assessed by an energy audit carried out by the local authority's energy efficiency unit.

If a home does not meet the minimum standard, the owner will be able to claim back all money spent within the first year after purchase on raising it to that level, through, for example, home insulation, up to the amount of stamp duty they paid when they bought the property (up to the maximum of £1000). This will help to cut pollution and save energy and give a valuable boost to the housing market.

Protecting the community

Over the past ten years recorded crime has risen faster than at any time in our history. Meanwhile, prison conditions have deteriorated and the public has lost confidence in the criminal justice system. Liberal Democrats will reverse this trend by:

- Creating safe and secure communities. We will give local authorities the powers to develop comprehensive community crime prevention programmes, improve services to victims and encourage Neighbourhood Watch and Safer City Programmes. We will pay special attention to the underlying social problems in high-crime areas, particularly to prevent young people drifting into crime.

- Putting more police officers on the beat. We will redeploy police resources in order to increase police presence in local communities and establish local neighbourhood offices. We will decentralise budgetary control to police subdivisions. We will encourage recruitment campaigns and training for promotion to increase the number of women and ethnic minority officers in the police force and especially in the higher ranks. Multicultural and anti-racism training will also increase confidence in the police among minority ethnic communities. We will support the creation by the police of new Racial Attacks Squads to monitor and coordinate action against racially-motivated attacks.

- Reforming the criminal justice system. We will establish a Ministry for Justice, merging the relevant functions of the Home Office and the Lord Chancellor's Department. We will create the post of Public Defender, equivalent in status to the DPP and responsible for investigating alleged miscarriages of justice. We will extend legal aid, ensuring that justice is more widely available. We will encourage 'restorative justice', in which mediation between victims and offenders provides reparations for those who suffer from crime.

- Radically reforming conditions inside prisons, reducing overcrowding, improving prison officers' morale and punishing offenders where possible within the community. We will create women's units in prisons where feasible. We will extend the rights and responsibilities of prisoners along the lines recommended by the Woolf Report, and create the post of Prison Ombudsman.

- Amend the provision of the Asylum Bill. We will introduce improved welfare and legal rights for genuine asylum seekers and establish substantive rights of appeal.

Ensuring a decent income for all

The tax and social security systems are long overdue for reform. Our objectives are to simplify and integrate the two systems, to mount a determined assault on poverty and dependence, and to protect our citizens from want.

We will work towards the eventual creation of a new 'Citizen's Income', payable to all irrespective of sex or status. For pensioners, the Citizen's Income will be well above the present pension, and for everyone else it will be about £12.80 a week (at present prices). Unpaid work will at last be recognised as valuable. Women caring in the home, for example, will receive an independent income from the state for the first time. The Citizen's Income will be buttressed by a single benefit for those in need, unifying income support and family credit, with supplements for people with disabilities and for child-care support. These reforms will ensure that every citizen is guaranteed a decent minimum income, whether or not they are in employment. Our immediate priorities, which will act as steps towards the Citizen's Income, include:

- Immediate improvements in benefits. We will increase Child Benefit by £1 per week for each child. Income support for under-25s will be paid at the full rate, an increase of £8.50 per week. We will give back to 16 and 17 year olds the right to claim income support. We will end immediately the minimum poll tax level of 20%, prior to the abolition of the tax itself. We will reform the Social Fund, removing its cash limit and converting most loans into grants.

- Increasing the basic state pension immediately by £5 a week for single pensioners, and by £8 a week for married couples. This higher basic pension will be paid to every pensioner, regardless of their contributory record, to end the indignity of means testing. After the initial increase, we will uprate the basic pension every year in line with average earnings. This will be paid for by abolishing SERPS, which does not help the poorest pensioners. People who have already built up SERPS entitlements will of course still receive their SERPS pension.

- Protecting the rights of members of occupational pension schemes. We will provide a statutory framework of protection, including employee representation on occupational pension trusts.

- Creating a comprehensive disability income scheme to give people with disabilities real financial freedom. We will increase Invalidity Benefit by 15%, extend mobility allowance and base payments on medical records rather than National Insurance contributions. In the longer term we aim to reimburse individuals in full for the additional costs of their disability.

- Creating a Carer's Benefit for the many individuals who forgo normal earnings to look after elderly or disabled relatives. We will convert Invalid Care Allowance into a Carer's Benefit, increasing its value by an immediate 15%, indexing its future level to earnings and altering the entitlement rules to enable carers to combine caring with part-time or even full-time jobs and to ensure that people will still be eligible even if the caring starts after the carer reaches pensionable age.

- Further improvements in benefits. We will, over the lifetime of a Parliament, phase out the differential in child benefit between the first child and subsequent children; reintroduce death and maternity grants; increase the family premium for income support and family credit, and reform the system of cold-weather payments.
- Unifying income tax and employees' National Insurance contributions so that the two taxes are collected and administered together and paid on the same income, whether from earnings, investments, capital gains or perks.

- Making the investment needed to end the recession, using the money borrowed by the Conservatives to pay for their pre-election tax cuts. We will also raise the basic rate of income tax by one penny in the pound to pay for the improvements essential to education. Our new tax rates will be as follows:

  - About 80% of tax payers will pay 26% income tax plus the 9% from National Insurance (a combined rate of 35%).
  - On earnings above £33,000, a combined rate of 42% will apply.
  - On earnings above £50,000 a combined rate of 50% will be paid.
  - Pensioners and ordinary savers will not pay the 9% National Insurance element on their incomes. Special provisions will also ensure that those on modest incomes most of which comes from investments, such as people who have been made redundant, do not pay this 9% on their savings.

A citizen's pension

At present many people do not receive the full basic state pension. If they have not paid enough tax because they have not earned enough during their working lives, people have to rely on means-tested benefits when they retire. Women in particular are badly affected, because they tend to have the lowest paid jobs and to spend several years looking after children.

Liberal Democrats believe that a pension should be a right for everyone. We will ensure that the basic state pension is paid as of right and end means testing for our poorest senior citizens.

We will introduce Housing Cost Relief, weighted towards those in need and available to house buyers and renters. People holding mortgages will have the choice of moving to housing cost relief or continuing to receive mortgage interest tax relief.

Widening horizons: investing in the arts

The arts benefit society in two ways. First, access to the arts is intrinsic to a high quality of life. Second, the cultural sector – the arts, crafts, design, and audiovisual industries – makes as great a net contribution to the economy as does the oil industry. We will:

- Create a new Ministry of Arts and Communications headed by a minister in the Cabinet. Liberal Democrats will raise investment in the arts to the EC average over five years.
- Reform and decentralise arts funding and organisation. We will decentralise many of the responsibilities of the Arts Council, increasing the roles of Regional Arts Boards and local authorities.
- Strengthen links between the arts and education. We will enhance practical arts teaching and library provision in schools and extend the provision of adult education for the arts and crafts. We will restore funding for public libraries to 1980 levels. We will abolish museum charges for school parties.
- Transfer responsibility for broadcasting to the new Ministry. The BBC is a major patron of the arts, and broadcasting itself combines a variety of arts and crafts. We will reform recent legislation affecting the independent channels to entrench the interests of quality broadcasting and to guarantee political independence. These interests will also be reflected in the impending review of the BBC's Charter, and our plans for cable television.
- Encourage participation within Europe – including in particular cooperation in the film industry, in protecting and enhancing our common heritage and in expanding opportunities for young artists of all kinds.

Encouraging a fit, active and healthy society

Sport is important for the economic, social and health benefits which it can bring and for its ability to enhance community identity. Liberal Democrats will:

- Create a UK Sports Commission to provide a voice for participants, spectators and administrators. State Sports Councils will continue to receive their core funds from government but the Commission will raise and distribute additional resources for the promotion of participation and excellence.
- Encourage sport across the community. We will encourage school to invest in sports facilities and open them up to the local community. We will establish Community Sports Plans offering tax relief to sports clubs that share facilities and coaching resources with local schools. We will encourage local authorities to transform football grounds into multi-sport venues.
- Encourage individual and corporate sponsorship, review the role of the Foundation for Arts and Sport and reconsider the Conservatives' hasty proposal for a national lottery.
- Maintain Britain's leading role in the fight against drug abuse in sport, ensuring adequate funding for testing programmes and education campaigns directed at participants.
- Enhance safety in the provision of sports grounds. We will put the safety of specta-

tors first in any legislation and make standards mandatory. We will take into account the size of grounds when setting safety standards. We will raise revenue for investment in safety by increasing levies on football pools and betting. We will require local authorities to include sports spectators on ground safety committees.

Guaranteeing equal opportunities

A forward-looking society places an equal value on the contribution of all its citizens – and benefits from the participation of all. Yet in today's Britain many groups of individuals are systematically discriminated against by a society which fails to recognise their right to equality of opportunity. Liberal Democrats will:

- Fight discrimination by incorporating the European Convention on Human Rights into UK law and then extending it into a full UK Bill of Rights. This will reinforce existing protection in British courts against discrimination on the grounds of sex, race, age, disability, religion or sexual orientation. We will set up a Commission of Human Rights to assist individuals to take legal action in cases of discrimination or other breaches of the rights guaranteed in the Convention.

- Strengthen the rights of women. We will guarantee equal pay for work of equal value; require public authorities and private contractors holding public contracts to be equal-opportunity employers and improve child-care support and facilities. Proportional representation for elections and modernising Parliamentary procedures will help to end the discrimination against women on elected bodies and in government at European, national and local levels.

- Extend the opportunities of young people. We will entrench young people's rights of representation on organisations which affect their lives and well-being such as college governing bodies. We will place a statutory obligation on local authorities to provide a comprehensive youth service in partnership with the voluntary sector, and we will invest in leisure and recreation facilities. Young people will have the right to confidential medical advice and treatment.

- Make old age a time of opportunity. We will introduce a flexible 'decade of retirement' for men and women, in which people may choose to retire and take a state pension at any time between ages 60 and 70 (the value of the pension increasing with the age of retirement). We will increase choice for elderly and retired people by encouraging openings in voluntary and part-time work, and widening the availability of education, the arts and recreational facilities.

- Protect the rights of ethnic minorities. We will reinforce legislation to ensure equal opportunities for all, in housing, employment, education and training, especially in inner-city areas. PR will greatly increase the possibilities of participation in the political process. We will repeal the 1981 Nationality Act, reform immigration legislation to make it free from racial discrimination and restore the right of entry to British passport holders. We will push for the extension of EC race discrimination legislation and ensure that the rights of black and Asian British citizens are respected throughout the EC. We will encourage changes to the education system which place a positive value on a pluralist, diverse and multicultural society.

- Guarantee equal rights for gay men and lesbians through changes to criminal law, anti-discrimination legislation and police practices. We will repeal Section 28 of the 1988 Local Government Act. We will create a common age of consent regardless of gender or sexual orientation.

- Work with people with disabilities and their organisations to draw up a charter of rights for people with disabilities. We will implement the 1986 Disabled Persons Act in full, giving priority to the development of advocacy schemes.

- We will fight discrimination by incorporating the European Convention on Human Rights into UK law and then extending it into a full UK Bill of Rights.

5. BRITAIN'S PARTNERS: EUROPEAN PARTNERSHIP FOR THE NEW CENTURY

Liberal Democrats will take decisive steps towards a fully integrated, federal and democratic European Community. We believe that by sharing sovereignty and pooling power, Britain and its partners will be better able to achieve common goals for the economy, the environment, society and security than by acting alone. Our aim is to create a citizens' Europe in which power lies as close to the citizen as possible.

Making Britain's European Presidency work

Very few of the proposals that we have set out in the preceding sections will be successful unless Britain is prepared to work in partnership within the Community. Following Maastricht, yet again Britain risks being left behind while the rest of Europe moves on.

Liberal Democrats want Britain to play a full role in creating a dynamic and democratic Europe. We will use Britain's six-month tenure of the Presidency of the Community's Council of Ministers to make a start on the real tasks that lie ahead: building a prosperous and integrated economy; correcting the democratic deficit, making Europe work for its citizens, not its institutions; widening the Community's membership; and helping to create a peaceful and stable new world order. We cannot expect Britain to influence the direction the Community takes in the next decade unless it is a full and enthusiastic member.

Our vision of the new Europe is of a federal community, where power is exercised at the lowest level consistent with good government. For us, federalism means decentralisation: passing powers down more than passing them up. The creation of Scottish, Welsh and English regional Parliaments therefore goes hand in hand with the promotion of more European cooperation and partnership, ensuring access to power for individuals and their communities right across Europe.

Building a citizens' Europe

January 1993 will bring the single market. Economic and monetary union will follow by the end of the decade. Yet the Community is still too much an organisation for businessmen and bureaucrats instead of citizens and communities. We want to mould Europe's future in the interests of Europe's people. Our priorities are:

- Economic and monetary union including the establishment of an independent European Central Bank and a single European currency. We will renounce the Conservatives' 'opt-out' clause and accept the timetable for EMU.
- Cooperation in research and innovation. We will encourage further collaboration within the EC on major scientific projects and the development of new technologies such as telecommunications, information technology and environmentally sustainable innovations.
- Action on the environment. Our environmental goals cannot be successfully achieved unless action is taken across the Community. The proposed European Environment Agency must be established, a European energy policy drawn up and environmental subsidies and penalties applied Community-wide.
- An active regional and social policy. The single market and economic and monetary union will expose regions and firms to greater competition. This will be beneficial in the long run, but the EC must assist in the transitional period. We will renounce Britain's social chapter 'opt-out' and argue for a more flexible framework of social policy across the Community. The EC should set down minimum standards of health and safety and employee rights, leaving national governments and enterprises to decide how to meet them, subject ultimately to the judgement of the courts.
- Fundamental reform of the Common Agricultural Policy. We will ease the transition from the present wasteful and inefficient price support mechanism to market prices and direct support for farmers' incomes to achieve environmental and social goals, to be funded by savings made from the present intervention payment system.

Creating a new democracy in Europe

The Community's structure gives far too much weight to the Council of Ministers at the expense of the European Parliament, and, most importantly, of the individual citizen. Further moves to European union, and enlargement, must depend on the institutions of the EC becoming truly democratic. We will:

- Set out the rights of the European citizen. We will work for a clear definition of the rights of the European citizen, and insist that these are common to all Community nationals. This must include common voting rights at local, national and European levels.
- Increase the democratic powers of the European Parliament. We will ensure that the Parliament becomes an effective partner with the Council in law-making, exercising in full the power of 'co-decision'.
- Introduce fair votes for the 1994 British elections to the European Parliament. The

British citizen must no longer be denied the fair voting systems enjoyed by the citizens of every other European country.

- Make the Commission more accountable. The Parliament must have the power to confirm or deny the Council's nominee as President of the Commission, and then to approve or not the President's choice of Commissioners – and subsequently to sack them if necessary. We welcome the provisions of the Maastricht Treaty as a first step.
- Increase democracy and accountability in the Council of Ministers. We will argue to extend majority voting in the Council to cover all areas of Community policy other than constitutional and crucial security matters. When passing laws, the Council should meet in public.
- Improve national scrutiny of Ministers' actions in Europe. We will create a new Europe Committee of the House of Commons, and give our reformed House of Lords (see page 48) a special role in scrutinising developments in the Community.
- Prepare for Community enlargement, welcoming EFTA members and, when they are ready, the new democracies of Central and Eastern Europe. A Community with more members requires reformed and dynamic institutions.

Further moves to European Union, and enlargement, must depend on the institutions of the European Community becoming truly democratic.

Sharing security; working for peace

The Gulf War and its aftermath have shown the crucial need for stronger and more effective world institutions capable of upholding international law and enforcing respect for human rights. Britain must ensure that the Community plays a pivotal role in the construction of a new security order in Europe, following the democratisation of Eastern and Central Europe. New initiatives for disarmament and for sharing security burdens will enable further reductions in levels of armaments to be made without endangering security. On the global stage, a stronger United Nations will be needed to underpin cooperation in tackling the world's problems. We will:

- Develop common European Community foreign and security policies. This will include a common approach to defence procurement and the gradual integration of Community members' armed forces under a joint military command. The burden of collective security in Western Europe should be shared more equally; we will press for contributions from all nations to the costs of joint forces such as NATO's proposed Rapid Reaction Force – of which Britain will provide almost half.

- Promote democracy and reform in Eastern and Central Europe by coordinating generous economic assistance to countries introducing democracy, guaranteeing human rights and reforming their economies.

- Assist the peaceful evolution of the Commonwealth of Independent States, the former USSR. We will help not just with food and financial aid and technical assistance, but also with the provision of military resources to shift food and supplies, and with scientific assistance to dismantle nuclear weapons.

- Develop a pan-European security framework. We will encourage the Conference on Security and Cooperation in Europe to develop monitoring, verification and mediation duties within the continent. We will press for NATO to guarantee the borders of Poland, Czechoslovakia and Hungary and to enter into talks with other governments in the region for similar guarantees.

- Instigate a comprehensive review of UK defence policy which will be dictated by a rigorous analysis of defence needs rather than by fixed monetary targets. The Review will cover the continuing need for contributions to collective security, the value of Britain's remaining extra-European commitments, and the potential for increasing our contribution to UN peacekeeping missions. Given the present hopeful international situation, we believe that further reductions in levels of armaments will be able to be made without in any way endangering security. Since the review will set out the framework for defence policy for years to come, we will halt any defence cut, and any order for a new weapons system, which might prejudice its outcome.

- Establish an Arms Conversion Agency to help arms manufacturers to diversify and convert out of the defence field, funded by savings made in the defence budget. Our proposed regional development agencies will also provide help to areas particularly affected. We will reduce spending on military research and development, and shift the resources saved into the civilian sector.

- Maintain a minimum nuclear deterrent. We believe that the UK needs to retain its independent nuclear deterrent, but that the escalation of firepower represented by the scale of the Trident replacement for Polaris is unnecessary and unhelpful. We will ensure that the total number of warheads on the four-boat Trident system is limited to no more than that currently deployed on the Polaris system, and our Defence Review will consider whether we can reduce this further without threatening security. Our Review will also examine the possibilities of future European cooperation in the provision of a deterrent force. We reject the Government's proposed replacement of British free-fall nuclear bombs with air-to-surface missiles.

- Propose new disarmament initiatives covering all categories of conventional and nuclear weapons. These will aim to eliminate non-strategic nuclear weapons from Europe, and to reduce the strategic weapons possessed by the US, the former Soviet Union, Britain, France and China – a vital step towards the day when individual nations' possession of nuclear deterrents ceases to be necessary.

- Act against the arms trade. Together with our Community partners, we will establish a register of all international arms sales, eventually to become a UN register. We will place a total embargo on arms sales to regimes which violate human rights, and work for further global agreements among suppliers to control arms sales and technology transfer. We will close the Defence Export Services Organisation and ensure that overseas aid is not linked in any way to arms purchases.

- Make the United Nations more effective. The UN Security Council should take a proactive role in peace-keeping before confrontation develops into conflict. We will work with our Community partners to ensure that funds are available for maintaining peace and security. The UN Military Staff Committee should be reinstated and a permanent peacekeeping force established, with member states contributing contingents on an annual basis. Because of the need to assign British forces to this and to European policing and disaster roles (on top of their present commitments), more general purpose infantry battalions will be required than the number currently planned by the Conservative Government.

Developing global prosperity

A secure, democratic and peaceful world can never be created while so much of the globe remains so desperately poor. Britain must play its part in developing prosperity, protecting the world environment, eradicating poverty, famine and disease, and promoting human rights and international cooperation.

This will include:

- Increasing overseas aid to reach the UN target of 0.7% of GNP over five years. We will increase aid especially to democratic countries carrying out policies which benefit the poorest, are environmentally sustainable and respect human rights. We will raise the proportion of aid given as grants instead of loans and place greater emphasis on supporting small-scale, community-based, labour-intensive projects. We will promote closer European cooperation, to make the best use of national and Community aid, and avoid wasteful duplication. We will rejoin UNESCO.

- Ending the commercialisation of aid which the current Government has practised and which substantially reduces its value to the world's poorest. We will reduce the proportion of UK aid tied to the purchase of UK goods and services and ensure that help to British exports is solely a function of the Department of Trade and Industry, rather than the ODA.

- Encouraging environmentally sustainable development. This includes the transfer of appropriate technology, the development of sustainable agriculture and forestry, sustainable use policies for the tropical rain forests and projects to prevent desertification, and the promotion of energy conservation and renewable energy schemes. We will provide technical help to develop methods of resource accounting and environmental protection and ensure that measures of sustainability are incorporated in decisions on development projects and programmes.

- Urgent action to tackle the growth in the world's population. Having doubled in the past fifty years to five billion, the world's population is expected to increase by a further one billion in the 1990s alone. We will give priority to support for family-planning programmes, education and employment opportunities for women, and basic provision for old age.

- Reform of the world trading and financial systems. We see the successful conclusion of the Uruguay round of the GATT world trade talks as an urgent priority. Global prosperity also requires the reversal of the net flow of resources from the global South. We will press the EC to coordinate international action to resolve the debt crisis, including reducing government-to-government debt, introducing regulatory and tax regimes to encourage commercial banks to reduce or write off debt, extending eligibility to IMF and World Bank loans, and encouraging, where appropriate, debt for development and debt for environment swaps. We will press for the progressive reduction of all tariff and non-tariff trade barriers, and in particular the removal of unfair trading barriers against developing countries.

6. BRITAIN'S DEMOCRACY: ELECTORAL AND CONSTITUTIONAL REFORM

Liberal Democrats, alone in British politics, recognise that unless we change Britain's system of government, we cannot change Britain's future. Without constitutional reform, we will not achieve our other objectives.

We believe in citizenship, not subjecthood – in the ability of all individuals to exercise power over the institutions that govern their lives. The creation of a modernised democracy therefore lies at the heart of all our proposals.

We recognise too that Britain's success in the next century will depend not just on changing what we do, but in changing the way in which we do it. However worthy its intentions, and however able its personnel, no government will be able to put Britain right unless and until it has modernised our constitution.

Fair voting for an effective Parliament

Our current 'winner takes all' system of voting has many faults. It is unfair, unstable and divisive. Government by minority is usually bad government: in no truly democratic country could a disaster like the poll tax have been pushed through in defiance of public opinion, wasting billions of pounds and causing misery to millions of people. Our top priority is therefore the introduction of fair votes for all elections at all levels of government.

Fair votes will make every elector's vote count. It will increase citizens' control over their elected representatives, by abolishing safe seats. It will eradicate the power of the extremist minority in political parties. It will lead to a better choice of candidates and ensure that more women and candidates from minority ethnic communities are elected. Above all, it will reduce tit-for-tat politics and introduce much greater stability into government, allowing individuals and businesses alike to plan for their future with confidence. We will:

- Bring in fair votes. We will introduce proportional representation for all elections at local, national and European levels. We propose the single transferable vote, by which electors cast their votes in multi-member constituencies based on natural communities.
- Introduce fixed-term Parliaments of four years, with a known date for the next

election, subject to an earlier election only if the government loses a special 'explicit' vote of no confidence.

- Reform the House of Lords. We will maintain a second chamber as a Senate, primarily elected by the citizens of the nations and regions of the United Kingdom. It will have power to delay all legislation other than money bills for up to two years.
- Improve the way Parliament works. We will give MPs greater influence over the executive by boosting the powers of Select Committees, improving staff backup for backbenchers and increasing financial and civil service support for opposition parties. We will improve the quality of legislation by establishing pre-legislative committees and better scrutiny of delegated legislation. We will improve the quality of debates by allocating time for business more fairly, timetabling Committee sessions of bills and ending Parliament's late-night sittings.

Bringing power to the people

Our system of government is far too centralised, and fails to make effective use of the talents and skills available across the country. We believe that political power is best exercised at the most local level possible, consistent with good government. We will:

- Introduce Home Rule for Scotland, with the immediate creation of an elected Scottish Parliament.
- Introduce Home Rule for Wales, with the immediate creation of an elected Welsh Senedd.
- Reform and strengthen local government, removing unnecessary tiers, restoring councils' independence and ensuring they are accountable to the people through a fair voting system.
- Create the framework for regional government in England. We will enable the establishment of fully democratic regional governments throughout England. We will set up a Strategic Authority for London as a priority. Preceding the new regional governments, we will establish regional development agencies throughout England, helping to boost economic development and prosperity.
- Decentralise power to the new national and regional governments. Economic development, housing, health, social services, roads and public transport, education and planning are functions which should be devolved from Whitehall and brought nearer the people they most affect.

Strengthening local government

The current Government's approach to local government finance – most notably through the poll tax fiasco – has been to destroy the independence of local authorities by reducing their powers to raise and spend revenue. The Liberal Democrat approach is exactly the opposite: we aim to take power away from Westminster and Whitehall, giving new powers to stronger, more independent and more democratic local councils – elected by fair votes. We will:

- Abolish the poll tax, cancel plans for the proposed Council Tax and introduce a Local Income Tax, related to ability to pay and collected by the Inland Revenue.

Local Income Tax is easy to understand, easy to administer, and fair. It works effectively in many other countries.

- Replace the Uniform Business Rate with Site Value Rating – locally administered and based on the taxation of land values (with exemption for agricultural land and domestic properties). This will create incentives to improve property, rather than leave it undeveloped. Administration will be easier and local accountability will be restored.
- Reform and strengthen local government. We will reform principal local councils into a unitary system based on natural communities and the wishes of local people. We will give the new authorities greater responsibilities – for example, over education, health, and planning – and freedom to ensure the delivery of services in ways they think best. Local authorities will be given a 'general power of competence', which will allow them to carry out any beneficial local action which neither duplicates the work of other public bodies nor breaks the law.
- Bring local government nearer to the people, by enabling the formation of a full network of community, parish, town or neighbourhood councils. We will ensure that all tiers of regional and local government publish a 'Charter of Services', giving citizens clear rights to standards of service, and remedies if these are not met.

Consulting local citizens

Liberal Democrats want local councils to be as responsive and accountable to their local citizens as possible. We will introduce across the country an initiative pioneered by Liberal Democrat-run councils such as South Somerset and Richmond.

We will require every council to conduct an annual survey of all its residents to gauge their views on the quality of local services. A summary of the results of the survey, compared to the previous year's findings, will be published with the annual demand for local income tax, so that every resident is able to tell what their council is achieving with the money they pay.

Ensuring citizens' rights and opportunities

No citizen is truly free unless all are. Individual citizens and minority communities themselves need protection against the power of the state and against discrimination and unfair treatment. Citizens must have rights of access to information about decisions taken by public authorities in their name. We will:

- Introduce a Freedom of Information Act, placing responsibility on government and other authorities to justify secrecy. We will reverse the present Government's encroachments on freedom of speech and association, such as the banning of trade unions at GCHQ. We will legislate to give individuals the right of access to their personal files, except in matters relating to national security, whether held by public or private bodies. Security services and intelligence agencies should be accountable to a committee of senior Privy Councillors.
- Enact a Bill of Rights by immediately incorporating the European Convention on Human Rights and its protocols into UK law. We will create a Commission of

Human Rights to help people bring proceedings under the Bill and to recommend changes in existing law and practice. In due course we will add rights and freedoms not currently included in the Convention, extending into a full UK Bill of Rights.

- Take tougher action against discrimination. Our Bill of Rights will guarantee effective protection against discrimination on the grounds of sex, race, age, disability, religion or sexual orientation. Our Commission of Human Rights will help individuals take legal action in cases of discrimination.
- End the bias against women's participation in the present political system. The introduction of fair votes and of sensible Parliamentary conditions will increase both the number of women candidates and the number of women MPs. In addition, we will use government's powers of appointment to ensure fair representation of women on public bodies.
- Improve the administration of the legal system with the establishment of a Ministry of Justice, separating responsibility for civil liberties and justice from that for order and security. We will establish a Judicial Services Commission to appoint judges.
- Adopt a written constitution, of which the Bill of Rights will form the centrepiece. We will create a Supreme Court to entrench and defend these fundamental reforms to the relationship between the citizen and the state.

Working for peace: Northern Ireland

Liberal Democrats reject simplistic solutions for Northern Ireland. We aim to confront the legitimate fears and aspirations of both communities. We accept that both the Unionist and Nationalist traditions are valid and legitimate; that Northern Ireland should remain a part of the UK until the free consent of the majority of its people is given to change; that the Republic of Ireland has a legitimate interest in the future of Northern Ireland; and that a partnership in government which allows both communities to participate is the only practical way in which to make progress.

Together with the Alliance Party, our sister party and the only non-sectarian political party in Northern Ireland, we believe that mutual respect, shared responsibilities and decentralised government are the only basis for a lasting solution to the troubles of Northern Ireland. We will work together to:

- Maintain the Anglo-Irish Agreement, unless and until an improved agreement emerges from cross-party talks to replace it.
- Strengthen the constitutional rights of individuals within Northern Ireland. The case for fair voting for all elections, to bring together communities and encourage cooperation, and for a Bill of Rights to protect individuals, is even more pressing in Northern Ireland than it is in the rest of the UK. We will reform the Diplock system, so that three judges preside over non-jury trials, and encourage the use of juries wherever possible. We will introduce a 110-day limit on the length of time for which a prisoner may be held before trial, repeal the broadcasting ban, and provide for the videotaping of police interviews with terrorist suspects.
- Support community-based organisations striving for peace and reconciliation and working to eliminate sectarianism and discrimination in religious life, education, housing and politics.

- Welcome the opportunities offered by the development of the European Community, in terms of economic assistance to Northern Ireland and also because it creates a framework for progress in the relationship between the UK and the Republic of Ireland.

OUR PLEDGE

What has been set out in these pages is a programme which could change Britain for good.

We could become a country of citizens, not subjects, striving for excellence rather than settling for second best. We could be economically prosperous, environmentally responsible and educated to our full potential. But the obstacle to national success is the British system of government itself. Until that outdated charade is swept away, Britain's decline will continue, whatever government may be in power.

That is why Liberal Democrats are putting constitutional change at the heart of our election campaign. The reform of our outdated and undemocratic voting system in particular is the change which will make other reforms possible and is the key to a successful future.

Because we believe in stable democratic government supported by a majority of the British people, we shall not only campaign wholeheartedly for fair votes in the coming weeks, we also make a pledge for the period after the election. Our aim will be the creation of stable government for a whole Parliament and a more democratic basis for future elections. Liberal Democrats will neither support nor participate in a government which turns its back on reform. Any minority government which tries to play games with the constitution in order to cling to power, promoting instability and dodging the moral challenge of democracy, will have to contend with us.

That is our pledge.

make the
difference

The Liberal Democrat Manifesto 1997

£2.45

LIBERAL DEMOCRAT GENERAL ELECTION MANIFESTO 1997

Make the difference

Date of Election	May 1 1997
Party Leader	Paddy Ashdown
Candidates	639
MPs	46
Votes	5,242,947
% of vote	16.8%

This will be the last election of this century. And one of its most important. We have ducked the challenges that confront our country for too long. It is time to face them. The choice you make will shape Britain's future for the next 50 years.

There are no quick fixes, no instant solutions. Eighteen years of Conservative government have left our society divided, our public services run down, our sense of community fractured and our economy under-performing. There is much to be done to prepare Britain for the next century and no time to waste in getting started.

Yet a terrible fatalism seems to grip politicians. Though the challenges are immense, the solutions we are offered are all too often puny. We are told we can't ask people to pay more for a better education. Or change the way we live to protect our environment. Or share more to give better opportunities to those who have less. Or modernise our politics to give people more say.

The Liberal Democrats reject this timidity.

We are in politics not just to manage things better, but to make things happen. To build a more prosperous, fair and open society. We believe in the market economy as the best way to deliver prosperity and distribute economic benefits. But we recognise that market mechanisms on their own are not enough; that the private sector alone cannot ensure that there are good services for everyone, or promote employment opportunities, or tackle economic inequality, or protect the environment for future generations.

We believe in a society in which every citizen shares rights and responsibilities. But, we recognise that a strong country is built from the bottom, not the top; that conformity quickly becomes the enemy of diversity. And that the imposition of social blueprints leads to authoritarian centralised government. Liberal Democrats believe that power and opportunity, like wealth, should be widely spread.

Above all, Liberal Democracy is about liberty. That does not just mean freedom from oppressive government. It means providing all citizens with the opportunity to build worthwhile lives for themselves and their families and helping them to recognise their responsibilities to the wider community.

Liberal Democrats believe the role of democratic government is to protect and strengthen liberty, to redress the balance between the powerful and the weak, between rich and poor and between immediate gains and long-term environmental costs.

That is the Liberal Democrat vision: of active government which invests in people, promotes their long-term prosperity and welfare, safeguards their security, and is answerable to them for its actions.

Much of what we propose here requires no money – only political will. But where extra investment is required we say where it will come from. This is a menu with prices.

The purpose of this manifesto is to widen opportunities for all.

And its aim is to build a nation of self-reliant individuals, living in strong communities, backed by an enabling government.

Rt Hon Paddy Ashdown

WHICH PARTY WILL MAKE A REAL DIFFERENCE TO MY CHILD'S EDUCATION?

Our aim: To make Britain the world's foremost learning society by 2010.

The problem: This country's education has been underfunded and undermined by repeated shifts in policy. Standards are too low, especially in core skills such as reading and maths. Britain is too low in the world league tables.

Our commitment: Liberal Democrats will make education the next government's top priority. We will invest an additional £2 billion per year in education, funded by an extra 1p in the pound on the basic rate of income tax.

Our first priority is to . . .

- Give children the best start by providing high quality early years education for every 3 and 4 year-old child whose parents want it.

Key priorities are to:

- Increase funding for books and equipment in schools. In the first year, we will double spending on books and equipment to overcome the effect of recent cuts.
- Reduce primary school class sizes so that within 5 years no child between 5 and 11 will need to be in a class of more than 30.
- Tackle the backlog of repair and maintenance to buildings with £500m additional investment over 5 years.
- Boost chances for all adults to improve their skills and get better qualifications.

Making the best start

Early years education is the essential building block for higher standards and achievement later on. Every £1 spent on high quality under-fives education raises standards in later life and adds up to £7 of value to the nation's economy. We will:

- Give children the best start by providing high quality early years education for every 3 and 4 year-old child whose parents want it. This will be the first call on our £2 billion annual programme of extra investment in education.
- Promote high standards in early years education. We will set minimum standards for care, curriculum and premises. We will ensure that those in early years education are supervised by qualified staff.
- Provide choice in early years education. We will scrap the bureaucratic voucher scheme. We will ensure a variety of provision from a wide range of public, private and voluntary providers.
- Raise standards in schools. We will raise standards in schools, especially in literacy and numeracy, which are still far too low.

We will:

- Improve teaching standards. We will set up a General Teaching Council, charged with improving teaching standards and making teaching a profession to be proud of again. We will provide more opportunities for professional development and reward excellence in teaching. We will help poor teachers improve, but if they cannot, we will ensure they do not continue to teach.
- Encourage schools to succeed. We will strengthen the inspection system so that it helps schools and we will extend inspection to monitoring Local Education Authorities (LEAs).
- Strengthen discipline in schools. We will support teachers in maintaining discipline and provide them with the means to do so – for example, by providing better access to special referral units. We will require every school to develop a policy to tackle bullying and truancy. We will launch a national Truancy Watch scheme. We will oblige LEAs to fulfil their responsibilities to educate pupils excluded or suspended from school.
- Measure achievement in pupils and schools. We will give every pupil a Personal Record of Achievement which will enable them to build up a set of nationally accredited qualifications and record their other achievements. We will require schools to publish meaningful information on their standards, achievements and plans for the future.
- Improve the National Curriculum. We will replace the National Curriculum with a more focused and flexible Minimum Curriculum Entitlement. We will ensure that religious education provides pupils with an understanding of the major traditions of belief in this country.
- Boost literacy. We will establish special literacy programmes involving parents with teachers in a drive to ensure that 90 per cent of all pupils reach their expected reading age by 2005.

Investing in schools

Extra investment for well-equipped classrooms and better-maintained buildings is essential if standards are to improve.

We will:

- Increase funding for books and equipment in schools. In the first year, we will double spending on books and equipment to overcome the effect of recent cuts. A typical primary school of 250 pupils will get an extra £16,000. A typical secondary school of 1,000 pupils will get an extra £110,000.
- Reduce primary school class sizes so that within 5 years no child between 5 and 11 will need to be in a class of more than 30.
- Tackle the backlog of repairs. We will invest an additional £500 million over 5 years in repairing crumbling and unsafe buildings.
- Support children with special needs. We will fully fund the implementation of the Code of Practice for Special Educational Needs.

A new partnership for schools

Involving parents in the education of their children and ensuring schools are supported by local communities are both essential to achieving higher standards and a better use of resources.

We will:

- Increase the role of parents in education. We will extend home/school/pupil links, develop home–school partnership arrangements and support parents with information and resources to help them help their child. We will require the schools inspection service to report on home–school partnerships as part of school inspections. We will promote school councils and guarantee automatic representation on governing bodies to staff and, where appropriate, students.

- Open up schools to the whole community. We will encourage schools to develop courses for parents, build links with local leisure organisations to open up school sports facilities to the community and work with local businesses to provide improved computer education.

- Give all schools more independence and allow them to develop their own styles and strengths. We will devolve as many powers as possible to schools and give them more control over their budgets. We will make new 'light touch' LEAs responsible for those functions that cannot be undertaken by individual schools on their own, such as coordination, planning and monitoring standards. We will bring grant-maintained schools and City Technology Colleges into this new framework and scrap the Funding Agency for Schools. Liberal Democrats are opposed to selection, but believe that decisions on this should be made by local communities through their local Councils and not by politicians at Westminster.

- Recognise the valuable role of church schools in the maintained sector. We will initiate a dialogue with all the major faiths about the role they wish to play in education in the future. Where any of the major faiths wish to establish publicly funded voluntary schools we will enable them to do so, provided that they enjoy substantial community support, offer acceptable programmes of study, provide equality of opportunity and are able to deliver the Minimum Curriculum Entitlement.

- Forge a new partnership with the independent sector. We will encourage independent schools to work with state schools. We will phase out the Assisted Places Scheme and use the money saved to enable LEAs, if they wish, to enter into local partnership schemes. These could include assisting the funding of pupils at independent schools. Pupils currently covered by the Assisted Places Scheme would, however, be protected until they finish their studies. We will require independent schools to offer the Minimum Curriculum Entitlement. We will extend charitable status to all schools without affecting total Council funding and maintain the VAT exemption on school fees.

Extending life-long learning

In the information age, education must be a life-long activity from which people can benefit anywhere and at any time, rather than being something that only happens in school.

We will:

- Widen access to further education. We will give every person an Individual Learning Account as the basis for life-long post-school education with contributions made by the state, individuals and employers. Our aim is that the state contribution will be at least equivalent to the cost of fees on approved courses. We will replace the Student Loans Scheme with a fair repayment scheme linked to salaries in later life. We oppose top-up fees for tuition. Our aim is to ensure that students on approved courses (including part-time courses) up to first degree level are treated equally.

- Promote flexible learning. We will create a higher standard credit-based system for all post-14 courses, including the current A-levels and degree courses. We will work with the private sector to link all schools to the Information Super Highway and ensure that they have the equipment and skills to take advantage of this.

- Promote training in the workplace. To support companies that invest in education and training, and to encourage others to do so, we will introduce a 2 per cent remissible levy on company payrolls. This would be deductible against the cost of providing accredited training or making contributions to the Individual Learning Account. Small businesses will be exempt. We will give Training and Enterprise Councils the leading role in forging local partnerships to meet youth training and employment needs.

- Expand training opportunities for young people. Our aim is to ensure that 16–19 year-olds receive the equivalent of at least 2 days a week education or on-the-job training.

- Boost chances for all adults to improve their skills and get better qualifications. We will ensure that all adults on approved courses or training have access to financial support, either through their Individual Learning Accounts or from their employer using our new remissible training levy.

- Improve the quality of tertiary courses. We will create a new Quality Council to ensure high standards and value for money in all post-16 education and training courses.

- Secure academic freedom. We will ensure the funding of university teaching and research, safeguard academic freedom and standards.

WHICH PARTY WILL BE BEST FOR MY JOB AND OUR FIRM?

Our aim: To end the cycle of boom and bust and equip Britain's economy to compete in the global market-place.

The problem: Despite the current pre-election mini-boom, the fundamentals of Britain's economy remain weak. We continue to be held back by instability in economic management, an underskilled labour force and chronic under-investment. Britain continues to consume too much and invest too little.

Our commitment: Liberal Democrats will lock in economic stability, encourage saving and promote enterprise. We will raise the quality of Britain's workforce through additional investment in education and training. As part of our strategy to build a sustainable economy, we will shift the burden of taxation from employment to the depletion of natural resources.

Our priorities are to:

- Provide stability in economic management to encourage long-term investment.
- Raise the quality of Britain's workforce and get people back to work.
- Promote enterprise and small businesses.
- Begin to shift taxation from jobs, wealth and goods to pollution and the depletion of natural resources.

Investing in Britain's future

Long-term investment and economic stability are crucial to future economic success.

We will:

- Secure stable prices and low interest rates. We will turn the Bank of England into a

UK Reserve Bank, free from political interference. We will charge the Bank with keeping inflation low and make it accountable to Parliament for achieving this goal. Lower inflation and greater exchange rate stability can be better secured by working with Britain's European partners. The best framework for this is a single European currency and it is in Britain's interests to take part in this. However, three conditions must be met before this can happen. First, the single currency must be firmly founded on the Maastricht criteria. Second, Britain must meet those criteria. Third, the British people must have said 'yes' in a referendum. If these conditions for a single currency are in place, Britain should join.

- Ensure responsible economic management. We will keep to the 'golden rule' of public finance: over the economic cycle, total borrowing should not exceed total investment. We will make the government accountable to Parliament for keeping to this rule, and subject it to independent monitoring. We will cut wasteful spending and ensure new spending delivers value for money.

- Build up Britain's capital assets. We will distinguish between capital and current spending in the national accounting system. We will promote effective public/private investment partnerships at both national and local levels, with Councils' borrowing carefully controlled.

- Put Britain's people back to work. We will enable long-term unemployed people to turn their unemployment benefits into 'working benefits' paid to an employer to recruit and train them. We will break open the poverty traps that stop unemployed people from working. Our plans for boosting investment in infrastructure, promoting small businesses and encouraging energy conservation will create hundreds of thousands of new jobs.

- Invest in a highly-skilled workforce. Our investment of an additional £2 billion a year in education and training will improve skills and increase the nation's knowledge base.

- Promote environmental sustainability. We will begin a long-term shift in taxation, reducing taxes on jobs, wealth and goods and shifting them to pollution and resource depletion. We will use new national indicators of progress which include measures of quality of life and environmental sustainability.

- Encourage people to save. Our aim is to extend the advantages of TESSAs and PEPs to a wider range of savers by developing a new save-as-you-earn scheme. We will encourage personal and portable pension plans.

Investing in enterprise

Small business, enterprise and self-employment are the engine of a modern dynamic economy and a vital source of new jobs and growth.

We will:

- Support small and medium-sized businesses. We will encourage the banks to develop new sources of private finance, including grants, equity finance and mutual guarantee schemes. We will seek to expand the sources of 'seed-corn' capital. We will legislate for a statutory right to interest on late debt payments. We will require the banks to develop new codes of banking practice for small businesses. We will cut red tape, for example by stopping European institutions interfering where they shouldn't and by preventing Whitehall departments 'gold-plating' European regulations with extra rules. We will, in the long-term, abolish the Uniform Business Rate and bring in a new, fairer local rating system. We will ensure that government purchasing gives special emphasis and easier access to small and medium-sized firms.

- Boost regional and local economies. We will set up regionally-based Development Agencies to build new partnerships between small businesses, local Councils, Business Links, TECs and local Chambers of Commerce. We will encourage these bodies to come together to provide 'one-stop shops'. We will enable Councils to raise capital for local infrastructure investment, where they work in partnership with the private sector. We will encourage industrial development by promoting geographical centres of industrial excellence.

- Invest in research and innovation. We will expand support for science and research by shifting government funds away from military Research and Development and into civil science and research, and improve specialist research facilities for industry. We will encourage regional technology transfer centres to bring together the resources of industry, universities and government laboratories.

- Promote tourism. We will bring together the marketing and infrastructure work of government, local Councils and tourist boards. We will ensure that local communities are involved in the planning of tourist developments from the earliest stages.

- Build new partnerships at work. We will give employees new rights to consultation and participation in decisions and give companies and their employees access to advice on the forms of partnership which best suit them. We will promote profit-sharing, mutual structures and employee share-ownership schemes. We will extend the benefits of the Social Chapter of the Maastricht Treaty to all UK employees, while resisting the adoption of new rules that unnecessarily harm job opportunities.

- Encourage a culture of long-term business investment. We will require companies to publish information on their long-term investment achievements, including environmental performance, research and development, and training. We will introduce greater shareholder control over directors' pay and appointments.

- Promote British exports. We will make export promotion and commercial activity a higher priority for British Embassies.

Making Britain more competitive

A competitive domestic economy is essential if British companies are to succeed in the global market.

We will:

- Strengthen the law on competition. We will tighten the rules on monopolies and adopt a pro-competition stance on take-overs and mergers. We will combine the Monopolies and Mergers Commission and the Office of Fair Trading into a single powerful body, independent of government and charged with promoting competition.

- Give consumers more power. We will promote the establishment of industry-wide Ombudsmen schemes to improve complaints procedures and consumer redress. We will strengthen customer guarantees, improve product standards and labelling, especially for environmental purposes, and encourage products that are easier to repair, reuse and recycle. We will insist on clear labelling for food products which include genetically modified ingredients.

- Reform the privatised utilities. We will combine the existing regulators into a single Office of Utility Regulation, reporting to a Cabinet Minister responsible for consumer affairs. This new office will contain a regulatory board for each industry and will be charged with protecting the consumer and ensuring that excess profits are used to reduce prices and increase investment in improved services. Starting with the water industry, we will encourage utilities to involve their consumers in ownership and control of their company, through mutual structures.

- Reinforce consumer and investor protection. We will introduce independent regulation of financial services and improve processes for redress (e.g. for mis-selling). We will protect pension and life assurance savings from fraud. We will work to maintain the City of London's pre-eminence as a financial centre and promote effective international banking standards.

'WHICH PARTY IS SERIOUS ABOUT MAKING OUR ENVIRONMENT CLEANER AND SAFER?'

Our aim: To end the cycle of boom and bust and equip Britain's economy to compete in the global market-place.

The problem: Despite the current pre-election mini-boom, the fundamentals of Britain's economy remain weak. We continue to be held back by instability in economic management, an underskilled labour force and chronic under-investment. Britain continues to consume too much and invest too little.

Our commitment: Liberal Democrats will lock in economic stability, encourage saving and promote enterprise. We will raise the quality of Britain's workforce through additional investment in education and training. As part of our strategy to build a sustainable economy, we will shift the burden of taxation from employment to the depletion of natural resources.

Our priorities are to:

- Cut taxes on things we want to encourage, like jobs, by taxing pollution instead. This will not mean more tax, it will mean taxing differently.
- Build environmental objectives into every government policy.
- Set tough targets to cut energy waste, reduce traffic congestion and control pollution.

A greener economy

Environmental protection must be built into every economic decision and every area of government policy.

We will:

- Set tough new targets for the reduction of traffic pollution and waste. This will help reduce global warming, cut air pollution and prevent waste. Our targets include cutting carbon dioxide emissions (the main cause of climate change) by 30 per cent from the 1990 level over the next 15 years.
- Cut VAT and taxes on jobs, and make up the difference by taxing pollution instead. This will help create more jobs and a better standard of living.
- Adopt a Green Action Programme. We will set targets for sustainability and bio-diversity, to be met by central and local government. We will measure these by using new indicators of quality of life, progress and wealth. The Prime Minister will report to Parliament each year on the country's success in meeting these environmental targets.
- Protect the local environment. We will pass stronger laws to conserve the country-side. We will cut road congestion and help local Councils make Britain's towns and cities healthier and cleaner places to live.
- Improve the way environment policy is made. Environment policy is currently buried, with housing and local government, in a huge single Government Department. We will put environment and energy policy within a separate, new department and ensure that all government departments and agencies pursue environmentally-friendly policies. We will give the Environment Agency stronger powers to enforce compliance with environmental laws.

Transporting people, tackling pollution

Travel delays and road congestion cost billions of pounds, and pollution damages the health of millions of people.

We will:

- Invest in public transport by building new partnerships with the private sector. We will enable Councils to introduce road pricing in the most congested urban areas and use the money to support clean and rapid public transport, and to improve cycle and pedestrian access. We will retain London Underground in public ownership and give it the right to seek private finance for new investment without an assured government guarantee.

- Treble the freight and double the number of passengers carried on Britain's railways by the year 2010. We will strengthen the powers of the rail regulators. We will require Railtrack to meet targets for greater investment and increased passenger and freight traffic. We will withhold public subsidies from Railtrack if the targets are not met and, in the case of persistent failure, use the funds to reacquire a controlling interest in Railtrack. We will provide for legislation enabling this.

- Encourage people to drive more fuel-efficient cars by cutting the annual car tax, from £145 to £10 for cars up to 1600cc, over the period of the next Parliament, funded by gradually raising the duty on fuel by approximately 4 pence per litre. Under our proposals, a person with a typical family car could drive up to 23,000 miles per year and still be better off – even in rural areas, where the average motorist only drives 11,700 miles a year. We will reform tax relief on company cars to encourage smaller cars and give people new incentives to use public transport for getting to work.

- Reduce the need to travel. We will reform the planning system so that people have easier access to shops, offices and facilities, and promote the use of information technology to decentralise work.

Warmer homes, saving energy

Official government figures show that half the energy used in Britain is wasted. This pushes up fuel bills, worsens pollution and speeds up global warming.

We will:

- Cut fuel bills and make homes warmer. We will launch a National Homes Insulation programme to end fuel poverty starting with the 2 million lowest income households. Our proposals will be funded by the Energy Saving Trust and the energy supply companies. This will save these households an average £85 per year and reduce global warming emissions. By contrast, cutting VAT on fuel bills to 5 per cent would save the average household only £19 per year.

- Cut taxes on people by taxing pollution instead. To encourage energy saving, we will gradually introduce a 'carbon tax' on fossil fuels, using the funds raised to cut

VAT and employers' National Insurance Contributions (the tax on jobs). This is a tax switch, not a tax rise, and will be phased in gradually.

- Improve energy efficiency. We will bring in new minimum standards for the energy efficiency of products, buildings and vehicles. We will cut VAT on energy conservation materials to 8 per cent – the same as for energy supplies.

- Promote renewable sources of energy and combined heat and power schemes. We will shift funds from nuclear research into decommissioning and nuclear waste management, and support research for renewable energy sources. We will not provide any government subsidies for nuclear generation. We support on-site dry storage of nuclear waste, pending the long-term development of safe alternatives. Nuclear stations will not be replaced at the end of their design life.

Protecting Britain's heritage

Britain's natural environment and heritage are being gradually destroyed.

We will:

- Clean up Britain's rivers and beaches and ensure that the costs of investment are spread fairly. We will require water companies to contribute to the cost of national environmental projects. We will reduce the need for new water developments by setting targets to reduce leakage and by promoting efficiency in water use. We will introduce a fairer system of charging for water and require water companies to share excess profits with their customers through rebates or investments in environmental improvements. We will end, within 10 years, discharges that cause unnecessary water pollution.

- Tackle marine oil pollution. We will implement tougher rules on shipping safety and bring forward the designation of marine high risk areas.

- Reform land use planning. We will make protection of the natural environment a major feature of the planning system through a new Wildlife Act. This will improve protection of National Parks, Heritage Coasts, Sites Of Special Scientific Interest and Areas of Outstanding Natural Beauty.

- Green the countryside. Our proposed new Countryside Management Contracts will help farmers to protect vital habitats and convert to more environmentally-friendly farming methods. We will use tax and planning reforms to protect rural areas, encouraging development on derelict land sites rather than green fields.

Thinking globally, acting locally

Most people understand the importance of thinking globally and acting locally. They want to play their part in protecting the environment. Government should help them do so.

We will:

- Encourage the manufacture of products that are easier to repair, reuse or recycle. We will introduce deposit refund schemes and back EU-wide standards for product design, energy efficiency and reuse.
- Help people to choose environmentally friendly products. We will press for comprehensive and understandable EU-wide ecologically friendly and energy efficient labelling schemes.

Promoting animal welfare

The way a society treats animals is a measure of its civilisation.

We will:

- Promote animal welfare. We will set up a compulsory national dog registration scheme. We will halt the trade in endangered species as pets. We will promote and extend training and qualification for those who work with livestock. We will insist on the enforcement of maximum time limits and for transporting live animals in the EU, a stricter timetable for banning veal crates and improved rearing conditions for pigs and chickens across the EU. We will create an Animal Protection Commission to enforce animal welfare laws and improve animal welfare standards. We will ban animal testing for cosmetics, weapons and tobacco products. We will review the law in order to reduce the use of animals in scientific experiments and seek the development of alternatives.

- Protect wild animals. We believe that the issues of hunting with hounds and coursing should be decided by free votes in the House of Commons. We will ban snares and leg hold traps. We will press for stronger international laws to protect endangered species. We will ban the importation of products derived from threatened wild animals.

'WHICH PARTY WILL MAKE ME FEEL SAFE ON THE STREETS AND SECURE IN MY HOME?'

Our aim: To give every person in Britain the security of a decent home in a safe, strong community.

The problem: Crime, homelessness and insecurity now threaten the very fabric of British society. Many people feel too frightened to leave their homes. Many do not have a decent home. Our country is becoming more and more divided, our sense of community is being lost and our shared values are being undermined.

Our commitment: Liberal Democrats will pursue practical measures to rebuild Britain's communities, tackle the causes of crime, reduce homelessness and make people safer in their homes and on the streets.

Our priorities are to:

- Put 3,000 more police officers on the beat.
- Build more affordable and secure housing.
- End, by the year 2000, the scandal of people being forced to sleep rough on the streets.
- Revive Britain's sense of community.

Housing

Boom and bust house prices, a shortage of decent homes and poor housing have wrecked the lives of millions and damaged Britain's economy.

We will:

- Build more houses. We will encourage partnerships between the public sector, the private sector and housing associations to build high quality homes to rent and buy. We will, within strict borrowing controls, give local authorities more powers to go directly to the market to raise finance for building new homes. We will begin the phased release of capital receipts from past sales of Council houses and allow the money to be used to build new homes.
- Give financial security to all, whether they rent or own their homes. We will introduce a new Mortgage Benefit for first time buyers. They will receive this instead of Mortgage Interest Tax Relief. Those holding current mortgages will retain Mortgage Interest Tax Relief. Our aim is, over time, to merge the new Mortgage Benefit and the current Housing Benefit into one system of housing cost relief, available to those who buy or rent and focused on those most in need.
- End the scandal of people being forced to sleep rough on the streets. We will ensure that by the year 2000 no one is forced to sleep on the streets. We will require every Council to set up self-funding rent deposit schemes to help homeless people take up private tenancies. We will fund more short-stay hostel places as the first rung on the ladder to permanent accommodation.
- Take action to tackle homelessness and raise housing standards. We will give Councils greater power to act on unfit private housing, where the landlord has failed to do so. We will strengthen tenants' rights to repair and, in the public sector, give them rights to take part in the management and development of their homes and estates. Our Empty Homes Strategy will enable local authorities to work with, and as a last resort require, landlords to bring empty properties back into use. We will end discrimination against those under 25 by scrapping the 'shared residency rule' when assessing housing benefit.
- Bring confidence back to the housing market by targeting low inflation and low interest rates.

Crime and policing

Crime and the fear of crime affect almost every person and every community in the country.

We will:

- Put 3,000 more police officers on the beat. Within one year, we will give police authorities the resources to put an extra 3,000 police officers on the beat. We will increase the time the police spend on preventing and detecting crime by reducing unnecessary paperwork and making greater use of new technologies.
- Tackle youth crime. We will widen the use of schemes that require offenders to repay their debt to society and to confront the consequences of their actions. We will, where appropriate, require parents to participate in support projects where their children have been involved in juvenile crime. We will develop schemes that target disruptive children from an early age. We will reserve custodial sentences for more serious and persistent offenders. Our voluntary Citizens Service will enable young people to get directly involved in crime prevention schemes.
- Strengthen the criminal justice system. We will make the justice system work more quickly and effectively and review sentencing policy. We will overhaul the Crown Prosecution Service. We will encourage the use of community sentences, as an alternative to prison, where the result is likely to be less reoffending, and use prison sentences where they are essential to public protection or to make punishment effective. We will concentrate resources on crime prevention and on increasing conviction rates, rather than spending billions on building prisons.
- Focus on crime prevention. We will require Councils to take the lead in establishing cross-community partnerships against crime, setting specific targets for crime prevention. We will give Councils powers and resources to support high-quality, targeted crime prevention initiatives.
- Wage war on drug abuse. We will give the Police and Customs and Excise the support they need to stop drugs coming into Britain. We will set up a Royal Commission charged with developing policies to tackle the drugs problem at its roots.
- Give victims a new deal. We will promote restorative justice, under which offenders can be required to compensate victims for the damage they have caused. We will ensure that the Victim Support movement and the Witness Support schemes play a full role in the criminal justice system. We will provide victims with the practical support they need to prevent repeat attacks.
- Strengthen public confidence in the police. We will make police authorities more responsive to local communities by increasing their elected membership and creating an accountable police authority for London. We will improve co-operation between police forces and work more closely with Britain's European partners to combat international crime, terrorism, drug trafficking and fraud. We will ensure that the police take further steps to reduce the level of racial and homophobic violence.

Rural communities

Britain's rural economy and communities have been transformed over the last fifty years. The challenge for the next fifty years is to protect and enhance the richness of rural life, while developing a thriving rural economy.

We will:

- Seek further reform of the Common Agricultural Policy (CAP). We will work to replace the CAP, which currently subsidises production, with Countryside Management Contracts – a targeted system of direct payments to support economic, social and environmental goals in rural communities. Countryside Management Contracts will enable farmers and landowners to choose from a wide range of options, for example, to improve the rural environment, maximise food quality, protect natural habitats or move to less intensive or organic farming methods.
- Help rural economies through a period of change. We will, in partnership with the agriculture industry, draw up a national strategy for farming in order to provide a framework for public policy and private decision-making over the next 10 years. We will promote agricultural research and development, and assist farmers wishing to diversify. We will promote local processing of agricultural products and expand support for small and medium-sized enterprises in rural areas.
- Tackle rural crime. We will put more police into rural areas, support Farm and Neighbourhood Watch schemes and give Councils the duty to set up crime prevention schemes with the local police. We will enable rural police authorities to introduce mortgage incentive schemes to encourage rural beat officers to live in the areas they serve.
- Enhance rural services. We will support smaller village schools through greater use of information technology and specialist teaching teams. We will encourage schemes that enable local communities to make use of school buildings and equipment. We will promote community hospitals and use them for more out-patient consultations.
- Provide more affordable rural housing. We will encourage housing authorities, Parish Councils and housing associations to set up partnership schemes with the private sector in order to build low-cost homes for first-time home buyers and social needs.
- Improve rural transport. We will give local authorities the power to improve the co-ordination of local bus services and to reopen closed railway stations, in co-operation with Railtrack.
- Strengthen the network of rural sub-post offices and village shops. We will encourage the Post Office to invest in new point of sale technologies, in order to provide access, through sub-post offices, to a wide range of customer services. Where post offices and village shops which are vital to their local community are threatened, we will enable local Councils to support them with up to 100 per cent rate relief.
- Protect the countryside. We will help landowners meet the environmental costs of increased access to the countryside. We will take action to reduce the use of chemicals in farming.
- Protect rural areas from urbanisation. We will penalise the use of greenfield sites, set and enforce targets for greater use of brownland sites and encourage over-the-shop accommodation in market town centres. We will review the excessive housing totals in the current structure plans and scrap the 'predict and provide' approach to housing development.
- Work to preserve fish stocks and protect the livelihoods of local fishing communities. Our aim is to scrap the Common Fisheries Policy and replace it with a new Europe-wide fisheries policy based on the regional management of fish stocks.

We will take firm action to end quota-hopping, begin the phased abolition of industrial fishing and strengthen decommissioning incentives.

- Promote safe food. We will set up a Food Commission, independent from MAFF and accountable to Parliament, maintain strict controls on the use of bio-technology and press for higher common food standards across the European Union.

Urban communities

Britain's towns and cities offer civic pride, accessible facilities and, potentially, a high quality of life. However, many suffer from alienation, joblessness, high crime rates, a run-down environment and loss of population. Urban areas should offer excitement, security and a strong sense of community.

We will:

- Boost local economic development and job opportunities. We will support local development corporations. We will build new partnerships between local government and the private and voluntary sectors, to regenerate local economies and promote community enterprise. We will link local training to local jobs. We will encourage the establishment of community banks and credit unions.
- Tackle urban crime. We will expand community policing, ensure that all new planning takes account of the need to deter crime and focus on crime prevention.
- Encourage public transport. We will enable Councils to co-ordinate bus and train services and give them powers to introduce urban road pricing schemes, using the revenue raised to invest in better public transport.
- Reform and strengthen elected local government. We will give local Councils greater control over their own affairs. We will create a strategic authority for London. We will encourage the use of 'planning for real' strategies, in which local people can make a direct input into major planning projects in their community.

Arts and media

Flourishing arts and a diverse culture are essential for a lively and open society. They can be engines of innovation that bring life to the economy. At the same time, the world is experiencing an information revolution as important and far-reaching as the Industrial Revolution. Britain must maintain a free and effective media capable of being a check on the abuse of power, and of giving people the information they need to make informed decisions.

We will:

- Tackle the concentration of media power. We will act to prevent media mergers or take-overs, except where these can be shown to advance quality, diversity and access. We will require the Independent Television Commission to protect the position of smaller regional ITV companies, within the network supply agreement.
- Maintain the role of the BBC as the benchmark of public service broadcasting,

committed to quality, diversity and universal access. We will protect the independence and impartiality of the BBC through its Board of Governors and its licence fee.

- Improve access to information technology and the Internet. We will ensure that everyone in Britain can have access, either individually or through a wide range of public access points, to a nationwide interactive communications network by the year 2000.
- Increase access to the arts. We will use the National Lottery to endow, house and improve access to the arts. We aim to move towards the European average for public funding of the arts. We aim to restore the principle of free access to national museum and gallery collections, starting with the removal of charges for school parties.
- Promote Britain's culture. We will promote film production in Britain. We will actively support the British Council and rejoin UNESCO. We will enhance the BBC World Service as a national asset.

'WHICH PARTY WILL CARE FOR THE NHS AND PUT MY PATIENTS FIRST?'

Our aim: To make year-on-year improvements in the health of Britain's people and the quality of the National Health Service.

The problem: The NHS has been squeezed between rising demand and government underfunding, and disrupted by repeated changes in government policy. Morale amongst NHS professionals is falling, and bureaucracy has grown at the expense of front-line patient care, while numbers of nurses and hospital beds have fallen.

Our commitment: Liberal Democrats will increase funding for the NHS and secure funding for the future. We will maintain the NHS as a comprehensive service, free at the point of need and funded primarily from general taxation. We will immediately tackle the crisis in the hospital sector, make the NHS more accountable and begin a long-term shift towards preventive medicine.

Our priorities are to:

- Halt all finance driven closures for 6 months, pending an independent audit of needs and facilities.
- Invest £200 million each year to recruit more staff for front-line patient care. This would be enough, for example, for 10,000 extra nurses or 5,000 extra doctors.
- Cut hospital waiting lists to a maximum of 6 months over 3 years.
- End the two-tier system in the NHS.
- Restore free eye and dental checks.

Raising standards in the NHS

Whilst many of the recent reforms to the NHS have been beneficial, they have resulted in the creation of a two-tier health service. The standard of health care a person receives is increasingly becoming a lottery. The length of time people have to wait, the chance of treatment being postponed and the quality of health care vary enormously from one part of the UK to another.

We will:

- Match NHS facilities to needs. We will place an immediate 6-month halt on the finance driven closure of beds and wards, and set up an independent audit of needs and facilities.
- End the built-in two-tier service in the NHS. We will end the present system where treatment depends on the type of GP people go to. We will treat all GPs equally, with a common basis for funding. We want all GPs to have the benefits of flexibility and access to services currently enjoyed by fundholders. Those who choose to manage their own affairs will be able to do so on their own or as part of a consortium. Those who do not will be able to leave management to the local health authority.
- Raise standards of care in all areas. We will set up a National Inspectorate for Health and Social Care to improve standards and promote patients' interests. This body will work with the Audit Commission to ensure that all spending is monitored and results in real improvements in patient care.

Funding the Health Service

The NHS is underfunded. Too much goes into bureaucracy and not enough into patient care. There is a crisis in the NHS, especially in hospitals. Morale is dropping, standards of care are at risk from underfunding and highly qualified doctors and nurses are leaving the profession.

We will:

- Invest more in the NHS. We will invest at least an extra £540 million every year in the NHS to pay for our policy priorities. This will be paid for by closing the loophole that allows employers to avoid paying National Insurance contributions on certain benefits in kind and by putting 5p on the price of a packet of 20 cigarettes. We will use these extra funds to tackle the crisis in staffing, especially in the hospital sector, and begin a shift to preventive care. We will ensure that the NHS budget keeps pace with increasing cost pressures.
- Shift money from unnecessary bureaucracy into patient care. We will move from annual to at least three yearly contracts between Health Authorities and Trusts, and shift the money saved into front-line patient care. We will replace time consuming local pay bargaining with a new national pay structure and a single NHS-wide Pay Review Body that covers all pay, from the cleaner to the chief executive.

Building on the best of the NHS

The NHS needs to be strengthened and improved.

We will:

- Cut waiting lists. We will cut waiting times between diagnosis and treatment to a maximum of 6 months over 3 years.
- Improve the quality of care and raise morale. We will recruit and train more professional staff. Our carefully costed plans would, for instance, pay for the equivalent of 10,000 more nurses or 5,000 more doctors. We will ban the use of 'gagging clauses' in employment contracts which prevent professional staff from speaking out against unsafe standards.
- Tackle the crisis in NHS dental care. We will require local authorities to ensure that the public has access to NHS dentistry in all areas.

Promoting good health

Britain has a health service that concentrates too much on curing illness rather than preventing it. A healthier nation and a more cost-effective NHS depend on shifting the emphasis towards prevention, tackling the root causes of ill health (e.g. poverty and homelessness) and making people more responsible for their own health.

We will:

- Make prevention a priority. We will immediately abolish charges for eye and dental check-ups and freeze prescription charges as the first steps in a radical shift of policy that emphasises the prevention of illness rather than treatment.
- Encourage people to take more responsibility for their own health. We will improve health education and promote healthy living. We will ban tobacco advertising and promotion and increase the duty on tobacco products. We will make the Health Education Authority truly independent and free to criticise government policy.
- Ensure that food is healthy and safe. We will create an independent and powerful Food Commission, separate from MAFF, and responsible to Parliament for food quality and safety.
- Put health promotion at the heart of government policy. We will require all government departments to assess the impact of their policies on health. Each year there will be an independent report, to be published and debated in Parliament, on the state of the nation's health.

Bringing health services closer to people

The local institutions of the NHS must become more accountable to those they serve and more responsive to patients' needs.

We will:

- Enable citizens to play a part in setting health policies in their area. We will build on current pilot schemes to bring together Health Authorities and Social Services Departments, within the framework of elected local authorities.
- Give local people a stronger voice on NHS Trusts. We will end the right of the

Secretary of State for Health to appoint members of NHS Trusts, Authorities and Boards. We will require at least half the membership of Trusts to be drawn from the population they serve. We will open up meetings of NHS Trust boards to the public and press, and give local people, staff and professionals speaking rights. We will guarantee direct representation from the staff of each Trust. We will give Community Health Councils improved rights to consultation and greater access to information and meetings.

- Give the public more say in setting priorities within the NHS. Difficult choices about priorities must be faced. They cannot be left to bureaucrats and health professionals alone. We will develop new ways of involving the public in setting health service priorities.

Giving patients more choice

Patients should have more choice over their type of treatment, who delivers it and when.

We will:

- Enhance the rights of patients. We will strengthen the Patients' Charter and include rights to treatment within a specified time, a choice of GP, information about the options for treatment, guaranteed access to health records and better redress.
- Ensure that action is taken to improve poor quality services. We will enable patients and staff to apply directly to our new National Inspectorate of Health and Social Care to carry out inspections and take action where deficiencies come to light.

Community care

Our aim is to create a society in which people, whatever their needs, can live their lives with dignity.

We will:

- Give people choice in the services they use and the way they are provided. We will require Councils to extend to those over 65 the right to arrange their own care privately, if they wish. This will promote independence and enable them to find better value for money.
- Care for carers. We will introduce a new Carer's Benefit, in place of the Independent Living Allowance, in order to meet more of the financial cost of caring. We will extend the Carer's Benefit, as resources allow, to those over retirement age and work to improve advice, information, training and counselling for carers. We will seek to increase access to respite care and ensure that carers and users are involved in decisions about care. We will draw up a Charter that sets out carers' rights and responsibilities.
- Establish high national standards for all community care services. Our new independent Inspectorate of Health and Social Care will publish codes of practice for residential and nursing homes, and have the power to close any home that consistently falls short of national standards. We will introduce national charging

and eligibility guidelines to ensure a 'level playing field' of provision and charges.
- Protect people from the excessive cost of care. We will, as resources allow, raise the threshold at which older people are required to make a contribution to their long-term care. We are committed to working on a cross-party basis, to establish a national agreement on a system for funding care services that does not penalise thrift.

'WHICH PARTY WILL CLEAN UP THE MESS IN OUR POLITICS?'

Our aim: To restore trust in British politics.

The problem: People know that British politics isn't working. Their politicians have lied to them, their Parliament has become tainted by sleaze and their government is out of touch and doesn't listen.

Our commitment: Liberal Democrats will modernise Britain's outdated institutions, rebuild trust, renew democracy and give Britain's nations, regions and local communities a greater say over their own affairs.

Our priorities are to:
- Restore trust between people and government, by ending secrecy and guaranteeing peoples' rights and freedoms.
- Renew Britain's democracy, by creating a fair voting system, reforming Parliament and setting higher standards for politicians' conduct.
- Give government back to the people, by decentralising power to the nations, regions and communities of the United Kingdom.

Restoring trust in politics
British politics remains far too secretive. We cannot rebuild trust in politics without making government more open and accountable.

We will:

- Safeguard individual liberties, by establishing a Bill of Rights. As a first step, we will incorporate the European Convention on Human Rights into UK law so that it is enforceable by the courts in the UK. We will set up a Human Rights Commission to strengthen the protection of individual rights. We will create a Ministry for Justice responsible for protecting human rights and overseeing the administration of the legal system, the courts and legal aid. We oppose the introduction of Identity Cards.
- Break open the excessive secrecy of government, by passing a Freedom of Information Act establishing a citizens right to know.
- Cut back the quango state We will scrap unnecessary quangos, handing their func-

344

tions over to elected bodies. We will require those that remain to meet in public and to list their members' interests. We will establish a fair, open and more representative appointment process for all quangos.

- Give people more say in decision-making. We will make greater use of national referendums for constitutional issues, for example, changing the voting system or any further transfer of power to European institutions. We will enable referendums to be held on specific local issues where there is public demand.

Renewing democracy

Britain's political institutions are outdated and unrepresentative.

We will:

- Modernise the House of Commons. We will reduce the number of MPs by 200 (one third) and introduce tougher rules for their conduct, behaviour and outside sources of income. We will improve drafting and consultation on legislation, and strengthen MPs' ability to hold the government to account.
- Create an effective and democratic upper house. We will, over two Parliaments, transform the House of Lords into a predominantly elected second chamber capable of representing the nations and regions of the UK and of playing a key role in scrutinising European legislation.
- Introduce a fair system of voting. We will introduce proportional representation for all elections, to put more power in the hands of voters and make government more representative.
- Make politics more stable. We will establish a fixed Parliamentary term of four years.
- Clean up party funding. We will reform the way political parties are funded and limit the amount they can spend on national election campaigns. We will make each party publish its accounts and list all large donors.

Giving government back to the people

Far too much power has been concentrated in Westminster and Whitehall. Democratic government should be as close to ordinary people as possible.

We will:

- Introduce Home Rule for Scotland, with the creation of a Scottish Parliament, elected by proportional representation, and able to raise and reduce income tax.
- Introduce Home Rule for Wales, with the creation of a Welsh Senedd, elected by proportional representation, and able to raise and reduce income tax.
- Create the framework to make existing regional decision-making in England democratically accountable, and enable the establishment of elected regional assemblies, where there is demonstrated public demand. We will create a strategic authority for London.

- Strengthen local government. We will establish a 'power of general competence', giving Councils wider scope for action. We will allow local authorities to raise more of their funds locally, give them greater discretion over spending and allow them, within strict limits, to go directly to the markets to raise finance for capital projects. We will, in the long-term replace Council Tax with a Local Income Tax, and replace the Uniform Business Rate with a fairer system of business rates, raised through local Councils and set in accordance with local priorities.

Northern Ireland

Peace in Northern Ireland depends on containing and ultimately removing the entrenched hostility between the two main communities in Northern Ireland.

We will:

- Establish a power-sharing executive for Northern Ireland, elected under a fair and proportional system of voting. We will press for a new constitutional settlement based on the protection of individual rights through a Bill of Rights, incorporating the European Convention.
- Give individuals more power and political responsibility. We will introduce a fair and proportional voting system for all elections, and reform and strengthen local government in the province.
- Ensure respect for civil liberties. We will introduce an independent procedure for investigating complaints against the security forces, and reform the Diplock system so that three judges instead of one preside over non-jury trials. We will urgently implement the North Report's recommendations for an independent commission to supervise parades and marches.
- Promote economic growth. We will strengthen the all-Ireland economy through the creation of effective cross-border agencies. We will invest in education and promote inward investment.
- Build on the Joint Declaration and the Framework Document, by working with the Irish Government to create agreement between as many of the constitutional parties as possible. Sinn Fein can only be admitted to this process if, in accordance with the Mitchell principles, they and the IRA turn their backs on terrorism. Meanwhile, we must remain vigilant and keep in place the present means for countering terrorism.

'WHICH PARTY WILL GIVE ME THE OPPORTUNITY TO MAKE THE MOST OF MY LIFE?'

Our aim: To widen opportunities for everyone in Britain to make the most of their lives.

The problem: Poverty, lack of training, low pay and discrimination deny too many people the opportunity to make the most of their lives. Meanwhile, the welfare system no longer meets the needs of a modern society. It locks too many into dependency and, too often, penalises those who wish to work and save.

Our commitment: Liberal Democrats will promote individual self-reliance, strengthen equality for all before the law and in employment, and work for a society that cherishes diversity.

Our priorities are to:

- Ensure that, by the millennium, every young person has had the opportunity to work, learn, train and make a positive contribution to society.
- Give women greater opportunities to play a full role in work and in society.
- Ensure dignity in retirement.
- Break open the poverty trap that makes people better off on the dole than in work.
- Modernise Britain's welfare state for the twenty-first century, building a new cross-party partnership for reform.

Breaking the poverty trap

Unemployment wastes the talents and denies people the opportunity to contribute to the well-being of their families and increase Britain's wealth.

We will:

- Help long-term unemployed people back to work. We will establish a self-financing Benefit Transfer Programme allowing those who have been unemployed for a year or more to turn their unemployment benefits into an incentive for employers to recruit and train them. The value of the benefit to employers will gradually be reduced.
- Break open the poverty trap. We will take nearly 500,000 low earners out of income tax altogether by raising tax thresholds. This will provide lower taxes and new incentives to work, while cutting the benefits bill and reducing tax for 99.5 per cent of all income taxpayers. This will be paid for by introducing a new top tax rate of 50p on taxable income of over £100,000 per year. We will replace Income Support and Family Credit with a simpler, more efficient Low Income Benefit that increases financial incentives for people going back to work.
- Modernise Britain's welfare system. We will initiate a comprehensive review of the welfare system to build a new framework for welfare and opportunity, on a cross-party basis. Our aim is to provide a more effective safety net for the disadvantaged, to encourage work, without compulsion, and to widen opportunities.
- Help parents to return to work. We will develop a national childcare strategy, drawing on public and private provision. We will, over time, extend tax relief on workplace nurseries to other forms of day nursery care.
- Establish a voluntary Citizens Service to give people, especially young people, up to 2 years' work on such projects as environmental conservation, crime prevention, housing renovation, social services and the armed services.

- Encourage a flexible labour market, while protecting the low paid with a regionally variable, minimum hourly rate.
- Crack down on social security fraud and tax evasion and shift the money saved into new policies to enhance opportunities. We will tackle the high levels of fraud and overpayment in the social security budget. We will stop tax evasion and close off tax avoidance loopholes.

Older people

Everyone in Britain should be able to look forward to a retirement of security, opportunity and dignity. Old people feel that they are fast becoming Britain's forgotten generation.

We will:

- Guarantee everyone an acceptable minimum standard of living in retirement. We will create an additional top-up pension for pensioners with incomes below the Income Support level. This will be indexed to earnings and tapered as outside income increases. The basic state pension will remain indexed to prices. We will start to phase out the expensive, unfair contributory system and base the right to a state pension on citizenship and residence.
- Enable people to choose when to start drawing a pension. We will bring in a flexible 'decade of retirement', between the ages of 60 and 70.
- Protect the rights of older people. We will legislate against discrimination on the grounds of age.
- Expand private pensions and give people more control over their pensions. We wish to see more people making provision for their old age. We will replace the State Earnings Related Scheme (SERPS) with a scheme under which all employees have personal or occupational pensions. Existing accrued SERPS will, however, be preserved. We will expand occupational and personal pension schemes by giving all employees an entitlement to participate in a pension scheme of their choice, funded by contributions from employers and employees. Pension rights will be fully secured if people change jobs. We will treat pensions as deferred income over which pension-holders have full rights of security, control and portability.
- Abolish standing charges for water and create a fairer system of charging.

Young people

We propose a new deal for young people, in which new rights and new responsibilities go hand in hand.

We will:

- Expand opportunities. Our aim is that every young person between the ages of 16 and 19 will have the opportunity to either work, learn, train or take a place on our new Citizens Service.
- Restore security to excluded young people. The withdrawal of benefit rights has

348

condemned thousands of young people to life out of work and on the streets, at great long-term public cost. We will restore access to benefits for 16 and 17 year-olds. In the longer term, we aim to scrap the lower rate of income support for those under 25.

- Ensure that young people can learn their rights and responsibilities, with citizenship classes in every school and parenting classes for young adults. We will give children and young people access to information about their legal rights and obligations, review the age of majority and ensure that young people are represented on bodies that especially concern them.
- Expand local youth services. We will require local Councils to provide a statutory youth service in partnership with the voluntary sector.

Families

Families, in all their forms, are a basic building block of society. But the nature of families is changing. This has brought new stresses which must be addressed. But it has also brought new attitudes, such as the sharing of family responsibilities, which should be encouraged.

We will:

- Give families more security. We will take nearly 500,000 low earners out of tax altogether, by raising tax thresholds. We will replace Income Support and Family Credit with a simpler, more efficient Low Income Benefit that helps people back to work. We aim to improve the support for those caring for older people and people with disabilities.
- Introduce fair and workable child support legislation. We will repeal the Child Support Act and abolish the Child Support Agency. We believe that parents should financially support their children at an appropriate level. Where there are disputes between the parents, these should be decided by the courts, not by an inflexible formula. We will create a new system of unified family courts to decide these questions, after they have heard all the evidence.
- Promote good parenting. We will encourage the provision of parenting classes for young adults. We will increase the role of parents in education by extending home/school/pupil links, and develop home–school partnership arrangements, to assist in addressing the needs of the child.
- Expand parental rights. We will introduce a statutory right to parental leave and develop Maternity Benefit into a new, flexible parental benefit to be shared between partners. We will ensure that fostering and adoption law is based on the suitability of prospective fosterers and the needs of the child.
- Help parents to return to work. We will, over time, extend tax relief on workplace nurseries to other forms of day nursery care. We will develop a national childcare strategy, drawing on public and private provision.
- Encourage flexible working patterns. We will encourage job sharing and family-friendly employment practices, especially in the public sector. We will give private sector employees approaching retirement age, or with responsibilities for young children, the right to negotiate reduced hours or a career break.

Women

There is still a long way to go before women in Britain have equal opportunities.

We will:

- Promote equality in the workplace. We will, over time, extend employment and pensions rights to part-time employees, on a pro-rata basis. We will bring in tougher obligations on employers to establish equal opportunities procedures and pursue the principle of equal pay for work of equal value.
- Make pensions fairer to women, by working to replace the contributory system with pension rights based on citizenship and residence in the UK. We will bring forward the introduction of pension splitting on divorce.
- Improve the services that women receive from the NHS. We will promote equal treatment of the sexes within the Health Service. We will set targets for the expansion of facilities which enable women to consult female health professionals.
- Make the legal system fairer to women. We will strengthen the civil law remedies for domestic violence and improve the treatment of rape victims by the court system. We will seek to improve the provision of refuge places for victims of domestic violence.
- Enhance the role of women in public life. We will tackle the under-representation of women on public bodies by setting a target that within a decade at least one-third of all those on all public bodies should be women. We will reform the procedures and facilities of the House of Commons to make them more accommodating to women and families.

Disabled people

Progress in equal opportunities for disabled people remains patchy and unacceptably slow.

We will:

- Guarantee the rights of disabled people. We will ban discrimination on the grounds of disability and pass comprehensive legislation securing the civil rights of disabled people. We will draw up a Charter of Rights setting out what our new Bill of Rights means for disabled people.
- Give disabled people more independence. We will introduce a Partial Capacity Benefit, building on the Disability Working Allowance, to assist those in work who cannot fully support themselves financially. We aim to increase financial support for disabled people who cannot find work and to make provision for the real costs of disability.
- Improve access. We will publish a code of practice to improve access to buildings and transport. We will require government departments, local Councils and public organisations to make their key public literature available in Braille or where appropriate, tape.
- Make education inclusive. As part of our £2 billion investment in education, we

will increase funding for, and enforce implementation of, the Code of Practice for Special Educational Needs.

Ethnic minorities

Despite progress over recent years, members of ethnic minorities are too often denied equal opportunities and have to face racism and discrimination on a daily basis. Diversity, pluralism and a multicultural society are sources of strength for Britain.

We will:

- Strengthen action against discrimination. We will create a new Human Rights Commission, combining the Commission for Racial Equality and the Equal Opportunities Commission. We will give statutory force to the Commission for Racial Equality's Code of Practice in employment, and ensure that Britain plays a leading role in strengthening anti-discrimination legislation throughout the European Union.
- Ensure equal opportunities for all. We will require local authorities and housing associations to ensure equal opportunities in housing allocation. We will expand access to mother-tongue teaching, for both adults and children, where this takes place through self-help and community groups.
- Free immigration laws from racial discrimination. We will ensure that immigration policy is non-discriminatory in its application. We will reform current immigration laws so as to enable genuine family reunions. We will restore benefit rights to asylum seekers and ensure that asylum claims are dealt with swiftly.
- Increase ethnic minorities' confidence in the police. We will encourage the recruitment of ethnic minorities into the police force and require action to be taken against discrimination within the force. We will tackle any discriminatory use of police powers, such as stop and search, and enhance police action to deal with racial attacks. We will encourage the use of aggravated sentencing for racially motivated crimes.

Lesbians and gay men

In a free and tolerant society, discrimination on any grounds is unacceptable. Diversity is a source of strength.

We will:

- Ensure equality before the law for lesbians and gay men through our new Human Rights Commission and the Bill of Rights. We will create a common age of consent regardless of gender or sexual orientation.
- Stop discrimination. We will outlaw incitement to hatred and discrimination in housing and employment, including the armed forces, on grounds of sexual orientation. We will repeal 'section 28' of the 1988 Local Government Act. We will reform the law, ensure that the police and local authorities deal more effectively with homophobic attacks, and encourage police forces to be more representative of the communities they serve.

'WHICH PARTY HAS THE VISION TO BUILD THE KIND OF WORLD I WANT TO LIVE IN?'

Our aim: To recast Britain's foreign policy and enable this country to play a leading role in shaping Europe and strengthening international institutions.

The problem: For too long British foreign policy has looked backwards to its imperial past. Britain's interests have been damaged by an attitude to Europe that has been, at best, ambivalent and, at worst, hostile. This attitude has also cost Britain opportunities for influence and advantage.

Our commitment: Liberal Democrats will ensure that Britain plays a leading role in shaping Europe, democratising its institutions and strengthening its role as a framework for prosperity, peace and security. Britain, with its world experience, expert armed forces and permanent membership of the UN Security Council, has a unique role to play in reforming international institutions for the next century.

Our priorities are to:

- Make the European Union (EU) work more effectively and democratise its institutions.
- Widen Europe to include the new democracies of central and eastern Europe.
- Create a strong framework for Britain's defence and security through NATO and European co-operation.
- Give Britain a leading role in reforming and strengthening the UN and other international institutions.
- Promote an enforceable framework for international law, human rights and the protection of the environment.

Positive leadership in Europe

Britain's interests can only best be pursued through constructive participation in an enlarged European Union. Our vision is of a European Union that is decentralised, democratic and diverse. A strong and united Europe, but one that respects cultural traditions and national and regional identities.

In seeking to reform the EU, our priorities are to:

- Give the British people a say. Reform that fundamentally changes Britain's place in Europe should only proceed if it has the explicit support of Britain's people. If there is any substantial change in Britain's relationship with the EU, the British people must give their consent through a referendum.
- Make EU institutions more democratic and accountable. We will give the House of Commons a more effective role in scrutinising European policy. We also want the Council of Ministers and the EC Commission to be more accountable to the elected European Parliament. We will introduce a fair and proportional voting system for British MEPs in time for the 1999 European Parliament elections.
- Make EU decision-making more efficient and effective. Europe cannot effectively

enlarge without improving its decision-making. We therefore favour the wider application of majority voting. But we will keep the veto on all issues relating to the constitution, budgetary matters and regulations on pay and social security. We support the use of the 'double majority', especially on matters such as foreign and security policy. Each member state must retain the unfettered right to make its own decisions on the commitment of its national troops.

Pursuing Britain's interests in Europe

Britain has much to gain from EU membership. This will take new leadership, a new approach and a renewed sense of national confidence.

Our aims in Europe are to:

- Enhance economic prosperity, by promoting the freedom of movement of people, goods, services and money throughout the EU and by completing the European Single Market, particularly in areas of financial services, pensions and air travel.
- Participate in a successful single currency. Being part of a successful single currency will bring low inflation and low interest rates. Staying out will result in less invest-ment and a loss of influence. However, three conditions must be met before Britain can join. First, the single currency must be firmly founded on the Maastricht criteria. Second, Britain must meet those criteria. Third, the British people must have agreed to it in a referendum.
- Strengthen the European framework for peace and security. Britain's security and national interests are best pursued in partnership with its European neighbours. We will work to strengthen European Common Foreign and Security policy to enable greater scope for united European action. Individual member states must be free to decide whether or not their national forces will take part in any particular action.
- Fight crime and protect citizens' rights through more effective co-operation between EU states' police and customs forces with greater democratic account-ability. We will work to improve European co-operation against cross-border crim-inal activity and allow free movement for Britain's people throughout Europe. The administration of border controls should remain with individual member nations until they can be confident that the EU's external borders are secure.
- Reform the Common Agricultural Policy, converting it into a system of direct payments to support economic, social and environmental goals in rural communities.
- Reform fisheries policies, scrapping the Common Fisheries Policy and replacing it with a new Europe-wide fisheries policy based on the regional management of fish stocks. We will take urgent action to end quota-hopping and begin the phased abolition of industrial fishing.

Strong defence in an uncertain world

The first decades of the next century are likely to be turbulent and unstable everywhere, including within and around Europe. Britain must maintain an effective security capability. This will best be achieved through NATO and European co-operation, and this country must continue to play a full part in both.

We will:

- Maintain a strong defence at home and enable the UK to play a leading role in keeping international peace. We will maintain Britain's overall defence capability at its current level, whilst ensuring UK forces meet current needs and are appropriate to potential threats.
- Retain Britain's basic nuclear capability through the Trident submarine force until such time as international multilateral nuclear disarmament can be achieved. We will restrict the number of nuclear warheads on Trident to the same number as previously deployed on Polaris.
- Resist the proliferation of weapons of mass destruction. We will press for the conclusion of a verifiable Comprehensive Test Ban Treaty. We will ensure that Britain plays an active part in talks to reduce the holdings of strategic nuclear weapons.
- Support the principle of common security. We support the extension of the security guarantees, from which western Europe has benefited, to the new democracies of central and eastern Europe. We support NATO and its enlargement.

Working for peace, security and sustainability

In an increasingly inter-dependent world, the security of a medium sized nation like Britain is best preserved within a framework of international law that is effective and enforceable.

Reforming the United Nations

Playing a leading role in strengthening and reforming the United Nations should be a central aspect of Britain's foreign policy over the next decade.

We will work to:

- Strengthen the UN's peacekeeping capability so that it can take earlier and more effective action to prevent or suppress conflict. This should include establishing fast track machinery for negotiations; permanent, on-call, peacekeeping forces made up from high-calibre troops provided by member states; the reinstatement of a Military Staff Committee; the establishment of a UN Staff College to train officers; and improvements to the UN's command control, communication and intelligence capabilities.
- Support the establishment of an International Criminal Court to deal with genocide and war crimes.

Protecting the global environment

Pollution and environmental degradation do not respect national borders. Countries must work together if the world's environment is to be protected.

We will:

- Take a lead in international environmental negotiations. We will press for tough and legally binding international targets for greenhouse gas emissions and other pollutants.
- Develop a global system of environmental protection. We will work for the creation of a global environmental organisation. We will promote an environmental equivalent of the Geneva Convention, to outlaw gross acts of environmental destruction in times of war.

Tackling world poverty

The elimination of global famine, pestilence and poverty is not only a moral challenge, it is also essential for the world's long-term stability and peace.

We will:

- Increase Britain's contribution to overseas aid. We will set out a timetable for sustained progress towards achieving the UN target for overseas development aid of 0.7 per cent of GNP within the next 10 years.
- Promote a timetable for debt relief to the poorest states including a programme for cancelling debt and the creation of new and additional resources for debt relief.
- Target Britain's bilateral aid where it is most needed. We will focus Britain's bilateral aid on the least developed countries and end the practice of tying aid.
- Require states that receive UK development assistance to respect the fundamental human rights of their people and suspend UK programmes where these standards are breached.

Controlling arms sales

The global arms trade fuels conflicts, hinders prosperity and robs the world's poor of resources. Its growth must be diminished.

We will:

- End the sale of British arms, war material, and 'dual use' technologies to regimes which abuse human rights, and strictly control arms sales to regions of tension or potential conflict.
- Seek a new international regime to control the arms trade. We will support tighter EU-wide restrictions on transfers of military technology to non-democratic regimes and press for the establishment of a mandatory UN register, in which all arms sales and transfers must be listed.
- Ban landmines. We will place an immediate and total ban on the production, stockpiling and export of anti-personnel landmines and work towards a global ban on landmine production.

Free and fair trade

Free and fair trade benefits all. The GATT Uruguay Round has successfully lowered barriers to international trade, but further reforms are needed.

We will seek action to:

- Enhance free trade by further reducing tariff and non-tariff barriers, especially against the poorest countries.
- Improve global labour standards by permitting countries to discriminate against goods produced by nations that maintain practices such as child, slave and forced labour. We will support the work of the International Labour Organization in raising labour standards throughout the world.
- Advance environmental objectives. We support the addition of an environmental sustainability clause to the GATT, setting out agreed principles of environmental policy against which trade measures can be judged.
- Reduce trans-national corporations' ability to abuse market power, through the development of a framework for global competition policy.

Liberal Democrats and your tax

A copy of our Annual Tax Contract will be delivered to each UK household following the Budget each year. Some of the information which would be included is provided here.
  This Annual Tax Contract will be in keeping with our four Tax Pledges:

1   No taxation without explanation
     Central Government should inform taxpayers of the ways in which their money is raised and spent, just as local councils now do.

2   No promises unless the bill is attached
     People have the right to know the Government's priorities and how much they will cost. When we make significant changes in our tax and spending priorities we will tell people where the money has come from. We will ask the National Audit Office to make sure that additional expenditure earmarked for specific projects is spent accordingly.

3   No more tax without tackling waste
     Each year we will set out the measures which we plan to implement in order to reduce wasteful expenditure and deliver best value for money to taxpayers. We will never raise taxes without first scrutinising Government expenditure for waste.

4   Fair tax for all
     Tax bands, rates and reliefs should ensure that everyone contributes according to their ability to pay and that the tax burden is fairly shared. We will aim to take more of those on low incomes out of tax completely. We will clamp down on tax avoidance and evasion. We will provide a mechanism for people to give their views on tax and spending priorities.

Costing our commitment

- We have issued alongside this manifesto a Costings Supplement to show in detail how our proposals will be financed.
- We will raise the basic rate of income tax by one penny in the pound – from 23p to 24p – to help finance our £2bn per year programme of Education investment.
- We will increase the amount of income which people can receive before they start to pay income tax by £200 per year to £4,245. This tax cut will be paid for by introducing a new rate of income tax of 50%, payable on taxable income of over £100,000 per year. Half a million people will be freed from income tax altogether.
- We will put 5p on a packet of cigarettes and use the money to restore free eye and dental checks for all and freeze prescription charges.

How these proposals would change your income tax

Main income tax changes:

- Around 70% of Adults will pay lower or unchanged income tax under our proposals.
- Around half of all income taxpayers would be better off or no worse off under our income tax proposals.
- Excluding those earning over £100,000 per year, the average income taxpayer will pay only around 45p extra per week in income tax under our plans.

Conclusion

In this manifesto, we have set out a practical, forward-looking programme to modernise Britain. Its central theme is the widening of opportunities. And its aim is to make Britain a nation of self-reliant individuals, living in strong communities, backed by an enabling government.

We do not duck the choices that have to be faced in this election.

And we do not pretend that they are easy – or free. High-quality education has to be paid for. As do decent public services and a more secure society.

You cannot, in the present climate, have these and tax cuts as well.

You have to choose.

We ask you to do so.

Your vote can make a real difference in turning our country away from short-term politics towards a more constructive long-term approach.

And with your support we believe we can make a difference too. Every vote we receive is a vote for better education, the modernisation of our politics, a cleaner environment, a better health service and more crime free communities.

Every vote we get and every seat we win will ensure that in the next Parliament, Britain, can at last face up to the challenge, as we enter the next millennium.

INDEX

ECSC *see* European Coal and Steel
  Community
education 15; *1923* 42; *1924* 47; *1929* 51; *1935*
  57; *1945* 64–5; *1950* 76; *1959* 100; *1964* 114;
  1966 131–2; *1970* 141; *1974* (Feb) 160–1;
  1979 197; *1983* 206, 216, 219–20; *1987*
  260–3; *1992* 285–6, 287, 289, 299–302; *1997*
  324–8, 329, 350–1; arts relationship 308;
  health 342; sectarianism 23; special needs
  259, 301, 326, 351; young people 349; *see
  also* schools
Education Act (*1902*) 31
Efficiency Audit Commission 214
elderly people: *1950* 75, 76; *1959* 101, 103;
  1964 113; *1966* 129–30; *1970* 140–1; *1974*
  (Feb) 160; *1974* (Oct) 178; *1983* 217, 220;
  1987 257; *1992* 287, 309; *1997* 348; care in
  the community 196; crime 228, 244, 245;
  housing 268, 269–70; water bills 296
electoral reform: *1922* 38; *1924* 48; *1931* 54;
  1935 58; *1945* 67; *1950* 75; *1955* 93; *1959*
  102–3; *1966* 128; *1970* 138, 141–2; *1974*
  (Feb) 165–6; *1974* (Oct) 174, 175, 180; *1979*
  186–7, 189; *1983* 206, 224–5; *1987* 239–40,
  242, 276, 277; *1992* 283, 287, 292–3,
  315–16, 319; *1997* 345; women 243; *see also*
  parliamentary reform; political reform
electricity 65, 100, 208, 250
eleven-plus exam 114, 131
Empire: *1900* 23, 24; *1906* 27, 28; *1924* 44;
  1931 54; *1945* 62, 66; *1950* 76; *see also*
  colonies
Employee Councils 212, 251
employers' liability 22
employment: *1929* 51; *1935* 57; *1945* 63;
  1950 72; *1964* 108–9, 109; *1966* 122; *1970*
  138–9; *1979* 193; *1983* 208–11; *1987*
  247–8, 249; *1992* 288, 289; *1997* 329, 330,
  347–8; child-care vouchers 291–2;
  Conservative/Labour conflict 91; energy
  215; family issues 349; health service 220;
  urban areas 339; women 350; *see also*
  industrial relations; trade unions; training;
  unemployment
Empty Homes Strategy 336
energy: *1923* 41; *1924* 46–7; *1945* 65; *1966* 123;
  1974 (Feb) 157–8; *1979* 187, 193, 197–8;
  1983 206, 208, 215–16; *1987* 265; *1992* 284,
  285; *1997* 332, 333–4; conservation 295;
  European policy 231; housing 304–5;
  sustainable development 314; *see also*
  power stations
Energy Commission 198
energy efficiency: *1979* 193, 197; *1983* 215;
  1987 265; *1992* 285, 295, 304, 305; *1997*
  333–4, 335

enterprise: *1923* 41; *1929* 51; *1951* 85; *1987*
  250; *1992* 288, 289, 290–1; *1997* 328,
  329–30, 332; urban areas 266, 339; *see also*
  private enterprise; small businesses
Environment Agency 332
environmental issues 10, 15; *1970* 137; *1974*
  (Feb) 153, 163–4; *1979* 186, 187, 197–9;
  1983 217, 223–4; *1987* 264–5, 276, 277; *1992*
  282, 284–5, 287, 293–8; *1997* 331–5, 338;
  agriculture 224, 252–3, 293, 334; Europe
  311; global 354–5; housing 304–5; rural
  areas 267; sustainable development 314,
  329; world trade 356
Environmental Protection Agency 295
equal opportunities: *1945* 67; *1950* 75; *1974*
  (Feb) 162; *1979* 191, 192; *1983* 227; *1987*
  239, 242, 243, 248, 252; *1992* 309–10; *1997*
  347, 350, 351
Equal Opportunities Commission 241
ethnic minorities: *1979* 192–3; *1987* 239, 242,
  252; *1992* 309–10; *1997* 351; police 305
Europe: *1950* 77; *1951* 82–3; *1955* 90; *1959*
  102; *1964* 114; *1966* 121, 132; *1970* 142;
  1979 188, 199–200; *1983* 207; *1987* 272–3;
  1992 283, 310–12; *1997* 352–3; arts 308;
  Conservative foreign policy *1923* 39–40;
  defence 273, 274, 312; developing countries
  314, 315; food standards 339; NATO 230;
  single currency 329; small business 330; *see
  also* European . . .
European Coal and Steel Community (ECSC)
  90, 158
European Common Foreign and Security
  Policy 353
European Community: *1966* 121; *1983* 231–2;
  1987 272–3; *1992* 281, 287, 310–12;
  Common Fishing Policy 253; dumping 250;
  joint research programmes 249; long-term
  prosperity 292; Northern Ireland 319;
  regional development fund 289; regional
  fund 267
European Convention on Human Rights:
  1979 191; *1983* 227; *1987* 241, 242, 243;
  1992 309, 310, 317; *1997* 344
European Defence Community 90
European Economic Community (EEC):
  1966 132; *1974* (Feb) 165, 166–7; *1974* (Oct)
  173, 181; *1983* 229; fishing industry 215;
  Northern Ireland 244; *see also* Common
  Agricultural Policy
European Environment Agency 311
European Monetary System (EMS) 232, 248,
  252, 277
European Parliament: *1974* (Feb) 166; *1974*
  (Oct) 181; *1979* 200; *1983* 231; *1987* 240,
  272; *1992* 311–12; *1997* 352; House of

Printed in Great Britain
by Amazon